4th Edition

The Essential Guide to

Workplace

Investigations

A Step-By-Step Guide to Handling
Employee Complaints & Problems

Lisa Guerin, J.D.

FOURTH EDITION	MAY 2016
Editor	SACHI BARREIRO
Cover Design	SUSAN PUTNEY
Book Design	TERRI HEARSH
Proofreading	IRENE BARNARD
Index	JULIE SHAWVAN
Printing	BANG PRINTING

Names: Guerin, Lisa, 1964-
Title: The essential guide to workplace investigations : a step-by-step guide to handling employee complaints & problems / Lisa Guerin, J.D.
Description: 4th Edition. | Berkeley, CA : Nolo, 2016. | Revised edition of the author's The essential guide to workplace investigations, 2013. | Includes index.
Identifiers: LCCN 2015049038 (print) | LCCN 2016000835 (ebook) | ISBN 9781413322736 (pbk.) | ISBN 9781413322743 (epub)
Subjects: LCSH: Employee crimes--Handbooks, manuals, etc. | Labor discipline--Handbooks, manuals, etc. | Violence in the workplace--Investigation--Handbooks, manuals, etc. | Discrimination in employment--Investigation--Handbooks, manuals, etc. | Sexual harassment--Investigation--Handbooks, manuals, etc. | Investigations--Handbooks, manuals, etc. | Labor laws and legislation--Handbooks, manuals, etc.
Classification: LCC HF5549.5.E43 G836 2016 (print) | LCC HF5549.5.E43 (ebook) | DDC 658.3/14--dc23
LC record available at http://lccn.loc.gov/2015049038

This book covers only United States law, unless it specifically states otherwise.

Please note

We believe accurate, plain-English legal information should help you solve many of your own legal problems. But this text is not a substitute for personalized advice from a knowledgeable lawyer. If you want the help of a trained professional—and we'll always point out situations in which we think that's a good idea—consult an attorney licensed to practice in your state.

Dedication

For my parents, whose five children gave them plenty to investigate.
In loving memory.

Acknowledgments

Many thanks to:

Amy DelPo, for her encouragement and suggestions.

Rich Stim, for his excellent editing and his sharp eye for the noir detail.

Sachi Barreiro, for her great ideas and strong editing.

Laura Lawson, **Dan Cafaro**, **Allen Smith,** and **Chris Anzalone**, of the Society for Human Resource Management, for their insightful comments on the manuscript and their assistance in making this project a reality.

Jathan Janove, of Bullard Smith Jernstedt Wilson, for his helpful advice on the manuscript on behalf of SHRM.

Kelly Perri and **Sigrid Metson**, for their tireless marketing efforts and their help in shaping the tone and structure of the book.

Drew Wheaton, Stephen Stine, and **Julia Burdette**, for their research assistance.

Susan Putney, for her wonderful cover design.

About the Author

Lisa Guerin, J.D.

Lisa Guerin is the author or coauthor of several Nolo books, including *The Manager's Legal Handbook: A Legal & Practical Guide for Employers, Dealing With Problem Employees: A Legal Guide, Create Your Own Employee Handbook: A Legal & Practical Guide for Employers*, and *Smart Policies for Workplace Technologies: Email, Blogs, Cell Phones & More*. Ms. Guerin has practiced employment law in government, public interest, and private practice where she represented clients at all levels of state and federal courts and in agency proceedings. She is a graduate of Boalt Hall School of Law at the University of California at Berkeley.

Table of Contents

Part II: Investigating Common Workplace Problems

Appendixes

PART

1

Investigation Basics

Workplace Investigations: An Overview

Chances are good that you picked up this book because you've become aware of a potentially serious problem at your company, and you're not quite sure how to handle it. Maybe you've heard a complaint or report of misconduct that sounds something like this:

"Every time I go into John's office, he's looking at porn on the Internet. It's really starting to offend me and some of the other women in the office."

"We've finished our internal audit, and the numbers just don't add up. I think we may have a thief on our payroll."

"Mark has been really angry lately. He keeps talking about his gun collection, and yesterday he told me that 'management is about to get what's coming to them.' I'm afraid of what he might do."

Now you're faced with some tough decisions: Whom should you believe? What really happened and why? How serious is this problem? What should you do about it? Can you handle this without creating legal problems for the company?

A complete, impartial, and timely investigation will help you answer these questions and figure out what to do. In fact, a proper investigation is one of the most important tools for maintaining a safe and productive workplace and keeping your company out of legal trouble.

Whether you're facing an immediate problem that requires investigation right now or you're interested in putting policies and procedures in place for the future, this book gives you the tools and information you need. Part I (Chapters 1 through 4) describes in detail the ten steps to a successful investigation of any kind of workplace problem. Part II (Chapters 5 through 9) takes a closer look at five common workplace problems—discrimination, harassment, theft, violence, and drug and alcohol use—and explains how to handle the special investigation challenges posed by each.

This chapter will help you get started. It introduces the benefits and basic components of a proper workplace investigation, including the actions you will have to take—and decisions you will have to make— along the way. (Each of these steps is covered in detail in Chapters 2 through 4.) It also covers some common investigation mistakes that can lead to legal trouble, with tips that will help you avoid them.

Investigations Require Judgment Calls

Although most investigations will require you to at least consider each of these ten steps, every situation is a little bit different. Workplace problems rarely land on your desk in a tidy package with an obvious solution. Instead, you'll often be faced with conflicting stories, documents that are open to different interpretations, and no clear answers about what happened and what you should do about it. You'll have to decide which problems merit a closer look, whom to interview, and what documents to review. And, when your investigation is complete, you'll have to decide what you think really happened based on the evidence.

All of these decisions are judgment calls, and no book can tell you how to handle every possible scenario you might face. However, if you follow the guidelines in the chapters that follow, keep an open mind, and use your best judgment, you should be able to handle most of the issues that come up.

The Benefits of an Effective Investigation

Although you might not be happy to learn that you have a workplace problem, investigating and resolving it in the right way can strengthen and protect your company. Among its many benefits, a proper investigation will help you:

- **Figure out what happened.** The immediate aim of any investigation is to get to the bottom of a problem. You won't know how to handle a situation until you know what really happened. And, acting before you have all the facts could lead you to discipline the wrong employee or allow a workplace problem to continue.
- **Deal with employee problems early.** An investigation will help you figure out who's behind a workplace problem, so you can take action before things get any worse. If you are dealing with a problem employee, he or she can be disciplined. An employee with a substance abuse problem can be identified and offered help. If employees are breaking the rules because they don't know what's expected from

them, you can implement training programs, work harder to publicize and distribute company policies, and make sure managers are
enforcing the rules.

- **Enforce company policies.** If a company doesn't enforce its own
  policies, employees quickly realize that they don't have to follow
  the rules. Showing employees that there are consequences for
  misconduct will help deter future trouble and keep employees on
  the right track.
- **Encourage reporting.** Investigating and dealing with problems
  quickly will encourage employees to come forward with their issues
  and concerns. This means that you'll hear about workplace trouble
  right away, before it has a chance to grow into a more serious
  problem.
- **Avoid or counter bad publicity.** A company that ignores complaints
  and problems gives the impression that it doesn't care about its
  workers or the law. And if your company's failure to deal with
  a problem becomes public knowledge—through a lawsuit, for
  example—it could really hurt the company's reputation.
- **Protect your company from lawsuits.** A solid investigation will help
  your company avoid or defend against lawsuits in the future. If
  someone who is injured by workplace misconduct—an employee
  who is sexually harassed, for example—sues your company, you
  can show that you took action right away, which will protect your
  company from liability in many cases. If an employee who was
  disciplined or fired as a result of your investigation files a lawsuit,
  you will be able to show that you acted reasonably and in good
  faith, which will undermine the employee's claims.

By the same token, however, a slipshod investigation can lead to
employee lawsuits, by giving employees the ammunition they need to
demonstrate that your company discriminated, spread false information, or treated employees poorly, among other things. And failing to
investigate at all is even worse: If an employee can show that company
management knew about a problem and didn't do anything about it,
the company will be legally responsible for any harm that employee
suffered as a result of its failure to act.

Your Role in the Investigation

This book addresses every aspect of workplace investigations, from start to finish. Depending on your role at your company, you may be responsible for all, most, some, or just a few of the actions and decisions described in this book. For example, you may be called upon to decide whether an investigation is necessary, but your company may then hire an outside investigator to handle the legwork. Or, you may be responsible for performing the investigation, but not for deciding what action should be taken based on your findings.

No matter what aspects of the investigation fall within your job description, you'll find the information you need in this book. We cover all of the duties associated with an investigation, to make sure that all of our readers are fully equipped to handle every part of the investigation for which they are responsible.

So how do you conduct the right kind of investigation? By being fair and thorough and making good faith efforts to get to the truth. Even if you come to the wrong conclusion, your company should be able to show that it was legally entitled to take action (for example, to discipline or fire an employee) based on the results of your investigation. As long as you investigated properly and your decisions were reasonable based on the information available to you, your company won't be held liable.

> EXAMPLE: Ralph was accused of sexually harassing two female coworkers. The company immediately performed a complete investigation, interviewing the women, Ralph, and a number of witnesses, including five that Ralph suggested. Based on these interviews, the company concluded that Ralph had in fact harassed his coworkers, and it fired him.
>
> Ralph later sued the company, claiming that he had a consensual affair with both women, no harassment had occurred, and the women were angry with him for two-timing them. (Ralph did not tell any of this to the company's investigator.) The jury found in Ralph's favor. However, an appeals court decided that it didn't matter what really happened. As long as the company conducted a fair and thorough investigation and reached a

good faith conclusion based on the information available to it at the time, it was not liable for firing Ralph based on the investigation's results.

Ten Steps to a Successful Investigation

Like any other project, the best way to tackle an investigation is to divide it up into manageable tasks. Fortunately, most workplace investigations follow a similar pattern, although the details can vary considerably. Once you become aware of a problem or complaint, you'll have to follow these ten steps:

1. **Decide whether to investigate.** Although there are some situations that don't warrant an investigation, you should generally err on the side of investigating. Sometimes, you won't know how serious a problem really is until you start asking questions. Chapter 2 explains how to decide whether to investigate, including how to scale the size of your investigation to the problem.

2. **Take immediate action, if necessary.** You might have to act right away, before you begin to investigate, to protect employees or the company itself. For example, an employee accused of serious sexual harassment or stealing company trade secrets should be suspended, with pay, until the investigation is complete. For information on taking interim measures—including tips that will help you avoid legal claims based on your pre-investigation actions—see Chapter 2.

3. **Choose an investigator.** If you won't handle the investigation yourself, you'll need to pick someone else to do it. The right investigator is experienced, impartial (and perceived as impartial by the employees involved), and capable of acting—and if necessary, testifying—professionally about the investigation. Chapter 2 explains these requirements, including when it makes sense to bring in an outside investigator.

4. **Plan the investigation.** Start by organizing your thoughts and information: What do you already know? What do you need to find out to decide what happened? Who might have relevant

information? What's the best way to get it? Some careful thought up front can help you avoid wasting time or overlooking important facts as you investigate. Chapter 2 explains how to prepare to investigate, including tips on letting others in the company know about your plans.

5. **Interview.** The heart of any investigation is gathering information. The most basic way to do that is by asking people questions. Typically, you'll have to interview the employee accused of wrongdoing, the employee who complained or was the victim, and any witnesses to the incident(s). You'll learn the most by asking open-ended questions that encourage disclosure without giving too much away. Chapter 3 explains how to conduct successful interviews, including whom to interview, what to ask, and how to get the facts you need.

6. **Gather documents and other evidence.** Documents play a role in many investigations and decide the outcome in more than a few. You might have to review personnel files, emails, personal notes, performance reviews, and other documents to figure out what really happened. You might also have to gather physical evidence, such as a weapon, photographs, drug paraphernalia, or pornographic magazines. You'll find information on gathering evidence, including a document checklist, in Chapter 3.

7. **Evaluate the evidence.** The most challenging part of an investigation—especially if witnesses disagree or contradict each other—is figuring out what actually happened. There are some proven methods of figuring out where the truth lies, which we all use in our everyday lives. Chapter 4 explains how to sift through the evidence and come to a conclusion. It also covers what to do if, despite your efforts, you can't get to the bottom of things.

8. **Take action.** If you conclude that an employee committed serious misconduct, you'll have to act quickly to avoid legal liability for that employee's behavior and to protect other employees from harm. Chapter 4 explains how to decide which actions to take after the investigation is complete, including how to communicate with the employees involved.

9. **Document the investigation.** Once your investigation is complete, you should write an investigation report that explains what you did and why. This will not only give the company some protection from lawsuits relating to the investigation, but it will also provide a written record in case of future misconduct by the same employee. Investigation reports are covered in Chapter 4.

10. **Follow up.** Your last step is to make sure the problem that led to the investigation has been solved. You'll need to follow through with the complaining employee and the accused employee, and you might have to take other steps—such as training employees or developing new workplace policies—to deal with systemic workplace problems. Chapter 4 explains how to follow up after the investigation.

RESOURCE

Get forms, checklists, sample investigation documents, and more. You'll find all of the forms, policies, and checklists described in this book—along with legal updates, audio interviews, a sample investigation file, and more—at this book's online companion page. Appendix A explains how to access these materials.

Common Investigation Mistakes

There are a number of legal traps waiting for companies that conduct an improper investigation or fail to investigate at all. Generally, these traps come in the form of lawsuits brought either by an employee who was a victim of inappropriate behavior in the workplace or by an employee who was disciplined or fired after being accused of misconduct. In either situation, a company that performed an incomplete, biased, or delayed investigation—or that never investigated at all—begins the lawsuit in a fairly deep hole. Not only has the company ignored its workers' legal rights, but it has also shown a lack of concern for its workers' well-being, a quality that many jurors (most of whom are or were employees themselves) find offensive.

In addition to these legal issues, companies that don't investigate problems or that conduct halfhearted investigations will face practical problems. These employers are sending precisely the wrong signals to employees, managers, and customers: that they don't want to hear about workplace problems, they don't really care what's going on in their companies and they won't enforce their own workplace rules.

What a Good Investigation Looks Like

Here's how one California employer won a lawsuit by conducting a timely, thorough, and fair investigation.

Lucky Stores (a supermarket chain) received two complaints from female employees that John Silva had sexually harassed them. After conducting a monthlong investigation, Lucky concluded that Silva had committed sexual harassment and fired him. Silva filed a lawsuit against Lucky, claiming that he didn't harass the women and, therefore, should not have been fired.

The court found in Lucky's favor because it had good reason to believe, based on its investigation, that Silva committed the harassment. The court detailed the qualities that made Lucky's investigation so reliable:

- Lucky chose Jeff Szczesny, a human resources representative who had been trained on how to conduct an investigation, to investigate the complaint. Szczesny was not involved in the underlying incident.
- Szczesny began investigating immediately.
- Szczesny interviewed 15 Lucky employees and documented the interviews. He asked open-ended questions and tried to elicit facts, not opinions. He encouraged the witnesses to contact him if they wanted to talk to him again.
- Szczesny told Silva of the charges against him and gave him a chance to tell his side of the story.
- Szczesny met again with important witnesses, including Silva, to give them a chance to hear new information and to clarify or correct their own statements.
- Szczesny memorialized the investigation in a written report, detailing the conclusions he reached and why.

Finally, failing to conduct a proper investigation will exact an emotional cost as well. Wrongly accusing an employee of serious misconduct not only invites a lawsuit, but also ruins that employee's reputation and relationships with coworkers. As if the legal and practical traps described above aren't bad enough, imagine how bad you'll feel if you make the wrong call and cause hurt feelings—or worse—for a blameless employee.

Fortunately, it isn't too hard to avoid these mistakes. By following the strategies outlined in this book—and using your common sense—you can keep your investigation on the right side of the law. Here are some common investigation errors, along with tips that will help you avoid them.

Failing to Investigate

If company management is aware of serious misconduct or dangerous activity in the workplace and doesn't do anything about it, the company could have significant legal exposure. Generally, any harm that comes to a company's employees—and sometimes, to people who aren't on the payroll, such as customers, clients, or bystanders—after the company has notice of a problem will be the company's legal responsibility. This means, for example, that an employee who suffers sexual harassment after a manager learns about the problem will be able to sue the company for damages.

Your company might also face a lawsuit if it fires an employee for workplace wrongdoing without first conducting an investigation. If that employee has an employment contract—whether written, oral, or implied—limiting the company's right to fire, that employee might sue for breach of contract if you don't investigate before terminating his or her employment. The lawsuit would claim that (1) the employee didn't commit the misconduct for which he or she was fired; (2) your company didn't bother to investigate to figure out what really happened; and, therefore, (3) your company didn't have good cause to fire the employee.

Usually, this won't be an issue because most employees don't have employment contracts that limit the right to fire. Instead, they are "at-will" employees, which means that they can quit at any time, and you can fire them at any time, for any reason that is not illegal (illegal reasons for firing include discrimination and retaliation). However, some employees have employment contracts that limit the employer's right to fire at will. For example, the contract might state that the employee can be fired only for "good cause" or for specified reasons (such as "gross misconduct" or "financial malfeasance"). If you fire the employee for reasons other than those stated in the contract, the employee can sue your company for breaching the contract.

Failing to Fire Dangerous Employees Can Lead to Lawsuits

Someone who is injured by one of your company's employees might have a legal claim against your company if management knew or should have known that the employee was unfit for the job, yet did nothing about it. These are called "negligent retention" or "negligent supervision" claims. Although these lawsuits have not yet appeared in every state, the clear legal trend is to allow employers to be sued for hiring or keeping on a dangerous employee.

Failing to investigate can give rise to this type of lawsuit. If you failed to perform an investigation that would have revealed that a particular employee posed a danger to others, your company could be on the hook for damages if the employee harms someone.

> EXAMPLE: John works at a machine plant. His coworkers notice that John has not been himself lately. His appearance is somewhat disheveled, he seems distracted, and he loses his temper easily. He complains that company management is trying to force him to retire, but that he "won't go quietly." Coworkers bring this to the attention of the human resources department but are told, "That's just John. He complains a lot, but he does high-quality work." A month later, John sabotages a major piece of equipment, which malfunctions and injures several employees and a few students visiting from a local vocational school. The company might face a lawsuit for negligent retention.

Negligent retention and supervision claims can always be brought by outsiders who don't work for your company. Your employees, on the other hand, may not be able to sue you for negligence. The workers' compensation insurance system, which guarantees compensation to employees who are injured in the workplace generally prohibits employees from suing their employers for injuries that are covered by workers' comp. For more on this issue, see Chapter 8.

An employee might also have a contract that hasn't been reduced to writing. For example, some employees have spoken agreements with the employer (known as oral contracts). Whatever the employer and employee agreed to orally will govern the employer's right to fire. In other cases, an employee might have an implied contract: a contract that was never explicitly agreed to, whether in conversation or in writing, but arose from the conduct and statements of the employer and employee. For example, if an employer tells a worker "as long as you do a good job, we'll keep you on," that could be interpreted as an implied contract restricting the employer's right to fire the employee unless the employee performs poorly.

To avoid the legal problems that can result from failing to investigate, take workplace problems seriously. Never ignore complaints of wrong-doing. Even if a situation seems simple or straightforward, always do some initial research before deciding that an investigation isn't warranted. And make sure you know all the facts before taking disciplinary action against an employee.

Delay

Even if you eventually decide to investigate and do a good job, your company can get into legal trouble if you wait too long to get started. If an employee suffers harm—from harassment or workplace violence, for example—after you learn about the problem but before you take action, your company will usually be legally responsible to the employee. The longer you postpone the investigation, the more serious that legal liability could be.

> EXAMPLE: Kristen worked as a checker at a grocery store. She complained that a coworker harassed her by calling her names, propositioning her, commenting on her appearance, and touching her. Kristen complained to the store's assistant manager several times; each time, the manager confronted the coworker, who denied the allegations. After Kristen's fourth complaint—two months after her first complaint—the accused harasser was transferred to a different shift, where he had no further contact with Kristen.

Kristen filed a lawsuit against the grocery store for sexual harassment. The employer tried to have her case thrown out, arguing that it stopped the harassment by transferring the alleged harasser. However, the court found that the store's two-month delay before taking action was too long, even if it eventually did the right thing by moving the alleged harasser to another shift. The court allowed Kristen's lawsuit to go forward.

Postponing the investigation could also lead the complaining employee to claim that he or she was retaliated against: disciplined or otherwise treated badly for making the complaint. (For more on this issue, see "Retaliation," below.) If the employee is threatened by the wrongdoer, given the cold shoulder by other employees, or disciplined by a supervisor for coming forward, that could well constitute illegal retaliation for which your company would be legally liable.

Of course, there's a simple solution: Don't delay your investigation. Once you learn of a serious problem or complaint, get moving right away. If you absolutely have to wait a bit before getting started (because the victim is on vacation, for example), document the reasons for the delay. (Chapter 3 explains how to do this.)

Inconsistency

Some companies get into trouble by acting inconsistently. In the employment arena, handling similar situations differently can lead to claims of discrimination. An employee might bring a discrimination lawsuit if he or she feels that the employer treated him or her differently because of a protected characteristic—an inherent quality, such as race or gender, that cannot legally form the basis for an employment decision.

Federal laws prohibit employers from making workplace decisions based on an employee's or applicant's race, color, national origin, sex, religion, age (if the employee is at least 40 years old), genetic information, or disability. These laws apply only to employers with 15 or more employees—or 20 or more employees, for age discrimination. In addition, almost every state has adopted an antidiscrimination law. Although some of these laws mirror the federal rules, some prohibit additional kinds of discrimination (based on sexual orientation or marital status, for example) and some apply to smaller employers. (For more on discrimination laws and protected characteristics, see Chapter 5. You'll find information on your state's antidiscrimination laws in Appendix B.)

If you aren't evenhanded in your investigations, you could risk a discrimination claim. For example, if you decide not to investigate a complaint against a white man for sexual harassment but you do investigate a harassment complaint against an African American man, you and your company might be accused of race discrimination. Similarly, if you don't investigate a claim of discrimination brought by a Muslim employee, that employee might argue that your decision was based on hostility to his or her religion.

> EXAMPLE: Kwik & Klean, a janitorial company, investigates an incident of sexual harassment. The company concludes that Tom, a white employee on one of the night crews, has been telling X-rated jokes and stories, which have made some of his female coworkers uncomfortable. Tom is given a written warning and is required to attend sexual harassment training.
>
> Several months later, a worker on a different crew complains that Eduardo, a Latino employee, has been making lewd sexual comments to coworkers. The company investigates and concludes that the complaint is valid. The company is concerned that it has had two incidents of harassment in the past few months and decides that it has to take steps to demonstrate its commitment to rooting out the problem, so it decides to fire Eduardo.
>
> Eduardo sues, claiming that he was treated more harshly than Tom because of his race. Even if the company's decision wasn't based on the race of either employee, it will have trouble defending its inconsistent treatment in court. Because the employees committed similar offenses, the best course of action is to impose similar discipline. The company can take other steps— like requiring sexual harassment training for the entire workforce—to show employees that harassment won't be tolerated.

Avoid discrimination claims by treating similar problems similarly. If you decide to investigate one claim but not another, make sure you have a valid, business-related reason for doing so. If you punish one employee more harshly than another, be prepared to justify the difference. And always check your motives: Most of us don't want to admit to any prejudice, but we all have preconceptions that can affect our decisions. Inconsistency is sometimes justified, but it can also be a sign of unconscious bias at work.

Retaliation

Your company may not take any negative action against an employee for coming forward with a harassment or discrimination complaint or for participating in a related investigation. As the U.S. Supreme Court has held, any action that could deter a reasonable worker from coming forward with such a complaint might constitute retaliation. (*Burlington Northern & Santa Fe Railway Co. v. White,* 548 U.S. 53 (2006).) The negative actions need not be a firing or demotion: Lesser forms of mistreatment might also qualify as retaliation, if they could discourage employees from bringing complaints. Although retaliation comes up frequently in harassment and discrimination cases, any complaint about workplace rights can give rise to a retaliation claim, if the employee who complained is fired or otherwise treated poorly as a result.

Most conscientious employers realize that punishing an employee for bringing a workplace problem to their attention is a bad idea, for legal and practical reasons. However, even savvy employers sometimes retaliate against an employee without intending to. This comes up most often when employees need to be separated for some reason. For example, if one employee is allegedly harassing another, your first instinct might be to move one of the workers to another position, so they won't have to work together. However, if you move the worker who complained, that worker might feel retaliated against for complaining, especially if the new position, workspace, or shift is less prestigious or desirable. If you must separate workers, either move the worker accused of misconduct or make very sure that the worker who complained is in favor of the change you propose.

An employee need not bring a formal complaint to be protected from retaliation. Title VII, the federal law that prohibits retaliation for reporting harassment and discrimination, says that those who "oppose" an illegal practice are protected from retaliation. The U.S. Supreme Court has held that this language protects not only employees who complain, but also witnesses and others who speak out against an illegal practice during a workplace investigation. (*Crawford v. Metropolitan Government of Nashville and Davidson County, Tennessee*, 555 U.S. 271 (2009).) In this case, Ms. Crawford was interviewed as part of an internal investigation into sexual harassment allegations, and she told the investigator that the accused employee had acted inappropriately toward her, as well. Following the investigation, Ms. Crawford was fired along with others who were interviewed; the alleged harasser was not. The Court found that Ms. Crawford could bring a retaliation claim even though she wasn't the employee who initially complained of harassment.

To protect against retaliation claims, warn everyone involved in an investigation that retaliation won't be tolerated. Ask the complaining employee—and perhaps his or her manager—to bring any instances of retaliation to your attention immediately.

CAUTION

Retaliation lawsuits can outlive the original complaint. Courts have held that an employee can sue an employer who punishes the employee for making a complaint even if the conduct the employee complains about doesn't violate the law. For example, an employee files a lawsuit, claiming that she was fired for complaining about sexual harassment by a coworker. The court decides that the coworker's conduct, while inappropriate, did not meet the legal standards for sexual harassment. However, the court might still allow the woman to sue for retaliation: Even though she wasn't sexually harassed, it is illegal for the employer to fire her for complaining about it in good faith.

Failing to Be Thorough

Performing an incomplete or sloppy investigation—by failing to interview key witnesses, neglecting to review important documents, or ignoring issues that come up during the investigation, for example—can have many of the same negative consequences as failing to investigate at all.

Employees Win Retaliation Cases at the Supreme Court

Although the Supreme Court under Chief Justice John Roberts is known as a friend to business, the Court is decidedly on the side of the employee in retaliation cases. In recent years, the Court has decided a handful of retaliation cases; employees have won them all. A couple of the most recent holdings:

- **An employee can sue for retaliation based on his fiancée's legally protected activity.** The Court found that a man could sue for retaliation after he was fired because his fiancée filed a sex discrimination lawsuit against their mutual employer. Even though one employee complained of discrimination and the other suffered the negative job consequence, the Court found that this sort of reprisal could dissuade employees from asserting their rights. (*Thompson v. North American Stainless, LP*, 131 S. Ct. 863 (2011).)

- **Oral complaints can give rise to a retaliation claim.** In a case under the Fair Labor Standards Act, an employee claimed that he was fired after making repeated oral complaints that the company time clocks were located in a place that required employees to clock in before donning their protective work gear, and to clock out before they took that gear off. As a result, employees were not paid for time that must be compensated under the law. The Court rejected the employer's argument that such a complaint must be in writing to form the basis of a retaliation claim. As long as the employee's complaint is sufficiently clear and detailed for the employer to understand it as an assertion of statutory rights, the employee is protected from retaliation. (*Kasten v. Saint-Gobain Performance Plastics Corp.*, 131 S. Ct. 1325 (2011).)

As these cases recognize, retaliation is particularly dangerous because it threatens the entire system of workplace law, which relies largely on employee complaints. Although discrimination and harassment are illegal, for example, government agencies don't have the resources to audit and police every private employer. Instead, employee complaints are the primary engine of discovery and enforcement. Courts have repeatedly shown that they will protect this mechanism, regardless of the form of the underlying complaint.

The employee who complained or suffered mistreatment might feel that his or her concerns weren't taken seriously and might sue for retaliation or for harm that continued during and after the investigation. An employee accused of misconduct might believe that your company wasn't interested in his or her side of the story or in finding out what really happened, which could lead to a lawsuit for wrongful termination or discrimination.

And worse, your company won't be able to rely on the results of your investigation in court: If an employee can show that you did an incompetent job, for example, by hiring an expert witness to testify that you didn't investigate properly, your company could be in an even worse position than if you never investigated in the first place. As great political scandals have shown, the "cover-up" can be more damaging than the underlying problem ever was. If your investigation appears to be inadequate, a jury might well wonder whether you were trying to hide deeper problems or protect someone important at your company, perhaps by making a scapegoat of the employee who was fired.

This is an easy mistake to avoid. Following the simple strategies and steps in this book will ensure that your investigation is thorough and proper, and will greatly increase the likelihood that it will be held up in court.

Compromising Confidentiality

Loose lips do more than sink ships: They can also torpedo a workplace investigation. From a practical standpoint, talking too much during the investigation—telling a witness what another witness said, revealing your personal opinion to one of the employees involved, or publicizing the complaint in the workplace, for example—can lead others to doubt your objectivity. They might believe you have already made up your mind and therefore aren't going to investigate fairly. Employees involved in the investigation might change their statements, either intentionally or subconsciously, based on what you say. And you can bet that if you're talking about the investigation, the entire workplace is talking, too, which will lead to a lot of gossip and lost productivity.

As a legal matter, an employee who believes you have maligned his or her reputation by spreading false information can sue for defamation. These claims are sometimes made by the target of the investigation, who argues that the employer falsely accused him or her of wrongdoing, resulting in unfair discipline and a damaged reputation, and perhaps even preventing him or her from getting another job.

> **EXAMPLE:** Tricia was fired from the Reader's Hideaway, a bookstore, after her register drawer was short on several occasions. Tricia claims that she didn't steal any money from the store and that another employee—David, the owner's son—used her register on each day that it was short. David denies taking the money, and the company never bothers to talk to other employees about what they've seen or otherwise investigate Tricia's claims further. When Tricia applies for other jobs and Reader's Hideaway is called for a reference, the owner says that Tricia was fired for stealing from the company. Tricia sues for defamation.

A defamation claim can also be brought by an employee who makes a workplace complaint, if you conclude that the complaint is false and make this belief public. In this situation, the employee's claim is that he or she was falsely labeled a liar. Even a witness who participated in a workplace investigation could accuse the employer of lying about what he or she said, if the employer's statements damaged the employee's reputation.

As explained in "Defamation Defenses," below, you can defend against a defamation claim by showing that your statement was true or, in some circumstances, that you made it in good faith and reasonably believed it to be true. If you speak with malice (that is, with the intent to cause harm), however, your statement probably isn't protected.

Defamation claims arise when investigators or employers talk too much or say things that they don't know to be true. The best way to avoid this mistake is to reveal information on a need-to-know basis only. Don't talk about the investigation, the evidence, or your conclusions with anyone except those who need to be in on the decisions. If you must make a damaging statement about an employee or former employee, stick to the facts and keep it short.

Defamation Defenses

Although employers can be held liable for harming an employee's reputation, the law recognizes that employers sometimes have to talk about former employees and the reasons why they are no longer employed. Here are a few legal defenses that will protect an employer that reveals limited information in good faith:

- **Truth.** Someone who is telling the truth can't be sued for defamation. In other words, if you tell someone that an employee was fired for pulling a gun on you, the employee can't make a claim for defamation if that's exactly what happened.

- **Good faith reference to a prospective employer.** Most states will not allow a former employee to sue an employer for defamation if the employer makes statements that it reasonably believes to be true to a prospective employer seeking a reference. Typically, these statements are "conditionally privileged": This means that the employer won't be liable as long as it acts in good faith (rather than with malice).

- **Good faith statement to a government agency.** An employer generally cannot be sued for responding in good faith to a government request for information about why an employee was fired. For example, you can tell the unemployment or workers' compensation office your reasons for terminating an employee without worrying about defamation claims. Similarly, statements made by an employer during official proceedings (such as a lawsuit or arbitration hearing) cannot give rise to a defamation claim.

A statement is in "good faith" only if it is not malicious (said with the intent to cause harm). In one case, for example, an employee's defamation claim against a coworker who accused him of stealing was allowed to go forward on this issue. The employee showed that the coworker could not have seen the alleged theft, that the items he was loading into a vehicle as part of his job looked nothing like the items he was accused of stealing, and that the coworker bore him a personal grudge because the employee had previously been in a relationship with the coworker's wife. Taken together, these facts could be enough to prove malice, which would defeat the coworker's claim that he acted in good faith. (*Curren v. Carbonic Systems*, 872 N.Y.S.2d 240 (2009).)

> ### Defamation Defenses (continued)
>
> The best way to avoid a defamation claim is to speak only to people who have a legitimate need to know why the employee was fired, and to only make statements that you know to be true. Conducting a proper investigation will help you figure out where the truth lies and, therefore, what you can safely say about the situation.

It's one thing to control what you say during an investigation, but it's much harder to control what employees say. Recently, a couple of government agencies have made investigation confidentiality a very tricky legal issue as well. Both the EEOC and the National Labor Relations Board (NLRB) have found that imposing broad confidentiality requirements on employees who participate in an investigation could violate laws prohibiting retaliation and unfair labor practices. Although both agencies recognize that a particular investigation might require employee silence (for example, if the employer reasonably fears that evidence could be destroyed), these decisions have to be made on a case-by-case basis. Blanket "gag rules" that apply to everyone involved in every investigation probably wouldn't make the cut, particularly if employees felt that they couldn't raise concerns or talk to their coworkers about workplace problems. For more information on this emerging issue, see Chapter 3.

Losing Objectivity

You've probably developed some personal opinions about most of the people you work with. It's human nature to like some people more than others. But you have to put these opinions aside and look objectively at the evidence when you conduct a workplace investigation. If you let your personal feelings and opinions hold sway, you might be accused of discrimination, and the results of your investigation could be called into question.

It can also be tough to stay objective if you have to investigate—and recommend discipline against—people who outrank you on the corporate ladder. But, if you let the offending employee's position in the company dictate the outcome of the investigation, you aren't doing your job properly.

The best antidote for this problem is to remember your role. When you investigate, you are acting on behalf of the company. If you feel unable to put your personal feelings aside, get some help. Ask someone else within the workplace (or hire an outside investigator) to conduct the investigation or get some advice from a lawyer.

> ⓘ CAUTION
> **You might not like what you discover.** You must follow the evidence wherever it leads, even if that means uncovering serious problems at your company or finding that a popular or high-ranking employee committed wrongdoing. You won't do your company any favors by turning a blind eye to these types of problems: Remember, your job is to figure out what's going on, so the company can take effective action to remedy the situation. Although your findings might make you unpopular or unhappy in the short term, you'll be doing the right thing in the long run.

Strong-Arm Interview Tactics

Some investigators are so intent on getting straight answers from the workers they interview that they restrain workers against their will. For example, an investigator might lock the door to the interview room, physically prevent the employee from leaving, or tell the employee something like "nobody's leaving this room until I find out what really happened." Using physical means to restrain an employee, or taking actions that lead the employee to believe that he or she is not free to go, can lead to a legal claim of false imprisonment.

You can avoid false imprisonment lawsuits by avoiding coercive tactics. If an employee indicates that he or she wants to leave the room or stop an interview, let him or her go. Your company is free to take disciplinary action against an employee who refuses to answer legitimate questions or participate in a workplace investigation. However, you can't use physical means or threats to prevent the employee from leaving.

Invading Employee Privacy

Don't become so zealous in your search for the truth that you invade employees' privacy rights. This can be a tough call; after all, conducting an investigation involves a certain amount of poking around, usually into things that someone doesn't want you to know about. However, if you cross the line from legitimate workplace concerns into private employee property or behavior, you could be inviting a lawsuit for invasion of privacy.

If an employee files a lawsuit for invasion of privacy, a judge will look at why both sides acted as they did: why the employee expected privacy and why the employer searched, monitored, or otherwise got into an area the employee felt was private. Then, the judge decides whose side of the argument seems most reasonable, in what is aptly called a "balancing test."

Searches

When investigating certain types of wrongdoing, you may need to search an employee's work area. For example, if an employee is accused of theft or drug use, you may want to look in the employee's desk or locker for the stolen items or the employee's stash. You will be on safest legal ground if your company has a written policy that reserves the right to search employee workspaces. This type of policy shows that employees should not have expected the contents of their desks or lockers to be private.

The more intrusive the search, the more compelling your reasons for searching must be. For example, if you want to search something an employee brings on company property, such as a lunch pail or backpack, you must have a fairly strong reason to search. And you probably should not undertake this kind of search unless your company has clearly warned employees, in a written policy, that these items are subject to search. If you want to conduct a really intrusive search—for example, turning out a worker's pockets or searching an employee physically—you are asking for trouble. If your investigation reaches a point where this type of search seems necessary, talk to a lawyer. (For more on workplace searches, see Chapter 7.)

Electronic Monitoring

As long as your company has a written policy letting workers know that it might monitor their email or use of the Internet, the company generally has the right to read employee email sent on company equipment or monitor which websites employees visit using the company's computer network. During an investigation, emails often provide crucial proof of misconduct, such as harassment, discrimination, or threats.

Monitoring in a BYOD Workplace

These days, many employers have "bring your own device" (BYOD) policies, in which employees are allowed to use their own mobile electronic devices—notably, smartphones and tablets—for work. This practice is popular among employees, who are often reluctant to carry an extra device just for work or abandon the device they are most comfortable with (usually the iPhone) for a corporate device (often a BlackBerry).

Employers can build loyalty by adopting BYOD, but it comes with a number of pitfalls, particularly in the area of security. Maintaining company trade secrets and confidential documents becomes much more difficult when those files are kept on devices the company doesn't fully control. And, if an employee with a BYOD device is accused of wrongdoing, the privacy issues are complicated. Can the company seize the employee's own phone to search it for lewd emails or downloaded pornography shown to a coworker? What if a manager keeps an electronic calendar on a BYOD device, and the dates of particular meetings and conversations with that manager become relevant to a discrimination claim? BYOD invites the mingling of personal and work-related information, in a way that can lead to confusion about what an employer may legitimately access. If your company has a BYOD policy, you'll want some legal advice on how to protect your company's security and maintain its right to inspect these devices.

EXAMPLE: Isaac complains that someone is sending him racist cartoons and jokes anonymously, using the office email system. The company has a written policy permitting it to monitor employee emails. The investigator reads the emails and asks for the tech department's help in figuring out where they originated. The employee who sent the offensive messages would have a hard time arguing that the company shouldn't have read the messages or traced them back to their sender.

Monitoring phone calls is another story. An employer is legally allowed to monitor employee conversations with customers or clients for quality control (although some state laws require the employer to inform the parties to the call—either by announcement or by signal—that someone is listening in). However, different rules apply to personal calls. Once the person monitoring realizes that a particular call is personal, the monitoring must stop immediately.

Avoiding Privacy Lawsuits

The best way to avoid violating employees' privacy rights is to limit your search or inquiry to only what you need to know. Exercise restraint: Don't search or monitor employees without a good reason. The further you stray from the complaint or alleged misconduct, the more likely you are to invade someone's privacy.

You can minimize legal exposure by making sure your company adopts written policies warning employees that it reserves the right to search desks, lockers, and email. If your company has a written policy warning that it might search, employees will have a tough time arguing that they reasonably expected those areas to be private.

Using Polygraphs Improperly

You might believe that the easiest way to get to the bottom of a workplace problem is to require everyone involved to take a lie detector test. In many situations, however, polygraph tests will only lead to trouble. A federal law, the Employee Polygraph Protection Act (29 U.S.C. §§ 2001–2009), strictly limits the circumstances in which an employer can require workers to take a lie detector or polygraph test, and it's not easy to meet the law's requirements.

From the Horse's Mouth: How a Plaintiffs Attorney Evaluates Company Investigations

In the best case scenario, no plaintiff's attorney will ever review your investigation. If you act promptly, investigate thoroughly, and take effective action to deal with any problems you find, hopefully the employees involved will be satisfied (or at least you won't give them grounds for a lawsuit).

But you can't please everyone all of the time. An employee who believes that the company didn't take effective action to stop harassment or discrimination, or an employee who is disciplined or fired for wrongdoing uncovered by your investigation, might seek out legal counsel. When they do, how will your investigation stand up? According to a recent SHRM article, plaintiff's attorney Nina Pirotti looks first to the company's investigation in evaluating the strength of a potential client's claims. She explained that she looks for five red flags signaling a possibly botched investigation:

- **Incompleteness.** If the investigator doesn't interview all of the relevant witnesses or try to dig deeper than the alleged perpetrator's denial, a plaintiff's lawyer will want to find out what should have been discovered.
- **Refusing to judge credibility.** Just because no one else witnessed a "he said, she said" incident, doesn't mean the investigator can't draw reasonable conclusions about what happened based on, for example, plausibility and circumstantial evidence. (See Chapter 4 for more on making these determinations.)
- **Poor questioning techniques.** If the investigator puts words in the witness's mouth, asks leading questions, or tries to intimidate the witness into giving a certain response, that could taint the investigation.
- **Failure to document or keep records.** It's not enough to investigate; your company will have to show that your investigation was thorough and sound, using your notes and investigation report as evidence. (Chapter 4 explains how to document your investigation.)
- **Investigator bias.** If the investigator has a personal relationship with a witness or otherwise has a stake in the outcome of an investigation, expect that fact to come up repeatedly at trial.

"Workplace Investigation Red Flags Raised," by Allen Smith (available at www.shrm.org).

An employer must fit within one of the law's narrow exceptions to have the legal right to test. (One of the exceptions applies to theft investigations; see Chapter 7 for more information.) And even then, the employer has to meet a long list of technical requirements before it can use the results of the test to make a disciplinary decision about an employee. Among other things, the employee must receive a variety of written notices, must receive the test questions in advance, cannot be asked certain types of questions, and must receive a copy of the test results. In addition, the employer must use a polygraph examiner who meets certain qualifications and reports the results of the test in a particular form.

It can be pretty tough to conduct a legal polygraph test under this law. Even if your company can meet the legal requirements, you'll have to decide how much weight to give the test results. Experts disagree about how easy (or difficult) it is to "beat" the test. Because of these legal and practical problems, it's usually best to just skip the polygraph testing altogether. If you are still inclined to test, make sure the situation falls within one of the law's exceptions, and hire a polygraph examiner who is properly certified and understands the law.

Getting Started

Although your company can reap a lot of benefits from con-ducting an effective investigation, that doesn't necessarily mean you'll enjoy every minute of it. Investigating can be unpleasant work. If you're looking into a sexual harassment complaint, for example, you might see or hear some pretty graphic things. If you're investigating a violence complaint, you might have to make difficult judgment calls to ensure the safety of employees and customers. And if you're investigating a complaint that involves employees whom you like or work closely with, your investigation may affect those relationships. All the while, you will probably feel some pressure to resolve the situation quickly, without creating legal liability.

In short, you're likely to experience some anxiety when investigating and dealing with workplace problems. The best way to alleviate this anxiety is through careful planning: Take some time before you begin your fact-finding to assess the situation and decide how to handle it.

Preparation can also help you avoid making mistakes that could come back to haunt you and your company. Sometimes, the worst investigation blunders are made before the investigation even starts: A company ignores a complaint, chooses an insensitive or biased investigator, or fails to take immediate steps to prevent further harm to its employees. It's often apparent only in hindsight, after a lawsuit is filed, that these problems could have been avoided by paying careful attention to pre-investigation details.

This chapter provides the information you'll need to prepare for a successful investigation. It explains how a problem requiring investigation might come to your attention, how to decide whether to investigate, what actions you might want to take before beginning the investigation, and how to plan for the investigation. It also covers how to choose someone to investigate a problem (if you aren't going to do it yourself), including the pros and cons of hiring an outside investigator.

Discovering Workplace Problems

The situation that triggers an investigation might come to your attention in any number of ways, but your company's obligation to investigate doesn't depend on how you find out about the problem. Some employers mistakenly believe that they have a duty to investigate only formal complaints. But this is wrong. No matter how your company learns of a serious workplace problem, it generally has a legal duty to resolve it, often starting with an investigation of the underlying facts. As a practical matter, if your company ignores misconduct, morale will drop, productivity will suffer, and employees will quickly learn that they don't have to follow workplace rules.

CAUTION

Once a manager knows, "the company" knows. Generally, a company is assumed to be aware of a complaint or problem once a manager, officer, or other person responsible for taking action (such as a human resources professional) knows about it. This is true even if the manager or other responsible person doesn't reveal the problem to anyone else. This is one reason why your company should have strictly enforced policies that require managers to immediately report problems to the appropriate person, such as a human resources representative or the company president. For an example, see the sample policy provided at this book's online companion page (Appendix A has information on accessing the page).

Some investigations do begin with a formal complaint. But you can't count on employees to bring every workplace problem to your attention. Employees sometimes choose not to complain because they don't want to be seen as troublemakers, they fear retaliation, or they simply hope the problem will go away on its own.

In some situations, employees may not even know about the misconduct because they're not being victimized by it. For example, if an employee is stealing from customers, it's possible that no other worker is even aware of the problem. And in some situations, no one wants to come forward because they are all implicated in the misconduct. For example, if employees are selling drugs in the workplace, you probably shouldn't expect their coworkers—who are also their customers—to let you in on the details.

Here are some of the many ways you might find out about a workplace problem requiring an investigation.

Formal Complaints

One advantage of starting an investigation with a formal complaint—in which an employee reports a problem directly to the appropriate person (typically, someone in the human resources department)—is that you can document the source and nature of the problem. A complaint gives your investigation a natural starting point; you can begin by getting the details directly from the complaining employee.

You should have a form for reporting complaints, with blanks to fill in the complaining employee's name, the date of the complaint, the details of the complaint, and so on. (You'll find a template complaint form at this book's online companion page; see Appendix A for details.) Although some companies require the complaining employee to complete a complaint form, this could create problems. Some employees will feel intimidated by having to commit their complaint to writing and will balk at this requirement. And you'll be at the mercy of the complaining employee's writing skills (and ability to pinpoint the problem). It's a better idea to have the person who takes the complaint—often a human resources representative or designated manager—fill in the complaint form. (See below for a sample completed complaint form.)

An employer can encourage formal complaints by instituting well-publicized complaint and open-door policies that encourage employees to come forward with their concerns. These policies can:

- give you an opportunity to deal with workplace problems immediately
- tell employees that the company cares about their concerns
- let managers know what their responsibilities are if they learn of a problem

- support other workplace policies (for example, an antiharassment policy or workplace violence policy) by demonstrating that employees will be held to these rules, and
- give your company some legal protection against harassment and discrimination lawsuits (see "Decide Whether to Investigate," below, for more information).

You'll find more information, including sample policies you can use in your workplace, at this book's online companion page; see Appendix A for details.

What If the Employee Doesn't Want to File a Complaint?

Most experienced managers and human resources professionals have faced this troubling situation: An employee comes to their office, shuts the door, and confides that another employee is causing trouble—perhaps by telling dirty jokes, threatening coworkers, or breaking workplace rules. The confiding employee may want advice, a shoulder to cry on, or simply a safe place to let off some steam about a bad situation. What the employee does not want is to make a formal complaint.

While you might be tempted to act as a friend and respect the employee's request to keep things quiet, that is rarely in the best interests of the company or the complaining employee. Once a manager knows of illegal workplace conduct, the company is on notice and has an obligation to deal with the problem, even if the employee doesn't want to file a complaint. And the complaining employee's situation isn't going to improve unless and until the company takes action.

This can be a tough situation for managers, particularly those who are friends with the employees who work for them. Prepare managers by letting them know that they must bring all complaints to the attention of the appropriate people, even if the complaining employee does not want to come forward. Managers can tell reluctant employees, "I know this is hard and you want to keep it quiet. But I have an obligation to report this, so the company can do something about it. That's the only way we can improve this situation."

CAUTION

Make sure your complaint policy and procedures can be understood by employees. The complaint process should be geared toward the employees at your company. For example, if many employees don't speak English, the policy should be made available in other languages. And, if your company employs minors, you must make sure the policy is straightforward enough for them to understand. In a case from the 7th Circuit Court of Appeals, the court rejected a fast food company's effort to dismiss a teenage employee's claim for failing to report harassment through the proper channels, finding that the company's poorly drafted policy wasn't a reasonable mechanism for taking employee complaints. The court found that the company's policy for reporting harassment was apt to confuse even the adults who worked there, let alone the many teenage employees. (*EEOC v. V & J Foods Inc.*, 507 F.3d 575 (7th Cir. 2007).)

Anonymous Complaints

Sometimes, complaints are made anonymously, through an unsigned note in a suggestion box, a letter or memo to a manager, or an unidentified phone message, for example.

An employee might complain anonymously for many reasons. An employee who is being harassed might fear retaliation from the wrongdoer or want to avoid being seen as a complainer. An employee who is threatened with violence or who witnesses illegal activities—such as theft or drug crimes—might fear for his or her physical safety or simply not want to talk to the police.

An anonymous complaint might also come from someone who isn't involved in the situation. For example, a coworker might complain anonymously on behalf of a friend who is too fearful to come forward. A customer, vendor, or client may want to report misconduct but not want to get involved. An anonymous complaint might even be made by someone outside the work environment, such as a concerned friend, spouse, or partner.

TIP

Publicly traded companies must have a procedure for making anonymous complaints about financial fraud. The Sarbanes-Oxley Act of 2002, a comprehensive federal law that seeks to protect shareholders from fraud, requires public companies to provide a way for employees to submit confidential, anonymous complaints about questionable accounting or auditing practices. This law also requires companies to adopt procedures for receiving, handling, and retaining such complaints. For more information, see Chapter 7.

Reports by Managers and Supervisors

Managers and supervisors are the company's eyes and ears in the workplace. Because they are on the front lines, they are most likely to witness developing problems. In some cases, managers or supervisors might hear rumors or gossip about improper activities; sometimes, they hear complaints directly from unhappy workers.

Rumors of Harassment

If a manager hears about harassment through the company grapevine, that is enough to trigger the company's obligation to act. Even if the manager doesn't directly witness the problem or receive an explicit complaint, the company is on notice once workplace rumors reach management. That was the recent finding of a federal District Court in refusing to throw out a sexual harassment claim. The Court found that two assistant managers had heard that a store manager had tried to hug, kiss, and touch female employees, and that he was involved in a sexual relationship with a 16-year-old subordinate. Even though the young employee never made a complaint of harassment, these facts, if proven true, would require the company to investigate and take action. (*EEOC v. Finish Line Inc.*, 940 F. Supp. 2d 777 (M.D. Tenn. 2013).)

Your company should train all managers to report any employee complaints, incidents of workplace wrongdoing, or even rumors of troublesome behavior. Requiring managers to report problems will allow your company to remedy the situation early. As a legal matter, once your managers are aware of a problem, the company is generally legally responsible for taking action to deal with the situation. If managers fail to report serious issues, your company may be on the hook for any harm that results, even if no formal complaint is made.

Indirect Complaints

Sometimes, an employee who is unwilling to bring a complaint will let a manager or human resources representative know about a problem indirectly. For example, an employee who receives a poor performance evaluation might explain that he or she has been unable to concentrate at work because of harassment. Or an employee who is interviewed as a witness in an investigation might raise a completely separate problem. Even though these workers are not making formal complaints, they are revealing a possible workplace problem that should be looked into.

Information From Departing Workers

Sometimes, a company learns of workplace troubles from an employee on the way out the door. For example, say that a worker quits, claiming that she has found another job. However, at her exit interview, the worker says that one reason for her departure is that her boss, whom she once dated, won't stop pressuring her to get back together with him. Once she's gone, do you need to look into this further?

The answer is a resounding "yes." The complaining employee's departure doesn't get rid of the potentially serious problem in your company. And, it doesn't preclude that same departing employee from suing for sexual harassment. The accused boss may be harassing others as well. And even if he's not, you have to take action against those who commit sexual harassment to demonstrate your company's commitment to rooting out the problem, both to the departing employee and to other workers. If your investigation reveals that the departing employee was harassed, you should also take steps to make things right for her, such as giving her a chance to return to her old job.

Workplace Observation

Sometimes, a workplace problem is obvious but the source of the problem is not. For example, you might see pornographic images in the lunchroom, money missing from petty cash, or baggies and marijuana cigarette butts left behind in the company parking lot. In these situations, you'll need to investigate to find out who's to blame.

Third-Party Reports

Sometimes, problems are brought to light by an outsider, such as a customer, a client, a vendor, a friend or family member of the victim, an administrative agency, a lawyer, or even the police. Regardless of how a problem becomes apparent, your company's obligations are the same: It must investigate and take action to deal with the situation, if necessary.

However, you might need to adjust your investigation procedures somewhat if outsiders are involved. For example, you might have an obligation to share what you discover with the police, if they are investigating an alleged crime in your company. These issues are covered in more detail in the chapters that follow. For now, simply remember that your obligation to investigate doesn't disappear just because you heard about a problem from an outside source, even if that third party or agency is investigating the situation on its own. Only your company can discipline its own employees and take other internal steps that are necessary (such as providing harassment training, developing procedures for dealing with workplace violence, or changing its internal financial controls) to make sure the problem is resolved.

RESOURCE

Listen to a sample complaint. At this book's online companion page, you'll find audio files of investigative interviews, including an intake session with an employee who's making a complaint. The page also provides forms, policies, and much more. Appendix A explains how to find the page and access these materials.

Investigating When an Outside Agency Is Involved

If an employee complains to an outside agency (such as the EEOC), some companies assume that they no longer have to perform an investigation. After all, the agency will investigate if it believes there's a problem, right?

Wrong. Once you learn of a problem, even if you find out because the employee files a complaint with an agency or a lawsuit, you have a duty to investigate. The sooner you learn what happened, the sooner you can take effective action to stop it. If you do nothing in the face of a formal complaint, you risk appearing indifferent to ongoing problems in your company; you also risk a much higher damages award, if your company loses the case.

EXAMPLE: Amanda West worked on an assembly line at Tyson Foods. Shortly after starting work, she told her trainer that her supervisor and coworkers were making sexual comments, whistling at her, making lewd gestures, and touching her. The trainer asked her not to go to HR and offered to move her to a different work area. (The trainer also told her she was "hot.") Despite the move, the harassment continued until West stopped coming to work after she was followed to her car one night. She reported the harassment during her exit interview; the HR manager with whom she met said he would investigate, but he did not.

West then filed a harassment charge with the EEOC. Upon receiving the charge, the company investigated, but very poorly. The investigator failed to interview several key witnesses. And, after the investigator submitted written statements she had gathered, the company took no action to stop the harassment. The company's shoddy investigation after West left was part of the evidence the jury considered in finding that Tyson was recklessly indifferent to West's right to work free of harassment, which led to an award of $1.2 million, including punitive damages. (*West v. Tyson Foods Inc.*, 374 Fed. Appx. 624 (6th Cir. 2010).)

If you learn of a problem only after an employee has retained a lawyer, filed a charge with an administrative agency, or even filed a lawsuit, you

Investigating When an Outside Agency Is Involved (continued)

should consult with an attorney right away. In this situation, you are starting the investigation in an adversarial position, and you know that someone will be looking closely to catch any errors or omissions. By talking to a lawyer, you can figure out the best way to protect your company as you try to uncover the truth.

 CAUTION

Don't let anyone destroy documents once you know a lawsuit might be in the offing. As you probably know, your company must keep a variety of personnel records for certain periods of time prescribed by law. Once the time period for retention is over, your company is usually free to dispose of the documents, unless the company knows that they might be relevant to a pending or possible legal action. If your company reasonably anticipates a lawsuit, it must retain these documents—in what's called a "litigation hold"— until the matter is resolved. For example, if the employee has complained to an outside agency (such as the Equal Employment Opportunity Commission) or hired a lawyer, you'll need to retain the relevant documents. A lawyer can help you figure out when a litigation hold is necessary, which documents to keep, and what you can do to protect certain documents from disclosure.

Decide Whether to Investigate

Not every workplace problem demands an investigation. To decide whether (and how extensively) you should investigate, you'll need to consider several factors, including:

- whether there is a dispute over what happened
- how serious the alleged misconduct is, and
- how similar complaints have been handled in the past.

Scale the Investigation to the Size of the Problem

Sometimes, a problem bears some further looking into but doesn't warrant a full inquisition. While you don't want to ignore a complaint or incident, you should also exercise your common sense about how deep to dig. For example, you should spend more time and resources on a complaint that one employee has threatened another with a gun than on a complaint that one employee parked in the other's space in the company lot, unless the facts take you in a different direction.

Although you should generally follow the ten investigation steps in any situation that requires a closer look, that shouldn't take much time in a fairly simple dispute. If the situation turns out to be more complicated, you can slow down and take a more detailed approach.

EXAMPLE: You are looking into the case of the errant parker, above. You decide that no immediate actions are necessary, that you will handle the investigation yourself, and that you will start by talking to Marie, the complaining employee. Marie tells you that she doesn't know who's been parking in her spot or why. You go to the parking lot, see that the offending car belongs to Jack, and ask him what's going on. He replies that he was recently assigned a parking space and thought the space was his. He says he will happily move his car to wherever he's supposed to park. The person in charge of facility issues tells you that Jack was assigned Space 35, and Marie has Space 53. You tell both employees, Jack moves his car, and it's over and done with.

Are you going to interview witnesses who may have seen Jack actually parking his car, ask Jack if he has a learning disability that might cause him to transpose numbers, or review Jack's and Marie's personnel files for signs of previous problems? Of course not. Going into any more detail would be a waste of time. You've gotten to the bottom of the problem and solved it.

Now change the facts a little. What if Marie, during your first interview, said, "I know that's Jack's car in my space. Ever since I told him I wouldn't go out with him, he's been trying to intimidate me. I found a really nasty note on my chair yesterday, and I'm pretty sure he

> **Scale the Investigation to the Size of the Problem (continued)**
>
> wrote it. One of our coworkers told me that he called me a bitch and said he was going to teach me a lesson." This is an entirely different situation. Now, you will have other interviews to consider, you have a document to look at, you will want to spend some time planning how you will question Jack, and you will probably want to review his personnel file.

Are the Facts in Dispute?

The first thing to consider is whether there is a disagreement about what really happened. For example, if one employee accuses another of making violent threats and the other employee denies making them, you'll need to investigate to figure out who's telling the truth. On the other hand, if everyone agrees on the basic facts, you can move on to figuring out how to deal with the problem.

Sometimes, employees agree on what was said or done but disagree about what it meant. For example, what seemed like an innocent request for a date to one employee might have seemed like harassment to another. These situations call for a closer look. Otherwise, you won't know if the incident was just a onetime miscommunication or part of a larger pattern of harassment. However, be prepared to adjust the scope of the investigation to fit the facts. If, after completing your interviews of the people involved, you conclude that you're dealing with a simple misunderstanding, that warrants a quicker investigation than if you conclude that the incident is just one example of a larger pattern of misconduct.

How Serious Is the Problem?

Sometimes, employees disagree over what happened, but the underlying problem is not serious. Who left the coffeepot on? Who was supposed to show up early to do inventory? In these situations, the simple fact that there's a dispute doesn't mean you have to investigate; just talk to the employees involved and resolve the situation.

Of course, if you discover that the seemingly minor issue is part of a more serious underlying problem, you may need to institute a full-scale investigation. Using one of the examples above, let's say that Jared didn't come in early to do inventory because he didn't know that it was his turn. In this case, you might make sure that Jared's manager institutes a reminder system to let employees know when they are assigned to do the inventory, and leave it at that. If, however, Jared knew he was supposed to show up but didn't because he's afraid to work alone with Patrick, who has made racist comments about him, that's a much more serious issue that calls for a comprehensive investigation.

Some companies make the mistake of investigating only allegations of potentially illegal behavior, such as harassment or theft. But there are many other types of incidents and issues that might warrant an investigation, such as violation of company policies, ethical concerns, misuse of company property, inappropriate dealings with clients or vendors, and much more. Although these issues might not involve potentially illegal behavior, they certainly merit a closer look and, possibly, disciplinary action. If you don't investigate allegations like these, you're missing an opportunity to root out workplace problems.

How Have Similar Problems Been Handled?

When you are deciding whether an investigation is warranted, think about how your company has handled similar incidents or complaints in the past. If it has generally investigated similar problems, you should consider doing so now. If legal trouble later develops, you will be able to show that your company was fair and consistent with its employees and treated their complaints with equal concern.

Take Immediate Action, If Necessary

In certain situations, you will need to take some precautionary steps right away, even before the investigation begins. If, for example, an employee complains that her supervisor has fondled her repeatedly, an employee threatens to bring a gun to work, or an employee appears to be stealing company trade secrets to give to a competitor, you don't have the luxury of waiting until your investigation is complete. If the safety of employees or your company is at risk, you'll have to take some action immediately to prevent further harm.

The actions you take will depend on the situation. In cases of misconduct between two employees (sexual harassment, insubordination, or fighting, for example), you might choose to separate the employees until the investigation is finished. By assigning one or both to different shifts, managers, or job responsibilities temporarily, you can alleviate the immediate problem and investigate more thoroughly.

CAUTION

Beware of retaliation. It is illegal to punish or otherwise take any negative action against an employee who comes forward with a good faith complaint of harassment, discrimination, illegal conduct, or health and safety violations. The most obvious forms of retaliation are termination, discipline, demotion, pay cuts, or threats of any of these actions. More subtle forms of retaliation may include changing the shift hours or work area of the accuser, or changing the accuser's job responsibilities or reporting relationships. Although it often makes sense to change the work environment so that the accuser doesn't have to report to or work with the accused, those changes cannot come at the accuser's expense. If one employee must move to a less desirable position temporarily, your best bet is to move the accused employee.

If one employee is accused or suspected of extreme misconduct (such as threatening or committing physical violence, sexual assault, or large-scale theft), you'll probably want to suspend that employee, with pay, while you investigate the situation. Similarly, if an employee is suspected of being under the influence of alcohol or illegal drugs at work, that's a potentially dangerous situation that warrants pulling the employee from the workplace and getting the employee safely home. When you suspend the employee, explain the complaint or behavior at issue and ask to hear the accused employee's side of the story. Assure the employee that you will investigate the incident and reach a decision as quickly as possible.

Avoid Unpaid Suspensions

No matter how egregious the misconduct an employee is accused of committing, it's always a bad idea to suspend employees without pay pending an investigation. From both a practical and legal standpoint, paid suspensions are less risky and less inconvenient for employers: less risky because a paid employee is not as likely to sue as one who isn't being paid, and less inconvenient because you don't have to interrupt your regular payroll system.

In some cases, you cannot suspend exempt employees (those who are not entitled to earn overtime pay) without pay. Even if the employee is entitled to earn overtime pay, however, you can still get in trouble for imposing an unpaid suspension. A suspension without pay signals that you believe the employee is probably guilty, which can cause bad feelings and potential legal problems. If your investigation shows that the employee didn't commit misconduct or that the misconduct was less serious than it appeared, you will probably have to provide retroactive pay anyway (along with an apology). It's easier to simply let the employee take a few days off with pay while you figure out what happened.

Choose the Investigator

This book assumes that you will generally be doing the investigating yourself. In some cases, however, it might make sense to choose someone else, whether from inside or outside the company. If you are unavailable, have a personal relationship with either the accused or the complaining employee, or, in a worst case scenario, are the accused or complaining employee yourself, you'll need to choose another investigator.

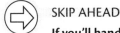

SKIP AHEAD

If you'll handle the investigation yourself, skip ahead to "Plan the Investigation," below.

The person you choose to investigate a problem will depend on various factors, including the size of your company, the identity of the complaining employee and accused employee, and the nature and severity of the problem. Regardless of how these factors play out, however, the investigator must meet a few essential job requirements: experience, impartiality, and professionalism.

Experience

The investigator should have some experience in investigating complaints, or at least some education and training on the subject. An experienced investigator will know what to look for, how to find it, and how to evaluate what he or she finds and, therefore, will probably do a better job than someone who hasn't tackled a project like this before.

Experience will also come into play if a complaining party files a lawsuit claiming that the investigation was faulty. If your investigator is inexperienced, a jury is more likely to second-guess his or her decisions, to question the quality of the investigation, and, ultimately, to disregard the findings altogether.

TIP

Train investigators ahead of time. Don't wait until you're facing a problem that you can't handle to start training other investigators. You need to be ready to start investigating serious problems as soon as you learn about them. This means that any other inside investigators you might use should be trained and ready to go before trouble starts.

Some situations call for an investigator with special expertise in certain issues. For example, if the investigation will involve figuring out technical matters (like whether an employee sabotaged a computer program or violated safety rules in a production line) or require advanced knowledge of a particular field (to determine whether an accountant was "cooking the books," for example), you should try to choose an investigator—or make someone available to assist the investigator—who has enough background to understand the details.

Should You Use a Team?

Some companies use a team of two or more investigators to look into workplace problems. The benefit of using a team is that you'll have an extra set of eyes, ears, and hands during the investigation. This means, for example, that one investigator can ask questions while the other takes notes, one investigator can gather evidence while the other sets up interviews, the investigators can collaborate when making decisions and recommendations about discipline, and both investigators will be available to testify about the investigation if the employer ends up in court.

However, there are also drawbacks to using a team. For one thing, two employees will be pulled away from their usual job responsibilities until the investigation is over, which can be a significant hardship for smaller employers. Some employees may feel intimidated by having to face two questioners, which might make it more difficult to establish rapport. And there's also the "too many cooks spoil the broth" problem: Unless the investigators carefully choreograph who will be responsible for what, there's a danger of duplicated effort and crossed signals.

It's probably best to use a team only for more serious or complicated complaints, including those that involve many employees, substantial misconduct, and/or a high possibility of legal trouble. Your company will reap the greatest benefits (of corroboration and efficiency) in these situations, and they warrant spending the additional time and money a second investigator will require.

Impartiality

The person who investigates must be perceived within the workplace—and particularly by the employees involved in the problem—as fair and objective. Someone who supervises, or is supervised by, either the complaining employee or the accused employee should not perform the investigation. Similarly, you shouldn't choose an investigator who has known difficulties with any of the main players, has expressed an opinion on the matter to be investigated, or has any involvement in the underlying problem. Here are some examples of situations when the investigator's impartiality could be challenged:

- The manager of a department is chosen to investigate an employee's claim of religious discrimination. Although the manager has no involvement in the underlying incident, he is a member of the same church as the complaining employee.
- The HR director decides to investigate alleged improper billing practices by the recruiters who work for her. If she were to find that the recruiters were not following the company's rules, she could be disciplined for failing to train and supervise them correctly.
- An HR representative is tapped to look into allegations that an employee is stealing company property. The representative and the employee carpool to work together.

In each of these situations, the circumstances suggest that it might be difficult for the investigator to be impartial. Even if the investigator were able to conduct a fair investigation, other employees and those outside the company might not trust the results.

Who's the Boss?

When choosing an investigator, you should consider where the accused employee ranks on the corporate ladder, and pick an investigator whose rank is higher, if possible. That way, you can avoid the appearance that the accused employee has any power over the investigator. If this isn't possible, take steps to insulate the investigation from the accused employee (by requiring the employee to take paid leave and refrain from talking to other employees during the investigation, for example). If employees—or a jury, if it comes to that—believe that the accused employee can intimidate the investigator or dictate his or her findings, they won't put much stock in the outcome of the investigation.

Once you have come up with a potential investigator, ask the employees involved if they believe that person can be fair and impartial. If they do not, choose someone else. Of course, in a small business, you might not have a wide range of potential investigators to choose from. In that case, just make sure that whoever does the job doesn't have an ax to grind with any of the employees involved in the problem.

Allegedly Biased Investigator Keeps Case in Court

Even if an investigator doesn't ultimately decide whether or how to discipline an employee, the investigator's alleged bias could hurt the company in court. The Supreme Court has held that a company may be liable for discrimination even if the ultimate decision maker had no discriminatory motive, if someone who had meaningful input into the decision was biased. If a manager takes action, motivated by bias, intending to cause the employee to be fired or disciplined, and the employee is fired or disciplined as a result, the company is liable. (This case, *Staub v. Proctor Hospital*, 562 U.S. 411 (2011), is referred to as the "cat's paw" case, after an Aesop's fable.)

An Oklahoma court has applied the same rationale to investigations: If an investigator is biased against the employee under investigation, and an independent decision maker takes action against the employee based on the investigator's findings, the company may be liable for discrimination. In the Oklahoma case, an employee presented evidence from which a jury could conclude that his manager controlled the investigation into his misconduct, was racially biased against him, and supplied the information that led to his termination. Even though there was no evidence of bias on the part of the person who made the ultimate decision to fire him, the investigator's alleged bias was enough to send the case to a jury. (*Bowdish v. Federal Express Corp.*, 699 F.Supp.2d 1306 (W.D. Okla. 2010).)

TIP

Document approval of the investigator. If the employees involved in the problem agree to the investigator (whether it's you or someone else), make a note of it in your file, including the date and time of the conversation.

This might be valuable evidence later, if an employee files a lawsuit and argues that the investigator was biased. Some employers also ask employees to sign a statement verifying that they have no concerns about the investigator's qualifications or impartiality. Although this could also be helpful evidence, it's probably overkill. Your signed statement is evidence of each employee's approval. And an employee who is asked to sign a statement like this may become suspicious that you are more concerned with avoiding a lawsuit than with solving the underlying problem.

Sometimes, the sensitivities of a complaining employee might also influence your choice of investigators. For example, some women might feel more comfortable discussing a sexual harassment complaint with a female investigator. Some larger companies try to make an investigator of each gender available for just this reason.

Professionalism

Professionalism is a quality that's sometimes hard to define, but we all know it when we see it. A professional behaves in a businesslike and dependable way, doesn't inject personal feelings or biases into workplace interactions, and remembers that he or she is always representing the company.

A professional demeanor is an essential quality for an investigator for several reasons. First, a good investigator has to keep his or her emotions in check. During an investigation, the investigator may hear or see things—such as X-rated or racist material, threats, or serious misconduct—that are disturbing. The investigator may also bear the brunt of employees' emotions, including anger at being the subject of an investigation, sadness and fear over making a complaint, and so on. In the face of these emotions, a good investigator must remain calm and try to get to the bottom of things.

Second, the investigator must be discreet and preserve the integrity of the investigation. At some point during an investigation, the investigator will begin to develop some ideas about what really happened: who's lying and who's telling the truth, who committed misconduct, and why.

Despite these hunches (no matter how well founded they may be), the investigator can't reveal his or her feelings. If the employees involved in the problem believe the investigator has already reached a decision before examining all of the evidence and hearing everyone's statements, they might come to distrust the investigation and any decisions that are based on it. This can lead to lawsuits challenging the fairness of the investigation. On the other hand, an investigator who conveys that he or she has not reached any decisions and will listen carefully and objectively to everyone's statements builds trust in the investigation and its outcome.

Third, the investigator may have to give testimony about the investigation in the future, to an administrative agency, an employee's lawyer, or even a judge or jury. If this worst-case scenario comes to pass, you'll want the investigator to convey confidence, poise, and objectivity. A professional demeanor will help the investigator convince outsiders that the company did the right thing. On the other hand, a jury might have doubts if the investigator is overly nervous, can't answer questions directly, or fails to make eye contact, even if he or she did a bang-up job on the investigation.

Hiring an Outside Investigator

In some situations, it makes sense to ask for professional help to investigate a workplace problem. Many law firms and private consultants will investigate workplace issues for a fee. You might consider bringing in outside help if:

- more than one employee complains about the same serious problem (for example, several women complain that a particular manager is harassing them)
- the accused is a high-ranking official in the business (such as the president or CEO)
- the complaining employee has publicized the complaint in the workplace or in the media
- the complaining employee has hired a lawyer, filed a lawsuit, or filed charges with a government agency, such as the Equal

Employment Opportunity Commission, the Occupational Safety and Health Administration, the Wage and Hour Division, or a similar state agency

• the accusations are extreme (allegations of rape, assault, threats, drug dealing, or significant theft, for example), or

• for any reason, no one is available to investigate the complaint fairly and objectively.

CAUTION

Some states require outside investigators to be licensed. If your state has this type of requirement, make sure that any outside investigator has a current license. Don't just take the investigator's word for it: Ask to see and copy the license itself. If your investigator is not properly licensed, you may not be able to rely on the results of the investigation in court.

You can get referrals for professional investigators through management newsletters, trade associations, other business contacts, and even listings in the yellow pages. The American Arbitration Association (AAA), a national provider of dispute resolution services, offers fact-finding services by trained, experienced investigators who are prequalified by the AAA to conduct independent investigations. You can find out more about these services at the AAA's website, www.adr.org. For complaints of discrimination and harassment, your state's fair employment practices agency may be able to provide referrals. These agencies are listed in Appendix B.

CAUTION

Your company is responsible for actions you take based on an outside investigator's findings. Hiring an outside investigator doesn't insulate your company from liability for the investigation or the decisions it makes based on that investigation (for example, to discipline or fire an employee accused of wrongdoing). Your company is ultimately responsible to its employees, even if it hires a professional to do some of the investigative work. You must work closely with an outside investigator to make sure that he or she receives all relevant information, conducts a thorough and fair investigation, and documents the findings. And although a professional investigator can certainly give advice about what action to take when the investigation is over, you or another company decision maker should always have the final say in disciplinary matters.

Reporting Requirements for Outside Investigators

Hiring an outside investigator used to have a very significant downside (other than the expense): Employers that hired outsiders had to comply with some legal technicalities that had the potential to derail the investigation. Under a law called the Fair Credit Reporting Act, employers that hired an outside investigator had to tell the accused employee that an investigation would be conducted, get the employee's written consent ahead of time, give a copy of the investigation report to the employee, and then wait for a "reasonable period" before taking any adverse action based on its contents.

These rules, which were extremely controversial, were relaxed in 2003. (Although the rules still apply to certain types of investigations, such as credit checks and background checks, they do not apply to workplace investigations of suspected misconduct, violation of the employer's policies, or violation of the law.) Now, employers are no longer required to warn the accused employee or get the employee's consent before hiring an outside investigator. If the employer decides to take action against the employee based on the investigation report, the employer must give the employee only a summary of the nature and substance of the report (which need not identify the employees interviewed). You'll find a form you can use to give this required notice at this book's online companion page. See Appendix A for details.

Hiring a Lawyer to Investigate

There are many good reasons to hire a lawyer to investigate. An experienced employment lawyer will know exactly what to look for and how to keep your company out of trouble. You can expect the lawyer to know the latest legal developments about investigations and workplace claims, including privacy issues. This specialized knowledge could be a real benefit, especially if your problem is factually or legally complicated.

Attorney-Client Privilege

Whenever you talk privately to a lawyer about legal matters, that conversation is protected by the attorney-client privilege, which means that no one can force you or the lawyer to reveal what either of you said. The purpose of the privilege is to encourage full disclosure, which allows the lawyer to give a candid assessment of your problem and sound advice about what to do next.

However, you can lose this privilege if you don't honor it. For example, if you tell another person what you said to your lawyer, your conversation with the lawyer is no longer privileged: You waived the privilege by revealing the statement. Similarly, if your company puts its lawyer on the stand to testify about what a great investigation he or she performed, the lawyer will have to reveal some conversations he or she had with company representatives. Once again, you've waived the privilege by allowing these statements to be revealed.

This is why some companies that have in-house counsel choose not to use an internal lawyer as the investigator. If your in-house counsel becomes a witness in a later legal proceeding about the investigation, your company could lose its attorney-client privilege as to conversations with the lawyer about the investigation. This means that not only the attorney's actions during the investigation may have to be disclosed, but also his or her advice and counsel. In this situation, companies often reserve their in-house lawyer for privileged conversations and advice, and leave the investigation to a nonlawyer employee or an outside lawyer or consultant.

Another advantage of using a lawyer to investigate is that many (though by no means all) lawyers are experienced in the courtroom. If the investigation is later called into question, the lawyer/investigator should have the presentation skills to come across as a strong witness on your company's behalf.

However, there is a drawback to having your lawyer perform the investigation: You may lose the attorney-client privilege. Usually, when you seek a lawyer's advice about a legal problem, your communications are privileged. This means that no one can force your company (or the lawyer) to reveal them. (See "Attorney-Client Privilege," above.) If the lawyer testifies as a witness for your company, however, you will probably lose the protection of this privilege. This means that the lawyer can be asked questions about what company representatives said and did throughout the investigation and about what advice the lawyer provided to you.

> **TIP**
> **Even if you decide not to use a lawyer to investigate, you can still seek the advice of a lawyer about your investigation.** By doing this, you get the best of both worlds: Your company will benefit from the lawyer's expertise, and your conversations will generally be protected by the attorney-client privilege. Of course, your company will also have to pay for the lawyer's time (unless you have in-house counsel). If you choose to go this route, ask the lawyer—before the investigation begins—how you can make sure that your conversations will stay confidential.

Plan the Investigation

Before you start to interview people and sift through documents and other evidence, you should come up with a careful investigation plan. During your planning, you will review the evidence available to you, then start thinking about what additional evidence might exist that will help you figure out what happened. You should also take a few steps to prepare your company for the investigation, including setting aside some time for the process and telling others what you'll be doing.

Review What You Know

At the outset, you will have some information available, such as an employee complaint, a report by a manager, or a suspicious situation (an employee who frequently seems to be out of it or money missing from a cash register, for example). Start your planning by figuring out what you already know. What misconduct is suspected or alleged? Your answer to this question will help you figure out what information you need to decide whether the allegation or suspicion is correct.

TIP

A timeline can help you sort through complicated facts. If there are more than one or two allegations, you might want to make a basic timeline to help you keep things straight. For example, if an employee alleges that she was harassed on five or six occasions over a period of months, plotting those incidents on a calendar or timeline may help you see patterns and figure out who might have witnessed the incidents. It will also remind you to ask, gather evidence, and draw conclusions about every incident.

Look over any available documents or other evidence related to the misconduct. Review the complaint or report (if applicable), gather and read through any paperwork relevant to the problem (such as personnel files, attendance records, correspondence, or performance reviews), and collect and review any other physical evidence (a weapon, illegal drugs, graphic images, or work materials, for example). Place these documents and items in a locked file cabinet or other safe place. (If you find illegal drugs, you should speak to a lawyer immediately; you may have to hand them over to the police as explained in Chapter 9.)

Planning for Serious Problems

In some cases, you might have to plan ahead to deal with a major problem. For example, if you suspect an employee of criminal activity (such as embezzlement, rape, or violence), you will have to decide whether to bring in the police. If you are facing issues that could lead to serious legal trouble (like allegations of widespread, egregious harassment or potential workplace violence), this is a good time to get some legal advice. If your workplace problem has been, or might become, publicized in the media, you will need a public relations strategy to handle the situation. If you are facing one of these difficult issues, get some expert advice about how to proceed.

You should also determine whether any company policies and guidelines might apply to the situation. For example, a sexual harassment policy, workplace violence policy, or noncompete agreement might be relevant.

Follow the Evidence Wherever It Leads

It's important to plan the investigation ahead of time, but it may be even more important to depart from your plan if new or unexpected information comes up. For example, imagine that an employee complained that her boss had sexually harassed her by repeatedly asking her out on dates. You've planned your investigation to speak to the complaining employee, her boss, and a few witnesses who may have heard or seen the proposals. However, when interviewing the first witness, you learn that the boss has also asked her out on dates. You also learn that the men in this work group routinely tell X-rated jokes, ask their female coworkers about their sex lives, and visit pornographic websites during work hours.

Should you stick to your original plan and just try to get to the bottom of the unwanted date requests? Not if you want to solve what is obviously a significant problem in this work group and protect your company from sexual harassment claims. Once you know this additional information, you should revisit your investigation plan. Because the problem is much larger than you thought, you will have to do a more extensive investigation to find out what's going on and who's responsible.

Figure Out What You Need to Know

Once you have gotten a sense of the information and evidence already at hand, you can start thinking about what you need to know or find out in order to make a decision about what happened. Whom will you need to interview? What additional evidence might exist? Are there any witnesses who might have helpful information?

Then, begin planning the interviews, including:

- **Whom to question.** Make a list of potential interview subjects. In some cases, only the complaining employee and the accused employee should be interviewed (if the complaint is about an incident that no one else witnessed, heard, or was told about later, for example). In other situations, there may be many potential witnesses. If the incident occurred during a staff meeting or company social event, there may be dozens of witnesses. In these cases, you should plan to ask both the complaining and the accused employee which workers were most likely to have seen or heard the disputed event.

- **What order to follow.** The complaining employee should be interviewed first, followed generally by the accused employee and then the witnesses. This order can be changed to accommodate employees' schedules, in the interests of moving as quickly as possible.
- **What questions to ask.** You need not script every interview question in advance. However, after reviewing Chapter 3, you should make some notes on topics you want to cover in each interview. As you interview each witness, you can review and add to these notes.

Prepare Your Company for the Investigation

Before you actually start asking questions and reviewing evidence, you should do a few things to make sure your investigation runs smoothly.

Schedule Time and Resources

First of all, give yourself enough time to investigate properly. You'll need to start right away and, depending on how complicated the problem is, you may need to spend a week or more interviewing, reviewing documents, sorting out the facts, drafting your report, following up with everyone, and so on. This means you might have to shift some of your work around, talk to your manager about freeing up some time, or postpone a project or two.

You might also need additional resources or support for the investigation. If you'll be interviewing employees on site, for example, you may need to book a conference room or other private space. And don't forget to include others in your planning, if necessary. For example, you might need assistance from the legal department, your supervisor, or a workplace partner in conducting your investigation (such as an IT expert, financial analyst, or co-investigator).

Inform the Employees' Manager

You should also prepare the manager(s) of the employees involved. You'll need to spend some time with the accused employee, complaining employee, and witnesses, and their manager will need to know where everyone is disappearing to. If you've decided to suspend the accused employee with pay while you investigate, that employee's manager should know about the decision.

In some cases, the manager will already know about the problem. For example, if the employee initially raised the issue with the manager, who escalated the issue to you, the manager will have a good idea of what's going on. Similarly, if the manager noticed a problem and reported it in the first place, he or she will know about it. In these situations, you can confirm to the manager that you will be investigating and explain how you will proceed.

If the manager isn't already in the loop, how much you tell him or her will depend on your company's practices and whether the manager is involved in the problem, among other things. Because the manager is the company representative who works most closely with the employees, it's a great benefit if you can tell the manager some basic information about the problem. That way, the manager can keep an eye on the situation, ensure that no one retaliates against the complaining employee, watch out for gossip and breaches of confidentiality, and make sure that there are no further problems once the investigation is over.

If, however, the manager is accused of wrongdoing, you won't be able to count on his or her help. In this situation, it often makes sense to suspend the manager with pay during the investigation, so employees will feel more free to express themselves and won't be subject to possible retaliation and intimidation.

Perhaps the trickiest situation arises when the perpetrator is unknown and, therefore, may be the manager. This could occur in a theft investigation, but it might also happen if racist or sexist graffiti or anonymous notes threatening violence start appearing in the workplace, for example.

In these cases, informing the manager of your investigation ahead of time might give him or her the opportunity to destroy evidence, put pressure on witnesses, and otherwise hamper your efforts. Your best course of action will depend on the facts: If it's possible to conduct interviews without the manager finding out (for example, by interviewing employees who work at remote locations), that might make sense. If not, you might start by interviewing the manager. This is one scenario where you may want to consult with a lawyer to help you figure out the best way to proceed.

Prepare Experts and Decision Makers

If you'll be working with anyone else on the investigation, you should get that person involved. For example, if you'll be working with the company's in-house or outside counsel, you should inform the lawyer about the investigation. If you'll be investigating and then handing your findings over to someone else in the company who will make disciplinary decisions, that person should be told that the investigation is about to begin. And, if you plan to seek outside help (from a forensic accountant, handwriting analyst, or workplace violence consultant, for example), now is the time to line up your experts.

Gather Information

Once you've decided that an investigation is in order, it's time to get to work. This chapter will explain how to gather the information you need to figure out what happened.

It's important to get started right away. This chapter explains how delay can derail your investigative efforts and offers some advice for dealing with unavoidable postponements. It also covers interviews, which are often your best source of information about workplace problems. You'll learn how to open and close an interview, what questions to ask complaining employees, accused employees, and witnesses, and other tips for successful interviewing.

In addition to interviewing, you may also have to do some workplace sleuthing. In some situations, paying a visit to the "scene of the crime"— the place where the alleged misconduct occurred—will help you sort out the truth. And in almost every investigation, you'll have to examine documents and other materials, such as inventories, performance evaluations, photographs, and attendance records, to figure out what happened.

Get Started Right Away

Delay is a common—and potentially costly—investigation mistake. Once you become aware of a serious workplace problem that requires an investigation, don't put off the inevitable. Ideally, you should begin investigating within a day or two of finding out about the problem, and complete the investigation within a week or two, depending on how complicated the allegations are. Of course, there will be times when outside circumstances and conflicting schedules lead to unavoidable delays. However, if you postpone the investigation unnecessarily, you will send the message that the company doesn't take the complaint seriously. And if the misconduct continues in the meantime, a court might find your company responsible for failing to investigate and take care of the problem right away.

TIP

Document unavoidable delays. If you can't start your investigation right away, document the reason for the delay in the investigation report. (Investigation reports are covered in Chapter 4.) For example, if the accused employee is out tending to a family emergency or the complaining employee is on vacation, make a note of these facts, the date you learned them, and the date the employee will return to work. These notes will help you prove, if necessary, that the company didn't cause the delay.

Conducting Interviews

In most investigations, interviews are the main tool investigators use to find out what happened. More often than not, investigators have to rely almost entirely on statements from the main players and witnesses, who may contradict each other. If the main participants flatly deny each other's claims, you'll have to sort out who is telling the truth.

How can you decide whose story is more credible in these "he said, she said" situations? The first step is to conduct interviews designed to elicit as much information as possible. The more information you can draw out of each witness, the easier it will be to figure out what happened and why. The general interviewing tips that follow will help you elicit the most useful responses, even from the reluctant or contentious witness. This section also includes specific ideas and questions for interviewing the person who complained (if there is one), the person accused, and witnesses.

Tips on Conducting Effective Interviews

Here are some guidelines that will help you conduct complete and informative interviews.

If the Employee Wants a Representative

As explained later in this chapter, union members who are accused of wrongdoing are entitled to bring a representative to any interview or meeting that could result in discipline, including your investigation interview. But what of other employees, or employees who aren't in a union? Often, the complaining employee asks to bring someone for moral support. How should you handle these requests?

As a legal matter, you generally don't have to allow the employee to bring someone to the interview. However, practical reasons dictate that you allow the request, with some ground rules. Having a representative might make the employee more comfortable and help the employee focus and remember details. What's more, if you refuse to allow an employee to bring someone along, you will either have to skip the interview entirely or try to require the employee to meet with you alone, which could feel coercive or even retaliatory to the employee. It's far better to allow the representative to attend, after explaining that you need to hear directly from the employee. Ask the representative not to interrupt or try to speak for the employee, but to simply be present and observe the proceedings.

An employee may want to bring a lawyer to the interview. Typically, this comes up when a complaining employee has already consulted a lawyer about a workplace problem (such as harassment). However, an employee accused of wrongdoing may also want an attorney present. Although you aren't legally required to allow the attorney to attend, the employee might refuse to cooperate otherwise. This will make it tough for your company to investigate and take appropriate action.

Of course, having an attorney present will make the process more formal, and it could be daunting for you. If there's already an attorney in the picture, it means there's a greater possibility of legal proceedings down the road. In this situation, consider talking to a lawyer to go over your options. It might make sense to bring in an outside investigator (perhaps one who's also a lawyer) once things reach this point.

Keep an Open Mind

Some investigators don't want to believe that serious misconduct or harassment could happen in their companies, and so tend to make light of possible wrongdoing. Others jump to the opposite conclusion, assuming that an employee would not complain without good cause.

As an investigator, your job is to avoid making assumptions. No matter how serious the problem or how straightforward the situation appears to be, don't reach any conclusions until you have gathered and evaluated all the facts. If you start your investigation believing you already know what happened, you will miss some important details. But if you keep an open mind until your investigation is complete, you will conduct more thorough interviews and receive more candid answers to your questions.

Don't ask:

Why did you pressure Maria to falsify her time card?

Ask:

Did you and Maria discuss her time card last week? What did each of you say?

Don't ask:

How could you steal from this company?

Ask:

When are your cash register shifts? Do you count the money in your drawer at the start of your shift? Do you count out your drawer at the end of your shift and write that total down for the manager? Your cash register has been short by quite a bit of money several times in the last month. Can you explain why that happened?

Ask Open-Ended Questions

Your goal when conducting an interview is to get as much information as possible. The best way to accomplish this is to ask open-ended questions. If you ask questions that suggest the answer you want to hear or questions that call only for a "yes" or "no" answer, you will be doing all the talking. Instead, ask the witness what he or she heard, said, or did, and why.

Don't ask:

Did you arrive at three o'clock?

Ask:

What time did you arrive?

Don't ask:

Did you hear John tell Ping that she would not be paid for her overtime work unless she agreed to have lunch with him?

Ask:

Did you hear John and Ping talking last week? Tell me what you heard.

Start With the Easy Questions

The employees you interview are likely to be nervous and uncomfortable. Employees suspected of wrongdoing will probably also be defensive, frightened about what may happen, and perhaps willing to lie to save their jobs. If you begin your interview by asking directly about the alleged misconduct, you will aggravate an already tense situation and limit the flow of information. Someone who feels accused or put on the spot is more likely to clam up. Also, if you cut to the chase too soon, you'll miss your chance to find out important details before the employee knows why you're asking questions (and, therefore, has an opportunity to tailor the answers accordingly).

The better course of action is to start with basic background questions about the employee's job, coworkers, daily schedule, and so on. You'll have to get to the tough questions eventually, but starting with a few softballs will put the employee at ease and give you the opportunity to ask about seemingly unimportant details that could prove very significant to your investigation. It will also help you get a sense of the employee's demeanor and body language when he or she is comfortable and telling the truth. Then, when you get to the tougher questions, you can see whether the witness reacts differently (for example, the witness stops making eye contact, starts fidgeting, or becomes much less certain of the facts). This will help you judge credibility.

Don't Start With:

You were seen leaving the workplace very late last Friday, with a bulky package under your coat. On Monday morning, the IT department found that several new modems and some other computer equipment were missing. Did you take these things?

Start With:

Tell me about your usual schedule. What time do you arrive in the morning? What time do you leave at night? Are you often one of the last ones here? Is your schedule fairly regular, or does it vary? What was your schedule like last week? Do you drive to work or take public transportation? Where do you park? Do you usually come in through the main front entrance or use one of the back doors? Which exit do you use when you leave at night?

Don't Start With:

Phyllis says that you refused to promote her to be a floor manager and that you have never promoted an African American employee to any management position. Did you refuse to promote her because of her race?

Start With:

How long have you worked here? What are your job responsibilities in your current position? Do they include promoting people? To what positions? About how many people have you promoted since you began working here? Tell me what you take into consideration when you're deciding whether to promote someone. Do interested employees have to fill out an application? Do you interview the applicants? Do you look at any documents, such as work samples, performance evaluations, or personnel files? Is there anything else you consider? How do you decide whom to promote?

TIP

Dig a little deeper if an employee's reaction seems odd. If an employee seems much more upset (or much less so) than you would expect, ask more questions. Although all of us react differently to unpleasant experiences, a response that strikes you as emotionally inappropriate could indicate that there's more to the situation than meets the eye.

Keep Your Opinions to Yourself

As your investigation progresses, you will inevitably start to develop some opinions about what really happened. You should not share these opinions with witnesses, however. If you suggest, through your statements or the tone of your questions, that you have already reached a decision, witnesses will be less likely to speak freely with you. Some witnesses might be afraid of contradicting your version of events; others might feel there is no point in explaining what really happened if you have already made up your mind. In the worst-case scenario, a witness might believe you are conducting an unfair or biased investigation and challenge the outcome in court. Avoid these problems by keeping your conclusions to yourself until the investigation is complete.

Don't ask:

I have already heard from several people that Sameh was absent from last week's mandatory meeting. Is that what you remember?

Ask:

Who attended last week's mandatory meeting? Was anyone absent?

Don't ask:

Can you confirm that Darrell punched Jeff on the loading dock?

Ask:

Where did you work yesterday? Did you see anything unusual? Tell me what happened. (If the witness claims not to have seen anything unusual, you might ask, "Did you see an incident between Darrell and Jeff?")

Focus on the Facts

On the television series *Dragnet*, Joe Friday had a simple interviewing technique: He asked his subjects to tell him "just the facts." If only it were that easy in real life. Many people have a difficult time distinguishing objective fact from subjective opinion when describing what they have seen and heard. Some witnesses might describe another person's motivations or thoughts, relate rumors as if they were known facts, or exaggerate. Your job is to separate the wheat from the chaff—that is, to isolate fact from opinion—then find out the basis for the witness's story. By helping your witnesses focus on the facts, you can prevent speculation and rumor from affecting your decisions.

If You Hear:

Lawrence has been out to get Graciela since the day he started working here. But I'm not surprised; he doesn't like reporting to a woman.

You Might Ask:

What have you seen or heard that leads you to believe Lawrence is out to get Graciela? Have you heard him say anything about her? Have you heard Lawrence say anything about reporting to a woman or make any disparaging comments about women in general?

If You Hear:

Everyone knew that Evelyn was going to lose her temper and get violent. It was just a matter of time.

You Might Ask:

What do you mean by get violent? Have you seen or heard Evelyn do anything that seemed violent or angry? Why did you believe Evelyn was going to lose her temper? What did she say or do to make you think she was on edge? When you say everyone knew, do you mean that you discussed this with others? Whom did you talk to about it, and what did they say?

Find Out About Other Witnesses or Evidence

Always look for leads. Ask every person you interview whether they know of other witnesses or physical evidence relating to the incident. If the witness is the accused or complaining employee, ask whether anyone else saw or heard the incidents in question. Ask whether they told anyone about the incident when it happened. Find out if they took any notes about the problem or if any workplace documents—emails, memoranda, or evaluations, for example—relate to the incident.

If You Hear:

Robert and I had a loud argument by the elevators. He told me I wouldn't get my raise unless I agreed to withdraw my complaint that he had harassed me. Afterwards, I was so upset that I ran back to my office in tears.

You Might Ask:

Was anyone else near the elevator when the argument took place? Did anyone hear what Robert said to you? Did you see anyone on your way back to your office? Did you talk to anyone about what happened?

If You Hear:

Julie sent me an email apologizing for giving me a bad review. She said her manager made her change my performance appraisal after I filed a workers' compensation claim.

You Might Ask:

Did you save Julie's email to you? Did she copy anyone on the message? Did you see the performance appraisal before it was changed? Do you have a copy?

Ask About Contradictions

Sometimes, one witness contradicts what another has said. The accused and complaining employees are perhaps most likely to contradict each other, but even uninvolved witnesses might give conflicting stories. The best way to deal with these inconsistencies is to ask about them directly. Once you get down to specifics, you may find that everyone agrees on what happened, but not on whether it was appropriate.

If the witnesses continue to contradict each other even after you have pointed out the conflicts in their stories—if the accused flatly denies the complaining employee's statements, for example—ask each witness why the other might disagree.

If You Hear:

I never sexually harassed anyone. I treat the women who work for me with respect.

You Might Ask:

A complaint was made that you touched Tanya's waist and hips several times while she was distributing paperwork to clients, and that you made jokes about her spending the night at her boyfriend's house. Did this happen? Have you ever touched Tanya? Did you say anything that someone might have interpreted in this way? Can you think of any reason why someone might have reported this if it weren't true?

If You Hear:

Darnell told us at last week's morning meeting that anyone who complained about safety problems in the warehouse would get in trouble. He basically threatened to fire anyone who reported an accident.

You Might Ask:

Other people in your work group described that conversation differently. They said that Darnell told all of you that he had reported two safety violations to his manager. They said that he encouraged you to bring any safety concerns to him and that he would bring them to the company's attention. Did this happen? Did you have a separate conversation with Darnell? Why do you think others remember the conversation differently?

Keep It Confidential

Complaints can polarize a workplace. Workers will likely side with either the complaining employee or the accused employee, and the rumor mill will start working overtime. Worse, if too many details about the complaint get out, you may be accused of damaging the reputation of the alleged victim or alleged wrongdoer.

You can minimize these problems by practicing confidentiality in your investigation. Tell each witness only those facts necessary to conduct a thorough interview. For example, accused employees deserve to hear the allegations against them, but peripheral witnesses don't need to know every detail. Set a good example by being discreet. Don't discuss the investigation in the lunchroom, keep your investigation materials in a locked cabinet when you aren't working on them, and avoid gossip.

Hold your interviews in a private space—one where you won't be seen or overheard by others in the workplace, and where others won't be able to see who comes to be interviewed. For example, a conference room with windows, a table in the company break room, or a centrally located office would be a bad choice. In some particularly volatile situations (for example, if violence is a possibility or employees have been threatened for coming forward), employees may be hesitant to talk to you in the workplace. In these scenarios, consider meeting an employee off-site, after work hours.

Recently, both the EEOC and the National Labor Relations Board (NLRB) have found that imposing broad confidentiality requirements on employees might be illegal. As discussed below, the NLRB has said that a rule prohibiting employees from discussing an ongoing investigation violates employee rights to discuss the terms and conditions of their employment. The EEOC has stated that threatening to discipline or fire employees if they discuss a sexual harassment complaint with anyone could be a form of illegal retaliation. Discussing harassment complaints with others is a form of "protected opposition" to illegal practices under Title VII. The EEOC has also indicated that such a confidentiality rule might lead employees to believe they could be disciplined or fired for discussing harassment with the EEOC, which is also illegal.

NLRB Rules on Confidentiality Requirements

In the case of *Banner Estrella Medical Center*, 358 NLRB No. 93 (2012), an HR consultant asked employees who had made internal complaints not to discuss the complaints with coworkers while the investigation was ongoing. The NLRB found that this request violated the National Labor Relations Act, which guarantees union and non-union employees the right to discuss the terms and conditions of their employment with each other.

According to the NLRB, a rule prohibiting employees from discussing an ongoing investigation is allowed only if the employer can show a legitimate business reason that outweighs the employees' rights. For example, the employer might have a legitimate need to protect a witness, to prevent the destruction of evidence, or to avoid the fabrication of testimony. However, even in this situation, the confidentiality requirement must be limited to the investigation for which it is necessary: Blanket confidentiality requirements for all investigations are not allowed.

Recently, the federal Court of Appeals for the D.C. Circuit weighed in on this issue. In that case (*Hyundai America Shipping Agency, Inc. v. National Labor Relations Board*, Case No. 11-1351 (D.C. Cir. 2015)), the Court agreed that a general confidentiality rule for all investigations was too broad. However, the Court declined to adopt the NLRB's more specific findings that a confidentiality requirement would be justified only if necessary to protect a witness or to prevent someone from tampering with testimony or evidence. Because this issue is still in flux, you should talk to a lawyer before asking employees to refrain from discussing an ongoing investigation.

Both of these opinions are relatively new, and it isn't clear yet how courts will rule on these issues. Also, both opinions criticize blanket "gag rules," not case-specific confidentiality requirements. For the time being, however, employers that tell employees they may not discuss an investigation could find themselves in legal trouble. If you want to go beyond asking the employee not to discuss the specific questions and answers given in your interview, get some legal advice first. There may be circumstances in which a broader confidentiality requirement is justified, but this area is evolving so quickly that it makes sense to get some legal guidance.

Don't ask:

Sylvia says that Roger asked her out several times and tried to bring her back to his room after the holiday party. She also says that Roger made a lot of X-rated jokes in front of clients, and that you might have heard some of these jokes during the meeting with Pets-Nation. Did you hear any of these jokes?

Ask:

Did you attend the pitch meeting with Pets-Nation? Who else was there? Do you remember anyone telling jokes during this meeting? Tell me what was said.

Don't ask:

Fernando has complained that Martin gave him a bad performance evaluation, and he thinks it's because Martin dislikes Latinos. Fernando believes that he has made more successful cold calls than anyone else on his shift. He thought you might be able to confirm this, since you compile the monthly productivity reports. Is this true?

Ask:

Do you compile monthly productivity reports? Do these reports contain the cold call success rate for each salesperson? Do you recall who had the highest success rate last month for the afternoon shift? May I see a copy of these reports for the last year?

Don't Retaliate

It is against the law to punish someone for making a complaint—or participating in an investigation—of harassment, discrimination, illegal conduct, or unsafe working conditions. And it is against your company's best interests to punish any employee who comes forward with a good-faith complaint, regardless of the subject matter. You want to encourage employees to bring problems to your attention, so they can be resolved before they start draining productivity or stirring up legal trouble. Employees will come forward only if they feel protected from retaliation, and witnesses will tell you the truth only if they know you will not kill the messenger who bears bad news. Assure all employees you interview that you want to hear their side of the story and that they will not face retaliation for coming forward.

If You Hear:

I'm having some problems working with Maurice, but I don't want to cause trouble.

You Might Ask:

I'm glad you brought this issue to my attention. We would really be in trouble if you kept this information to yourself and your team's work suffered as a result. No one in the company will take any action against you for coming forward. Now, what has been happening with Maurice?

If You Hear:

I've seen some pretty heated conversations between Maria and Simone, but it's really none of my business. I don't want Simone to think that I'm not a team player.

You Might Ask:

I need to find out what's been going on between Maria and Simone, and anything you can tell me about those conversations will help me get to the bottom of this. If there are problems in your work group, everyone's work suffers and everyone feels uncomfortable. No one will be allowed to retaliate against you for speaking to me. Both Maria and Simone have been told that these issues would be investigated, and they both understand that they cannot retaliate against anyone involved in the investigation. What have your heard Maria and Simone say to each other?

Ask Interviewees to Contact You With New or Additional Information

People sometimes freeze up when they're put on the spot. It's very likely that a witness might remember some significant detail—or learn new information—after the interview is over. To make sure you stay in the loop, close every interview by thanking the witness and asking him or her to contact you if anything else comes to mind.

Some witnesses might intentionally hold back important information during the interview, while trying to decide whether to come clean. If you offer every witness an opportunity to continue the conversation, you are more likely to get the full story. And should the investigation be challenged in court, you will be able to show that you made every effort to gather all the facts.

Don't Say:

Have you told me everything you remember about these incidents? Because you won't be able to change your statement once I start talking to other witnesses.

Say:

Please remember that my door is always open, if you remember anything later or you want to add to your statement. Also, if you learn of any new information that relates to the complaint, please bring it to my attention right away.

Document Your Interviews

Take notes during every interview. Include the date, time, and place of each interview, the name of the witness, and whether anyone else was present. Don't just record the witness's conclusions; include all the important facts that the witness relates or denies, using the witness's own words whenever possible. These notes will help you remember what each witness said later, when you are making your decision. They will also help you defend your investigation in court, if it is challenged as biased or incomplete.

Before the interview is over, go back through your notes with the witness to make sure you got everything right. It's a good idea to have the witness sign either your notes (if they are legible) or a written statement of what was said during the interview. If you decide to use a written statement, write the first draft yourself. That way, you can make sure to include all of the important facts the witness told you. Give the draft to the witness and encourage changes, additions, or deletions. (Of course, if the witness makes a change that contradicts an earlier statement to you, you should ask about it.)

These statements are great evidence of what a witness told you at the time. A witness who later claims to have said something different will have to explain why he or she signed the statement.

Start your notes from each interview on a clean piece of paper. That way, you won't have to worry about the witness seeing your notes from other interviews.

Don't Write:

I spoke to Joan today. She said that Richard has been acting strange lately but she hasn't really seen any fights between him and Sam. She thinks Richard might act out violently sometime soon.

Write:

I interviewed Joan Suzuki today, June 14, 20xx, regarding Sam Levine's complaint (see complaint form in file). We met in my office at 3 p.m. I asked Joan whether she had seen any incidents between Richard Hart and Sam in the last two weeks. Joan said that she thought Richard had been acting very strange lately. When I asked her to explain, she said that Richard seemed "distracted and angry," and that he had been complaining to others in the work group about his ex-wife's petition for an increase in child support. Richard told her that Sam had denied his request for a raise and that Sam was responsible for all of his problems. Joan also said that Richard had made several jokes during shift meetings about "going postal," and that he told Sam, "You will be the first to go." This is the only incident she has seen between Sam and Richard. Joan said that she was frightened by Richard's change in behavior.

Joan confirmed that Jose, Jocelyn, and LeShawn were at the meetings where Richard made these jokes. I thanked her for her information and encouraged her to come forward with any additional information immediately. I explained that retaliation is prohibited and asked her to let me know if she faced any reprisals for coming forward. I assured her that Richard has been suspended pending the outcome of the investigation, and that the company would act swiftly to deal with the situation as soon as the investigation was complete.

You'll find audio tracks of investigative interviews at this book's online companion page. You'll hear the right way—and the wrong way—to take a complaint, interview the complaining employee, and interview the accused employee. You can find a sample investigation file, including notes from additional witness interviews, at this book's online companion page; see Appendix A for details.

Speak Into the Microphone

You might think it would be easier to dispense with all the notes and statements and just tape your interview sessions, on video or audio. Taping does offer accuracy, but it tends to make things complicated. For one thing, you'll need to know how to operate the equipment (or have someone at the interview who does, which could raise confidentiality concerns). And you'll have to contend with employee anxiety: Most employees will be less comfortable (and more nervous) having their interviews taped. This means that you'll have to work harder to build rapport and trust. Finally, when it comes time to use the tape to remember what was said (for example, when you write your report or have to defend your investigation in court), you'll have to fast forward and rewind your way through the conversation until you find the exact statement you need.

For these reasons, most investigators prefer to simply take notes. But this doesn't mean that you should deny an employee's request to tape record the interview. If you refuse to allow an employee to tape, you open the door to later claims that your notes are incomplete or false. You might even start to look a bit shady. ("The investigator didn't write down everything I said. I asked if I could tape the interview, but she wouldn't let me.") If an employee asks to record an interview session, give the okay, but only on the condition that you receive a copy of the tape right away.

Whatever you do, don't tape employees' statements without their knowledge and written consent. In some states, it is illegal to record a conversation unless both parties consent. Secret taping can lead to an invasion of privacy lawsuit, or even criminal prosecution.

Interviewing the Complaining Employee

If the investigation is triggered by a complaint, then you should start by interviewing the complaining employee. Your goals are to put the employee at ease, explain the process, and find out, in as much detail as possible, exactly what happened.

TIP

Handle a distressed employee with care. If the complaining employee is really upset, you may have to alter your usual interviewing procedures to avoid exacerbating the problem. For example, if the employee wants to take some time off work, you might have to postpone your interview for a few days. Or, you might allow the employee to bring a friend or family member to the interview for moral support. If you do make an accommodation like this, document it in the investigation file, especially if it requires you to delay the investigation.

Where to Start When No One Complains

In some situations, wrongdoing is clearly taking place, yet no employee has complained. Perhaps the real victim is the company, rather than a particular employee (as is often the case when employees steal). Or maybe someone has made an anonymous complaint. Whom should you interview first when no employee has come forward?

You could start with someone who has general or background knowledge of the problem. For example, if racist graffiti suddenly started appearing on the walls of a particular work area, you could start by interviewing the manager in charge of those employees to find out who usually works there, what schedules they work, whether there seem to be any racial tensions among the workers, and so on. If money is missing from the cash register, you might start by asking the bookkeeper when and how the problem became apparent and who has access to the cash. Of course, if you don't know who's responsible for the misconduct, the person you interview for background information may turn out to be the perpetrator; keep this in mind when you ask your questions.

Getting Started

Begin the interview by letting the employee know how the process will work and what to expect. Here are some points you should make at the start of the interview:

- Explain that you will be investigating the employee's complaint by interviewing witnesses and gathering evidence.
- State that you expect the employee to give you complete and accurate information and to answer all of your questions truthfully.
- Explain that, if the investigation reveals misconduct, the company will take appropriate steps to deal with the situation.
- Assure the employee that you will maintain confidentiality to the extent possible, but that it will be necessary to reveal some details of the complaint in order to find out what happened.
- Explain what retaliation is and that the company prohibits it. Ask the employee to come to you immediately with any retaliation concerns.
- Ask whether the employee has any questions or concerns about the process.

You can provide some of this information in writing as well. For example, some investigators routinely provide written notice to everyone they interview explaining the importance of cooperating with the investigation, maintaining confidentiality, and reporting any retaliation immediately. This isn't strictly necessary, but it's a good way to under-score the witness's obligations and demonstrate that the company is taking the matter seriously. You'll find a sample investigation notice that you can adapt for your own use, along with other forms, samples, and policies, at this book's online companion page; Appendix A explains how to access these materials.

TIP

Follow up on employee concerns. If an employee seems overly worried about confidentiality or other employees finding out who complained, find out why. Sometimes, these concerns indicate legitimate fears about retaliation. Ask whether anyone told the employee not to come forward or threatened to take some retaliatory action. If the employee claims to have been threatened or otherwise warned against complaining, add that to your list of things to be investigated, ask the employee to tell you immediately of any further threats, and monitor the workplace carefully for any sign of retaliation.

Don't compromise your impartiality. Make sure that the complaining employee feels comfortable coming forward, but don't sympathize so strongly that you lose your neutrality. Remember, you don't know what happened yet: The complaining employee may be a brave voice crying in the wilderness or may be the boy who cried wolf. Avoid statements implying that you believe the employee is telling the truth, like "What happened to you must have been awful" or "I'm so sorry for what you've been through."

Some investigators begin by thanking the complaining employee for coming forward. While this is an encouraging gesture that can get the interview off on the right foot (and convince the employee to answer your questions fully), it can also improperly signal that you believe the employee's story. If you choose to give thanks, say something like "Thank you for coming forward with this information. We plan to look into it right away."

When Emotions Run High

Employees often find it difficult to come forward with a complaint, especially about discrimination or harassment. Many employees complain only as a last resort, after trying informally to stop the misconduct. An employee who complains may be wrestling with difficult feelings of embarrassment, anger, sadness, fear, and reluctance to come forward.

When an employee finally does decide to complain, these emotions may spill out during the interview. The worker may cry, become angry, or even try to "take back" the complaint. Your best response is to listen and be understanding. Assure the employee that you know this is difficult and emotional, and that you want to get to the bottom of things. If the complaining worker tries to rescind the complaint, explain that you will have to investigate anyway, and you would like the worker's cooperation. If the employee is afraid of the accused employee, think about immediate steps you can take to calm these fears, such as separating the workers.

Don't try so hard to sympathize that you lose your objectivity in the investigation, however. Remember, your job is to remain impartial, uncover all of the facts, and then make a reasoned, objective decision.

Sample Questions

Once your introductory statements are out of the way, you'll start your questioning. Of course, the questions you ask will depend on the nature of the complaint. No matter what the complaint is about, however, you'll want to cover the basics: who, what, where, when, how, and (sometimes) why. Here are some sample questions to consider:

- What happened? If the complaint involves several incidents or a pattern of misconduct over a period of time, ask about each separately. Start with the most recent problem and work backwards.
- Who was involved? What did that person say or do?
- What was your response or reaction, if any?
- When and where did the incident(s) take place?
- Why did you decide to come forward now? (Ask only if the incident took place well before the complaint.)
- Did anyone witness the incident(s)?
- Did you tell anyone about the incident(s)?
- Do you know of anyone who might have information about these incidents?
- Have you been affected by the incident(s)? How?
- Do you know of any similar incidents involving other people?
- Do you know of any evidence—documents or otherwise—relating to the incident(s)?
- How would you like to see this problem resolved? (Make clear that the company will ultimately decide how to handle it, but you'd like to hear the employee's opinion.)
- Is there anything else you'd like to tell me?

Once you have finished your questions, go back through your notes with the employee to make sure you got everything down correctly. Double-check dates, names, and times. If you plan to ask the employee to sign a statement rather than your notes, prepare that document now: you can let the employee take a break while you pull it together.

Conclude the interview by giving the employee some idea of what to expect. Tell the employee that you plan to interview the accused worker and any other witnesses, review any additional evidence, and complete the investigation as soon as possible. Finally, ask to be contacted with any new or additional information about the complaint.

Interviewing the Accused Employee

Imagine what it's like to be accused of wrongdoing in the workplace. If you actually committed misconduct, you probably wouldn't be eager to admit it; if you were wrongly accused, you would likely be upset, even angry. Keep this in mind when interviewing the accused (or suspected) employee. As the investigator, you'll have to assure the employee that you'll make a fair decision while also trying to uncover the truth.

Getting Started

As in your interview with the complaining employee, you should start by explaining the process. Here are some topics you should cover at the outset:

- Let the employee know that a complaint has been made (or a problem has come to your attention) and that you will be investigating the situation.
- Assure the accused employee that you have not yet reached any conclusions and that you will listen carefully to everyone involved before taking any action.
- Explain that you expect the employee to give you complete, accurate information and to answer all of your questions truthfully.
- Explain that you will keep the investigation as confidential as possible, but that you may need to disclose some facts in order to conduct a proper investigation.
- Tell the employee that retaliation is forbidden, and explain what retaliation is.
- Ask if the employee has any questions or concerns about the investigation.

Union Members Have the Right to a Representative

Union members have the right to bring a union representative to any investigative interview that could result in disciplinary action against the employee. (This is referred to as the employee's *"Weingarten"* right, named after the case that decided the issue.) This right was extended to nonunion employees in 2000, but that extension was short-lived: The National Labor Relations Board (NLRB) overruled itself in 2004 and once again limited *Weingarten* rights to union members.

The employer has no obligation to inform the employee of this right. However, the employer must allow a representative to attend the interview, if requested by the accused employee.

Sample Questions

The questions you ask the accused will, of course, depend on the nature of the complaint and the employee's responses. Remember to begin with the easy questions and background details, then work your way up to the harder issues. Here are some sample questions to consider:

Sample Questions

- What is your typical workday like? What time do you arrive, what time do you leave, what are your responsibilities?
- Do you supervise any employees? What are their names and positions?
- [State the allegations one at a time.] Did this happen? What can you tell me about it?
- [If the accused employee says the allegations are false:] Could someone else have misunderstood your actions or statements? Have you had problems working with anyone? Do you think someone might have made up these incidents? Why?
- [If the accused employee does not completely deny the allegations:] What happened? When and where?
- Did anyone witness the incident(s)?

- Did you tell anyone about the incident(s)?
- Do you know of anyone who might have information about the incident(s)?
- Do you know of any documents or other evidence relating to this situation?
- Is there anything else you'd like to tell me?

> **TIP**
>
> **Silence is golden.** If you're having trouble digging information out of an accused employee, take a page from therapists and counselors—trained experts at getting others to talk about uncomfortable things—and try a little silence. If an employee is giving you short answers and holding back information, let the silence deepen. Instead of immediately asking another question, wait a bit. Look at the employee expectantly. (Those who really want to get into character might even try a "Hmmm" or "I see.") You'll be surprised at how often this prompts employees to add something to a previous answer or try a bit harder to explain their side of the story.

When you're through with your questions, review your notes with the employee; ask the employee to sign off on your notes or a written statement summarizing the interview.

Again, close the interview by telling the accused employee what will happen next. Explain that you will interview witnesses and review other evidence before reaching a final conclusion. Stress again that retaliation is strictly prohibited. And ask the employee to bring any new or additional information to your attention at once.

Interviewing Witnesses

There are many kinds of witnesses. Some have seen or heard, firsthand, the misconduct at issue, while others have only heard rumors. Some will be privy to an entire dispute, while others have only a bit of information to share. And some may have an ax to grind (or favor to curry) with either the complaining or the accused employee.

When you interview witnesses, your goal is to find out what they know without revealing any information unnecessarily. While the accused employee has the right to know what allegations have been made, third-party witnesses have no such right. What's more, you have good reasons to maintain confidentiality. If the allegations turn out to be false, you could get into legal trouble for publicizing them unnecessarily. Even if no lawsuit is in the offing, you can cut down gossip by keeping a tight lid on the investigation.

It can be tough to figure out whom to interview as a witness, especially if the complaining employee and/or accused employee suggest a number of candidates. You'll want to interview anyone who allegedly heard or saw something important. Sometimes, however, an employee (particular one accused of wrongdoing) will suggest witnesses who can attest to his or her good character; "Ask Mary or Scott; they know I would never do anything like this!" Although witnesses like this won't add much to your investigation, you might decide to interview one or two, so the employee knows you are taking his or her suggestions seriously.

You shouldn't simply pick and choose, or decide to interview only a set number of witnesses, however. If you decide not to interview a witness suggested by another employee, you should have a good reason, documented in your investigation report (see Chapter 4).

Getting Started

Once again, begin with an opening statement. Here are some topics to include:

- Explain that you are investigating a workplace problem and that you believe the witness might have information that will help you figure out what happened.
- Let the witness know that you have not come to any conclusions about what happened.
- Explain that you expect the witness to give you complete and accurate information and to answer all of your questions truthfully.
- Explain what retaliation is and that it's strictly prohibited. Ask the witness to come to you with any concerns about retaliation for participating in the investigation.

- Ask whether the employee has any questions or concerns about the investigation process. (You may find yourself having to explain that you cannot answer some of these questions, particularly if the witness asks who complained or who else is being interviewed.)

Sample Questions

When deciding what to ask a witness, think about who suggested the witness and why. Did the complaining employee tell you that the witness saw the misconduct? Did the accused employee tell you that he or she confided in the witness after an incident? Sticking to the facts the witness is supposed to know will help you keep things confidential. Here are some questions to consider for third-party witnesses:

Sample Questions

- Do you work with [the complaining employee or accused employee]?
- If the person may have witnessed the incident, ask what the witness saw or heard. For example, "Were you in the lunchroom last Friday? What time? Who else was there? Did you hear Mark and Sarah talking to each other? What did each of them say?"
- When and where did this take place?
- Did you tell anyone about the incident?
- Did [the complaining employee] tell you anything about the incident?
- Did [the accused employee] tell you anything about the incident?
- Have you personally witnessed any other incidents between [the complaining employee] and [the accused employee]?
- Have you heard these issues discussed in the workplace? When, where, and by whom?
- Have you ever had any problems working with [the complaining employee or the accused employee]?
- Is there anything else you'd like to tell me?

As with all interviews, review your notes with the witness when you are through with your questions. Make sure you wrote everything down correctly and that your notes include all of the important details. If you plan to ask the employee to sign a statement rather than your notes, prepare that document now.

When your questions have been answered, thank the witness for participating. And ask the witness to return to you with any further information.

Interviewing Nonemployees

In some situations, you might want to interview someone who doesn't work for the company: a customer who overheard racist comments, a bystander who saw some employees fighting on the street, or a friend or partner in whom an employee confided. Handle these interviews with special care. Talking to someone outside the company can lead to problems. From a legal standpoint, an accused employee is more likely to take offense—and possibly contemplate a defamation lawsuit—if people outside the company learn of the allegations. On the practical side, unless the witness is willing to sign a confidentiality agreement, the company has no way to enforce its confidentiality rules against outsiders, which means your company's dirty laundry might get aired in public.

You may have to run these risks if the witness is crucial to the investigation. For example, if a customer is the only witness to an employee theft or a sexual harassment incident, you need to find out what that person saw. If you find yourself in this situation, stay on your best behavior. Remember, you will be representing the company to the outside world, and you'll want to make it look good. And the witness is under no obligation to talk to you: You're really asking for this person's help, and you should make that clear from the start.

When interviewing an outside witness, confidentiality is especially important. Conduct the interview off-site, at a place that's convenient for the witness. Don't reveal anything unnecessarily, including the names of the employees involved or what you suspect might have happened. Be sure to thank the witness for helping you get to the bottom of things. And provide your contact information so the witness can get in touch with you if anything else happens or comes to mind.

Gathering Other Evidence

In some cases, there will be no evidence of wrongdoing other than witness statements. Much workplace misconduct is interpersonal, conducted face-to-face rather than in writing. If the alleged misconduct consists of verbal or physical harassment, threats, or violence, there may be no document or other tangible piece of evidence related to the incident.

Sometimes, however, documents and other physical evidence play an important role in the investigation. If one employee accuses the other of sending threatening emails, for example, you'll want to get your hands on those messages. Or if an employee is accused of bringing a weapon to work or drinking on the job, you'll want to look for the "smoking gun" (or the empty bottle).

And in some cases, you might want to pay a visit to the scene of the alleged misconduct. This could give you important clues about who's telling the truth, what questions to ask, and which witnesses to interview.

> CAUTION
>
> **Don't pretend to be someone you're not.** Investigators who use a false identity to try to gather information can get in a lot of trouble. For example, in a case involving Hewlett-Packard, an outside investigator allegedly got a board member's phone records by calling the telephone company and pretending to be the member. (The investigator was trying to figure out who was leaking confidential information.) The investigator faced multiple criminal charges. This type of investigating can lead to legal problems and very harmful publicity.

Documents

In every investigation, ask yourself what types of documents could help you figure out what happened. Think about the records your company keeps in personnel files, attendance reports, inventories, computer records, and so on.

In some investigations, documents play a starring role. For example, if an employee claims that her coworkers sexually harassed her by sending X-rated messages and images over the office email system, those emails might be the most important evidence you can gather.

TIP

Get technical help to uncover the history of important electronic documents. Sometimes, you'll need to know who sent an electronic document, when it was created, who else received it, and whether it was altered. In these situations, your company's I.T. department may be able to help you get the information you need. If not, it might be worth the expense to hire outside help to recover this data.

More often, however, documents play a supporting role by providing important background information. For example, if an employee complains that a supervisor has discriminated against him, you might review the employee's personnel file to see how the supervisor has documented their exchanges. Or, if an employee is accused of stealing company equipment, inventory records can help you figure out exactly when the goods disappeared.

Documents might also help you pin down crucial details. For example, attendance records can corroborate (or contradict) an employee who claims to have been out of the office on a particular day. Or, if an employee accuses a supervisor of changing her performance review after she complained of harassment, you can use documents to find out when the complaint was made, when the performance review was drafted, and whether the review was changed at any time.

Here is a checklist of documents that may figure into your investigation. Of course, not every workplace will use all of these types of documents, and not every document on the list will be relevant to a given investigation. But this list will give you a starting point when you start considering which documents might be helpful.

Document Checklist

☐ Company policies

☐ Emails

☐ Postings to company bulletin boards (electronic or corkboard)

☐ Correspondence

☐ Performance evaluations

☐ Work samples

☐ Written warnings and other disciplinary records

☐ Customer complaints or comments

☐ Commendations

☐ Documents signed by the employees involved (such as hiring agreements, employment contracts, and other agreements)

☐ Attendance records (for regular work hours, required meetings, or training sessions, for example)

☐ Payroll records

☐ Time cards or other records showing hours worked

☐ Work schedules

☐ Inventory records

☐ Expense reports

☐ Computer records (of Internet sites visited, productivity, and so on)

☐ Cash register receipts

☐ Purchase orders

☐ Productivity reports (such as records of sales completed, deadlines met, or projects finished)

☐ Sales receipts

☐ Equipment logs

☐ Results of drug or alcohol testing

☐ Notes taken by an employee involved (for example, in a diary, calendar, or journal)

☐ Files from any previous investigations of the same employees or same types of incidents

☐ Photographs (for example, of sexist cartoons posted in an employee's workspace)

TIP

Look for documents that are not in official personnel files. Many supervisors make a habit of keeping their own working files on the employees who report to them. These files often contain documents that never find their way to the employees' official personnel files. For example, a supervisor will probably give an employee's final performance review to the human resources department to place in the employee's personnel file. However, the supervisor might keep old drafts of the review, the employee's comments on the review, and informal notes on the employee's performance in a working file. To make sure that you get your hands on every important document, ask supervisors for all documents they have on the employees involved in the incident, whether or not those documents appear in the employees' personnel files.

If a document is relevant to your investigation, take good care of it. Make a record of where you found it and store it in a secure location. If you plan to use the document in your interviews (for example, to show to the accused employee), don't bring the original; make a copy. That way, you won't have to worry about writing on the document or losing it. If your company later faces a lawsuit relating to the investigation, you will want to be able to show where important documents came from and, more important, that they have not been altered.

EXAMPLE: Sanjiv is accused of sexually harassing a coworker, Linda. During your investigation, Linda gives you several handwritten notes that Sanjiv gave to her. These notes include sexually explicit comments and threats to harm Linda if she doesn't agree to have a relationship with him. As a result of your investigation, Sanjiv is fired.

Sanjiv sues the company for wrongful termination, claiming that he never harassed Linda and that the company really fired him for complaining about health and safety violations. He claims that the investigation was biased and that the notes were doctored to give the company a reason to fire him. He agrees that he wrote part of the notes but claims that the offensive language and threats were added by someone else. You should be able to defeat these arguments if you can show that you recorded the date you received the notes, indicated that Linda gave them to you, placed them in a secure location, and did not remove them from that location until you were asked to hand them over in the lawsuit.

Other Evidence

Misconduct doesn't always leave a paper trail. Sometimes, the path is cluttered with bulkier objects, such as discarded plastic baggies, a knife hidden in a desk drawer, or confidential company data stored on a flash drive. In the most extreme cases, you might need to test this evidence to determine its relevance. For example, you may need to check for fingerprints or test for the presence of illegal drugs.

Always consider the range of possible evidence that might exist. If you find evidence like this, store and label it carefully. Indicate when and where you found the evidence, then place it in a secure location. This could be important later, if you must prove that the evidence has not been tampered with.

> ⓘ **CAUTION**
>
> **If you find contraband, talk to a lawyer.** If you come across illegal evidence, such as controlled substances or an unregistered or illegal weapon, contact a lawyer right away to find out whether you should report it to the police. If you hang onto items that are illegal to possess, you could find yourself facing criminal liability.

Clues From the Scene

It's often a good idea to visit the place where the alleged misconduct took place. This will give you a better understanding of what the witnesses are describing and give you ideas for additional witnesses or follow-up interview questions. It might even convince you that someone is—or is not—telling the truth.

For example, imagine that an employee has complained that another employee raised his voice to her and threatened to harm her one morning in the hallway outside her office. You go to the hallway at about the time when the incident allegedly happened. You notice that the employee's office is next door to a kitchenette, which employees are allowed to use. During the five minutes you spend there, you see 20 different employees come to get coffee, put their lunches in the refrigerator, or just talk to their coworkers. These are all potential witnesses to the incident. You should ask the complaining employee if she noticed any of them nearby when she was threatened. If nobody heard the threats, despite all of this traffic, the complaining employee's story starts to sound a bit far-fetched.

On the other hand, imagine that you went to the hallway and noticed that the complaining employee's office was next door not to a kitchenette, but to an equipment room full of noisy machinery. You don't see anyone else while you're investigating. In this situation, it wouldn't hurt the complaining employee's credibility if there were no witnesses to the threats.

Follow-Up Interviews

Once you complete your interviews and review any other available evidence, consider setting up another interview with the accused employee, especially if you have heard new allegations or information since your last interview. If witnesses have added significant details or documents have surfaced supporting the complaining employee, it is probably a good idea to get the accused employee's response to these additional facts. Courts are more likely to find an investigation was fair and thorough—and its outcome reliable—if the accused employee is given the opportunity to respond to all the evidence before the company makes a final decision.

You should also consider another interview with the complaining employee. If the accused employee or witnesses have denied the complaining employee's allegations or offered reasons why the complaining employee might not be telling the truth, you should let the complaining employee respond.

Make and Document Your Decision

Now you're facing what may be the hardest part of your job as investigator: reaching a conclusion about what happened and what to do about it. You have interviewed all the witnesses. You have gathered all of the relevant evidence. But how do you decide who is telling the truth and who is lying? How do you figure out what actually occurred and why?

Because every investigation—and every person involved in an investigation—is a little bit different, there's no single formula to apply that will always lead you to the right answers. However, there are some guidelines that will help you sort through conflicting stories. This chapter offers some tried and true strategies for evaluating the results of your investigation and reaching a decision.

After you have made your assessments, you must decide whether wrongdoing occurred and what, if any, corrective action to take (if that's part of your job). You must document your investigation and decisions. And, even after the investigation is written up and filed away, you'll want to take a few steps to make sure that you've really dealt with the underlying problem. For example, you may want to follow up with the affected employees and think about whether any workplace changes are necessary to avoid similar problems in the future.

Evaluate the Evidence

If there is no dispute about what actually happened, you can skip right to "Decide Whether Misconduct Occurred," below. However, if there are important disagreements among the witnesses—and particularly if the accused worker denies the facts of the complaint—you will have to figure out where the truth lies.

Look at the Facts

To begin, review the evidence you have gathered and your notes from interviews. If there are multiple allegations, go through each one separately. Are there any facts to which everyone agrees? What are the major points of contention? As to each of these disputes, what did the witnesses say? Are there any documents supporting one version over another?

Some investigators find it helpful to group the evidence into two categories: disputed facts and undisputed facts. If you can make a decision based solely on the undisputed facts, then you don't really have to decide which witness(es) you believe; they've all agreed on the important points. If the undisputed facts don't give you enough to go on, think about which disputed facts will have to be resolved in order to reach a conclusion. Focus on these facts—and on each witness's version of these facts—as you consider credibility issues (discussed below).

> EXAMPLE: Mimi is evaluating the evidence she has gathered in her investigation of missing products from an electronics store. Here are the undisputed facts her investigation has revealed:
>
> 1. The missing products are all high-ticket items; each is worth several hundred dollars or more.
> 2. The products were signed for by the receiving department but could not be located on the stockroom shelves when customers tried to buy them. In other words, the items disappeared from the stockroom, not from the showroom floor or in transit between the manufacturer and the electronics store.
> 3. Franklin and Debbie are the only two employees who were working in the stockroom when each of the thefts occurred.
> 4. Franklin recently bought a new Land Rover and took a cruise to the Bahamas.
>
> Is this enough information for Mimi to decide what happened? Nope. The only fact that points to Franklin as the culprit is his recent change in spending habits, and there could be lots of reasons for that. So Mimi has to move on to consider the disputed facts. She realizes that these disputed facts are the most important:
>
> 1. Debbie claims that Franklin disappeared for an hour or so during each shift when items were taken. Franklin claims that he is frequently asked to work in other areas of the store and that he was probably working elsewhere at the time.
> 2. Franklin claims that his wife recently inherited a large sum of money from her deceased grandfather, which paid for their new car and cruise.

3. Several employees claim to have seen Franklin's car parked at the loading dock (which backs onto the stockroom) on occasion. Franklin denies that he has ever parked near the loading dock and says these employees must be mistaken.

Mimi can now focus her energy on assessing these key disputed facts. As sometimes happens, Mimi realizes that she might have to gather some more information to make a final decision. For example, she might briefly interview the managers who were working when Franklin claims to have been asked to work in a different part of the store, to find out if anyone reassigned Franklin. She might also perform a quick public records search online to see what she can find out about Franklin's grandfather-in-law.

Assess Credibility

When you're faced with conflicting stories—as happens in many investigations—you will have to consider each person's version of the facts. Evaluating credibility and determining who's telling the truth can be difficult, but the following guidelines will help you sift through the evidence:

- **Plausibility.** Whose story makes the most sense? Does one person's version of events defy logic or common sense? Based on your visit to the scene (see Chapter 3), could the employees involved have heard and seen what they claimed to have witnessed? Should they have heard and seen things that they did not admit?
- **Source of information.** Did the witness see or hear the event directly? Did the witness report firsthand knowledge or rely on secondhand statements from other employees or rumors?
- **Detail.** How general or specific was each person's statement? If a witness gave a detailed statement, were those details supported by other evidence? Did the accused or suspected employee deny the allegations in detail or only generally?
- **Corroboration and conflicting testimony.** Are there witnesses or documents that support one side of the story? Does the evidence contradict one person's statements? Do the witnesses support the person who suggested you interview them? If there are conflicts, are they over minor or significant issues?

- **Contradictions.** Was each person's story consistent throughout your questioning or on a second telling? Did any of the witnesses contradict themselves during your interview? If so, did the change involve a minor issue or a matter of substance?

- **Demeanor.** How did the witnesses act during the interview? Did the accused employee have a strong reaction to the complaint or no reaction at all? Did the complaining employee seem genuinely upset? Were any witnesses' reactions unusual, based on their typical demeanor or behavior? Judging demeanor can be tough—even for the experts—and you certainly shouldn't base your conclusions on demeanor alone. But you should consider any reactions that are particularly strong or unexpected.

- **Omissions.** Did anyone leave out important information during the interview? Is there a sensible explanation for the omission? Did an accused or suspected employee admit an important detail only after being confronted with it?

- **Prior incidents.** Does the accused employee have a documented history of this type of misconduct? Has the complaining employee made previous complaints? Have there been other incidents between the complaining and the accused employee?

- **Motive.** Does either the complaining worker or the accused worker have a motive to lie about, exaggerate, or deny the incident? Is there any history between these employees that affects their credibility? Do any of the witnesses have a special loyalty to—or grudge against—any of the employees involved?

TIP

Reopen the investigation, if necessary. Sometimes, your evaluation of the facts and credibility assessments will lead you to only one definite conclusion: You need more information. This is not uncommon. You might not see important lines of questioning or gaps in the evidence until you analyze all of the facts. If you think you need more information, it's much better to continue the investigation than to make a decision that might later be called into question.

Put It All Together

Once you've examined all of the facts and weighed each witness's credibility, you will probably begin to see the real story, or at least the way that things are most likely to have played out. Often, investigators find that one version of events is implausible or that it makes a lot less sense than another version of the events. In investigations, as in science, the adage holds true: The most obvious explanation is often the correct one.

However, the web may remain hopelessly tangled even after you've considered every angle. In that case, you might have to end the investigation by admitting that you cannot figure out what really happened. If there is evidence on both sides and it really could have happened either way, it's better to throw up your hands than to take disciplinary action that isn't supported by the evidence. (See "Take Action," below, for more on how to handle these situations.)

> **EXAMPLE:** Stuart complained that Marcus threatened to fire him for taking time off to report to jury duty. Stuart said that Marcus made this threat in the lunchroom on April 28. Marcus seemed very surprised by this allegation; he agreed that he spoke to Stuart in the lunchroom about his jury summons but said only that he hoped Stuart didn't get picked to sit on a jury because jury duty can be so boring. Marcus suggested that the investigator speak to several witnesses, all of whom confirmed his side of the story. Marcus also said that Stuart had seemed upset since his last performance review, when Marcus noted that Stuart hadn't met several of his performance goals for the year. When the investigator interviewed Stuart a second time to get his reaction to this, Stuart admitted that the witnesses were there but insisted that they must have misunderstood what Marcus said. He also admitted his bad feelings about the performance review.
>
> In this case, the investigator can conclude that there was no wrongdoing. All of the witnesses support Marcus's version of events. Stuart cannot explain this discrepancy. Marcus has also offered a reason for Stuart's complaint, which Stuart has not denied.
>
> **EXAMPLE:** Same as above, but one witness (a friend of Marcus's) confirms Marcus's version of the conversation, and one witness (a coworker with

whom Stuart often eats lunch) confirms Stuart's version. Although Stuart admits his bad feelings about the performance review, he points out that he went to Marcus's manager shortly after his evaluation to talk about the review. The manager confirmed Marcus's opinion of Stuart's performance and explained how Stuart could improve. Stuart says that he felt more comfortable with the evaluation after this conversation, although Marcus was upset that Stuart went over his head and complained. Marcus denies being upset about this.

What should the investigator do now? Without more evidence, the investigator cannot reach a conclusion. Both Stuart and Marcus claim that the other had a motive to lie, and both claim to be telling the truth. In short, this one could go either way.

Get a Second Opinion

Except in the most clear-cut situations, it's a good idea to ask someone else to review your investigation and the conclusions you've reached. This will help you make sure that you've considered all the angles, documented everything properly, and made an objective decision based on the evidence.

If possible, choose someone who is fairly high up in the company and has some distance from the situation, such as a human resources director for a different region. Give this person all of your investigative documents and evidence, then ask whether your decision seems justified. This person may point out gaps in your documentation or ask questions that you hadn't considered. A lawyer can also help you make sure that your investigation and conclusions are sound.

Decide Whether Misconduct Occurred

Once you have evaluated the evidence and reached some factual conclusions, you will have to decide whether company policies were violated or misconduct occurred. This decision will dictate what further actions you should take and what you should tell the employees involved.

Misconduct and Discipline: Who Decides?

You may not be responsible for deciding whether discipline should be imposed. In many larger companies with dedicated human resources departments, the investigator is responsible only for reaching factual conclusions about the situation under investigation—that is, for deciding what probably happened—not for making decisions about discipline. Even in smaller companies, the investigator won't always be responsible for discipline, depending on where he or she ranks on the company ladder. Tailor your report and conclusions to your responsibilities: If you don't make disciplinary decisions, limit yourself to writing down your conclusions about what happened, not what should be done about it.

At this point, you may be wondering what, exactly, constitutes misconduct. For the most part, it isn't hard to tell whether an employee has crossed the line that separates eccentric behavior, jokes, or silliness from actions that are worthy of discipline. However, there are some gray areas, where it can be tough to distinguish misconduct from a misunderstanding.

EXAMPLE: Over the course of several months, $300 has gone missing from petty cash. Numerous employees saw Claude taking money from the petty cash drawer on three separate occasions. When you ask Claude about it, he denies taking the money and calls his coworkers liars. Based on these facts, it looks like Claude has committed misconduct.

Now assume that employees have seen Claude taking the money, but they've also seen Claude putting money back into the drawer. No money is missing from the petty cash account. When you ask Claude about it, he immediately admits taking the money but says that he always paid it back. He assumed that this was okay because his supervisor also borrows from petty cash. Now, the situation is less clear. Claude hasn't lied, and technically he hasn't stolen. He may have exercised poor judgment, but his supervisor's actions led him to believe his actions were okay. He should be told that he has violated company policy and perhaps be given a warning, but severe disciplinary measures aren't called for. His supervisor should also be warned and, perhaps, disciplined for violating company policy.

In "Take Action," below, you'll find information on what to do once you've decided whether wrongdoing occurred, or you've decided that you can't reach a conclusion. If you're having trouble making these distinctions, however, here are some guidelines that may help:

- **The law.** Are the employee's actions illegal? Has the employee committed actionable harassment, stolen from the company or its customers, used or sold illegal drugs, or threatened to harm someone?

- **Written company policies.** Does the employee's conduct violate company policies, as expressed in the employee handbook or in other documents that are distributed to employees?

- **Company practices and procedures**. Did the employee violate a rule that is known in the workplace, even if it isn't written down?

- **Common sense.** Was the employee's action obviously inappropriate or dangerous, even if it isn't illegal or explicitly prohibited by company policies? For example, an employee decides to play a prank on the supervisor who just gave him a bad review by disassembling the supervisor's car and reassembling it on the factory floor, which disrupts an entire shift of work and creates a hazard for employees on the floor. It's not clear that this is illegal, and many companies won't have had the foresight to explicitly prohibit car assembly in the workspace, but this employee's conduct is deserving of discipline.

What these criteria have in common is that, in each case, employees have fair notice of what constitutes misconduct. If actions are prohibited by law, violate written or understood company policy, or don't pass the laugh test ("I didn't know I'd get in trouble for calling in a false fire alarm when our biggest client was here; that's not in the company handbook!"), then it's fair to label those actions misconduct and take appropriate corrective action. On the other hand, if an employee's actions are not illegal, against company policy, or obviously inappropriate (like Claude's loans from the petty cash drawer, in the example above), it might not be fair to take action against the employee. Instead, this might be an opportunity to create or revise company policies, inform employees about the company's expectations, or even provide some training.

Take Action

After you have decided whether wrongdoing occurred, you will have to take action based on your findings. This section describes how to handle each of the three conclusions you might reach:

- no misconduct occurred
- you can't decide whether misconduct occurred, or
- misconduct occurred.

No Misconduct

There are several types of situations in which you might find that no misconduct occurred. If there was some incident between the complaining and the accused employee, but nothing happened that is illegal or prohibited by company policies, you might find that no misconduct occurred. In these situations, you should consider whether the accused employee's behavior (and/or the complaining worker's conduct) warrants counseling or warning.

> EXAMPLE: Sabine complains that Henry, a coworker, asked her to go out on a date with him, then seemed unhappy when she turned him down. Henry agrees that this happened, acknowledges that he was disappointed when Sabine declined, but says that he has not asked her out or had any social interaction with her since. Both agree that the incident has not affected their jobs or their ability to work together. This is not misconduct, but you might want to make sure Henry knows that any further advances towards Sabine could violate company policies on harassment.

In rare cases, you might conclude that the complaint was false. If the complaining employee acted in good faith but was mistaken (for example, if he or she misunderstood an incident or was confused about the accused employee's actions), you probably won't have to take any further action once the misunderstanding is cleared up. On the other hand, if the complaining employee acted maliciously—that is, the employee intentionally fabricated the complaint—discipline against the complaining worker may be order. Consider the employee's motives, how serious the allegations were, and the disruptions to your company in determining an appropriate response. (See "Handling False Complaints," below, to learn why caution is required in this situation.)

Inconclusive Results

In some cases, you may be unable to figure out what happened. If the results of your investigation are inconclusive, you should tell both the complaining and the accused employee that you hit a dead end.

If your investigation uncovered confusion about a particular policy (such as what constitutes sexual harassment or what is required under a safety rule), some workplace training might be in order. If you can't figure out whether company policy was violated or who is behind a problem, at least you can take steps to prevent future misconduct.

> **EXAMPLE:** Jon claims that his boss, Maureen, said she wouldn't give him a raise because he refused to clock her in each morning at 8 a.m. (she would sometimes arrive at work ten to 15 minutes late). Maureen denies Jon's claims but admits that she has been warned about her tardiness and that she has joked with Jon about clocking her in. Maureen also says that she does not plan to give Jon a raise because his work performance has been slipping; her statement is supported by productivity records. No witnesses have seen or heard anything relevant. In this situation, it's not clear what happened. You might want to warn Maureen that having another worker clock her in is a violation of company policy that will result in discipline, but otherwise there isn't much you can do.

Misconduct

You may find that the accused employee engaged in misconduct that requires discipline. If so, and if you are responsible for determining disciplinary measures, choose a corrective action that will be effective in ending the wrongdoing and signaling that the company takes it seriously. And no matter what disciplinary measures you come up with, implement them immediately.

Handling False Complaints

Sometimes, an employee makes a complaint that turns out, after a thorough investigation, to be false or unfounded. Some employers are tempted to punish the complaining employee in this situation. After all, investigations disrupt the workplace, cost time and money, and can cause considerable stress for employees wrongly accused of misconduct. But think twice before taking action against an employee who brings a complaint. If the employee had a good faith reason for complaining, any disciplinary action against that employee might constitute retaliation.

A complaint is in good faith if the employee honestly and reasonably believes the complaint to be true. Even if an investigation proves that the employee was mistaken, you cannot take action unless the complaining employee acted maliciously or recklessly. For example, imagine that Sarah accuses Bernice of stealing from the cash register. If Sarah made up the allegation to get back at Bernice for dating Sarah's former boyfriend, Sarah should be disciplined for making the complaint. However, if Sarah saw Bernice taking money from the register and reasonably believed that Bernice was stealing, Sarah should not be disciplined, even if it turns out that Bernice had permission to take the money to purchase company supplies.

Savvy employers discipline complaining employees only when they can prove that the complaint was false, was motivated by bad intentions, and caused the company or another employee harm (including damage to a falsely accused employee's reputation). And they do so only after consulting with an experienced lawyer. An employee who is disciplined for complaining might turn around and sue for retaliation. Even if you believe you had good reason for imposing discipline, a jury might see it otherwise. And juries are quite willing to make employers pay in these situations: Some of the highest damages awards in employment cases go to employees claiming retaliation.

Here are some factors to consider when trying to decide on an appropriate corrective action:

- **Severity.** How serious was the misconduct? If there was a victim (for example, an employee who was harassed or threatened), how was the victim affected by the accused employee's actions? What effect did the accused employee's actions have on the workplace?

- **Consistency.** Have other employees committed similar types of misconduct in the past? How were these incidents handled? Being consistent when you discipline employees will help you avoid charges of discrimination and unfair treatment.

- **Policy.** Does the company have a progressive discipline policy? Where does this misconduct—and this employee—fall on your company's scale?

- **History.** Have there been any similar prior incidents involving this employee? Does the employee have a history of disciplinary problems?

- **Knowledge.** Did the employee know that his or her conduct was prohibited? Did workplace rules and policies clearly spell out the company's expectations? An employee who knowingly violates a rule often deserves harsher discipline than an employee who wasn't aware of his or her transgression.

- **Evidence.** How strong is the evidence of wrongdoing? Remember, your company may have to defend whatever action you take in court. Do you have strong, firsthand, corroborated evidence of wrongdoing? If you are going to take harsh disciplinary measures, make sure the evidence you've gathered will support your decision.

Once you have decided how to discipline the wrongdoer, take care of it immediately. Meet with the employee to inform him or her of the results of the investigation and the discipline that will be imposed. Follow your company's policies on discipline, including documenting your decision.

If the Complaining Employee Is Unhappy

Even if you take immediate and effective action against the wrongdoer, the complaining employee may be upset. The complaining employee may believe a harsher punishment should have been imposed, may be upset by damage to his or her reputation or work opportunities, or may not believe the wrongdoer will shape up.

Your company is under no obligation to impose the punishment your complaining employee favors. Your obligation to the company, the accused employee, and the rest of your workforce is to be fair and reasonable. However, you should listen carefully to the complaining employee's concerns. Perhaps the employee who claims that the wrongdoer will never change is worried about retaliation or further misconduct. If so, you can assure the complaining employee that you will deal swiftly with any such behavior. An employee who claims to have suffered because of the misconduct may have a point: If the employee was unfairly denied a promotion, raise, or time off, for example, you should consider conferring these benefits retroactively.

Although complaining employees may well have their own axes to grind, they can also help you figure out whether you have chosen an effective remedy. If the resolution you've chosen isn't going to work, better to hear about it now when you can fix the problem than later in a lawsuit.

CAUTION

If you discipline an employee based on findings by an outside investigator, you must provide a summary of the investigation report to the employee. As noted in Chapter 2, using an outside investigator brings some of the provisions of the Fair Credit Reporting Act into play. If you decide, based on the investigator's report, to impose discipline, you must provide a summary of the nature and substance of the report to the disciplined employee. This requirement doesn't apply if you investigate in-house. You'll find a sample form you can complete and provide to the employee at this book's online companion page; see Appendix A for details.

You must also meet with the complaining employee. Explain that the wrongdoer has been disciplined and describe any steps you will take to prevent further problems. Give assurances that the employee can come to you with any concerns about the situation.

Some employers apologize to the complaining employee for the misconduct. This is a nice gesture, and one that can go a long way toward making employees feel that their concerns were taken seriously. However, if you offer an apology, choose your words with care. Avoid saying things that could be construed as admitting that what happened is the company's fault. There is a world of difference between "We're so sorry that this happened" and "We're so sorry that we allowed this to happen."

Document Your Decision

If you've followed the advice in this book, you've already documented every step of your investigation. At this point, you should have:

- a written complaint or your notes from meeting with the complaining employee, if there is one (if the investigation was based on something other than a complaint—for example, an audit revealed missing funds or sexist graffiti appeared at a work site—you should have notes about the incident)
- notes from your other interviews, and
- copies of any relevant documents, policies, photographs, or other physical evidence relating to the investigation.

You should also make a note of any proposed witness who was not interviewed and why. For example, if an employee accused of sexual harassment suggests that you speak to his friend and coworker, who can attest that he "wouldn't sexually harass anyone," you could reasonably choose to save your interviews for those who actually know something about the incident.

Some investigators, particularly consultants who specialize in conducting investigations, prepare formal investigative records. Although you don't have to prepare a formal document with index tabs and footnotes, you should preserve your notes from the investigation and write a brief report of what you did and why. Remember, you might have to prove to a jury that you acted reasonably and that your conclusions were sound. If you have documented the reasons for your decision, you will have an easier time remembering the details and convincing the jury that you considered all the angles before taking action. You will also have a contemporaneous record (that is, one made at the time of the investigation) of what you did and why. This type of document is much more persuasive to a jury than one created after the fact to present in a courtroom.

Prepare an Investigation Report

When you sit down to write your investigation report, remember your audience. If your company is sued for anything related to the investigation—for example, because of the underlying incident or because of the punishment imposed on the wrongdoer—the document you write today could end up in the hands of a lawyer suing your company (and later, in the hands of a judge or jury). If this worst-case scenario comes to pass, your report will be put under a microscope. Any important omissions, inappropriate comments, or random musings could come back to haunt you.

Because of the unfortunate possibility that your report might be evidence in a lawsuit someday, it can be hard to figure out how much detail to include. Your documentation doesn't have to memorialize every thought that crossed your mind during the investigation, nor should it. If you include a lot of extraneous detail, the jury might have trouble following your decision-making process. But make sure to write down all of the major decisions you made and why.

For example, if you did not believe a witness's statement, make a note of that and the reasons for your skepticism. Similarly, if you concluded that no misconduct occurred, write down all of the reasons for your decision. If you write extensive notes but later claim to have left out an important detail, the jury may well believe that you are trying to build a case after the fact.

If you conclude that the employee committed misconduct, you should certainly say so. However, you should avoid saying that the employee broke the law or committed a legal violation (for example, that the employee sexually harassed someone). The reason is simple: In many cases, the company can be liable for an employee's illegal conduct. If you state in an investigation report that an employee committed an illegal act, you have conceded your company's liability. If it later turns out that you were wrong, that other facts mitigate your company's responsibility, or that your company may have a valid defense, this admission will be very hard to undo. You're far better off simply saying that the employee committed misconduct, violated company policies, acted inappropriately, or used poor judgment.

If the results of your investigation were inconclusive, you should document the reasons why you were unable to sort things out. Note the conflicting evidence carefully. This documentation will be invaluable if similar allegations are later made against the accused employee. You will have a record of previous problems to support any discipline you might impose for future misconduct.

Your documents should include a notation of the discipline (if any) you imposed on the wrongdoer. This information should also go in the wrongdoer's personnel file. If your meeting with either the wrongdoer or the complaining employee was eventful (for example, there was heated argument or significant commentary), you might want to include some notes from that meeting as well.

You'll find a template for completing an investigation report, a sample investigation report, and other sample forms and policies at this book's online companion page. Appendix A explains how to access the page.

Where to Keep Investigation Records

Now that you've documented your investigation, what should you do with your notes, the investigation report, and other documents from the investigation? Create a separate investigation file to be kept with the company's other confidential records. The investigation file should be treated like an employee's medical records: It should be kept confidential and revealed only on a strict need-to-know basis. Don't put the investigation report in any employee's personnel file. In most states, employees have the right to inspect the contents of their personnel files.

If you took corrective action against an employee, that employee's personnel file should include a memo or other documentation of the discipline imposed. It should also indicate that a separate investigation file exists on the incident. That way, if another incident arises involving the same employee, the investigator will know to look in the confidential investigation file for information on the previous problem.

What Goes in the Investigation File

Put all documents relating to the investigation in the confidential investigation file, including:

- the complaint, if there is one
- copies of any company policies pertaining to the incident(s) investigated
- copies of any documents you considered in reaching your conclusion
- photos, diagrams, notes, and other evidence relating to the investigation
- copies of the written instructions you gave to witnesses regarding cooperation, retaliation, and confidentiality (see Chapter 3)
- your notes from interviews, signed by the witness
- your investigative report, and
- copies of any disciplinary action taken as a result of the investigation.

You'll find a sample investigation file for a sexual harassment case, along with other materials and resources at this book's online companion page. See Appendix A for more information.

CAUTION

Don't toss documents without speaking to a lawyer. Some investigators throw away their notes once they have written a final investigation report. However, this can be very risky. If the incident under investigation—or the investigation itself—turns into a lawsuit, you might be accused of destroying evidence. If you have a lot of extraneous paper you'd like to get rid of or you're concerned about a particular document, get some advice from a lawyer before you throw anything away.

Investigation Report Checklist

Here are some important facts your investigation report should include, if applicable:

☐ the date of the incident(s) under investigation

☐ if there is a complaint, the date of the complaint and name of the employee who complained

☐ why the investigation was initiated (for example, an employee complained, a fight broke out, or an employee was suspected of being under the influence of drugs at work) and the basic facts to be investigated

☐ who conducted the investigation

☐ when the investigation began

☐ what documents or other evidence were gathered

☐ where documents or evidence were found (for example, in an employee's personnel file, pinned to the company bulletin board, or in an employee's desk drawer)

☐ when documents or evidence were gathered

☐ any company policies that are relevant to the incident under investigation

☐ who was interviewed

☐ the date of each interview

☐ a summary of each witness's statement

☐ a summary of any other important facts (for example, things you may have noticed when visiting the scene of the incident)

☐ your conclusions and how you came to them

☐ any important issues left unresolved, and

☐ any action taken in the workplace (for example, discipline against the wrongdoer or workplace training).

Should You Speak to Other Employees?

Investigations can be very disruptive, especially if the allegations become widely known in the company. Of course, you'll need to talk to the complaining and accused employee once the investigation is complete, but should you say anything to other employees who know about the situation?

This can be a tough issue to sort out. On the one hand, you must treat the investigation confidentially, both to avoid legal claims (for defamation or unfair treatment, for example) and to avoid poisoning the atmosphere for anyone. An employee who is investigated—and disciplined—for telling a racially inappropriate joke, for example, probably doesn't want the whole company to know about that lapse in judgment. And, an employee who makes a complaint may worry about being branded as a "tattletale" or as someone who "isn't a team player." On the other hand, an investigation can become the elephant in the room for a department: Everyone knows something about it, many participated in it, but nobody knows what happened. This can lead to rumor, gossip, and lack of productivity; it can also lead to lack of trust in the company, if a problem is perceived as not being dealt with.

One solution is to make a limited statement, to only those employees who were involved, acknowledging that there was an investigation (without divulging who was investigated or for what), thanking everyone who participated, and stating that the matter is now concluded. This is appropriate where a department or group of employees knows about the investigation. For example, if all three of the Accounts Payable clerks were interviewed because their manager was accused of creating a sexually hostile environment, some closing statement to that department is in order. It's also a good idea to state that the company must respect the rights of the employees involved, and keep the investigation and its outcome confidential; employees are likely to have questions you aren't at liberty to answer, and a statement like this will head many inquiries off at the pass. You can also tell employees to come to you if they have any concerns going forward. This will help your company watch out for retaliation or signs that the corrective action you took might not be working.

Follow Up

You've finished your investigation, taken action if you've found work-place wrongdoing, written your report, and filed it away. So now you can rest on your laurels, right? Not yet. There are still a few things you should do to make sure that you've effectively dealt with the underlying problem.

Meet With Employees

Check in periodically with the complaining employee, if there is one. Make sure that the misconduct has stopped, that no retaliation has taken place, and that the employee is comfortable in the workplace. If you learn of any problems during these conversations, take action right away.

In some cases, you may also want to follow up with the accused employee, if that employee is still with the company. Ask whether the employee has any concerns relating to the investigation, and whether things are getting back to normal.

Verify Corrective Actions

You'll want to make sure that any corrective actions you recommended were taken. Was the wrongdoer actually disciplined? For example, was a written warning placed in the personnel file, or did the employee actually serve a recommended suspension? If the wrongdoer was told to complete a training program, a rehabilitation program, or counsel-ing (for example, on anger management), has it happened? If you recommended a change in reporting relationships, has that taken place?

Consider the Big Picture

Some investigations reveal company-wide problems that should be addressed. Did your investigation turn up significant confusion about company rules or appropriate workplace behavior? Are managers in need of some advice or training on dealing with employees and employee problems? Did you discover that previous incidents had been swept under the rug or improperly documented? If you answer "yes" to any of these questions, you need to take some action. Your company's employees may need training on company policies, proper management practices, record keeping, or legal requirements.

PART

II

Investigating Common Workplace Problems

Investigating Discrimination

Investigating claims of discrimination can be complicated. Because the essence of most discrimination claims is that the complaining employee was treated differently from other employees because of a protected characteristic (race, gender, religion, and so on), a thorough investigation will of course require you to look at how the complaining worker was treated. However, you will also need to look at how other workers were treated, how the employee accused of discrimination has acted in the past, and whether the reasons the accused employee gives for the challenged decision or action are consistent and legitimate.

Because you will need to gather potentially sensitive information about a number of employees, these investigations can easily mushroom. To handle a discrimination investigation successfully, you'll need to figure out exactly what information you need and how to get it. If you aren't thorough enough, the investigation might not hold up in court or convince complaining employees that their concerns have been taken seriously. If you go overboard in your information gathering, however, you could create unnecessary delays and risk compromising the confidentiality of the investigation.

An investigation of discrimination is likely to trigger an emotional response, as well. Employees who feel they are being judged based on a protected characteristic rather than their performance are likely to be angry, particularly if they are members of a group that has historically been mistreated in this country. An employee accused of discrimination will probably have a very strong reaction as well; being labeled as a bigot does not sit well with anyone.

This chapter will give you the information and strategies you need to conduct a thorough and effective discrimination investigation. First, it explains the law of discrimination, including common types of discrimination claims. Then, it describes how the ten steps to an effective investigation (as explained in Part I) apply to discrimination cases, paying special attention to the unique considerations that arise in these investigations.

What Is Discrimination?

It is illegal for an employer to make job decisions based on a person's race, religion, gender or other "protected characteristics" (as explained below) rather than on that person's ability to do the job. This rule applies to every aspect of the employment relationship, from hiring to promotions, job assignments, pay raises, leaves of absence, working conditions, performance evaluations, demotions, discipline, and firing.

Discrimination is prohibited by federal, state, and some local laws. The Equal Employment Opportunity Commission (EEOC) enforces federal antidiscrimination laws, and state fair employment practices agencies handle violations of state law. Appendix B includes a list of local EEOC offices and contact information for state fair employment practices agencies.

Protected Characteristics

Federal, state, and local laws determine which characteristics are protected. Under federal law, employers may not make job decisions based on an employee's race, color, national origin, genetic information, religion, gender (including pregnancy), disability, citizenship status, or age (if the employee is at least 40 years old). Virtually every state and some localities also outlaw discrimination on these bases, and many protect employees from discrimination on bases not explicitly covered by federal law, such as sexual orientation or marital status. You can find information on your state's antidiscrimination laws in Appendix B.

Race and Color

Discrimination on the basis of race or color might include segregating employees of a particular race in certain jobs, making decisions based on stereotypes about race, treating an employee differently for associating with people of a particular race, making decisions based on conditions that correlate to race, or making distinctions based on skin color.

Here are some examples:

- A department store chain routinely channels white employees to sales jobs, while Latino employees are placed mostly in restocking and warehouse positions.

- A delivery company refuses to hire Asian applicants as truck drivers; the hiring committee believes Asians are poor drivers and are more likely to get in accidents.

- A consulting firm doesn't promote a white employee whose husband is Lebanese; the firm's principals often bring their spouses when they entertain important clients, and they are afraid their clients will feel uncomfortable around an Arab American.

- A restaurant chain has many African American employees; however, the chain routinely assigns lighter-skinned African Americans to wait tables and seat customers, while African Americans with darker skin are channeled to jobs washing dishes and busing tables.

Retaliation Charges at an All-Time High

The Equal Employment Opportunity Commission (EEOC), the federal agency responsible for administering and enforcing laws that prohibit discrimination, collects statistics on how many discrimination charges are filed with the agency each year, and on what basis. In each of the last 15 years, there were more charges alleging race discrimination than any other type, followed by sex discrimination. In recent years, however, the most frequently filed charge was not for any type of discrimination, but for retaliation. Charges of disability discrimination have also increased since Congress amended the law to provide stronger protections for employees with disabilities.

Which Antidiscrimination Laws Apply to Your Company?

Not every antidiscrimination law applies to every employer. For the most part, whether your company has to follow these laws depends on its size and location. Federal antidiscrimination laws (listed below) apply only to employers with more than a minimum number of employees.

Name of Law:	Discrimination Prohibited on the Basis of:	Applies to:
Title VII	Race, color, religion, sex, or national origin	Employers with 15 or more employees
Age Discrimination in Employment Act	Age (40 or older)	Employers with 20 or more employees
Americans with Disabilities Act	Physical or mental disability	Employers with 15 or more employees
Equal Pay Act	Sex (wage discrimination only)	All employers
Immigration Reform and Control Act	Citizenship status, national origin	Employers with 4 or more employees
Civil Rights Act of 1866	Race, ethnicity	All employers
Genetic Information Nondiscrimination Act	Genetic information	Employers with 15 or more employees

States also have antidiscrimination laws; some apply to smaller employers, and many outlaw additional types of discrimination. Your company must follow all laws that apply to it, whether federal, state, or local. To find out what types of discrimination are prohibited in the state(s) where your company does business, see the chart "State Laws Prohibiting Discrimination in Employment," in Appendix B.

English-Only Rules

Some employers have adopted "English-only" rules that require employees to speak only English in the workplace. These rules can be discriminatory based on national origin, but they are sometimes legally justified. An English-only rule will not be considered discriminatory as long as there is a legitimate business justification for the rule. For example, a rule might pass muster if a team of employees is working together and English is their only common language, or if safety or customer service requires it.

> EXAMPLE: An auto parts factory imposes an English-only rule for its line workers, who must work together using heavy machinery. Such a rule is probably justified by safety concerns. However, if the factory prohibited workers from speaking other languages even on breaks and while making personal telephone calls, that would be a tougher sell. Similarly, if the company imposed a rule that prohibited workers from speaking only certain languages (such as a "no Spanish" rule), that would be discriminatory.

National Origin

An employer discriminates based on national origin when it treats an employee differently because of ethnicity or country of ancestry, or because of traits closely linked to ethnicity (such as surname, accent, language, cultural identity, and so on).

Examples of national origin discrimination include:

- An airline doesn't allow anyone who appears to be from the Middle East to work in any position that involves dealing with passengers.
- A hardware store that serves a predominantly white neighborhood refuses to promote an employee who has adopted a traditional African style of dress.
- A Chinese restaurant hires only people with Asian features and surnames to wait on customers.

- An automotive supply store disciplines Latino employees more severely than white employees for unexcused absences and tardiness.

Employers can legitimately make job decisions based on an employee's accent only if the accent significantly interferes with the employee's ability to do the job. For example, a business might transfer an employee with a heavy Indian accent from a software help desk position to a job that doesn't require customer contact. Such a transfer would be legitimate if customers had complained that they could not understand his instructions; the same transfer would be illegal if the employee was transferred simply because he had an Indian accent, not because the accent impaired his ability to do the job.

Gender

An employer discriminates based on gender when it makes decisions based on an employee's sex, stereotypes about men and women, or pregnancy. (As explained in "Sexual Orientation and Gender Identity" below, the EEOC considers discrimination against gay, lesbian, and transgender employees to be a form of sexual discrimination as well.) Here are some examples:

- A consulting business does not assign women to positions that require significant travel; the company owner believes that women have greater responsibilities at home and will be reluctant to leave their families.
- A manager refuses to promote a pregnant woman to a position for which she will need substantial training; the manager thinks, "we'll just spend all that money to get her up to speed, then she'll quit to stay home with her kids."
- The manager of a sporting goods store assigns only men to work in its golf section, assuming that its customers for golf equipment— who are mostly male—will be less inclined to listen to a woman's advice about clubs and shoes.

Employers must treat pregnant women just as they treat other workers who are temporarily disabled for other reasons. If the employer grants some accommodation requests and not others, it must have a neutral business reason for the difference in treatment. However, such a policy might still be illegal if it places a significant burden on women and the business reason for the policy isn't strong enough to justify this burden.

> EXAMPLE: Marcie works as a file clerk, which requires her to file documents and occasionally lift and move boxes. When she becomes pregnant, her doctor restricts her from lifting more than ten pounds. Marcie asks her boss for an accommodation. If the company routinely provides accommodations to anyone with a lifting restriction, it must grant Marcie's request as well. If, however, the company has granted only requests by employees who were injured on the job, Marcie may not be entitled to an accommodation. It depends on whether that policy significantly burdens women (for example, because a number of other pregnant women have requested accommodations and have been denied) and whether the company has a strong business justification for the policy.

Employers may not impose special rules on pregnant women. For example, an employer may not prohibit a woman from working past a certain point in her pregnancy or require her to take a certain amount of leave after having a baby.

Age

It is illegal to base employment decisions on a worker's age, but only if the worker is at least 40 years old (this is the federal law; some states protect workers of all ages from discrimination). A company discriminates based on age by, for example, excluding older workers from certain job opportunities, refusing to hire or promote older workers, making decisions based on stereotypes about age, or providing more expensive benefits to younger workers.

Here are some examples:

- A computer software company hires mostly younger workers as programmers; although older workers apply, the hiring team assumes that they will have a harder time mastering the technology and staying on top of new developments.
- A company that provides human resources training has a team of trainers who are mostly in their 20s and 30s; the company wants a

dynamic, energetic group of trainers, and so has screened out most of the older workers who have applied for training positions.

- A small publishing company automatically stops paying for its workers' health insurance when they reach the age of 50. Because older workers are more likely to use their health benefits and therefore more expensive to insure, the company simply cuts them off the plan.

CAUTION

Benefits issues can be complicated. The law recognizes that certain benefits become more expensive as workers age (and that older workers are more likely to take advantage of them). Although employers cannot discriminate against older workers by offering them less expensive benefits, they can often give older workers a different benefit plan, as long as the employer spends the same amount on benefits for older and younger workers. This is true only of certain benefits, however, and Obamacare has added some new wrinkles. The rules on age discrimination in benefits are complex; if you have questions about your company's benefits programs, talk to a lawyer.

Disability

Disability discrimination occurs when an employer makes job decisions based on an employee's disability, the fact that an employee has had a disability in the past, or the employer's perception that the employee has a disability (even if that perception is incorrect). A disability is a physical or mental impairment that substantially limits a major bodily function or a major life activity (such as the ability to walk, talk, see, hear, breathe, work, or take care of oneself), without taking into account any medications or other "mitigating" measures the employee is using (such as a prosthetic limb or hearing aid) to remedy the effects of the condition. Courts tend not to categorically label certain conditions as disabilities; instead, they consider the effect of the particular condition on the particular employee.

EXAMPLE 1: Gerard has suffered from depression. Before he started taking medication, he was often unable to get out of bed in the morning and could not take care of himself. Once he began treatment, Gerard improved to the point where he now has a fairly active schedule and enjoys his life again. Because Gerard's condition limited his major life activities in its unmitigated state, he has a disability under the Americans with Disabilities Act (ADA), even though his medication has alleviated some of his problems.

EXAMPLE 2: Jamal sometimes stutters when he talks. Although the stutter is noticeable, Jamal can easily be understood when he speaks. Jamal probably doesn't have a legally recognized disability. However, if his employer decided not to promote him to a position that involved dealing with customers because of his stutter, that could be discrimination. Although Jamal does not have a disability, his employer is treating him as though he has one.

Although a company may not discriminate based on an employee's disability, it is not legally required to hire or keep on employees who cannot do the job. If the employee cannot perform the job's essential functions, even with a reasonable accommodation, the employer is not required to hire or retain that employee. (See "Reasonable Accomodation," below, for more information.)

EXAMPLE: Jean suffered a spinal cord injury in a car accident and is paralyzed from the waist down. She uses a wheelchair to get around. Because Jean is substantially limited in the major life activity of walking, she has a legally recognized disability. Jean applies to work as a secretary in a law firm. She can perform all of the job's essential elements—typing, transcribing, answering phones, and so on—but her wheelchair won't fit under the desk. Raising the height of the desk is a reasonable accommodation that will allow her to do the job. Because Jean is qualified and can do the job with an accommodation, she is protected from discrimination.

Now suppose Jean applies to oversee a private campground. The job responsibilities include traveling through the campground twice a day to collect fees and check on campers, providing emergency first aid treatment to campers as necessary, and helping campers with problems that may arise (for example, getting a car out of a ditch or helping to pitch a tent).

Jean may not be qualified for this job. Her wheelchair cannot travel over the forested and rocky campground trails, and her ability to assist campers will be limited. The employer could legally decide not to hire Jean because she cannot perform the job's essential functions.

Religion

An employer may not make job decisions based on an employee's religious beliefs or practices. (Employers also have to make reasonable accommodations for employees' religious beliefs, in certain circumstances; see "Reasonable Accommodation," below.) Here are a few examples of religious discrimination:

- A group of friends who attend the same evangelical church go into business together; they refuse to hire anyone who does not share their faith.
- A company owner who is a self-proclaimed atheist tends not to promote religious employees to managerial positions; he believes that those who are religious have trouble exercising authority and thinking for themselves.
- A company that manufactures and distributes organic health supplies has a monthly company meeting, during which all employees must participate in a traditional Native American blessing ceremony.

Citizenship Status

An employer may not discriminate against employees based on their citizenship status, as long as they are legally authorized to work in the United States. Those who are legally authorized to work in this country include:

- citizens or nationals of the United States
- aliens lawfully admitted for permanent or temporary residence
- aliens admitted as refugees, and
- aliens granted asylum.

However, there are a couple of exceptions to this general rule. First, an employer may make job decisions based on an employee's citizenship status if federal law explicitly allows it (this exception generally applies only to government employers and some federal contractors). Second, an employer may give preference to a citizen or national of the United States over an equally qualified alien.

> EXAMPLE: Khalid, a refugee from Afghanistan, and Judy, a United States citizen, apply for a position at a blood bank. If both are equally qualified, the blood bank may hire Judy rather than Khalid simply because she is a citizen. However, if Khalid has better qualifications, the bank may not hire Judy based on its preference for a U.S. citizen.

Genetic Information

The Genetic Information Nondiscrimination Act (GINA) makes it illegal for employers to gather or use employee genetic information, and it requires employers to maintain the confidentiality of any genetic information they obtain through legal means. Genetic information includes the results of genetic testing or the manifestation of a particular disease or disorder in the employee's family.

Employers may not make employment decisions based on an employee's or applicant's genetic information, or the genetic information of an employee's or applicant's family member. For example, an employer may not refuse to hire an applicant because she carries BRCA1 or BRCA2 (the genes thought responsible for most inherited breast cancers) or fire an employee because he carries the trait for sickle cell anemia. Whether the employer is motivated by stereotypes or stigma associated with particular conditions or by a desire to reduce health care costs, decisions like these are illegal.

There are a handful of situations in which an employer might obtain genetic information about an employee without violating GINA, including when such information is provided to comply with the medical certification requirements of the Family and Medical Leave Act and when the employer uses genetic monitoring to determine the biological effects of toxic substances in the workplace. Genetic information gathered pursuant to one of these exceptions must be kept confidential and treated as a medical record. Even if an exception applies, however, the employer may not use the information as the basis for employment decisions.

Sexual Orientation and Gender Identity

A number of states, cities, and counties ban discrimination against LGBT employees. If the state or local government where your company does business prohibits discrimination based on sexual orientation and/or gender identity, your company may not make job decisions based on these traits. This means, for example, that it may not prefer heterosexual employees for promotion over gay and lesbian employees, and it may not require transgender employees to comply with the dress and grooming policies of the gender they were assigned at birth, rather than the gender with which they identify.

If your company does not have to comply with a state or local law prohibiting discrimination against LGBT employees, the legal landscape is less clear. Title VII, the primary federal law that protects employees from discrimination, does not explicitly prohibit employers from discriminating on the basis of sexual orientation or gender identity. In recent years, however, the EEOC has interpreted Title VII's prohibition on sex discrimination to include discrimination based on these characteristics.

In the last few years, the EEOC and a few federal courts have found that Title VII protects transgender employees from being fired because of their perceived failure to conform to the gender they were assigned at birth. An employee who is transitioning from female to male, for example, may face discrimination for wearing masculine clothing, using a traditionally male name, or using the men's restroom. This issue is in flux, however, and federal courts are not consistent on this issue; many continue to hold that transgender employees are not protected by Title VII.

The EEOC has also recently taken the position that discrimination based on sexual orientation is also a form of illegal sex discrimination under Title VII. Treating a lesbian or gay employee less favorably because he or she doesn't conform to gender-based stereotypes of femininity or masculinity, for example, would violate this interpretation. Similarly, treating an employee differently because he or she is attracted to, dates, or marries someone of the same gender would also be illegal under this interpretation.

These interpretations and cases are relatively new, and LGBT rights may be one of the most quickly evolving areas of the law right now. If you have questions about how courts would apply the law in your area, talk to an experienced employment lawyer. Remember, too, that management decisions can be inappropriate or ill-advised even if they are legal. A supervisor who categorically refuses to promote gay employees, for example, is harming employee morale and depriving your company of the full contribution of every member of its workforce, whether or not that supervisor is also breaking the law.

Legal Claims of Discrimination

The classic legal theory of discrimination—sometimes called "disparate treatment"—is that an employer made a job decision based on a person's race, religion, or other protected characteristic. Most of the examples and the discussion above focus on disparate treatment discrimination, because it is by far the most common type of discrimination claim employees might make. You'll find more information on disparate treatment claims below.

There are two other types of discrimination claims:

- An employee who makes a disparate impact claim alleges that a seemingly neutral company policy, practice, or requirement had the effect of discriminating against a protected group. For example, a woman might claim that an employer's failure to hire anyone who could not lift 60 pounds had the effect of discriminating against women. These claims are described in "Disparate Impact," below.

- An employee who brings a reasonable accommodation claim argues that the employer failed to make reasonable changes in work rules, schedules, practices, equipment, or the physical layout of the workplace that would have allowed him or her to do the job. For example, an employee who is hard of hearing might claim that an employer's failure to purchase TTY communications equipment made it impossible for her to be promoted to a sales position. These claims, which apply only in cases of disability or religious discrimination, are explained in "Reasonable Accommodation," below.

It's important to learn the legal standards for each of these theories so you can recognize when an employee is complaining about something that might be illegal. Keep in mind, however, that you may want to take some corrective action even if your investigation reveals that an employee might not be able to prove discrimination in court. For example, if your investigation reveals that a manager accused of race discrimination is not making decisions based on race, but is favoring employees who are his friends outside of work over their coworkers, you will probably want to address that manager's behavior.

Disparate Treatment

In a disparate treatment case, an employee claims to have been denied a job benefit or treated negatively because of a protected characteristic. Most disparate treatment claims involve firing, discipline, failure to promote, or inconsistent application of work rules.

The elements of a disparate treatment claim—what an employee must prove to win a lawsuit—depend on the employee's allegations. However, an employee usually must start by showing that:

- he or she has a protected characteristic
- he or she was denied a job benefit or subjected to a negative job action (for example, did not receive a promotion, was not allowed to take time off, was disciplined more harshly than other employees, or was fired)
- he or she was qualified for the benefit (for example, the employee met the requirements for the promotion) or was undeserving of the negative job action (for example, the employee received a negative evaluation despite good performance), and
- employees who do not share the complaining employee's protected characteristic received the benefit or were not subjected to the negative job action (for example, male employees were not fired or a white person got the promotion).

Once the employee makes this showing, the employer must give a legitimate, nondiscriminatory reason for the decision the employee is challenging. To win the lawsuit, the employee must then show that the employer actually acted out of discriminatory motives (lawyers call this "pretext," because the employee must show that the employer's stated reason is just an excuse or pretext for discrimination).

Most of the disputes in discrimination lawsuits are over this last issue: why the employee was treated differently. To show that the company was motivated by bias, an employee generally must come up with something more than the simple fact of different treatment. For example, it isn't enough to show that a woman didn't get a promotion that went to a man: The female candidate must also show some evidence that the decision was motivated by discrimination.

"Me Too" Evidence

Employees who sue for discrimination often try to present evidence that other employees also faced discrimination (called "me too" evidence). In 2008, the U.S. Supreme Court held that the trial court must decide, on a case-by-case basis, whether "me too" evidence is admissible. (*Sprint/United Management Co. v. Mendelsohn*, 552 U.S. 379 (2008).) In that case, the plaintiff claimed she had been fired because of her age and wanted to present testimony from other employees who also believed that they had suffered age discrimination. The trial court said that testimony from other employees was relevant only if they were complaining about the same supervisor and about events that happened close in time to when the plaintiff was fired. Because they were not, the trial court refused to allow them to testify.

The Supreme Court could have ruled that "me too" evidence should never be admitted or should be allowed only if it pertains to the same decision maker, or made some other blanket rule as to when this evidence will and will not be permitted at trial. Instead, the Court found that the trial court must look at the facts and legal theories of each case to determine whether to admit the evidence. For those investigating discrimination claims, this case makes it even more important to look at the big picture: If other employees also feel that they have faced discrimination, it's better to find out about it (and remedy the situation, if necessary) during your investigation than at trial.

Often, this evidence takes the form of comments by decision makers, such as the supervisor who says, "I'd like to bring in a more youthful, dynamic group of salespeople" before choosing a younger employee over an older employee, or the manager who makes frequent sexist jokes, then promotes only men to be in charge of accounts.

An employee can also try to prove discrimination by showing that the company's explanation for an employment decision doesn't hold water. For example, a company promotes a white employee to a managerial position, stating that he had more supervisory experience than a Chinese American employee who was not promoted. If the Chinese American employee can show that he actually had more years of supervisory experience and better qualifications for the job, the company's rationale starts to look a little suspect.

If the employer's rationale is really weak and the evidence of different treatment is strong enough, an employee may not need direct proof that the employer was motivated by bias.

> EXAMPLE: Curtis, who is African American, claims that he was disciplined more harshly for horseplay than white employees. Curtis says that white employees who engaged in the same behavior received a verbal warning, while he was fired. The company contends that Curtis's behavior merited harsher discipline because he damaged company equipment (he accidentally knocked a postage meter off of a table and broke it), while the white employees to whom he compared himself did not.
>
> However, Curtis's lawyer reviews company records and discovers that each of the four employees who have been fired for horseplay is African American—and that the company has relatively few (about 5%) African American employees. The lawyer also discovers that ten white employees have been disciplined for horseplay, but none received any discipline harsher than a verbal reprimand. What's more, three of these white employees damaged company equipment. In this situation, Curtis might win a discrimination claim, even without any evidence that his supervisor made racist remarks or that the company has an explicit policy of only firing African Americans. The company's explanation doesn't pass the blush test—and the numbers are pretty powerful evidence that something else is going on.

> **CAUTION**
>
> **Beware the cat's paw.** A company can be guilty of disparate treatment discrimination if an employment decision is tainted by bias, even if the person who took action against the employee had no intent to discriminate. In these "cat's paw" cases (named after an Aesop's fable), one supervisor takes action against an employee with the intent to discriminate, and another supervisor makes the ultimate decision. For example, a supervisor might give an employee a series of poor performance reviews because of the employee's race, then a higher-level supervisor decides to fire the employee based on the reviews (and with no discriminatory intent). The ignorance or innocence of the final decision maker won't protect the company if another person's bias poisoned the process.

Disparate Impact

An employer may commit illegal discrimination even if it didn't intend to make job decisions based on race, gender, or another protected characteristic. Under the theory of disparate impact, an employer discriminates if it adopts a neutral policy that has a disproportionately negative effect on a protected group. For example, an employer that requires all employees to have a college degree may exclude more employees of certain races. Similarly, an employer that imposes a height or strength requirement for some positions may screen out disproportionately large numbers of women.

Of course, these types of requirements may be perfectly legitimate. For example, a person who works loading and unloading heavy packages in a warehouse, felling trees, or rescuing people from burning buildings must have some strength to do the job. Recognizing this, the law allows employers to defend against a disparate impact claim by showing that the rule or requirement is job-related and necessary to the business.

> **EXAMPLE 1:** Delivery Co. delivers packages across the country for its customers. Delivery Co. requires all of its warehouse workers to be able to lift and carry 50-pound packages. Because the warehouse workers spend a large portion of their day carrying heavy packages, this requirement is job-related and necessary to the business, even if it screens out disproportionate numbers of women.

Slightly Different Rules Apply to Age Discrimination

Until the Supreme Court decided the case of *Smith v. City of Jackson*, 544 U.S. 228 (2005), it wasn't clear whether employees could sue for age discrimination based on disparate impact. The Supreme Court decided that these claims are allowed, but what the employer and employee have to prove is a bit different than for other types of discrimination claims.

In an age discrimination disparate impact case, the employee must point to a specific practice (such as a screening test) that led to the disparity. And, the employer can escape liability by showing that its practice was based on a reasonable factor other than age (RFOA). The RFOA is an affirmative defense, which means the employer must prove it at trial. In 2012, the EEOC issued regulations explaining how the defense works. Among other things, the regulations define an RFOA as a "non-age" factor that is objectively reasonable when viewed from the position of a prudent employer mindful of its obligations under the ADEA. The employer must show both that the employment practice it used was reasonably designed to achieve a legitimate business purpose, and that the employer applied the factor in a way that reasonably achieves that purpose.

A court must consider all of the relevant facts and circumstances in deciding whether an employer has adequately proven an RFOA. Among the things a court can consider when deciding whether an employer's practice or policy counts as an RFOA are:

- the factor's relationship to the employer's stated business purpose
- whether the employer defined and applied the factor fairly and accurately, including whether managers and supervisors received training as to how to apply the factor in making decisions to avoid discrimination
- whether (and how much) the employer limited supervisors' discretion to evaluate employees subjectively, particularly if the factor is known to be subject to negative stereotypes based on age
- whether the employer assessed the adverse impact of its practice on older employees, and
- how much the practice harmed older workers (in severity and number) and whether the employer took steps to reduce that harm, given the burden involved in taking such steps.

EXAMPLE 2: Delivery Co. also delivers letters, contracts, and blueprints for business clients. Some warehouse workers deal exclusively with these documents, while others handle the packages. If Delivery Co. applied its "50-pound rule" to all warehouse workers, it could face a sex discrimination claim. The document handlers don't need to lift heavy packages, so the rule is neither job-related nor necessary to the business as applied to them.

Disparate impact claims often arise in the hiring context. For example, an employer that requires all applicants to take a written, standardized test might screen out disproportionate numbers of minority applicants, which could result in a disparate impact claim. Layoffs and other group firings could also result in a disparate impact claim if the employer uses firing criteria that result in a disproportionate number of protected workers losing their jobs. Generally, however, disparate impact claims are much less common than disparate treatment claims.

Reasonable Accommodation

In some situations, an employer may be required to take action based on an employee's protected characteristic in order to avoid discriminating. For example, in order to avoid discriminating against a worker with a disability, an employer may need to install a handrail in the bathroom. This may sound counterintuitive: Isn't it discriminatory to make decisions based on an employee's protected characteristic? Usually, the answer is yes. However, the law recognizes an exception to this general rule when an employee, because of religious beliefs or a disability, needs some changes to workplace rules or equipment in order to do the job.

Religion

Employers are legally required to reasonably accommodate an employee's religious practices unless doing so would create an "undue hardship." These claims often come up in regard to scheduling. For example, an employee whose religion prohibits working on the Sabbath might request a schedule change to take that day off. Religious accommodation claims might also involve dress codes. For example, an employee whose religion requires a particular style of dress might ask the employer to make an exception to its usual rules about employee grooming and attire.

EXAMPLE: Alicia is a Seventh Day Adventist. She works as a hygienist in a large dental practice. Her employer has informed her that it plans to begin staying open on weekends in order to attract more clients. The employer says that every hygienist will be required to work either Saturday or Sunday each week. Alicia tells her employer that her religious beliefs prevent her from working on Saturdays. As an accommodation, the employer agrees that Alicia can work on Sundays and have Saturdays off every week.

An employer does not have to accommodate an employee if doing so would cause an undue hardship. Although the law isn't entirely clear about what constitutes an undue hardship, there are a few rules. If the accommodation would require more than ordinary administrative costs (for example, the cost of making a payroll or scheduling change), then the employer doesn't have to provide it. Similarly, an employer cannot be required to override a seniority system to accommodate an employee's religion. If granting the accommodation would deprive another employee of a transfer, shift preference, or other benefit, the employer doesn't have to provide it.

EXAMPLE 1: Rory is a salesperson for an upscale furniture store. His employer institutes a dress code requiring all employees to wear professional attire and requiring male employees to wear their hair no longer than their shirt collars. Rory's religious beliefs prohibit him from cutting his hair. As long as Rory is neat and clean, his employer can't claim that accommodating his request for an exception to the dress code is an undue burden. It won't cost anything, and the employer will have a tough time proving that Rory's long hair will interfere with business.

EXAMPLE 2: Rachel works as a salesperson in a small antique store. During her shifts, she works with one other employee for most of the day; each works alone when the other takes a lunch break. Rachel joins a religious group that believes in strict gender separation. The group's adherents are prohibited from interacting with persons of the opposite sex other than their spouse, their family, or clergy members. Rachel asks her employer to accommodate her religious beliefs by allowing her to serve only female customers. This accommodation would create an undue hardship: Her employer would have to either lose customers or hire another employee for the lunch hour, and Rachel's coworker would have to take on extra work.

Disability

Accommodating a worker with a disability means providing assistance or making changes in the job or workplace that will enable the worker to do the job. For example, an employer might provide an accessible parking space, install ramps, or change the height of desktops and other facilities to accommodate a worker in a wheelchair; provide a quiet, distraction-free workspace for a worker with attention deficit disorder; or allow a worker who is fatigued from chemotherapy sessions to take more frequent breaks during the day.

It is the employee's responsibility to inform the employer of the disability and request a reasonable accommodation; the employer need not guess at what might help an employee do the job. Once an employee starts this conversation, however, the employer is legally required to brainstorm with the employee to figure out what kinds of accommodations might be effective and practical (the law calls this an employer's duty to engage in a "flexible interactive process"). Although an employer is not required to provide the precise accommodation a worker requests, it must work with the employee to try to come up with a reasonable solution.

However, your company is not required to provide an accommodation if doing so would cause the business "undue hardship." The law imposes more responsibility on employers to accommodate disabilities than religious beliefs. While any cost beyond an administrative burden creates an undue hardship in a religious accommodation claim, an employer can be legally obligated to shell out some money to accommodate a worker with a disability. In determining whether a particular accommodation creates an undue burden, courts consider:

- the cost of the accommodation
- the size and financial resources of the business
- the structure of the business, and
- the effect the accommodation would have on the business.

If the cost of the accommodation is significant when compared to the business's resources, the employer probably doesn't have to provide it.

Similarly, if providing an accommodation would impose significant changes on the way the company does business, it isn't required.

> EXAMPLE 1: Jon has attention deficit disorder. He finds it difficult to concentrate on a project if there is any background noise or activity. Jon works in the financing department of a large car dealership. He tells his employer of his disability and requests to be moved out of his cubicle near the showroom floor to an office with a door that closes, farther away from the wheeling and dealing. The company has some unused space upstairs and agrees to convert some of it into an office for Jon. This is a reasonable accommodation.

> EXAMPLE 2: Gerrie works as a route supervisor for a company that sells and delivers bottled water. She arrives at work before anyone else, reviews the schedule for the day, and determines which driver will make each pickup and delivery. She then creates a route assignment for each driver, which the drivers receive when they arrive at work. Gerrie tells her employer that she suffers from depression and that the medication she takes for her condition makes her groggy in the morning. She asks if she can change her schedule and come in several hours later. Because the customers expect their water on time, and because the drivers cannot begin their deliveries until Gerrie gives them their route assignments, her requested accommodation probably poses an undue hardship. Allowing Gerrie to come in late would substantially disrupt the company's business.

Ten Steps to an Effective Discrimination Investigation

In discrimination cases, your investigation will almost always begin with an employee complaint. Unlike harassment or employee theft, discrimination cannot really be anonymous, and it always has a victim. You are most likely to hear about discrimination directly from the employee who feels mistreated. If that employee doesn't come forward, you may hear a complaint from another employee, such as a coworker or supervisor who feels that an unfair decision was made.

RELATED TOPIC

Read Part I first. This section explains how to apply the basic investigation steps covered in Part I of this book to a discrimination investigation. If you haven't read Part I, you should do so before getting into this more specific material. The discussion that follows assumes that you are already familiar with basic investigation procedures.

Here are some of the ways you may learn of a discrimination claim:

- **Formal complaint.** An employee may use your company's complaint policy to complain of discrimination.

- **Performance evaluation.** An employee may raise a discrimination issue during a performance review. For example, the employee might believe that the evaluation itself is discriminatory ("I was rated poorly because my project was three days late, but my white coworker turned in his project three weeks late, and he was rated higher than me"). Or the employee might use the performance evaluation as a forum to raise discrimination concerns ("I'm wondering why I always seem to get the projects that don't involve client contact. I'm concerned that it might have something to do with the fact that I'm older than the other account managers").

- **Exit interview.** An employee leaving the company may be more willing to be frank about problems within the company. For example, the employee might say that he is leaving because he believes he is being discriminated against. Or, he may raise a more systemic issue. For example, an African American employee might say, "I finally decided to take another job offer because I noticed that only white employees are promoted to management positions, no matter how many employees of color apply. I felt that I would never move up the ladder here."

- **Administrative charge.** Before an employee can bring a lawsuit alleging discrimination, he or she may have to file a charge with the EEOC or a similar state fair employment practices agency. If an employee (or former employee) files an administrative charge, your company will be notified and receive a copy of the charge. In most cases, your company will also be asked to respond to the charge and give its side of the story. This means you'll have to investigate, so that you will know whether you need to take action and what to tell the agency.

The Government May Investigate, Too

If an employee files a charge of discrimination with a government agency, that agency may perform its own investigation. This does not relieve you of your obligation to investigate and take action. Your company still has a legal duty to prevent and remedy discrimination once you learn of it in any way, including through an EEOC or state agency charge. However, government agency involvement will affect your investigation in one important way: You should consult with an attorney. What you do and say during the investigation should be carefully choreographed, to avoid giving the complaining employee fodder for a lawsuit.

Talk to an attorney immediately after you receive the employee's charge. Unless the agency dismisses the charge right away or your company decides to settle, you will have to prepare a written response relatively quickly. (The agency might dismiss the charge if it is fundamentally flawed—for example, the employee filed it too late—or if the employee asks for the dismissal, in order to file an immediate lawsuit.) Your company may also have to turn over documents, make employees available for interviews with the agency's investigator, and allow the investigator to make a site visit to your company. All of this material could become evidence in any lawsuit arising out of the charge, which is why it's so important to have legal advice when deciding what to say, what to hand over, and how to handle the matter internally, from communicating with employees to managing the employee who complained (if that person is still an employee).

To learn more about agency investigations, check out the EEOC's fact sheet, "The Charge Handling Process." You can find it—as well as many other helpful resources on discrimination and harassment—on the EEOC's website, www.eeoc.gov/employees/process.cfm.

- **Letter from an attorney.** This is possibly the least desirable way to find out about a discrimination claim. If an employee asks a lawyer for help in dealing with potential discrimination, your first notice of the problem may come in an envelope with an "Esquire" in the return address. Many lawyers will recount the facts as their clients have related them, then ask your company to respond within a certain period of time. If your company is the unfortunate recipient of one of these letters, investigating is a must; you should also bring in your company's lawyer to help you decide how to respond.

Once your company is aware of a claim of workplace discrimination, you are ready to use the ten basic investigation steps, as described below.

Decide Whether to Investigate

When dealing with discrimination claims, an employer should generally err on the side of investigating. The Supreme Court has held, in the case of *Kolstad v. American Dental Association*, 527 U.S. 526 (1999), that an employer may not be liable for punitive damages for discrimination by managers and supervisors, as long as the employer makes good faith efforts to prevent discrimination. (Punitive damages are damages intended to punish the employer for especially egregious conduct, in order to deter future discrimination; they often make up the largest part of a damages award in a discrimination case, sometimes totaling two, three, or ten times the amount of other damages awarded in a case.)

The Court didn't specify exactly what constitutes good faith efforts, but it suggested that having an antidiscrimination policy and responding appropriately to complaints of discrimination—by performing an investigation and taking disciplinary action against wrongdoers—could protect an employer from these types of damages. In light of this decision, it makes sense to investigate most claims of discrimination.

However, not every claim of discrimination is a claim of *illegal* discrimination. Discrimination is illegal only if it is based on a protected characteristic, as explained above. Discrimination on other bases—for example, because of an employee's hair color, fashion sense, or sense of humor—is not illegal.

EXAMPLE: Yvonne claims that she wasn't promoted to a customer service position because she favors outlandish outfits in loud colors. She says this is unfair because her attire has nothing to do with her ability to serve customers. Yvonne may be right and she may be wrong, but she has not been illegally discriminated against. No law prohibits an employer from making decisions based on an employee's clothing style, per se.

However, if Yvonne claims that she didn't receive the promotion because she wears a hijab (a body covering or head scarf worn by some Muslims), she could have a discrimination claim. Although the employer's decision was based on her clothing, that clothing is strongly associated with a particular religion and ethnicity. Therefore, the employer's decision could be discriminatory.

Discrimination or Harassment?

Sometimes, it can be hard to tell whether an employee is complaining of discrimination or harassment. As a legal matter, harassment is a form of discrimination. Like discrimination, harassment is mistreatment based on a person's protected characteristic. While discrimination most often results in a negative job action (such as losing a promotion, getting fired, or being denied a job benefit), harassment can consist solely of demeaning behavior, like racist jokes, sexual innuendo, or repeated negative comments about an employee's disability or ethnicity.

In some harassment cases, however, an employee complains that the harassment resulted in a negative job action. For example, in a sexual harassment case, an employee may allege that she was denied a promotion or fired because she refused to submit to sexual demands.

If you get confused about whether an employee is complaining about discrimination or harassment, take heart: The way you classify the claim is not as important as what you do about it. In either situation, you will be looking at whether an employee was mistreated because of a protected characteristic. And in either case, your job will be to figure out what happened, document your findings, and take action to make sure that the mistreatment stops.

Thorough Investigation Defeats Punitive Damages Claim

Under the *Kolstad* case, an employer can avoid punitive damages by making good faith efforts to prevent discrimination. An example from a federal Court of Appeal demonstrates how this defense works. William Dominic complained that he had been sexually harassed by his boss, Patricia Fant. Fant was put on paid leave during the subsequent investigation, in which the company interviewed every person suggested by Dominic. In consultation with a lawyer, the company decided that most of Dominic's claims were not substantiated by the investigation and that there were no grounds to terminate Fant. They took steps to minimize Dominic's interactions with Fant, warned her about retaliation, and told her that she had acted unprofessionally.

Although Dominic didn't complain of any further harassment, he claimed that Fant retaliated against him following the investigation. The company asked for more information, but Dominic refused to provide it, claiming attorney-client privilege. Fant denied the allegations. The company again interviewed other employees and concluded that there was no retaliation. The company hired a law firm to conduct a fresh investigation into Dominic's claims. The law firm concluded that the company's investigation had been adequate and that there was no evidence of illegal harassment or retaliation. The company again counseled Fant and required her to take supervisor training classes, and spoke with her daily about her communications with Dominic. The company also conducted sexual harassment training. Dominic was allowed to work from home for a period of time; after returning briefly to work, he went out on leave and eventually resigned.

Dominic filed a lawsuit claiming sexual harassment and retaliation. The jury found in his favor, awarding him a total of more than $413,000, $250,000 of it for punitive damages. The court of appeal reversed the punitive damages award, however. The court found that the company had investigated Dominic's claims, some of them more than once. During the investigations, employees were asked neutral and open-ended questions that were not suggestive. The company hired outside experts to review its work. And, it minimized the interaction between Fant and Dominic, allowing him to report to another manager and to work from home. This evidence showed that the company acted in good faith and therefore could not be assessed punitive damages. (*Dominic v. DeVilbiss Air Power Co.*, 493 F.3d 968 (7th Cir. 2007).)

> ! CAUTION
> **Remember state laws.** Many states prohibit discrimination based on characteristics that are not covered by federal law, such as marital status or weight. Check the chart in Appendix B—and contact your state fair employment practices agency—to find out your state's rules.

If you decide that an employee has not alleged illegal discrimination, you still might want to investigate. After all, you can't say for sure that a judge or jury will agree with you. Even if a decision looks legitimate to you, it might look like discrimination to someone else. And, even if you're fairly certain that your company is on safe ground from a legal perspective, you may still want to take some action. For example, say that an employee alleges that his manager allows workers who play for the company's softball team to leave early once a week to attend games, while everyone else has to be at their desks until five o'clock. Discrimination on the basis of softball? Not from a legal perspective, but it may be a poor management practice that you'll want to look into and possibly stop.

Take Immediate Action, If Necessary

Before you start your inquiry, you will have to decide whether some immediate action is necessary to prevent further incidents and to protect the integrity of your investigation. You should consider taking action before the investigation if:

- **The accused employee continues to make managerial decisions.** For example, if the vice president who approves promotions is accused of discriminating against older workers, you might not want the VP to fill any new vacancies until the investigation is complete.
- **Tension between the accused employee and the complaining employee has escalated significantly.** In this situation, you may have to change reporting relationships until you sort things out.
- **The alleged victim and/or witnesses appear to be intimidated by the accused employee.** This might be the case, for example, if the complaining employee says that her supervisor threatened retaliation if she complained.

Whatever course you take, you must be very careful to avoid retaliation (or the appearance of retaliation). The Supreme Court has held that any action that could deter a reasonable employee from complaining of discrimination may constitute retaliation, depending on the facts of the case. (*Burlington Northern & Santa Fe Railway Co. v. White*, 548 U.S. 53 (2006).) If you separate employees by placing the worker who complained on administrative leave or by moving that worker to a less desirable shift or work area, you could be accused of retaliating.

Your safest strategy in these circumstances is to move the accused employee or suspend him or her with pay until you complete the investigation. (Unpaid suspensions pending an investigation are a bad idea, for reasons explained in Chapter 2.) When you tell the accused employee about the change, emphasize that it's temporary, that no conclusions have been made about the truth or falsity of the allegations, and that the company does not view the transfer or suspension as punitive. If you must take an immediate action like this, complete the investigation as quickly as possible to minimize workplace disruption.

CAUTION

Don't take action against those close to the employee, either. Once an employee makes a complaint, you must be careful about how you treat not only that employee, but his or her close associates as well. In 2011, the Supreme Court found that an employer committed retaliation when it fired an employee's fiancé (who also worked for the employer) three weeks after the employee filed a charge of discrimination with the EEOC. Even though the employer did not take action directly against the employee who filed the charge, the Court found that firing someone's fiancé would likely dissuade a reasonable employee from making a complaint in the first place. And, the Court didn't limit its holding to spouses or engaged couples: If employees have a close relationship, disciplinary action against one may count as retaliation against the other. (*Thompson v. North American Stainless*, 562 U.S. 170 (2011).

> ### Time Off for the Complaining Employee
>
> If an employee who complains of discrimination wants to take some time off, find out why. If the employee has been threatened with retaliation or is being shunned by coworkers for making a complaint, these are facts you need to know. Also, make sure the employee doesn't feel forced to take time off. Explain that retaliation is prohibited and that you will investigate as quickly as possible.
>
> If an employee simply wants to take some time to catch his or her breath, you can arrange for a brief period of paid leave. However, make sure that the employee will be available to participate in the investigation.

Choose the Investigator

You can find tips on choosing the right investigator in Chapter 2. However, there are a couple of additional things to consider when choosing an investigator for a discrimination claim.

Impartiality

An employee who alleges discrimination believes that he or she was treated unfairly—and that other workers were favored—for illegitimate reasons. It follows, therefore, that the person who investigates such a claim must not only be objective and impartial, but also be perceived in the workplace as objective and impartial.

Of course, this is an important consideration in any investigation, but it is especially crucial when investigating discrimination. Make sure you (or your chosen investigator) have no connection to the employees involved, have no role in the alleged discriminatory acts, and have no history of problems or controversy on issues of race, gender, and so on.

> EXAMPLE: Fiona alleges that her employer does not promote women to higher levels of management; she says this "glass ceiling" has kept her from getting several promotions. The company is considering asking

Brian to investigate Fiona's claims. Brian has no connection to Fiona or to the promoting supervisors, and he doesn't participate in promotion decisions. However, Brian sits on the board of directors of an exclusive, all-male country club, and has been interviewed in local papers defending the club's membership policy. Even if Brian could investigate Fiona's claims impartially, he is the wrong choice as an investigator. Fiona and other women he interviews could reasonably question his ability to look fairly at a sex discrimination claim, and he wouldn't have much credibility if the company had to defend his investigation in a lawsuit.

When to Use an Outside Investigator

In some situations, it makes sense to bring in an outside investigator. Consider hiring a professional in these situations:

- Widespread discrimination is alleged (for example, that the company never promotes women, fires disproportionate numbers of older workers, or bends the rules only for white workers).
- Discrimination by a high-ranking company official (such as the CEO, president, or chairman) is alleged.
- An employee challenges a company practice or policy as having a disparate impact on a particular group (see "Disparate Impact," above). These cases require an investigator to review statistics and information about lots of workers and potentially affect a large number of people.
- The charges have been publicized in the community and/or media.
- An employee has filed a charge of discrimination with the EEOC or a similar state fair employment practices agency.
- An employee has hired a lawyer or filed a lawsuit.

Plan the Investigation

Because discrimination investigations almost always begin with an employee complaint, you'll have a natural starting point for your investigation planning. And because discrimination complaints will almost always require an investigator to dig deeply into personnel files and other written records, you should spend some time gathering the documents you will need to make your decisions.

Examine the Allegations

Your first planning step is to carefully review the complaint. Consider these issues:

- **Who complained?** What is the employee's protected characteristic? Did the employee allege that other employees were also discriminated against?
- **What's the nature of the complaint?** What type of discrimination is alleged? Does the employee claim that he or she was discriminated against, or is the employee challenging a company policy or practice that affects a group of employees? Did the employee request a reasonable accommodation for a disability or a religious practice? If so, what was the accommodation? What effect would the accommodation have had on the company, and what would it have cost?
- **Who is accused of discrimination?** Is it a high-ranking company official? Does the employee accuse this person of making bigoted comments and holding biased views, or is the employee complaining about a single personnel action? Is the employee accusing one person of discrimination, or is the charge leveled at a group of people or the entire company?
- **What's the employment decision at issue?** Is the employee alleging a failure to promote, improper firing, unfair application of workplace rules and procedures, or failure to accommodate a disability or religious practice? Who was responsible for making the decision complained of?
- **Has the employee named any witnesses?** You should plan to interview anyone who heard or saw anything relating to the complaint. You may need to consider interviewing "similarly situated" employees as well. For example, if an employee is complaining of being denied a promotion, you may need to speak to other employees who applied for the position and the employee who eventually received it.

Based on your answers to these questions, you can begin to structure your investigation and determine what documents and other evidence to gather, whom to interview, and what questions to ask.

CAUTION

Courts caution employers to cast a wide net in discrimination investigations. Some courts and juries have penalized employers for inadequate investigations of discrimination. The flaw in these investigations is often the employer's failure to look at the big picture: whether the company treats employees who share the complaining employee's characteristic differently than those who don't. If an employee alleges that Latinos are not promoted, or that women are denied work benefits (such as a company car) that are granted to men, for example, you will have to look beyond the complaining employee and the accused wrongdoer to examine company-wide practices. In these examples, your investigation might include examining which employees were promoted and which were not, or how many company cars have been issued and to whom.

Documents and Other Evidence

Discrimination investigations often rely heavily on documents. To adequately examine an employee's allegation that an unfair decision was made, you'll need to find out the basis for the decision and what information the decision maker relied on. Generally, this means you'll spend some time looking at personnel files, performance evaluations, employee qualifications, and other paperwork. Particularly if an employee alleges that another worker was unfairly selected for promotion, you will have to closely examine evaluations, recommendations, work samples, and other evidence of performance to figure out whether there was a legitimate, business-related reason for choosing one employee over the other.

In most situations, you will also want to look at similar employment decisions made by the accused employee in the past, to see if you can find a pattern (or lack of one). For example, if an employee alleges that he wasn't promoted because of his age, you should look at previous promotion decisions made by the same supervisor. Has the supervisor consistently promoted younger workers, or have older workers been promoted in the past?

Here are some documents that might be relevant in a discrimination investigation:

- Company policies, including policies on discrimination and policies on the specific job action in question. For example, if an employee alleges that he was unfairly denied a promotion, you'll want to examine any company policies or other written materials that describe how promotion decisions should be made. If an employee claims to have been disciplined unfairly, you'll want to look at company discipline procedures.

- Personnel files, including the files of the complaining employee and the accused employee. If the employee complains of being denied a benefit, you also may want to examine the personnel file of any employee who received the benefit, to figure out whether the decision was justified.

- Performance records, if the decision was (or should have been) based on employee performance. For example, in a promotion case, you'll need to examine the work records of the employee who was denied the promotion and the employee who received it.

- Attendance records or sign-in sheets from antidiscrimination training.

- Any other records related to the employment decision at issue. For example, if an employee complains that he was disciplined more harshly for unexcused absences than other employees, you will want to examine attendance records to find out how many times each employee was absent.

Interviews

Once you've finished your investigation planning, you'll have some ideas about which employees you should interview. Start by interviewing the employee who complained. Next, move on to the employee (often a supervisor or manager) accused of discrimination. Then, interview any witnesses, other employees who were involved in the contested decision, other employees who received the benefit the complaining employee was denied, and/or other employees who share the complaining employee's protected characteristic and report to the same supervisor (to find out whether they feel that they've been treated fairly).

Start every interview with some opening remarks to set the employee at ease, explain the process, and answer questions. You should also distribute a written notice regarding the investigation (you'll find a sample at this book's online companion page; see Appendix A for more information). Next, proceed to your specific questions, remembering to follow up on any new information raised by the witness's responses. Close the interview by letting the witness know what will happen next and inviting the witness to come to you with any concerns or additional information. And conduct follow-up interviews if any new information comes to light.

Getting Started

Some of your opening comments will be the same, no matter whom you're interviewing. Some of them will be geared more specifically toward a complaining employee, an accused employee, or a witness. The opening statement you make to every person you interview should cover these points:

- **The purpose of the meeting.** The information you give here will depend on whom you're interviewing. You can tell the complaining employee that the company will be investigating the complaint and that the purpose of the meeting is to gather as much information as possible. Tell the accused employee that a complaint has been made, that you're investigating, and that your role is to gather as much information as possible. A witness can simply be told that you're investigating a workplace problem and you believe the witness might have some relevant information.

- **The investigation process.** Explain that the company will be investigating the problem and interviewing other employees and will take appropriate steps if it finds that misconduct occurred.

- **Confidentiality.** Explain that you will maintain confidentiality to the extent possible, although it will be necessary to reveal certain details in order to conduct thorough interviews and reach a decision. (See "Requesting Employee Confidentiality," below, for information on gag rules in an investigation.)

- **Retaliation.** Explain that retaliation is prohibited and that the company will take immediate steps to discipline anyone who retaliates based on the complaint or investigation. Ask the employee to come to you with any concerns about retaliation.
- **Questions or concerns.** Ask whether the employee has any questions or concerns about the process.

Requesting Employee Confidentiality

Investigators, professional and otherwise, have routinely informed employees they interview that the investigation and underlying incidents must be kept confidential. Recently, however, rules like these have come under fire from government agencies. As explained in Chapter 3, the National Labor Relations Board (NLRB) and the EEOC have both issued opinions invalidating broad "gag order" rules in workplace investigations, finding that such a rule could result in retaliation or in violating employee rights to discuss workplace conditions and issues.

If your company disciplines or fires employees for discussing a discrimination or harassment complaint, it could face a retaliation charge. However, a particular investigation might call for a more limited confidentiality request. For example, if the complaining employee tells you that the accused employee has threatened to destroy evidence or intimidate witnesses, you may have a very good reason to ask for confidentiality, at least until you have confronted the accused employee. If you are facing a situation like this, in which you fear that your investigation could be compromised if employees discuss the matter, ask an attorney to help you decide how much confidentiality you can require without crossing the legal line.

When you interview the accused employee, emphasize that the company has not reached any decisions about what happened. Explain that you are interested in hearing what everyone has to say before making a decision or taking any action. Because you will probably have to reveal the name of the complaining employee (as explained below), spend some extra time discussing retaliation: what it is, that the company prohibits it, and that employees who engage in retaliation will be subject to discipline. Although the accused employee will probably want to know the allegations right away, you are better off postponing this discussion until later in the interview, after you have had a chance to gather some important background information. Explain that the accused employee will have the opportunity to hear and respond to the allegations before the interview is over.

For witnesses, your opening remarks can be brief. The witness doesn't need to know who complained, who is accused, or what the specific allegations are. Once you have explained that you are investigating a workplace problem and have talked about confidentiality and retaliation, you can begin asking your questions.

Questions for the Complaining Employee

The questions you ask the complaining employee should focus on getting all of the details about the job action or decision at issue, as well as the employee's reasons for believing that the action was discriminatory. Your questions should be geared toward the specific employment decision in question. Here are some sample questions to consider when investigating a complaint that the employee was passed over for some job benefit, a complaint that the employee was fired or otherwise disciplined, and a reasonable accommodation complaint.

Sample Questions

Employee Did Not Receive Benefit

- What benefit were you denied [for example, a promotion, a job transfer or schedule change, time off work, a raise]?
- Why do you believe you were denied the benefit?
- Did you have to apply for the benefit? If so, when and how did you do so? If not, did you make it known that you wanted the benefit? How, when, and to whom?

- Do you know who made the decision to deny you this benefit? Do you report to this person? If so, when did you begin reporting to this person? Describe your work relationship to this person.
- How did you find out that you were denied the benefit? Who told you, if anyone? What did that person say? How did you respond? When did this happen?
- Have other employees received this benefit, either now or in the past? Did any employees receive this benefit instead of you? What are their names?
- [If the employee is alleging that another employee improperly received the benefit:] Do you believe that you should have received the benefit instead? Why?
- Why do you believe that this decision was based on your [protected characteristic] rather than your qualifications?
- Aside from this decision, is there anything else that leads you to believe you were discriminated against? Have you heard anyone make comments about [employee's protected characteristic]? If so, who made them, when, and what did they say?
- How has not receiving this benefit affected you? Have you had to spend any money, or lost potential income, because you did not receive the benefit?
- How would you like to see this situation resolved? [Make clear that the company can't promise this outcome.]
- Do you know of anyone who might have information about this decision?
- Do you know of any documents relating to your complaint?
- Is there anything else you'd like to tell me?

Employee Was Disciplined or Fired

- When were you fired or disciplined?
- Who told you about the firing or discipline? What reasons did that person give for the firing or discipline? What did you say in response, if anything? Do you know of any documents relating to this discussion?

- Do you know who made the decision to discipline or fire you? Is that person your supervisor? If so, for how long have you reported to that person? Describe your work relationship with that person.
- Do you know of anyone else who was involved in the decision to discipline or fire you? Describe your work relationship with that person.
- Were you told that you were fired or disciplined because of misconduct, performance problems, or other work-related reasons? Describe any incidents that were given as the basis for your firing or discipline. Are these allegations accurate? If not, why do you believe you were accused of these things?
- Do you know of others who were not fired or disciplined for the same misconduct or behavior? What are their names? When did these incidents occur?
- Why do you believe the decision to discipline or fire you was based on your [protected characteristic]?
- Aside from this decision, is there anything else that leads you to believe you were discriminated against? Have you heard anyone make comments about [employee's protected characteristic]? If so, who made them, when, and what did they say?
- How has being disciplined or fired affected you? Have you had to spend any money, or lost potential income, as a result?
- How would you like to see this situation resolved? [Make clear that the company can't promise this outcome.]
- Do you know of anyone who might have information about this decision?
- Do you know of any documents relating to this decision?
- Is there anything else you'd like to tell me?

Employee Was Denied an Accommodation

- Did you request an accommodation? If so, what did you request, when, and from whom? If not, did you make your need for an accommodation known in some other way? How, when, and to whom?
- Why did you request an accommodation? How would the accommodation you requested have assisted you?

- [If employee has a disability:] What is your disability? How does your disability affect your everyday activities? Describe the essential functions of your job. Are you able to perform these essential functions? How would the accommodation have helped you in this regard?

- [If employee requested an accommodation for religious reasons:] What is your religion? What are the religious beliefs or practices that require a modification to our usual work rules or practices? How would the accommodation have helped you in this regard?

- How did you find out that your request for an accommodation was denied? Did you receive written notice? If you were told in person, who told you? What did that person say? Do you report to this person? If so, for how long? Describe your work relationship to this person.

- Do you believe your requested accommodation was reasonable? What do you think the company would have had to do to provide the accommodation? If you know, approximately what would the accommodation have cost?

- How has the denial of your request affected you? Have you had to spend any money, or lost potential income, because you did not receive the accommodation?

- How would you like to see this situation resolved? [Make clear that the company can't promise this outcome.]

- Do you know of anyone who might have information about this decision?

- Do you know of any documents relating to this decision?

- Is there anything else you'd like to tell me?

Questions for the Accused Employee

The questions you ask the accused employee should focus on the reasons for the challenged decision. Because discrimination complaints usually challenge a job decision or action, the accused employee is almost always a manager (in other words, someone with the authority to make those decisions or take those actions). You will want to explore the accused employee's work history, treatment of other workers, and similar decisions or actions taken in the past. Here are some sample questions geared toward the type of discrimination alleged.

CAUTION

You must allow the accused employee to respond to the allegations. Some investigators are so eager to keep the interview civil—or to protect the complaining employee's privacy—that they never actually confront the accuser with the allegations. This is a big mistake, one that could undermine the legitimacy of the entire investigation. Courts have held that accused employees who never learn precisely what they are accused of haven't had a fair opportunity to tell their side of the story, to offer the names of relevant witnesses, or to explain why the complaining employees might have made the accusations. You don't necessarily have to say who complained, but you should say whom the employee is accused of discriminating against. And don't worry about privacy concerns: You have a very compelling business reason for revealing this information.

Sample Questions

Employee Did Not Receive a Benefit

- Do you supervise any employees? What are their names? How long have you been a supervisor/manager? Have you had any managerial training? If so, when, for what, and who conducted the training?
- Do your responsibilities include deciding who gets [the benefit at issue—for example, promotions, raises, time off]? How do you make these decisions? Are there company guidelines or policies on the topic? What criteria do you consider? How often do you decide whether to [promote someone, give someone a raise, grant a request for time off]?
- Do you supervise [the complaining employee]? How long have you worked together, and in what positions? Describe your work relationship.
- Did you decide [the action at issue—for example, not to give the complaining employee a raise, who would be promoted to account manager, not to give the complaining employee time off]? If not,

who made this decision? If you made the decision, did anyone else have input? Who?

- Explain the basis for your decision. What did you consider? Are there any documents that you looked at? Did you create any documents, notes, or memos in the process of making the decision?

- [If the complaining employee alleges failure to promote:] Who received the promotion? Why? Why did you decide not to promote [the complaining employee]?

- [If the complaining employee alleges denial of another benefit:] Have you given other employees this benefit [for example, time off, raises, or shift changes]? If so, what are their names, and why did they receive the benefit? Why did you deny [the complaining employee] the benefit? How is [the complaining employee]'s situation different from that of the employee(s) who received the benefit?

- Describe the qualifications for the position or the criteria for receiving the benefit. Did [the complaining employee] meet those criteria or qualifications? If not, in what ways?

- Who told [the complaining employee] of your decision? If it was you, what did you say? How did [the complaining employee] respond? If someone else relayed your decision, who? Do you know what that person said? Why didn't you tell [the complaining employee] yourself?

- [The complaining employee] thinks [he or she] should have received the benefit because [state the complaining employee's reasons]. Did you consider that when making your decision? If so, why did [the complaining employee] not receive the benefit? If not, why not?

- [The complaining employee] thinks your decision was based, at least in part, on [complaining employee's protected characteristic]. What is your response to that? Can you think of any reason why [the complaining employee] might think that?

- Do you know of anyone who might have information about this decision?

- Do you know of any documents relating to this decision?

- Is there anything else you'd like to tell me?

Employee Was Disciplined or Fired

- Do you supervise any employees? What are their names? How long have you been a supervisor/manager? Have you had any managerial training? If so, when, for what, and who conducted the training?
- Do your responsibilities include deciding whom to discipline and fire? How do you make these decisions? Are there company guidelines or policies on the topic? What criteria do you consider?
- [If the complaint is about a termination:] How many employees have you fired in the past few years? What are their names? Why were they fired? Were there other employees that you considered firing? If so, what are their names, and why did you decide not to fire them?
- [If the complaint is about discipline:] How many employees have you disciplined in the past few years? What are their names, and for what were they disciplined? Were there other employees that you considered disciplining? If so, what are their names, and why did you decide not to discipline them?
- Do you supervise [the complaining employee]? How long have you worked together, and in what positions? Describe your work relationship.
- Who decided to fire or discipline [the complaining employee]? If it was your decision, did anyone else have input?
- Why did you fire or discipline [the complaining employee]? Tell me every factor you considered in reaching this decision. Did you rely on any documents in making your decision? Did you prepare any documents about the decision?
- Have you fired or disciplined other employees for similar conduct? Who, when, and for what reasons? Are there any documents relating to these decisions? What is the [protected characteristic—for example, race, age, or religion] of each of these employees?
- Did you tell [the complaining employee] that he or she would be disciplined or fired? If so, what did you say? How did [the complaining employee] respond? If someone else delivered the news,

do you know what that person told [the complaining employee]? Why didn't you tell [the complaining employee] yourself?

- Was the employee fired or disciplined for misconduct, poor performance, or other workplace problems? Does the employee have a history of these kinds of problems? Are these problems reflected in the employee's performance evaluations? Have you ever disciplined this employee before for the same problem? If so, when, what did you say, and how did the employee respond?

- [If the employee was fired:] Has the employee been replaced? By whom? What is this person's [complaining employee's protected characteristic—for example, race or national origin]?

- [The complaining employee] believes [he or she] should not have been disciplined or fired because [give the complaining employee's reasons]. Did you consider that in reaching your decision? Why or why not?

- [The complaining employee] believes that [complaining employee's protected characteristic] played a role in your decision. What is your response to that? Can you think of any reason why [the complaining employee] might think that?

- Do you know of anyone who might have information about this decision?

- Do you know of any documents relating to this decision?

- Is there anything else you'd like to tell me?

Employee Was Denied an Accommodation

- Do you supervise any employees? What are their names? How long have you been a supervisor/manager? Have you had any managerial training? If so, when, for what, and who conducted the training?

- Do your responsibilities include deciding whether to change work rules, schedules, or other workplace issues to accommodate an employee's disability or religious practices? How do you make these decisions? Are there company guidelines or policies on the topic? What criteria do you consider? How often do you decide whether to accommodate an employee's disability or religious practice?

- Do you supervise [the complaining employee]? How long have you worked together, and in what positions? Describe your work relationship.
- Did [the complaining employee] ever ask you to make a workplace change to accommodate a disability or religious practice? If so, what did the employee request? How did you respond? If not, has [the complaining employee] ever spoken to you about a disability or religious practice? What did [the complaining employee] say, and how did you respond? Has [the complaining employee] ever asked you to make a workplace change for any reason? What was the change? How did you respond?
- If a request for accommodation was made, did you deny the request? What did you consider in making your decision? What would the company have had to do in order to fulfill the request? What would the request have cost the company? Did you discuss the request with anyone else? Did you get input from anyone else in making your decision?
- Did you tell the employee that the request was denied? If so, what did you say, and how did the employee respond? If not, who told the employee? What did that person say, and how did the employee respond, if you know? Why didn't you tell the employee yourself?
- Did you offer the employee an alternative accommodation? If so, what did you offer, and how did the employee respond? What would the company have had to do in order to provide the alternative accommodation? What would the request have cost the company? If not, can you think of any other accommodations that would meet the employee's needs?
- Do you know of anyone who might have information about this decision?
- Do you know of any documents relating to this decision?
- Is there anything else you'd like to tell me?

Questions for Witnesses

When questioning witnesses, your goal is to gather information without giving too much away. To plan your questions, consider who suggested the witness and why. Did the witness play a role in the employment decision at issue? Did the witness see or hear allegedly discriminatory conduct or statements? Did the witness receive a benefit that was denied to the complaining employee, or was the witness otherwise treated differently than the complaining employee? Is the witness another possible victim of discrimination?

Start by explaining, in very general terms, why the witness is being interviewed (that you are investigating a workplace problem and you believe the witness might have information that will help you figure out what happened). Then, move into questions that will help you figure out how the witness fits into the picture (if at all). Finally, find out what the witness knows. Start with general questions like these:

Sample Questions

General questions

- How long have you worked at the company? What positions have you held? What is your current position? What are your job responsibilities? To whom do you report? Who reports to you?
- Do you work with [the complaining employee] or [the accused employee]? How would you describe their work relationship with each other?
- [Your next questions will depend on what the witness said, did, or knows. Here are some examples.]

For a witness who played a role in the decision

- Are you responsible for deciding or participating in decisions about [the decision at issue—for example, who gets promoted, who gets fired, or whether the company will grant an employee's request for an accommodation]? How many such decisions do you make or participate in each year? What is the process for making these decisions? What do you consider in making these decisions?
- Were you involved in the decision to [fire, promote, deny time off to] [the complaining employee]? What was your role? What did you consider in making this decision? Whom did you talk to about

the decision? Did you consider any documents in reaching this decision? Did you create any documents?

- Have you been involved in any previous decisions to [deny time off, promote, fire] an employee at the company? What are the names of these employees? What did you decide? Why?
- What role did [the accused employee] play in this decision?
- [The complaining employee] believes that [protected characteristic, such as race or age] played a role in this decision. How do you respond to that? Can you think of any reason why [the complaining employee] might think that?
- [The complaining employee] believes the decision was unfair because [give reason, such as he had more seniority than the employee who was promoted, or she was told she would receive a raise by February]. Did you consider that in making your decision? Why or why not?

For a witness who may have seen or heard something

- Describe your typical workday.
- Has [the complaining employee] ever spoken to you about [the accused employee]? Has [the accused employee] ever spoken to you about [the complaining employee]?
- Have you seen any interactions between [the complaining employee] and [the accused employee] that made you uncomfortable? Describe them to me.
- [If the witness may have seen or heard the incident, ask questions to figure out whether the witness was there and what happened.]
- Have you ever heard [the accused employee] make any comment about [the complaining employee's protected characteristic, such as national origin or disability]? If so, what did the accused employee say?

For a witness who received the benefit

- Did you recently [apply for a promotion, receive a raise]? When? Who made the decision? Did you have to apply? If so, what materials did you submit?

- Do you know of any other employees who applied for the benefit?
- When did you learn that you would receive the benefit? Who told you? What did that person say? How did you respond?
- Do you know what the qualifications or other criteria are for receiving this benefit? Do you meet those qualifications or criteria?

No matter what your reason for interviewing the witness, make sure to ask whether the witness knows of anyone else who might have information about the complaint or knows of any documents or other evidence relating to the complaint.

Closing the Interview

Once you have finished your questions, review your notes with the person you interviewed. Make sure you got everything right and that your notes include all of the important details; have the witness sign your notes or a written summary of the interview. Remind the employee (especially the accused employee) that retaliation is prohibited. And, ask the employee to come to you immediately with any new information.

This is all you have to tell witnesses. When you close interviews with the complaining and accused employees, let them know what will happen next. Tell them that you'll interview them again if any important new information comes up.

Follow-Up Interviews

If any new information comes up during your investigation, you should conduct follow-up interviews with the complaining or accused employee. Both employees should have the opportunity to respond to new allegations or defenses to make sure that you have a complete understanding of the facts when you make your decision and to give you the opportunity to gauge credibility. It is especially important to let the accused employee know of any additional allegations that come up during the investigation. If you don't, the accused employee may claim, in court, that he or she was denied the opportunity to respond and, therefore, that the investigation was not thorough or fair.

EXAMPLE: Roy claims that Anna unfairly denied him a promotion because of his race and national origin (Asian). You interview Roy and Anna, focusing primarily on the promotion decision. You also interview Rachel, a witness whom Roy suggests because she has told him that she believes Anna is biased against Asians. Rachel tells you that she and Anna used to be friends outside of work until one night when Anna, after a few drinks, made a number of racist comments about Asians and Asian Americans, including Roy and other Asians who report to her. One of the comments, according to Rachel, was "Asians think they're better than everyone else—well, they're not going to get any positions of power in this company while I've got anything to say about it." Before you wrap up the investigation, you should go back to Anna to confront her with these allegations and allow her to respond.

Gather Documents and Other Evidence

Most discrimination claims allege that the employer made an unfair job decision, one based on the employee's protected characteristic, rather than appropriate work considerations (such as performance, ability, skills, and so on). Your job as an investigator is to find out the real reason for the allegedly discriminatory decision, and this will require you to carefully review employment-related records to see whether they support—or contradict—the accused employee's stated rationale.

You should always start by gathering up any relevant policies (such as an antidiscrimination policy, or a policy relating to the job decision in question) and the personnel files of the complaining employee and the accused employee. These records should yield quite a bit of information, including:

- **Whether company policies spell out a procedure for making the decision in question.** For example, if an employee complains that she was unfairly denied an annual raise, examine workplace policies on raises (if there are any). Are employees promised an annual raise? Does the policy list the criteria for awarding or denying raises?
- **The complaining employee's work history at your company.** Has the employee had a history of performance problems? Has the

employee been promoted repeatedly, received raises, or otherwise been rewarded? For how long has the employee reported to the accused employee? Examine the employee's evaluations and other work records during that time: Are they generally consistent with the employee's work history, or do the records reveal a change in treatment? Has the employee complained of discrimination before? If so, how were those incidents handled?

- **The accused employee's history at your company.** Has anyone else ever accused this person of discrimination? If so, how were those situations resolved? What are the accused employee's qualifications as a supervisor? Has the employee received training or coaching in that area? Who else reports to the accused employee? What similar decisions has the accused employee made in the past? For example, who else has been promoted or denied a raise?

Once you have examined these records, you will want to look at documents relating to the employment decision in question. For example, if an employee complains that she was not promoted because of her gender, you should gather up any documents relating to the promotion decision. These might include the applications of everyone who applied for the position, any other written materials (such as performance evaluations, work samples, or written tests) the supervisor considered in deciding whom to promote, and any written notes the supervisor took when interviewing candidates.

After you've reviewed documents relating to the decision that is the subject of the complaint, you'll want to widen your net to look at similar decisions made by the same decision maker in the past. Using the same example, if a supervisor is accused of sex discrimination for failing to promote a woman, you'll want to look at other promotions by the same supervisor. If the supervisor has never promoted a woman even though plenty of qualified women have applied, you'll want to follow up on that. Similarly, if the supervisor has a history of promoting women, that might lead you to believe that the explanation lies in something other than the complaining employee's gender.

Evaluate the Evidence

In many discrimination cases, everyone agrees on what happened. Unlike a sexual harassment case, for example, in which the complaining employee and the accused employee may tell very different stories about what each said and did, a discrimination case is often based on some undisputed facts. An employee did not receive a promotion, was not granted time off work, was disciplined, was demoted, or was fired. The dispute in discrimination cases is often over the reasons for these actions. In other words, everyone may agree about what happened, but they disagree about why.

In these situations, it can be tough to get to the bottom of things. Motivation—why a person does something—can be very difficult to gauge. You'll have to rely on outward indications of intent, including plausibility, corroboration, and consistency.

- **Plausibility.** Whose story makes the most sense? Does the employee's version of events ring true? Has the decision maker given a common-sense, nondiscriminatory reason for the challenged decision?

- **Corroboration.** If the complaining employee alleges that the decision maker made biased comments, did anyone else witness them? Do personnel files, performance evaluations, and other documents support the decision maker's rationale? Or do they support the complaint?

- **Consistency.** This is probably the most important factor to consider in many discrimination claims. A discrimination claim is, at its core, an allegation of inconsistent treatment. Does the evidence support the decision maker's stated reason for action? Has the decision maker been consistent in applying the rules? Has the decision maker used the same objective criteria to judge all employees? Have these criteria been used consistently over time?

> EXAMPLE: Manuel requested a week off to attend his mother's funeral in Mexico and help his siblings wrap up her personal affairs. He complained that his request was denied because of his race and national origin; he tells you that white employees have been allowed

to take time off for family matters. Manuel's supervisor agrees that he denied Manuel's request but claims that he was only following company policy, which requires employees to have worked for the company for at least one year before taking time off. After examining the attendance records of the other employees who report to this supervisor, you discover that two employees, both white, have taken time off during their first year of employment. When you ask the supervisor why they were allowed to take time off, he responds that they both had serious personal emergencies: One had to stay home to care for her child for a week while her nanny was in the hospital, and the other had a fire in his home, which required him to miss work for a week while he moved his family's belongings out and met with contractors and insurance adjusters.

Has this supervisor acted consistently? Not really. He has bent the rules for some employees and not others. Does he have a principled reason for distinguishing between Manuel's situation and that of the other two employees? Again, not really. A mother's death is a serious personal problem; although Manuel could miss her funeral, the employee with child care problems could have hired a temporary babysitter and the employee with the fire could have moved his family after work hours. The long and the short of it is that this supervisor has acted inconsistently, in a manner that—intentionally or not— has favored white employees. Whether or not Manuel could win a discrimination lawsuit, he has brought an important problem to light, which the company should deal with right away.

Of course, some discrimination cases involved disputed facts. If a supervisor is accused of making racist or sexist comments, the supervisor may deny the statements altogether or claim to have said something different. For example, if an employee claims that her supervisor told her that she should stop working after having her baby, the supervisor might respond, "That's not true. What I said was that many women decide to quit their jobs after having babies, and that I understood why they made that decision." In these situations, you'll have to decide which version of the facts makes the most sense; review the guidelines in Chapter 4 for help in sorting things out.

As you evaluate the evidence, remember that conduct may be improper even if it's not clearly illegal discrimination. In the example involving Manuel, above, a court may not find in Manuel's favor, at least, not without some other evidence that the supervisor's decisions may have been based on race or national origin (such as racist comments or a long history of denying Mexican Americans' requests for time off). However, the supervisor's explanation is unsatisfactory and raises the question of why these other workers got to take time off when Manuel did not. This supervisor's decisions are unpredictable and confusing to employees and have led at least one person to suspect that bias is at work. This is a situation you'll want to deal with as improper managerial conduct, whether or not it amounts to illegal discrimination.

Take Action

If you find that discrimination occurred—or that improper management decisions were made, even if you aren't convinced that they were intentionally discriminatory—then you should take corrective action. Your two goals in taking action are:

- to end the discrimination or other questionable management behavior, and
- to put the victim where he or she would have been had decisions been made appropriately.

Ending the Problematic Behavior

It can be very tough to decide what to do about a discrimination claim. If you face a really cut-and-dried case, in which a supervisor made bigoted comments or made employment decisions based on biased views, firing is clearly appropriate. However, cases like this are not that common. A more likely scenario is this: A supervisor makes employment decisions that aren't entirely consistent and objective but also aren't clearly discriminatory. What you decide to do in these situations will depend, in part, on the supervisor's explanation for the actions, your company's criteria for making the type of employment decision that's been challenged, and the supervisor's willingness to respond to the problem.

EXAMPLE: Toby is a regional manager for a large company. In the last year, he has promoted three employees to be site supervisors, all of them men. One of the women who applied for this position complained of sex discrimination. Toby claims that he promoted the best-qualified candidates; however, the woman who complained had more experience and better performance evaluations than two of the men Toby chose. When you asked Toby about this, he says that the woman "looked fine on paper, but she didn't seem very assertive during the interview. She was very soft-spoken, and she didn't strike me as someone who could supervise a bunch of people on a hectic job site."

What do you do now? Well, Toby had a reason for failing to promote the woman. The problem is, that reason is kind of subjective; and it could have some correlation to the gender-based stereotype that women are less assertive, less confident, and less comfortable holding positions of authority than men. Of course, it could also be true that this particular woman lacked the confidence necessary for the position. In this situation, you could look at:

- **The job description for the position.** Is a certain level of assertiveness necessary for this position? Is that explicitly stated or is it obvious from the nature of the job?
- **The qualities of the selected candidates.** If all three of the men are confident wielding authority, Toby's explanation makes more sense. If, on the other hand, one or more of the men is known as shy and diffident, then it starts to look like Toby didn't apply the same standards to everyone.
- **The qualities of the rejected candidates.** If there were a number of female candidates whose qualifications were at least as good as any of the men who got the job, that raises some questions.
- **Toby's reaction.** If Toby reveals that bias played a role in his decisions ("very few women are going to have what it takes to supervise one of these sites"), there's clearly a big problem. If, however, Toby is willing to examine his decision-making process carefully, he'll be more likely to respond to training and advice about how to make these decisions more objectively in the future.

The action you take must stop the discrimination. However, if you are too severe in your response, you might be facing a lawsuit from the employee accused of discrimination. The only way to walk this fine line is to make the punishment fit the crime. Consider:

- the severity of the behavior
- how many incidents there were
- the harm to the victim
- whether the law was violated
- whether workplace policies were violated
- whether the accused employee holds a position of authority in the company, such as officer, manager, or supervisor (discrimination by a higher-level employee is more serious and requires a heightened response)
- how the company has dealt with similar incidents in the past
- the accused employee's attitude toward the incident, and
- the accused employee's history at the company. Does the employee have a record of similar problems, or is this a onetime lapse from an otherwise stellar worker?

Restoring the Victim

If you find that improper conduct occurred, you should take steps to right the wrong. If the complaining employee suffered some negative job action, it may be appropriate to undo the damage. Here are some actions you might consider:

- Remove negative performance evaluations or disciplinary warnings from an employee's file, if doubt has been cast on the fairness of those documents.
- If an employee was suspended without pay, make sure the employee is paid for that time.
- If an employee has been unfairly denied a transfer, promotion, raise, or other job benefit, grant the benefit retroactively.
- If an employee has been demoted or fired, reinstate the employee, with pay retroactive to the date of the decision.

Sometimes, you may have to work with an employee to figure out how to deal with a problem in the past. Remember Manuel, who was denied time off to attend his mother's funeral? There's no obvious way to undo this damage, but the company may be able to give Manuel a related benefit instead. For example, the company might give Manuel a week of paid leave to use whenever he wishes or make a donation to a charity in his mother's name.

In some situations, you may not know whether discrimination occurred, but you do know that the employment decision was not made properly. In these cases, it may not be appropriate to just give the complaining employee the denied benefit (such as a promotion or job transfer), because that wouldn't really be fair to others. At the same time, however, you should take some action to rectify the situation. The solution might be to make the decision again, this time using fair, job-related criteria that are consistently applied to everyone.

> **EXAMPLE:** Jim has worked for a law firm for a couple of months as a file clerk. Jim has extensive experience and training as a paralegal, but the law firm had no paralegal positions open when he applied. When a paralegal position became vacant, Jim applied. Tom, who supervises the paralegals, hired someone from outside the firm. Jim alleges that this decision was based on his age (he is 62 years old, and the person Tom hired is 28). Tom responds that he assumed Jim didn't have the right experience for the position, because he was working as a file clerk. Tom admits that he didn't even look at Jim's application. The firm hires paralegals regularly; on average, a paralegal is hired every several months. Tom has hired dozens of paralegals for the firm in the past; many of them have been over the age of 40.
>
> What do you do now? Clearly, Tom's decision was flawed. However, there's no clear indication that it was based on Jim's age. And, now, you've got someone else in the picture: the new employee who got the paralegal job. In this situation, your best move might be to promise that Jim will be considered for the next available position. (And, if Jim gets the position, you might also consider raising his pay to the paralegal level, retroactive to when his application should have been considered in the first place.) Because the firm hires so frequently, Jim won't have to wait long to be considered. And you won't have to displace a worker who has already been hired.

Document the Investigation

Document your discrimination investigation by following the guidelines in Chapter 4. Remember, if an employee files a lawsuit based on the investigation (or the alleged discrimination you investigated), your documentation could well end up in the hands of a judge or jury. Make sure to write a report that's complete and professional and fully supports the conclusions you reached.

 CAUTION

Don't create evidence that can be used against your company. If you investigate a really egregious situation in which you believe rank discrimination took place, you might be tempted to state this conclusion in your report. This is a temptation you should resist, however. Remember, if the affected employee decides to file a lawsuit, your company will generally be liable for discrimination by supervisors and managers. If you state, in your report, that discrimination occurred, you will be tying your company's hands in the courtroom. The employee's lawyer will tell the jury, "The company's own investigator admitted that my client was a victim of discrimination"; you can imagine how the argument goes from there. The better strategy is simply to state that company policies were violated and that the manager or supervisor acted inappropriately or unprofessionally, and leave it at that.

Follow Up

Once the investigation is complete, it's a good time to think about how the company can prevent future problems. For example, did your investigation reveal racial insensitivity, ignorance about the needs and contributions of disabled workers, or a general lack of understanding among different groups of employees? If so, some diversity training may be in order. You might also consider training for company managers, if you discover that they were making inconsistent or haphazard managerial decisions, or if they simply weren't clear about their obligations under the antidiscrimination laws.

This is also a good time to examine any company practices that the investigation has called into question. Do managers understand the company's criteria for promotions? For discipline and termination? Are these criteria fair, objective, and job-related?

You should also follow up with the employees involved in the complaint. Retaliation can be a problem if the accused employee continues to work for the company, especially if you determined that the complaint was unfounded. An employee who was accused of discrimination and ultimately vindicated is likely to be angry, and may feel justified in taking out some of that anger on the complaining employee. To guard against this problem, meet with the complaining employee a few times after the investigation to make sure that everything is going smoothly and that no retaliation is taking place. You should also meet with the accused employee to make sure that things are getting back to normal.

If an employee raised any reasonable accommodation issues, you may need to follow up on that as well. If the employee and the company were able to come up with an accommodation, check in with everyone involved to make sure that the accommodation is working. If the employee's suggested accommodation ultimately created an undue burden on the company, you may need to spend some time with the employee (and perhaps the employee's manager), trying to come up with an alternative accommodation that will be effective.

Investigating Harassment

You've probably heard about the multimillion-dollar verdicts some employees have won in harassment lawsuits. Maybe you've even seen news reports about huge companies facing class action claims and government investigations for mistreating women, people of color, or workers with disabilities. These stories demonstrate that claims of workplace harassment can do serious damage to a business, in bad publicity and in dollars and cents. It's no wonder why most employers feel some anxiety when they get a complaint of harassment.

Harassment claims can also be uncomfortable to investigate. If you're looking into a complaint of sexual harassment, for example, you may need to pry into personal relationships, sexual misconduct, graphic language, and more. For other types of harassment claims—such as racial harassment or harassment based on disability—you may hear disturbing accounts of bigotry and insensitivity. And no matter what type of harassment you're investigating, you can be sure of one thing: The people involved will have very strong feelings about the situation and about how the company decides to handle it. This can put a lot of pressure on you to maintain your objectivity, stay focused on the facts, and make the right decision.

The good news, however, is that investigating these complaints properly can help your company avoid legal liability for harassment. And you'll have plenty of guidance on what you need to do to stay out of trouble: The Supreme Court has decided several cases explaining an employer's obligation to investigate harassment complaints. And the Equal Employment Opportunity Commission—the federal government agency that enforces laws prohibiting discrimination and harassment—has issued some written guidelines for employers on how to investigate harassment. Although harassment investigations can be challenging, the information in this chapter will help you do the job right and keep your company out of legal trouble.

This chapter explains the law of harassment: what it is, what it isn't, and what employers are obligated to do about it. It covers both sexual harassment and other types of workplace harassment. You'll also find information on how to apply the ten investigative steps described in Part I to claims of harassment.

What Is Harassment?

Some workers are quick to claim harassment whenever they feel that a supervisor is being tough on them or they're being treated unfairly:

- "These deadlines are too tight. Forcing all of us to meet them is harassment!"
- "Making us smoke outside the building when it's this cold out is ridiculous. I feel like we're being harassed."
- "Just because I forgot to call in sick, my supervisor called me to find out where I was. She shouldn't be calling me at home, regardless of the reason. This is harassment."

Complaints like these generally don't meet the legal definition of harassment. Harassment is an offshoot of the laws that prohibit workplace discrimination, which means that harassment is illegal only if it is based on a person's race, gender, age, disability, or other protected characteristic. Such characteristics are determined by federal laws—such as Title VII, the Americans with Disabilities Act, and the Age Discrimination in Employment Act—and by state and local laws that prohibit discrimination. (For more on antidiscrimination laws, see Chapter 5.) General complaints about working conditions don't meet this standard unless the employee is being subjected to tougher supervision or more onerous rules because of, for example, race or gender.

> EXAMPLE: Carla wants to leave work early two days a week to get a graduate degree. She works for a department store that does not offer flexible scheduling. Her supervisor tells her that she can't take the time off because company policy prohibits it and because it would be difficult to find someone to work her station for just a few hours a week. Her supervisor offers to let her take those days off entirely, but she would have to work on the weekend instead. Although this is unfortunate for Carla, it isn't harassment.
>
> Now suppose Carla's supervisor has usually accommodated employees' requests to take time off for personal pursuits. In fact, Carla had spoken to her supervisor before she signed up for school, and her supervisor assured her that he would rearrange her schedule. However, when Carla told her supervisor that she would be attending divinity school to become

a minister, his attitude changed. He was not as friendly toward her and seemed to avoid her at work. When she asked to meet with him to work out the scheduling details, he told her that he wasn't willing to lose an employee for several hours each week just so she could "go to Bible school." Carla may have a valid claim of religious harassment if she was subjected to different rules because of her religious beliefs.

The general rules that apply to all harassment cases are discussed in "Harassment: The Basics," below. There are a couple of additional issues that are more likely to come up in sexual harassment cases; these are covered in "Sexual Harassment," below.

Harassment: The Basics

Legally speaking, harassment is unwelcome workplace conduct based on the victim's protected characteristic. Sometimes, the victim is required to put up with the unwelcome conduct as a condition of continued employment. In this situation (sometimes called "quid pro quo" harassment), the victim's job, promotion opportunities, or other benefits are tied to the harassment. For example, a supervisor might tell an employee, "I'm not going to give you that promotion unless you agree to go on a date with me."

A second type of harassment, called "hostile work environment" harassment occurs when the employee is subjected to unwelcome conduct that is so severe or pervasive as to affect the terms and conditions of employment. This type of harassment might take the form of constant ridicule, belittling comments, teasing, or sexual come-ons.

Harassing Conduct

As noted above, workplace mistreatment can be construed as harassment only if it is based on a protected characteristic. Under federal law, protected characteristics include race, color, national origin, sex, disability, age (40 and older), genetic information, and religion. Many states expand this list to include marital status, gender identity, and other categories. And some cities and counties prohibit additional types of discrimination.

(See Chapter 5 for more information on protected categories; Appendix B provides information on state antidiscrimination laws.)

What kinds of conduct constitute harassment? Anything from derogatory jokes to name-calling and slurs to threats and outright physical violence. Harassment may take the form of actual comments about an employee's protected characteristic or it may be more subtle. For example, an employer may treat workers of a certain ethnicity better than other workers. Here are some examples:

- A Jewish office worker is subjected to jokes about the Holocaust and is assigned to a bookkeeping position because "Jews know how to handle money."
- An African American salesman works at a car dealership. His coworkers make racist comments about nonwhite customers; after he tells them that he finds their comments offensive, they start referring to themselves jokingly as "the KKK."
- A clerical worker with cerebral palsy is mimicked by her supervisor, who ridicules her speech and the way she walks, blames her for errors she did not commit, and tells her coworkers that "she is incompetent, but we can't fire her because she's disabled."

Unwelcome Conduct

To constitute illegal harassment, conduct or statements must be unwelcome to the victim. In many harassment cases, this isn't really an issue. Someone who is referred to in offensive or derogatory terms, made fun of because of age or disability, or threatened with racial violence can be assumed to find the conduct unwelcome. However, this sometimes is a disputed issue in sexual harassment cases, because some sexual advances, comments, or jokes might not offend their target. (See "Sexual Harassment," below, for more information.)

There may be a legitimate question of welcomeness in some cases that don't involve sexual harassment. For example, if an older worker frequently refers to himself as "gramps" or "the old-timer" and makes jokes about his "senior moments," other employees may feel that he doesn't mind being teased about his age. Similarly, workers who share a protected characteristic (such as the same ethnic background or sexual orientation) may feel comfortable exchanging jokes about it but quite uncomfortable hearing the same kinds of comments from someone else.

Severe or Pervasive

In a hostile work environment case, the harassment must be severe or pervasive. Generally, this means that there must be a pattern of harassment or a series of incidents over time. One teasing comment, request for a date, or even use of a bigoted epithet probably does not constitute harassment by itself. On the other hand, courts have found that a single act can be harassment if the act is truly extreme, such as rape or a racially motivated physical assault.

There's no clear line or "magic number" of incidents when name-calling, teasing, and such cross the line to become harassment. Courts will look at all of the circumstances in deciding whether harassment has occurred. This means that the court will consider all of the incidents in context. The more egregious each incident is, the fewer that will be necessary for an employer to be held liable.

CAUTION

It may be inappropriate even if it isn't illegal. This section explains how the law defines harassment. However, you shouldn't base your decision to investigate solely on whether the alleged conduct meets these legal standards. For one thing, you can't predict with utter certainty how a judge or jury will decide a particular harassment claim. More important, behavior doesn't have to be illegal to violate your company's standards on proper workplace behavior. A few isolated sexual jokes or bigoted comments can quickly escalate into a full-blown harassment claim. Even if they don't, they will certainly create an uncomfortable atmosphere for at least some of your workers. If you investigate, you can put a stop to this type of unprofessional behavior right away, before legal trouble develops.

Terms and Conditions of Employment

In order for a court to determine that harassment occurred, the conduct must affect the terms and conditions of the victim's employment. There are several ways this might happen. If the harasser is a supervisor or someone else who has the right and authority to make job decisions, harassment might take the form of a negative job action, such as firing, failure to promote, demotion, discipline, a pay cut (or refusal to grant a pay raise), or an undesirable transfer, reassignment, or change in job duties or title.

However, harassment can occur even if the victim is not subjected to a negative job action like this. The victim can make a hostile work environment claim if he or she reasonably finds the workplace to be abusive or hostile as a result of the harassment. The keyword here is "reasonable." It is not enough that the victim believes the workplace is hostile; the circumstances must be such that a reasonable worker in the victim's position would also find the workplace hostile. This rule ensures that employers won't be liable to hypersensitive employees who see harassment behind every smile and gesture.

Who's a Reasonable Worker?

The "reasonable person" test for harassment can be tough to figure out. After all, reasonable people can differ on what constitutes harassment or whether a particular situation has crossed the line from sophomoric to abusive.

The law says that employers (and juries, if it comes to that) must consider the situation from the viewpoint of a reasonable worker in the victim's position. This means that the typical sexual harassment claim must be considered from the perspective of a reasonable woman, and a case of racial harassment against an African American employee must be looked at from the vantage point of a reasonable African American. This rule is an effort to acknowledge the fact that different groups in our society may react differently to particular actions, words, and comments.

Sexual Harassment

Sexual harassment is defined in essentially the same way as other types of harassment: It's offensive, unwelcome sexual conduct that affects the terms and conditions of the victim's employment, either because the victim's submission or failure to submit to the behavior is the basis for job-related decisions (like firing or demotion) or because it is sufficiently severe or pervasive as to create a hostile work environment. However, sexual harassment cases tend to spend more time analyzing whether the behavior was welcome, due to the fact that not all sexual or romantic behavior in the workplace is offensive to the recipient.

It's safe to say that harassment based on race, disability, and so on is rarely a misguided effort to establish a closer relationship with the victim. Although such harassment is sometimes meant as a joke, its victims tend not to find it very amusing. In contrast, behavior that could be construed as sexual harassment under certain circumstances might not bother the recipient at all. After all, some requests for dates are accepted happily and lead to mutually satisfying relationships. While one person might find sexually explicit comments and jokes offensive, another might find them flattering and flirtatious. In an era when everyone spends so much time on the job—and, according to some surveys, a majority of us have had a relationship with someone we met at work—the law can't presume that every sexual advance or provocative comment is offensive.

At the same time, of course, it is very disturbing to be subjected to unwanted sexual attention, to be told that you have to submit to sexual advances in order to get ahead, or to work in an environment where X-rated jokes are the order of the day.

Unwelcome Harassment

Sexual harassment is unwelcome when the victim finds it offensive rather than flattering or innocent. Notice the focus on the victim: Unlike the reasonableness standard discussed above, unwelcomeness is in the eye of the beholder. It's subjective, which means that when you are investigating a sexual harassment claim, you will want to ask the victim how he or she felt about the alleged harassment and what impact it had on him or her.

Who's Harassing Whom?

The majority of sexual harassment claims involve a male harasser and a female victim. However, courts have recognized harassment claims by women against men, men against men, and women against women. And the Equal Employment Opportunity Commission (the federal government agency that enforces antidiscrimination and harassment laws) reports that harassment claims by men have been steadily increasing. For the last few years, such claims have made up more than 17% of all sexual harassment charges filed under federal law (these statistics don't indicate the gender of the harasser).

Regardless of the gender of the victim or harasser, the same standards apply: The victim must be subjected to unwelcome sexual conduct that affects the terms and conditions of employment.

Keep in mind that what may be welcome to one employee could be unwelcome to others. For example, a group of men enjoy teasing and making sexual jokes with the office receptionist, an attractive young woman. The receptionist finds the jokes amusing and harmless, and sometimes tells one herself. This isn't illegal harassment of the receptionist, because she finds the conduct welcome. However, a female secretary who shares space with the receptionist finds these comments offensive and disruptive. Although none of the jokes are directed at her, she finds them unwelcome and must put up with them to do her job. She may be a victim of sexual harassment.

Prior Relationships

Remember all of those consensual relationships that began at work? Well, common sense tells us that many of them are bound to end at some point, which means that all of the drama, hurt feelings, and denial that can accompany a relationship's demise might find their way into the workplace.

Claims of Sexual Favoritism

If a worker is required to submit to sexual advances in order to get some type of job benefit (such as a promotion or desired assignment), that worker has a pretty good sexual harassment claim. But what about the other workers, those who weren't put under sexual pressure but also didn't get the job benefit? According to the EEOC, these workers may also have a legal claim against the company for harassment. Even though they weren't directly subjected to harassment, their job opportunities suffered because of sexual harassment against another employee.

What if the favoritism is based not on harassment, but on a consensual relationship? Some courts have found that this type of favoritism cannot give rise to a harassment claim, but the California Supreme Court has held that other employees might have a harassment claim even if the employee(s) who received the benefits do not. While an isolated incident of sexual favoritism—such as giving a plum job assignment to a girlfriend— might not be actionable, the court found that the situation is different if favoritism is widespread. If, for example, a manager is having sexual relationships with several employees, all of whom receive job benefits that aren't provided to others, the manager is sending a message that the only way to get ahead at work is to have sex with the boss. This might be actionable harassment.

Whether the courts in your state decide to follow California's example or not, one thing is clear: Managers should not be favoring their paramours with job benefits that are not available to other employees. Basing employment decisions on personal relationships or other factors that are not directly related to the job is a poor management practice. Even if it doesn't lead to a lawsuit, it will certainly lead to resentment, poor morale, and increased employee turnover. If you hear of sexual favoritism at your company, you should investigate and take action to stop it, even if it wouldn't provide sufficient fodder for a successful lawsuit.

Unfortunately, it also means that sexual harassment claims might not be far behind. Some sexual harassment claims are brought by a victim who used to be in a consensual relationship with the harasser. This is a particular danger when one member of the former couple supervises the other or holds a position that provides an opportunity to make decisions about the other's future at the company. The subordinate employee might claim that she is being punished for ending the relationship or that she is being subjected to advances that are now unwanted. In extreme cases, one employee might even make a false claim of harassment against the other, out of spite or anger over the breakup.

If you learn, during the course of your investigation, that the alleged harasser and victim used to be romantically involved, you'll probably have to ask some questions about that relationship so you can figure out how it plays into the harassment allegations. This can be a sticky situation for investigators, as it requires you to get into some issues that the parties might think of as private. (You'll find tips below that will help you handle this type of problem.)

Sex-Based Harassment

Sexual harassment may take the form of sex-based harassment: harassment that is based on sex but is not sexual in nature. In these cases, the harasser is not interested in having a sexual relationship with the victim(s) or otherwise "sexualizing" the workplace with jokes and stories but instead wants to intentionally create a hostile environment for workers of a particular gender (almost always women). Often, these claims are made by women working in traditionally male professions.

Although women in these cases have clearly been subjected to a hostile work environment because of their sex, there are none of the traditional signs of sexual harassment, such as requests for dates, dirty jokes, and sexualized comments about women's bodies. Instead, harassing conduct in these cases might include sabotaging the tools, vehicles, or work of female employees; soiling or defacing women's work spaces, lockers, or restroom facilities; subjecting women to dangerous work conditions; displaying cartoons or telling jokes that depict violence towards women; and making comments about women's inability to do the job.

Legal Liability for Harassment

In 1998, the Supreme Court decided two cases that spell out when an employer will be legally responsible for harassment. In these cases, the Court held that employers that have an antiharassment policy and investigate harassment complaints quickly and fairly can avoid liability in certain kinds of cases, even if the employee proves that he or she was harassed.

Generally, your company has a legal duty to take effective action to stop harassment as soon as management learns of it, whether the harasser is a supervisor or a coworker of the victim. But in some cases, your company will also be held responsible for harassment committed by a manager or supervisor, even if no one in human resources knew what was going on. The Supreme Court and the Equal Employment Opportunity Commission (EEOC), the government agency charged with handling complaints of discrimination and harassment, have come up with the following rules for employer responsibility for harassment.

An employer is generally responsible for harassment by a manager or supervisor if the harassment results in a "tangible employment action"—an action that significantly changes the harassed employee's job status, like getting fired, demoted, or reassigned. This is true even if the employee never complained and the employer had no idea what was going on. The logic behind this liability is that when managers and supervisors make these types of decisions, they are acting as agents of the company. Therefore, if their decisions are influenced by discrimination, the company is responsible.

Who's a Supervisor?

These rules—which make employers liable for harassment that results in a negative job action, even if the employer isn't aware of it—apply only to harassment by supervisors. So which employees qualify as supervisors? According to the EEOC, a supervisor is someone who either has the authority to make or recommend decisions affecting the employee or has the authority to direct the employee's daily work activities.

However, an employer is not necessarily responsible for harassment by a manager or supervisor that doesn't result in a tangible employment action, such as a manager who tells racist jokes or repeatedly asks an employee out on dates. In these cases, an employer can defend itself by showing that:

- the employer exercised reasonable care to prevent and promptly correct any harassment, and
- the employee unreasonably failed to take advantage of opportunities the employer offered to prevent or correct the harassment (for example, by failing to make a complaint).

The first step requires employers to make efforts to create a harassment-free work environment. A company can do this by training employees and managers to recognize and report harassment, by adopting a policy prohibiting harassment and a complaint procedure that encourages employees to come forward, and by investigating harassment complaints quickly and fairly. If the employer takes these precautions and a harassed worker delays in making a complaint or fails to complain at all, the employer will not be responsible for harassment that occurred prior to the complaint.

However, certain employees may occupy such a lofty position on the corporate ladder that they are something more than supervisors. These employees—which might include corporate officers, the president, the CEO, an owner, or a partner, depending on how the company is organized—generally have the authority to act on the company's behalf in all matters. Therefore, if they harass employees, the law will presume that the company knows about it, even if the harassment doesn't result in a negative job action. In these situations, employers can't rely on the defense described in this section: The company will always be liable for harassment by these high-ranking employees.

FORM

Need an antiharassment policy? A sample antiharassment policy, which you can modify to fit the needs of your workplace, is available at this book's online companion page; see Appendix A for more information.

The policy behind this defense is pretty simple: If an employer has an antiharassment and investigation policy that it follows faithfully, the employee has to use it if he or she wants the problem to stop. If an employee fails to make a complaint, the employer has no notice of the problem and, therefore, no reason to investigate or take action. But in order to take advantage of this protection, the employer must make clear to employees that their complaints will be investigated fully and fairly. The only way to drive this point home is to investigate every harassment complaint. That way, no employee can argue that he or she didn't report harassment because the employer would not have done anything about it. Remember that once the employer learns of this second kind of harassment—through a complaint or in any other way—it is responsible for any harassment that continues after that point. This gives the employer an incentive to investigate and take action quickly.

Sometimes, harassment is committed by someone who doesn't have the authority to make job decisions involving the victim. For example, a coworker might display pornographic images to an employee during meetings, or a vendor might pressure an employee to go out on dates. In this situation, the company is liable if it knew (or should have known) about the harassment and failed to take prompt, effective action to correct it.

> EXAMPLE 1: Sheila's boss, Roger, has asked her out several times. She has turned him down each time, explaining that she has no romantic interest in him and would prefer to keep their relationship professional. Roger refuses to approve Sheila's scheduled raise because she will not go out with him. Roger's employer will be legally responsible for Roger's harassment, even if Sheila never complains about it, because she has been subjected to a negative job action.

> EXAMPLE 2: Katherine works on the production line in an auto plant. Her coworkers and supervisor, mostly men, constantly tell sexual jokes and refer to women in crude terms. The top executives in the company visit the plant. Although the men are on their best behavior during the official tour, several executives remain in the building afterwards to review paperwork

and overhear the men's crude remarks. The company will be liable for any harassment Katherine suffers after the visit. Although she has not made a complaint or suffered a negative job action, the company now knows about the harassment and has a duty to take action.

EXAMPLE 3: Same as Example 2, except the executives never visit the plant. If Katherine wants to hold the company responsible for her harassment, she will have to make a complaint to put the company on notice of the problem. If Katherine fails to make a complaint, she can hold the company responsible only if she can show that (1) the company had no policy against harassment, or (2) the company did not take complaints seriously, failed to investigate, or failed to act on reported problems. For example, if Katherine can show that several women from her plant had complained in the past few years and nothing had been done about the problem, the employer will be liable despite her failure to complain.

For more information on employer liability for harassment by supervisors and managers, check out the EEOC's guidelines, "EEOC Enforcement Guidance on Vicarious Employer Liability for Unlawful Harassment by Supervisors" (June 1999), available from the EEOC's website at www.eeoc.gov/policy/docs/harassment.html.

CAUTION
Check your state's laws. Although many states have adopted the rules explained in this section and most others are likely to adopt them, there may be a few states that buck the trend. States that have stronger anti-harassment laws—and are therefore more likely to hold employers responsible for harassment—might not follow the Supreme Court's lead. For example, a state that uses a strict liability standard will hold the employer liable for all harassment, whether management participated in it or not, and whether the company knew about it or not. In this situation, it's even more imperative that a company do all it can to prevent harassment in the first place. An employment lawyer can help you figure out how your company can protect itself.

Ten Steps to a Successful Harassment Investigation

This section explains how to apply the basic investigation steps covered in Part I of this book to a harassment investigation. If you haven't read Part I, you should do so before getting into this more specific material; the discussion that follows assumes that you are already familiar with basic investigation procedures.

Decide Whether to Investigate

When you're dealing with possible harassment, it's best to err on the side of investigating, even if the allegations don't seem that serious. As explained above, failing to investigate harassment claims can have serious consequences not just for the claim you decide not to investigate, but for future claims of harassment that might be made against your company.

But this doesn't mean you have to jump into investigative high gear every time an employee utters the "h" word. First, figure out whether the employee is complaining about conduct based on a protected characteristic (race, gender, disability, and so on). If not, you may still want to look into the incident further, depending on the allegations, or refer them to an appropriate person in management for further consideration.

> **EXAMPLE:** Roland complains to the human resources department about his supervisor, Marie. Marie was recently hired to improve the performance of the sales department. Roland complains that Marie has imposed deadlines on the department that are difficult to meet and has required everyone to attend sales training, even if they have years of experience. She has arranged a standing meeting with every employee once a week to review their sales figures and talk about ways they could improve their numbers. Roland claims this is harassment: "She's working all of us like dogs. She's always there, looking over someone's shoulder, telling them what they're doing is wrong. Our group is really demoralized. It feels like she doesn't respect our experience and opinions."

Even though Roland used the term "harassment," he isn't complaining about illegal harassment based on a protected characteristic. Although Marie's management style isn't winning her any friends, she is applying it equally to all, regardless of race, gender, and so on. This isn't a complaint that demands an investigation. However, it is a legitimate concern that should be communicated to Marie and her supervisors. The company may decide that Marie is doing exactly what it hired her to do and urge her to keep up the good work. Or it may decide to tell Marie to back off a bit and try using some management techniques that are a bit more successful at motivating her employees.

Even if the conduct appears to be based on a protected characteristic, the situation may not call for a full-blown investigation. There may be cases in which the alleged conduct is minor, everyone agrees on what happened, and a simple discussion with both parties (carefully documented, of course) will put the matter to rest.

EXAMPLE: Mark asks Georgia, his coworker, to have dinner with him one night after work. Georgia declines, telling Mark that she has a boyfriend. Mark says, "Well, he's a very lucky man." Nothing further happens between them, but Georgia tells her supervisor about the incident and confides that it made her a bit uncomfortable to know that Mark finds her attractive. You interview Georgia, who confirms what she told her supervisor and says that Mark has never asked her out again or acted inappropriately towards her. Mark tells you that Georgia's statement is accurate. He says that he won't approach her socially again: "I don't want to make her uncomfortable. In fact, I feel kind of bad for asking her out in the first place."

In this situation, you won't have to interview witnesses, comb through files, and carefully weigh the evidence. Once you've talked to the two employees involved, made sure that Mark understands that he shouldn't bother Georgia, (or retaliate against her for complaining), explained the outcome to Georgia, and documented your conversations, you're done. Of course, a few different facts could lead to a different conclusion. For example, if Mark's response was "I can't believe my bad luck; she's the third person in my department I asked out this month, and they all turned me down," or Georgia said, "I think Mark felt comfortable asking me out because our supervisor is always joking and making comments about the supposedly wild sex lives I and the other women in our department have," then you've got a more serious problem on your hands that will require a more extensive investigation.

! CAUTION

When there is no complaint. Remember, your company has an obligation to investigate harassment, no matter how you find out about it. Although you may learn of harassment through an employee complaint, there are lots of other ways harassment might come to your attention. For example, a supervisor might notice racist graffiti on the walls of the employee locker room, overhear an X-rated joke, or see employees picking on a disabled coworker. An employee might make an anonymous complaint of harassment or raise the issue in an exit interview. Your duty to investigate kicks in as soon as you know of the allegations, regardless of how they surface.

Take Immediate Action, If Necessary

Before you begin your investigation, you will have to decide whether some immediate changes are necessary in the workplace to prevent further harm and to ensure that the investigation won't be disrupted. You should consider taking steps to separate the alleged harasser from the alleged victims when:

- Very serious allegations—for example, unwanted sexual touching, sexual assault, violence, threats, or extremely abusive verbal harassment (such as the use of offensive racist epithets)—have been made.
- Ongoing harassment is alleged.
- The alleged victim(s) and/or witnesses appear to be intimidated by the alleged harasser.

You must be very careful to avoid retaliation (or the appearance of retaliation) when you decide what to do. If you separate the employees by moving the worker who complained to another shift or a different work area, you could be accused of retaliating: "As soon as I complained, they moved me to the night shift, while the person who harassed me got to continue working his usual shift, just like nothing happened."

The best way to avoid these types of charges is to move the harasser or suspend him with pay while you investigate. When you tell the alleged harasser about the change, emphasize that it's a temporary situation, that no conclusions have been made about the truth of the allegations, and that the transfer or suspension is not punitive. If you must take an immediate action like this, make extra efforts to complete the investigation quickly, to minimize workplace disruption.

Time Off for the Complaining Employee

Sometimes, an employee who complains of harassment asks to take some time off. If you face a request like this, find out exactly why the employee wants out of the workplace. For example, if the employee has been threatened with retaliation or her coworkers are shunning her because she made a complaint, these are facts you'll need to know. Explain that retaliation is prohibited and that you will investigate as quickly as possible.

If an employee simply wants to take some time to catch her breath, you can arrange for a brief period of paid leave. However, make sure that the employee will be available to participate in the investigation.

If criminal allegations have been made—of sexual assault, physical violence, or serious threats—you might be wondering whether you should call the police. In this situation, you should talk to a lawyer right away. There are pros and cons to having the police involved: They can use a wide range of investigative methods and bring the force of the state to bear when trying to get to the truth, but they also have their own priorities, which may differ from those of your company. A lawyer can help you weigh the alternatives and decide what to do. Of course, the victim can always report the incident and, if this happens, you should cooperate with the authorities.

Choose the Investigator

Chapter 2 explains the qualities that make an investigator particularly effective, such as professionalism, experience, and impartiality. Those considerations always apply, no matter what type of problem you're investigating. However, there are a few special issues to consider when you're choosing an investigator for a harassment complaint.

Your Company's Chances in Court Depend on Its Investigator

Because the Supreme Court has held that a prompt, complete, and impartial investigation could shield you from liability for certain types of harassment, a company's ability to defend itself in a harassment case could well depend on the investigator. Will the investigator handle the job carefully and quickly, without letting personal feelings get in the way? Will the investigator be able to testify professionally and accurately in court, in a manner that a jury will believe?

 CAUTION

Watch out for claims of bias. Some courts have disregarded a company's efforts to investigate—and the conclusions of the investigation—if any of the employees involved in a harassment claim perceived the investigator to be biased. This means you must be especially careful to choose an investigator who is beyond reproach, and to confirm with the complaining employee and the accused employee that they are comfortable with the investigator. The investigator should not be someone who directly supervises or has a personal relationship (or a history of negative encounters) with either worker. For more on choosing an unbiased investigator, see Chapter 2.

Of course, these are important questions to ask yourself when choosing an investigator for *any* type of workplace problem. But they are particularly important in cases of harassment, because the Supreme Court's decisions have virtually guaranteed that the quality of the investigation will be on trial, if your company is faced with a lawsuit.

Sensitivity

Harassment claims can be particularly uncomfortable, for alleged harassers and alleged victims alike. In a sexual harassment case, for example, the investigator may have to ask about prior relationships, sexual comments, flirtations, and more. To investigate a case of racial harassment, the investigator might have to ask the victim to repeat racial slurs and offensive statements that are deeply disturbing. Many of us are reluctant to reveal or talk in detail about these kinds of incidents, which means the investigator must be especially skilled at drawing people out and encouraging them to speak openly.

Some experts recommend choosing an investigator who shares the victim's protected characteristics (to the extent possible), to encourage the victim to open up. This is often sound advice. For example, many women would feel more comfortable (and less embarrassed) discussing sexual harassment with another woman. And a victim of racial harassment might feel that an investigator of the same race is more likely to understand how offensive certain statements or actions were.

However, you won't always be able to follow this advice, particularly if your company is a small business. No company will have the wherewithal to come up with a "demographically correct" investigator for every claim, and that's okay. Your main concern is to find an investigator who can listen attentively and carefully to everyone and who won't come to the investigation with preconceived notions about what happened.

When to Use an Outside Investigator

As explained in Chapter 2, it makes sense to consider hiring an outside investigator in certain circumstances. You may want to bring in a professional investigator for a harassment claim if:

- An employee has raised allegations of sexual assault, rape, or violence motivated by bias.
- Several employees have complained about the same problem (for example, a group of African American employees complain of widespread racial harassment).

- The accused harasser is a high-ranking company official (in this situation, employees might not believe that an investigator who works for the company can be impartial).
- An employee has filed a lawsuit or an administrative charge (with the Equal Employment Opportunity Commission or a state antidiscrimination agency) based on the harassment.
- An employee has hired a lawyer because of the harassment.
- The allegations have been publicized in the media.

Plan the Investigation

Although you might become aware of harassment in any number of ways (see Chapter 2), you will often be dealing with an employee complaint of inappropriate behavior. This gives you a leg up on the investigation. You'll have some basic information before you begin your interviews, and you'll be able to plan your investigation accordingly.

You won't always have a complaint to work from, however. If a manager happens to notice X-rated cartoons or racist graffiti on the walls, for example, or if you receive an anonymous complaint of harassment, you'll have to begin your investigation without knowing who may have committed wrongdoing or who may have been harmed by it.

When Someone Has Complained

If an employee has complained of harassment, that complaint is your natural starting point for planning the investigation. Using the complaint as your guide, these questions will help you define the scope of your inquiries:

- Who complained? Is there more than one complaining employee? If not, does the complaining employee allege that other employees were also harassed?
- What misconduct is alleged? Is the victim alleging harassment based on a protected characteristic? Is the victim alleging that he or she suffered a tangible job action—such as demotion, failure to get a raise or promotion, or a change in job duties—or a hostile work environment?

- Who is the alleged wrongdoer? Is there more than one alleged harasser? What position does the alleged harasser hold?
- How many incidents of harassment does the victim allege?
- Has the victim named any potential witnesses?
- Where did the alleged incidents take place? Is the alleged misconduct limited to one work group, one shift, or one area of the workplace, or is it more widespread? Are there any employees who may have witnessed them?

The answers to these questions will help you decide whom to interview, what documents or other evidence may be available to shed some light on the allegations, and what kinds of questions you'll need to ask. Of course, you may not know the answers to all of these questions right now. If the victim made a bare-bones complaint, for example, you might not find out any details until you actually begin to investigate. In this situation, simply keep these questions in mind as you conduct your initial interview with the complaining employee.

When There's No Complaint

Where should you start when there's no complaining employee? As always, start with what you know. How did the alleged harassment come to your attention? Did a manager or another employee report it? If so, what did that person notice? If you received a report of interpersonal harassment—that is, one employee harassing another—consider starting with the alleged victim. Even though that person hasn't come forward, he or she is probably in the best position to tell you exactly what happened.

You might learn of possible harassment that isn't focused on a particular victim (for example, that certain employees frequently use foul language or refer to others in racist or ageist terms, that sexually explicit images or jokes have been posted on an employee bulletin board or online message board, or that employees with disabilities have been the victims of anonymous practical jokes). In cases like these, you may wish to start by talking to someone who manages the work group where the problem arose to find out which employees may be involved, what schedules they work, how the employees seem to get along, and so forth.

If the information you begin with isn't sufficient to identify the alleged harasser(s), remember that anyone you interview to gather background information could be involved in the wrongdoing; plan your questions accordingly.

Documents and Other Physical Evidence

No matter how you learn of the harassment, part of your investigation planning should include gathering relevant documents. The following types of documents may help you figure out whom to interview and what questions to ask:

- the company's harassment policy
- the personnel files of the alleged harasser and the complaining employee or victim (if there is one)
- any allegedly harassing documents, including emails, correspondence, cartoons, postings on company property, or notes
- performance evaluations and other documents reflecting personnel decisions, if the complaining employee claims to have suffered a negative job action as a result of the harassment, and
- attendance records for any company trainings on harassment.

You should also consider whether any physical evidence other than documents might exist. If someone has reported sexist graffiti in the locker room, for example, you will want to photograph the graffiti and record exactly what it says. Other types of evidence that may be relevant in a harassment investigation include:

- objects given to or left for the victim, including gifts, suggestive clothing, sexual toys, offensive items (like a noose or Ku Klux Klan imagery), or pictures
- photographs from company events where harassment allegedly took place (such as a company holiday party or other social event), and
- work-related items connected with the alleged harassment. For example, if the victim alleges that her toolbox was tampered with, his briefcase or computer was defaced, or his equipment was sabotaged, you will want to collect those items (or at least photograph them and take careful notes of the apparent damage).

Interviews

Once you've finished your investigation planning, you'll have some ideas about which employees you should interview. If an employee has made a complaint, you should generally start by interviewing that person. If no employee has complained, you can start by interviewing whoever noticed the problem, a manager in the work group where the problem exists, or any known victims.

No matter whom you're interviewing, you should start the interview with some opening remarks to set the employee at ease and explain the process. You should also give the witness a written notice regarding retaliation, and so on. (You'll find a form you can use for this purpose at this book's online companion page; see Appendix A for more information.) Next, proceed to your specific questions, remembering to follow up on any new information raised by the witness's responses. Close the interview by letting the witness know what will happen next and inviting him or her to come to you with any concerns or additional information. And conduct follow-up interviews if any new information comes to light.

Getting Started

Some of your opening comments will be the same, no matter whom you're interviewing. Some of them will be geared more specifically toward a complaining employee, an accused employee, or a witness. The opening statement you make to every person you interview should cover these points:

- **The purpose of the meeting.** The information you give here will depend on whom you're interviewing. You can tell the complaining employee that the company will be investigating the complaint and that the purpose of the meeting is to gather as much information as possible. The accused employee will need to be told that a complaint has been made, that you're investigating, and that your role is to gather as much information as possible. A witness can simply be told that you're investigating a workplace problem and you believe the witness might have some relevant information.

- **The investigation process.** Explain that the company will be investigating the problem and interviewing other employees and will take appropriate steps if it finds that misconduct occurred.
- **Confidentiality.** Explain that you will maintain confidentiality to the extent possible, although it will be necessary to reveal certain details in order to conduct thorough interviews and reach a decision. (As explained in Chapter 5, it's risky to require employees not to talk about the investigation or underlying incidents.)
- **Retaliation.** Explain that retaliation is prohibited and that the company will take immediate steps to discipline anyone who retaliates based on the complaint or investigation. Ask the employee to come to you with any concerns about retaliation.
- **Questions or concerns.** Ask whether the employee has any questions or concerns about the process.

When you interview the accused employee, emphasize that the company has not reached any decisions about what happened. Explain that you are interested in hearing what everyone involved has to say before making a decision or taking any action. Because you will probably have to reveal the name of the complaining employee (as explained below), spend some extra time discussing retaliation: what it is, that the company prohibits it, and that employees who engage in retaliation will be subject to discipline. Although the accused employee will probably want to know the allegations right away, you are better off postponing this discussion until later in the interview, after you have had a chance to gather some important background information. Assure the accused employee that he or she will have the opportunity to hear and respond to the allegations before the interview is over.

For witnesses, your opening remarks can be brief. The witness doesn't need to know who complained, who is accused, or what the specific allegations are. Once you have explained that you are investigating a workplace problem and talked about confidentiality and retaliation, you can begin asking your questions.

Questions for the Complaining Employee or Victim

Harassment is usually a pattern of incidents rather than one single event. Because the complaining employee will probably be describing several separate occurrences, you need to be especially careful to ask precise questions and take clear notes; otherwise, you could easily get confused about the details. Experienced investigators advise discussing each incident separately. First, ask the complaining employee to tell you briefly about every incident. Then, go through the list and ask for the details of each, starting with the most recent problem and working backwards. Here are some sample questions you can tailor to the facts of your investigation:

Sample Questions

- What happened? How many incidents have there been?
- Who was involved? What did that person say or do?
- How did you react? Did you say anything to [the accused employee]? What did you say? Did you react physically [for example, by leaving the room, slamming a door, crying, or blushing]?
- Prior to these incidents, what was your relationship like with [the accused employee]? Did you work together frequently? Did you have any problems working together? Did you socialize outside of work?
- When did each incident take place? How often did they occur? When did they begin?
- Where did each incident take place?
- Was anyone else present? Could anyone else have witnessed the incident(s)?
- Did you tell anyone about the incidents? Whom did you tell? What did you tell them?
- Do you know of any similar incidents involving other people?
- Have you been affected by the incidents? How? Did you take any time off as a result of the incidents? Did you seek medical treatment or counseling?
- Are there any documents or other kinds of evidence relating to the incidents? Did you take notes or keep a journal recording these incidents?

- When did you first complain about these incidents [if the employee says she complained earlier and nothing was done]? Whom did you complain to? What did you say? What did the person you complained to say? [If the employee only complained after a delay:] Why did you decide to come forward now?
- How would you like to see this problem resolved?
- Is there anyone who might have information about these incidents that you'd like me to interview?
- Is there anything else you'd like to tell me?

> **TIP**
>
> **Act like a reporter.** When interviewing the complaining employee, follow the universal rule of journalists everywhere: Ask who, what, where, when, and how (and sometimes why) for each incident. By sticking to these open-ended questions, you'll elicit as much information as possible while keeping the witness focused on the facts.

Questions for the Accused Employee

Your interview with the accused employee is likely to be a tense affair. An employee who committed misconduct may try to evade your questions or lie about what happened. An employee who has been wrongly accused is likely to be upset at both the complaining employee and the company, for taking the allegations seriously. Either way, you may be facing a defensive and combative interview.

One way to defuse the tension is to emphasize that the company has a legal obligation to investigate the allegations and that you haven't reached any conclusions yet. Explain that the purpose of the investigation is to figure out what really happened. Assure the employee that you are eager to hear what he or she has to say and that you will be interviewing witnesses and examining documents to help you get to the truth.

Asking About a Prior Relationship

If the complaining employee and the alleged harasser used to be romantically involved, you will have to ask about that relationship. What each party says about the relationship, why it ended, and how it affects their work relationship will help you figure out whose story is more credible.

But proceed with caution: Once you start asking about personal matters—and we can all agree that our romantic relationships fall into this category—you risk invading an employee's privacy. The best way to avoid this problem is to limit your questions to issues related to work and the complaint. In most cases, you could safely ask about when the relationship started, when it ended, who ended it and why, how the parties have gotten along at work since the breakup, and what relevance each party thinks the prior relationship has on the current situation. (For example, does the complaining employee think that she's being harassed because she ended the relationship, or does the accused harasser think his former paramour has made a false complaint out of jealousy or anger?)

In some situations, you might find yourself asking more intimate questions, based on the information that comes out in your interviews.

EXAMPLE: Rosalie complains that Xavier, her coworker and former boyfriend, is harassing her. She says that he hangs around her desk all of the time and asks her a lot of questions about her personal life. She says she has told him to stop, but he persists in asking her out and asking whether she's dating anyone else. She decided to complain when she found a sex toy on her desk. She says, with some embarrassment, that she and Xavier had used a similar toy when having sex, and that finding it on her desk convinced her that Xavier was not going to stop bothering her.

When you interview Xavier, are you going to ask him about the sex toy? Ordinarily, you should stay very far away from any questions about sexual practices. In this case, however, you need to find out who left the item on Rosalie's desk, and the evidence so far points to Xavier. Just make sure to limit your questions to what you need to know to resolve the complaint. (In other words, you can ask whether Xavier put the item on her desk, but not why the couple used it or "How the heck does this thing work?")

TIP

You work for the company. It can be tough to interview an angry witness, particularly one who blames the company—or even you, personally—for the investigation. You may hear things like "I can't believe you think I did this," "I won't sit here and be accused of this nonsense," or "I'm outraged that anyone would take these allegations seriously." To avoid taking these kinds of statements personally, just remember that you are playing a very important role for the company. Your job is to find out what happened and resolve the situation, and you should explain this to the accused employee.

Because the accused employee is likely to be defensive—and may have something to hide—you'll have to plan the order of your questions carefully. Start with easy, basic questions about the employee's work. This will allow both of you to ease into the interview and will give you the opportunity to gather potentially important facts while the employee's guard is down.

EXAMPLE: Ricardo, a Mexican American supervisor at a company that manufactures food products, complains that another supervisor, Jessica, has harassed him based on his national origin. He says that Jessica constantly teases him about his accent and the foods he likes to eat and tells jokes about Ricardo being an illegal alien. Ricardo is responsible for giving biweekly safety presentations to the line workers. As a fellow supervisor, Jessica is neither required nor expected to attend these meetings, but Ricardo says she has attended the last five meetings and made comments about his accent.

If you start your interview with Jessica by saying, "Ricardo claims that you've been attending his safety meetings and making inappropriate comments about his accent. Is this true?," Jessica now thinks to herself, "Aha! They're saying I did something wrong at these safety meetings." This could give her a reason to lie or make up an innocent explanation for her attendance.

If you start your interview instead by asking, "Tell me about your job responsibilities," then following up with questions about whom she supervises, what she does in a typical workday and workweek, and whether she is required to attend or run any regular meetings with other workers,

Jessica may not know what you're fishing for, and won't have a chance to shape her answers to put herself in the best possible light. This means you'll have a better chance of getting an honest answer.

CAUTION

You must allow the accused employee to respond to the allegations. Some investigators are so eager to keep the interview civil—or to protect the complaining employee's privacy—that they never actually get around to confronting the accuser with the allegations. This is a big mistake, one that could undermine the legitimacy of the entire investigation. Courts have held that accused employees who never learn precisely what they are accused of haven't had a fair opportunity to respond, to offer the names of relevant witnesses, or to explain why the complaining employee might have made the accusation. You don't necessarily have to say who complained, but you should say whom the employee is accused of harassing. And don't worry about privacy concerns: You have a very compelling business reason for revealing this information.

Once you are done with the background questions, tell the accused employee what the allegations are and ask for a response. As you did with the complaining employee, go through each allegation chronologically (starting with the most recent incident and working backwards), asking whether the accused employee was present at the time and place alleged, who else was present, what happened, and how everyone reacted. Give the accused employee the opportunity to offer any explanations, denials, alibis, and witnesses for each alleged incident. Here are some sample questions to consider:

Sample Questions
- What is your typical workday or workweek like? What time do you arrive? What time do you leave? What are your job responsibilities?
- Do you supervise any employees? What are their names and positions?
- How would you characterize your working relationship with your direct reports? Your coworkers?

- [Tell the accused employee what misconduct is alleged or suspected.] What is your response to these allegations?
- Did these things happen? [If the accused employee does not completely deny the allegations:] What did happen? When and where?
- How did [the alleged victim] respond? Did [the alleged victim] indicate that your statements or actions were offensive?
- Did anyone witness these incidents?
- Have you told anyone about these incidents?
- Have you kept any notes or a journal about these incidents?
- What is your work relationship like with [the alleged victim]?
- [If the accused employee denies the allegations:] Could another person have misunderstood your actions or statements? Do you think someone made up these incidents? Why?
- Have you ever used foul language in the workplace?
- Have you ever used racial epithets in the workplace? [Ask about other biases as appropriate, based on the allegations.]
- [For sexual harassment complaints:] Have you ever seen [the alleged victim] outside of work? Have you ever had a social relationship with each other? A romantic relationship? Have you ever asked [the alleged victim] out on a date? What was [the alleged victim]'s response?
- Have you ever been accused of harassment? How was the issue resolved?
- Have you had any training on workplace harassment issues?
- Are you aware of the company's antiharassment policy?
- Do you know of anyone who might have information about these incidents?
- Do you know of any documents or other evidence relating to these allegations?
- Is there anything else you'd like to tell me?

Questions for Witnesses

When questioning witnesses, your goal is to gather information without giving too much away. To plan your questions, consider who suggested the witness and why. Did the witness see or hear the misconduct? Was the witness told of the misconduct? Is the witness privy to some details of the relationship between the complaining employee and the accused?

Start by explaining, in very general terms, why the witness is being interviewed. State that you are investigating a workplace problem and you believe the witness might have information that will help you figure out what happened. Then, move into questions that will help you figure out if the witness could have seen or heard the alleged incidents. Finally, find out what the witness knows. Here are some sample questions to consider:

Sample Questions

- Describe your typical workday or workweek. Who is your supervisor? Where is your workstation? What time do you typically arrive at work each day? What time do you leave?
- Do you work with [the alleged victim] or [the accused employee]? How would you describe their work relationship?
- Has [the alleged victim] ever spoken to you about [the accused employee]? Has [the accused employee] ever spoken to you about [the alleged victim]?
- Have you seen any interactions between [the alleged victim] and [the accused employee] that made you uncomfortable? Describe them to me.
- [If the witness may have seen or heard the incident, ask questions to figure out whether the witness was there and what happened.]
- Have you heard these issues discussed in the workplace? When, where, and by whom?
- Have you ever had any problems working with [the alleged victim] or [the accused employee]?
- Do you know of anyone else who might have information about these incidents? Are there any documents or other evidence that you know of relating to these incidents?

EXAMPLE: If the complaining employee says that the witness was present when her supervisor told a racist joke, you might ask: Did you attend a meeting to discuss sales techniques last Monday? What time was the meeting? Were you present for the whole meeting, or did you leave the room at any time? Who else was at the meeting? Do you remember any comments Tom made at the meeting?

If these questions don't get you the information you need, you'll have to ask more specific questions, like: Did Tom tell any jokes at the meeting? Do you remember him making any comments about Native Americans? What did he say?

Closing the Interview

Once you have finished your questions, review your notes with the person you interviewed. Make sure that your notes include all of the important details. Remind the employee about retaliation, especially the accused employee. And ask the employee to come to you immediately with any new information.

This is all you have to tell witnesses. When you close an interview with the complaining or accused employee, let them know what will happen next. Tell them that you'll interview them again if any important new information comes up.

Follow-Up Interviews

If any new information comes up during your investigation, you should conduct follow-up interviews with the complaining and accused employee. Both employees should have the opportunity to respond to new allegations or defenses, to make sure that you have a complete understanding of the facts when you make your decision and to give you the opportunity to gauge credibility. It is especially important to let the accused employee know of any additional allegations that come up during the investigation. If you don't, you may be accused of unfairness for refusing to give him or her an opportunity to give his or her side of the story.

> EXAMPLE 1: Siri complains that her supervisor, Jeff, is sexually harassing her. She says that he has persistently asked her out and has recently told her that he will not recommend her for promotion unless she agrees to go on a weekend trip with him. When you interview Jeff, he says that he has never asked Siri out or invited her away for the weekend, but that

he has told her that he cannot recommend her for promotion because her performance has been slipping in recent months. He also says that Siri responded that she would get the promotion, regardless of his recommendation. In this case, you should definitely reinterview Siri and find out how she responds to Jeff's comments.

EXAMPLE 2: Emily complains that a coworker, Gabe, has harassed her because she is a member of Jews for Jesus. She says that Gabe frequently taunts her because of her religion, making comments like "If the Jews really liked Jesus, they wouldn't have killed him." You interview Gretchen, who works with both Emily and Gabe. Gretchen tells you that Gabe has made offensive anti-Semitic comments to her on several occasions, including calling Emily a "kike" and saying that Hitler had the right idea. Before you wrap up the investigation, you should go back to Gabe and confront him with these new allegations.

Gather Documents and Other Evidence

Unless harassment has escalated to physical touching or violence, it is primarily accomplished through communication. Racist epithets, pornographic images, demeaning jokes, slurs, or cartoons become harassment only when they are conveyed to another person who finds them offensive. Sometimes this communication is carried out in writing, at least in part. In a harassment investigation, part of your job is to gather any written communications relating to the problem. This could include emails, letters, notes, and items posted in cubicles, on company bulletin boards, or in shared company spaces (such as locker rooms, restrooms, or the mail room).

If the victim alleges that harassment resulted in a negative job action —for example, denial of a promotion, raise, or desired transfer—there should be a paper trail. Consider whether performance evaluations, payroll records, or other personnel documents will shed some light on what happened.

Official company documents might also corroborate or raise doubts about one person's story. For example, an employee complains that his supervisor harassed him by making fun of his disability during a meeting with a client. The supervisor denies the harassment and contends that he wasn't even in the office on the date of the alleged incident; he was on a long-planned vacation with his family. In this situation, you could take a look at schedules and attendance records to find out the truth.

Finally, physical evidence (other than documents) may play an important role in the investigation. If the complaining employee claims that the alleged harasser left gifts or offensive objects (such as some racy lingerie or a photo of a mass murderer), try to track down those items. Ask about photographs of offensive items, if they aren't still available. For example, several female employees complain that a cake baked in the shape of a naked woman was served at an office function. Obviously, the cake is long gone, but someone may have taken a picture of it (or you might be able to find out which bakery supplied the creation).

Evaluate the Evidence

Sometimes, there are many witnesses to harassment. For example, an entire work group may hear a supervisor's racist jokes or sexual come-ons. If the victim is complaining of a hostile work environment, other workers may have seen or heard something. Often, however, harassment occurs behind closed doors, and only the harasser and harassee really know what happened. If you're facing this type of investigation and you've received conflicting stories, your credibility determinations will be especially important.

Review the factors listed in Chapter 4 as you try to figure out where the truth lies. Two factors can be especially relevant in harassment cases: corroboration and motive.

- **Corroboration.** Even if no one else was in the room when the alleged harassment took place, you can still try to corroborate other details of each person's story. For example, a secretary complains that her boss called her into his office several times a week to tell her racist jokes a friend sends him by email. Although no one else was in the room, you might find other corroborating evidence. Did anyone see her entering or leaving his office? If so, did she appear to be upset? Did she tell anyone about the incidents? Has he told similar jokes to other employees? Can his emails be retrieved?

• **Motive.** Does either party have a motive to lie? Has either party told any other employees that he or she might make a false claim or false denial? Does the alleged harasser have any reason to act—or not to act—as the victim has claimed? Especially in sexual harassment cases where the parties have a prior romantic relationship, it's important to consider any reasons they might have for their actions and statements.

Take Action

If you find that some form of harassment occurred, your company has a legal obligation to take prompt corrective action that is reasonably calculated to end the harassment. The right corrective action is one that:

• stops the harassment
• prevents harassment from recurring, and
• restores the victim to the position he or she would have held absent the harassment.

Employers face some tough decisions when considering how to deal with harassment. On the one hand, an employer will be legally liable for any harassment that occurs following a complaint. In other words, the action you take must be effective at stopping the harassment. If it isn't, your company will be on the hook for any further incidents. On the other hand, an employee who is punished too severely might have a separate legal claim against your company for breach of contract, discrimination, or defamation, depending on the circumstances. The only way to walk this fine line is to make the punishment fit the crime. Consider:

• the severity of the incidents
• how often they occurred
• how many incidents took place in total
• the harm to the victim
• whether the law was violated

- whether workplace policies were violated
- whether the harasser holds a position of authority in the company, such as officer, manager, or supervisor (harassment by a higher-level employee is more serious and requires a heightened response)
- how the company has treated similar incidents in the past, and
- the harasser's history at the company; does the employee have a record of similar problems, or is this a onetime lapse from an otherwise stellar worker?

(For more information on choosing an appropriate response to wrongdoing—and on what to do if your investigation is inconclusive or reveals that no wrongdoing took place—see Chapter 4.)

Finally, don't forget the victim. Your company has a legal obligation to undo any harm the victim suffered as a result of the harassment. This could include:

- reinstating a victim who was fired for refusing to acquiesce to harassment
- restoring any job benefits or promotions a victim lost as a result of the harassment
- removing negative evaluations or critical comments in the victim's personnel file, if they arose from the harassment, and
- crediting the victim with any paid leave taken as a result of the harassment.

Document the Investigation

Document your harassment investigation just as you would any other workplace investigation. (See Chapter 4 for details.) Because of the Supreme Court's decisions creating a potential defense for employers who promptly investigate claims and take other steps to prevent harassment, you can expect that your report will end up in the hands of a jury if an employee files a lawsuit based on the underlying incidents. Make sure to write a report that's complete and professional and fully supports the conclusions you reached. (You'll find a sample report of a harassment investigation—along with policies, forms, and more—at this book's online companion page. See Appendix A to find out how to access these materials.)

If the Harassment Stops, You Made the Right Call

When courts have to decide whether an employer took appropriate corrective action, they focus on whether the harassment stopped. The ultimate test of whether an action was appropriate is effectiveness: Actions short of serious disciplinary measures can pass this test if they work.

EXAMPLE: Hattie, a housekeeper at a veterans medical center, complained that her coworker, Oliver, had grabbed her and put his arms around her twice during a work shift in September of 1996. Hattie reported the incidents to her supervisor, who investigated, confronted Oliver and told him the allegations were serious, and warned him to stay away from Hattie. Hattie told her supervisor that she was afraid of Oliver, although he hadn't done anything else to her since the incidents. A month later, Hattie filed a charge of sexual harassment; in response, Oliver was switched to a different shift, which overlapped Hattie's shift by an hour and a half.

Hattie sued for sexual harassment, complaining that her employer was required to "discipline" Oliver and that telling him to stay away from her and changing his shift didn't constitute discipline. The court disagreed. Because the employer took action that was effective in ending the harassment, the court found that it had met its obligation to take prompt remedial action. (*Star v. West*, 237 F.3d 1036 (9th Cir. 2001).)

If the harassment continues, however, the same corrective action might be insufficient. In the case of *Grego v. Meijer* (239 F.Supp.2d 676, W.D. Ky., 2002), an employer told the harasser that his comments were inappropriate and told him to leave the plaintiff alone. However, the court found these actions to be insufficient, because the victim had twice reported the harassment, the employer was aware that other women were being harassed by the same man, and the harassment continued after the reports.

Follow Up

Once the investigation is over, take some time to consider what you discovered. If you concluded that harassment—or even inappropriate behavior short of harassment—occurred, think about whether your company's policies against harassment and misconduct could use some revamping. Do employees understand what types of conduct violate company policy? Is there some confusion over whether particular types of behavior—joking around, teasing, flirtatious comments, or references to an employee's race or religion—are appropriate in the workplace? You may need to update company policies against harassment to ensure that everyone understands what's allowed and what's prohibited.

This is also a good time to consider harassment training. Many companies and workplace consultants offer harassment training, often in separate sessions for managers and employees. If your employees don't seem to get the difference between an innocent compliment and an offensive come-on, training can help make these distinctions clear.

You should also follow up directly with the employees involved in the incident, particularly if an employee complained of harassment. Retaliation can be a problem if the alleged harasser remains in the workplace, and it may be more likely if that employee was cleared of wrongdoing. The employee probably feels pretty upset about the allegations and the investigation, and that anger may naturally be directed at the employee who complained. The accused employee may feel entitled to take this frustration out on the complaining employee, because the company found that the allegations weren't supported by evidence.

To guard against this risk, meet with the complaining employee regularly after the investigation ends. You might hold these meetings every couple of weeks for a month or so, then check in once a month for a few months to make sure that no retaliation is taking place. You should also meet with the accused employee a few times to make sure that things are getting back to normal and that there have been no repercussions as a result of the investigation.

Investigating Workplace Theft

Some readers might be tempted to skip this chapter, thinking to themselves, "Our company couldn't have a theft problem; our employees wouldn't steal from us." Well, guess again. According to a 2014 survey conducted by the National Retail Federation, retailers lose more than $15 billion a year to employee theft, which is almost as much as they lose to shoplifters. And experts estimate that up to one-third of small business closures and bankruptcies are due to employee theft.

Perhaps the most surprising statistics are not about the dollars lost to employee theft, but about employees' willingness to steal. According to a 1998 survey by The Security Group of Cahners Business Information, 66% of employees would steal if they saw others getting away with it, and that's on top of the 13% who will steal regardless. These statistics show that an employer's response to theft can make a huge impact. A company that investigates and punishes thieves shows other employees that they shouldn't expect to get away with anything. Given these facts, it's imperative for companies to investigate every internal theft, no matter how large or small.

Theft investigations differ from investigation of workplace violence, harassment, or discrimination in several ways:

- **The company is usually the victim.** This means that you probably won't have to anticipate a potential lawsuit from an employee who was harmed by theft, so proving that your company took appropriate action to stop the misconduct won't be your foremost concern (as it often is in other types of investigations). It also means that you probably won't have a complaint or an interview to fill in the basic facts, which is why documents are the backbone of many theft investigations.

- **Theft is unlikely to be reported.** Most employees are not highly motivated to rat out their coworkers, especially if they are stealing from the company rather than from a particular individual. So, unlike other investigations, the real trick in a theft investigation is learning about the problem in the first place. This chapter describes some of the warning signs of various types of theft, so you'll know what types of situations warrant a closer look.

- **Theft investigations are whodunits.** Unlike a harassment or discrimination investigation, in which you sort out conflicting stories to determine whether something improper occurred, a theft investigation is usually about one thing: catching a thief. This means that you'll want to gather all of your evidence—and, usually, conduct all of your other interviews—before you confront your suspect.
- **Employers want payback.** In addition to stopping the flow of stolen money or property, you'll also want to get the company's cash or goods back, if possible.

Because theft investigations are unique, this chapter differs slightly from others in this book. First, it describes some common types of scams, rip-offs, and embezzlement that can occur in the workplace. This information will help you figure out if your company has a theft problem that requires investigation.

As in the other chapters in Part II, the second part of this chapter explains how the ten steps to an effective investigation work when you're faced with employee theft. But you will notice that the order of the steps is slightly different. Here, you'll look at documents before you conduct your interviews. You can't confront or interview a workplace suspect until you have examined all of the evidence that supports your position; this will help you elicit a confession, if possible. This chapter also addresses other unique features of a theft investigation, including tips for minimizing theft and dealing with insurers.

How Employees Steal

Most employee theft is never discovered. In most cases, employees get away with theft. The money is never returned, and the employers never figure out that profits are trickling out through the back door. That's why the real trick in a theft investigation is figuring out that theft has occurred in the first place.

The bad news is that the methods and means available to employee thieves are unlimited; thieves invent new ways to rip off their employers every day. The good news is that a handful of schemes and patterns come up again and again and account for much of the theft most employers are likely to face. By familiarizing yourself with these methods—and the telltale signs of workplace thievery—you'll know when your company might have an employee theft problem on its hands, which in turn will help you figure out when you need to investigate.

Follow the Money

No matter how an employee steals from an employer, the net result is the same: The employee has more money, while the company has less. The employee's newfound wealth is one key to discovering employee fraud. An employee who suddenly has fancy cars, a new summer home, and expensive clothing and jewelry (and no good explanation of how it all came about) is someone you'll want to talk to if you uncover a theft problem. Tread carefully when making inquiries, however, because snooping into an employee's personal finances can leave you open to an invasion of privacy claim. (See "Plan the Investigation," below, for more information.)

Why Do Employees Steal?

The most basic reason employees steal is because they can. In other words, the opportunity is there, and the employees believe they won't get caught or suffer any consequences. (Your company can nip this kind of theft in the bud by making it difficult to steal and by disciplining those who do steal.)

In addition to plain old opportunism, some other common reasons for workplace theft are:

- financial need (sometimes caused by problems like gambling or substance abuse)
- revenge for perceived mistreatment by the employer, and
- excitement. Some employees report stealing to see if they can get away with it or because they are bored.

Employee theft can be broken down into four basic categories:
- schemes for stealing money
- schemes for stealing property
- false disbursement schemes, which trick the company into paying money to the employee, and
- conflicts of interest, in which the employee uses his or her position in the company to favor particular vendors, suppliers, or other third parties.

Stealing Money

Employees can steal money in a variety of ways, from simply pocketing cash rather than putting it in the register to developing elaborate schemes for diverting funds (and covering their tracks). Here are some common ways employees steal money, and a few warning signs of a money theft problem.

> **TIP**
> **Stolen cash can be put on a gift card.** Each of the schemes in this section involve stolen money—but that doesn't mean an employee has to take it out of the store in cash. Gift cards are an increasingly common way for employees to take their booty. For example, an employee can void out a sale or enter a false refund and put the money on a gift card, or load up their own card with a customer's money while giving the customer a card with a lower balance. And, employees don't have to spend that card on store merchandise: They can sell them for cash or on the Internet to the highest bidder.

Skimming

In a skimming scheme, an employee steals money before it is entered into the company's records. Any employee who is responsible for receiving payments to the company can skim. This includes an employee who runs a register, records customer payments, does the company's books, or otherwise acts as an intake point for money coming into the company. Skimming can be tough to detect because it doesn't "unbalance" the company's books. Because the money is taken before it is entered into the records, the thief doesn't have to make up a reason why the money disappeared or make false entries in the company's accounting system.

EXAMPLES OF SKIMMING:

- **Failing to ring up or record sales.** The employee charges the customer and pockets the money, and the company never knows the sale was made. The skim can be accomplished at a cash register or anywhere else money comes in (for example, at customers' homes for an outside salesperson).
- **Diverting checks.** The employee endorses the incoming check on behalf of the company, then on his or her own behalf. The employee then cashes the check or deposits it in a personal account.
- **Under-ringing sales.** The employee records the sale for a particular amount, charges the customer more, and then pockets the difference.

 WARNING SIGNS

Skimming. Most types of skimming work by the following equation: The customer is receiving goods or services, but the employee—rather than the company—is getting paid for them. Therefore, most of the warning signs of skimming involve discrepancies between how much work your company is doing (or how much product it is moving) and how much money it is taking in.

Red flags for skimming include:

- lower revenues than expected
- increased inventory shrinkage (that is, goods are disappearing in numbers that are not accounted for in sales)
- declining cash sales as a percentage of total sales (because most employees want to pocket cash, these are the sales that don't get recorded), and
- customer complaints (a customer who notices an overcharge is likely to complain, but some customers will also tell you if they notice an employee who fails to ring up a sale, or if they receive a canceled check endorsed to someone other than the company).

Lapping

Lapping is a more complex method of theft that resembles a pyramid scheme. The employee steals some money as it comes into the company, then uses subsequent incoming payments to make up the difference. As long as the employee keeps up the scheme, the shortfall won't be noticed.

> EXAMPLE: Sam is the bookkeeper at a small company that supplies uniforms to institutional customers. All of the payments from customers go through Sam, who enters them in the company's books and deposits them into the company's bank account. Sam receives a payment for $100 from one customer, which he diverts to his own bank account and does not enter into the company's records. The next day, Sam receives a payment for $300 from a second customer. He credits $100 to the first customer's account, then waits for another payment to make up the shortfall to the second customer—and so on, and so on.

Many lapping schemes eventually collapse under their own weight. The employee won't be able to resist the temptation to take more and more money, which creates a larger and larger discrepancy to be hidden. At some point, there won't be enough money coming in to make up the shortfall. By the time this happens, however, your company might be out many thousands of dollars.

WARNING SIGNS

Lapping. Lapping is a pretty complicated affair, which requires the employee to keep careful track of precisely which Peter was robbed to pay which Paul, and by how much. Here are some of the red flags of lapping:

- a money-handling employee who never takes a day off work; if the lapper isn't in the office to apply incoming payments to shortchanged accounts (and to handle any queries about whether and when certain payments were made), the whole system will fall apart
- delays in posting customer payments
- a slowdown in incoming payments and/or an increase in late accounts, and
- customer complaints.

Void/Refund Schemes

Anyone who has ever worked a register knows about the void function, which zeroes out a sale that has already been entered. Voiding is legitimately used when the cashier enters an incorrect amount or a customer decides not to buy an item after all. However, it can also be used to back money out of the system, which the employee can then steal.

Refund schemes are similar: The employee enters a false refund, then pockets the "refunded" money. Employees can also use an employer's promotional refunds or discounts to steal money. For example, an employee who can lay hands on a stack of cards offering "$10 off any purchase of $50 or more" can apply the cards to sales (unbeknownst to the customer), then pocket the $10 discount on each transaction. Similarly, a waiter can use "buy one entrée, get one free" promotional ads to get some quick cash by applying the discount to tables that paid in full.

Either method can be used at cash registers or at any other point where money comes into the company.

> **EXAMPLE:** Joanna is a cashier in a drugstore. The store offers customer refunds on items that have not been used and are returned in their original packaging within 30 days of purchase. The cashiers are responsible for checking the condition of the item and making sure the customer shows a receipt; the cashier is supposed to cross the returned item off of the receipt, return it to the customer, then tender the refund, using the "refund" key on the register to record the money paid out. Joanna gets a lot of use out of that refund key—she records at least a refund a day, to the tune of several hundred dollars a week, then pockets the money at the end of her shift.

WARNING SIGNS

Void/refund schemes. In void and refund schemes, the company pays out money (to the employee) for returned or "unsold" items, but those items never find their way back to the shelves. Therefore, as in a skimming scenario, these schemes result in depleted inventory and shrinking cash. Here are some of the red flags of void and refund frauds:

- increased refund and void transactions
- cash sales declining as a percentage of total sales (again, because the employee wants to be "paid" in cash)

- irregularities in refund paperwork (missing documents, illegible customer names, duplicates)
- one employee getting particularly high numbers of voids, refunds, or customers taking advantage of a promotional offer, and
- voids or refunds issued at the end of a shift.

Stealing for the Customers

Some customers make out pretty well from employee theft: friends and family members of a dishonest employee at the cash register. Dishonest employees often give favorite customers free or heavily discounted merchandise, in what the retail industry calls "sweethearting." Discounts used to be accomplished through under-ringing sales (punching in a lower price) or simply not ringing some items up. These days, when scanners register the price in many stores, it's often accomplished through not scanning every item purchased (or not scanning any at all). If items aren't scanned at all, this is essentially shoplifting, given away through increased merchandise shrinkage and shady employee behavior at the register (such as directing the sweetheart customers to wait to have their sales rung up or taking them ahead of other customers, often because the employee is waiting for an unsupervised opportunity to do the deal).

Ripping Off Customers

Schemes to steal from customers (rather than from the company) are very troubling for business owners. Although the company isn't losing money directly off its bottom line, its employees are ripping off the very people it most wants to please. Because this kind of theft depends on customer ignorance, it doesn't always work. All it takes is a customer complaint or two, and you'll uncover the whole scheme, as long as you are vigilant.

The most common way employees steal from customers is simple overcharging. For example, a waiter might charge a diner for something the diner didn't order or receive, or a cashier might ring up an item twice or charge more than the store does for an item. If the customer doesn't notice, then the employee takes the money attributable to the overcharge. These schemes can get more elaborate and more costly as well. An employee might steal customer credit card numbers to use for personal purchases, for example.

> **WARNING SIGNS**
>
> **Stealing from customers.** When employees steal from customers, the customers themselves are your early warning system. Here are some red flags of this type of theft:
> - customer complaints, especially when most of them point to the same employee
> - frequent "errors" and voids attributable to the same employee (these are the signs that the customer caught on to the overcharge, and the employee had to correct the bill), and
> - increased contacts from credit card issuers. Customers have the option of protesting an overcharge or unauthorized use of their credit card to their credit card issuer, which must then investigate the situation. If you start hearing about a number of questionable charges by your company, you know you have a problem on your hands.

Larceny

An employee commits larceny by taking money after it has been entered into the company's records. These are the least imaginative—and easiest to detect—theft schemes, because the losses will show up in your company's books eventually.

> **EXAMPLES OF LARCENY:**
> - A cashier takes $20 or $30 from the register during each shift.
> - An employee responsible for making bank deposits takes cash out of the deposit bag, then alters the deposit slip to show the lower amount.
> - An employee steals money from the petty cash drawer.
> - An employee writes company checks payable to "cash" or to him- or herself.

WARNING SIGNS

Larceny. An employee who commits larceny makes either no efforts or halfhearted efforts to cover up the crime. Therefore, the red flags of larceny are all about discrepancies between how much money your company should have and how much money it actually has, including:

- cash register drawers that are always short
- bank deposits that don't match total sales, as shown by receipts, register tapes, and so on
- cash missing from anywhere the company keeps it (the petty cash account, a safe, the area where the company keeps change for registers)
- company checks that are missing or out of sequence, and
- company checks made out to "cash" or to an employee, or excessive numbers of checks that are recorded as void.

Stealing From Other Employees

Some workplace thieves target their coworkers. For example, you may face a rash of missing wallets or personal items stolen from employee offices. This type of theft is less common than stealing from an employer, for two reasons: (1) While employees may perceive stealing from the company as a "victimless crime," stealing from a coworker directly harms a particular person, which makes it harder for the thief to justify; and (2) very few employees would hesitate to turn in a thief who was stealing from them, while many employees would be reluctant to turn in a coworker who was ripping off the company.

The warning signs of a thief who is ripping off coworkers are pretty straightforward: Employees will notice money or items missing. In addition, watch out for employees who spend time in another employee's work space when that employee isn't there, or in a common area, such as a locker room or changing room, without a good reason. Some employees try to avoid detection by committing theft when they know other employees won't be in their usual places: before work hours, after work hours, during lunch, or during times when all employees are supposed to be elsewhere, such as during a fire drill, companywide event, or mandatory training.

Stealing Property

Although most workplace thieves are after money, some will go after other things, such as merchandise, raw materials, equipment, trade secrets, and so on. It's easy to understand why employees steal money: They can use it immediately, to purchase whatever they want. But stealing property is different. Unless the employee wants the item for personal use (as might be the case with a computer or jewelry), the employee will have to convert the item into cash or some other compensation. This means that those who steal goods may be selling goods online, or may be working with an outsider, such as a fence or a competitor who wants to buy the goods.

Theft of Goods

If you take a look around your company, you'll probably find lots of things an enterprising thief could take. If your company is in the manufacturing industry, its raw materials and finished product could be stolen. If your company is in retail, its merchandise is up for grabs. And virtually every business uses some equipment, from computers and phones to tools, building supplies, and heavy machinery.

Common shipping and receiving theft schemes include under-counting goods received—or shorting customers on goods shipped—and keeping the extra stuff; categorizing received items as damaged; or fudging paperwork to make it look like more goods are legitimately leaving the company than are actually being ordered by customers.

> **EXAMPLE:** Roger works in the warehouse of a computer store. When he receives shipments from suppliers, he sometimes sets aside equipment like modems or speakers, which he steals at the end of his shift. To keep his theft from showing up when inventory is taken, Roger sets aside the invoice, alters the numbers, and submits a color photocopy of the doctored document.

Employees who steal merchandise often act just like shoplifters. They take your products and slip them into purses or bags, stuff them into coat pockets, or spirit them off to their cars during a break or after work hours.

Equipment thieves sometimes concoct stories to explain away the missing property. For example, an employee who has a company-issued laptop computer might falsely claim that it was stolen from the employee's car or home.

> **WARNING SIGNS**
>
> **Thefts of goods.** An employee who steals goods needs some way to get them out of your company and sometimes needs a third party to sell them to. Here are a few red flags:
> - employees who are in the wrong place at the wrong time, take frequent breaks, or carry bags or wear bulky clothing
> - employees who meet with outsiders on or near company property
> - employees who leave work with large packages
> - shipping and receiving paperwork that has been altered or is missing, and
> - inventory numbers that don't add up.

Intellectual Property Theft

The real value of many businesses lies not in their equipment or their merchandise, but in their intellectual property (IP): the trade secrets, customer lists, formulae, recipes, business methods, and other intangible information that make the company a success. An employee who steals these assets can wreak enormous havoc on a company. Usually, these assets are what give the company an edge over competitors. Once the information is out, the competitive edge is gone.

Some IP thieves sell business secrets to competing companies, while others use the secrets to start their own competitive businesses, publicize the information as acts of revenge, or give the secrets to subsequent employers.

> **EXAMPLE:** Harold works for a sports food company that manufactures energy bars, drinks, and gels. The company recently developed a new line of energy bars that are salty rather than sweet—the end result is a bar that tastes like potato chips or pretzels rather than cookies or candy. The bars have proven enormously popular with athletes, and competitors are trying desperately to reverse engineer the product. Harold downloads the company's recipes and sells them to a competitor, who then claims to have independently cracked the code.

WARNING SIGNS

IP theft. Unfortunately, employers often learn of IP theft only after the horses have left the barn. Here are some red flags:

- An employee leaves to start a competing business.
- Competitors suddenly develop products that are similar to your company's or start calling on your company's customers.
- Unusual attempts are made to access physical areas of your company or portions of its computer system where trade secrets are kept. Employees who are in the wrong place at the wrong time—in the workplace or in cyberspace—bear a closer look.
- The number of computer password violations increases, indicating that someone is trying to get into sensitive files.

CAUTION

Watch out for identity theft. Sometimes, a workplace thief steals a customer list not to do business with them, but to misuse their identities for financial fraud. Whenever personal information is stolen from your company, whether from customers or from other employees, identity theft may not be far behind. In these situations, your company might have an obligation to notify those whose identifying information has been stolen, so they can take steps to prevent fraud by, for example, putting a security freeze on their credit report.

Fake Disbursements

In a fake disbursement scheme, an employee gets the company to pay money to the employee on false pretenses. Rather than simply stealing the money, the employee submits phony invoices, expense reimbursements, or other paperwork so that the company will disburse money to the employee. In effect, the employee submits illegitimate requests through legitimate company channels to commit the crime. Here are a few of the most common types of fake disbursements.

Phony Vendor/Supplier and Other Billing Schemes

Many an employer has paid money to a nonexistent vendor: a company or account set up by an employee, who then submits fake invoices or other requests for payment to the company. An employee might also set up a false vendor in order to overcharge the company for goods. For example, an employee might establish a company to purchase raw materials the employer uses to make its products, then sell the materials to the employer at a steep markup.

> **EXAMPLE 1:** George is in charge of buying materials for a clothing manufacturer. The company buys buttons in huge quantities from a variety of suppliers. George sets up his own company and purchases buttons from some of his employer's biggest suppliers. Then, in his role as buyer for the clothing company, he purchases buttons from his own company, at a sweet 100% markup.

> **EXAMPLE 2:** Hannah is a bookkeeper for a company that provides human resources training to businesses across the nation. The company has some on-staff trainers, but it also uses consultants to provide training in distant locations. These consultants submit invoices for payment. Hannah starts drafting her own invoices and slipping them in with the consultants' requests for payment. The invoices are submitted in the name of "HHH Training," a name she also uses to open a bank account. When the checks are cut, she simply deposits the HHH Training check in her new bank account.

An employee can also set up a phony billing scheme using the company's existing vendors. For example, an employee might copy a legitimate invoice and submit it twice: The first check goes to the vendor, and the second goes to the employee. A more elaborate version of this scheme involves refunds. The employee submits the invoice twice and actually pays the vendor twice. When the vendor realizes the error and refunds the second payment, the employee keeps the money.

WARNING SIGNS

Phony vendor schemes. In a phony vendor scheme—as in other fake disbursement scenarios—an employee covers the theft with false paperwork. This means that your first clue to the problem will often be a document that doesn't look quite right.

Here are some red flags to phony vendor schemes:

- new vendors who are unknown to the company
- invoices that lack the usual information, such as a taxpayer ID number, address, or phone number, or are not printed on letterhead
- duplicate invoices or invoices that appear to have been altered
- invoices that don't contain the usual billing detail, or that request nice round numbers (for example, if most of your consulting invoices list hours expended on various types of tasks and an hourly rate, you should question an invoice that requests a flat $5,000 without explanation)
- vendors who have the same name (or initials), address, or telephone number as one of your employees
- canceled vendor or supplier checks that have been endorsed by one of your employees, and
- increased costs for vendors, suppliers, or materials.

Expense Schemes

If employees are entitled to claim expense reimbursements, your company is at risk of paying out money for expenses that were never incurred. For example, an employee might claim false expenses, claim that personal expenses were incurred for business purposes, or make unauthorized charges on a company credit card.

> EXAMPLE: Marvin takes a three-day business trip for his employer. He submits an expense reimbursement form claiming that he spent $150 a night on a hotel room, about $50 each day on food, $50 on cab fare to get from the hotel to customer locations, and $300 taking a client and her husband to a fancy restaurant for dinner. In fact, Marvin stayed with his brother-in-law, ate fast food, took public transportation, and had dinner at the client's home. Less money spent on bus fare and hamburgers, Marvin can clear almost $1,000 in phony reimbursements from a single trip.

WARNING SIGNS

Phony expenses. The documents an employee submits in order to be reimbursed are often the key to unraveling expense fraud. Here are some red flags:

- failure to submit receipts for claimed expenses
- receipts that have been doctored or photocopied, do not clearly show the merchant and amount of sale, are not dated, or appear to claim duplicate expenses (for example, two receipts for dinner on the same day)
- expense claims for personal items
- expense claims that are higher than they should be (for example, an especially high rate for a hotel room or meal), and
- expense claims that are just below the limit for an internal audit. Some companies routinely approve expense claims up to a certain amount but will look more closely at a claim that exceeds the limit. An employee whose expenses always approach the audit limit without crossing it might be gaming the system.

Conflicts of Interest

In a conflict of interest scheme, an employee uses company resources or a company position to create illegitimate moneymaking opportunities. These schemes often involve hiring preferred vendors or suppliers, either in exchange for a bribe or kickback or because the vendor has some financial connection to the employee.

Bribes and Kickbacks

An employee who takes money to help an outsider get business with the company is participating in a bribe or kickback scheme. A bribe is a simple payment up front for the privilege of getting work; a kickback is a payment of a percentage or portion of the money the outsider makes from the company.

> EXAMPLE: Ron is the office manager for a large medical practice. His responsibilities include making sure that the vending machines are stocked and that coffee, snacks, and other amenities are available to the staff. A new vendor who is trying to break into the field offers Ron a 5% kickback to get the contract for coffee service at his company. Ron agrees and soon begins collecting a monthly payment from the vendor.

WARNING SIGNS

Bribes and kickbacks. These schemes involve third parties: not only the company that is paying the employee, but also the companies that are left out in the cold because they are not paying the employee. Here are some red flags:

- vendor complaints; if your company's usual vendors suddenly find themselves out of a contract, they might complain (and if an employee tries to hit up an unwilling company for a bribe, you might hear about it)
- new and unknown vendors
- increased costs; a vendor who has to pay a bribe or kickback is going to have to charge more to cover that cost and an employee who is receiving a kickback wants the vendor to earn as much as possible from your company
- increasing inventory or services (because the employee wants your company to buy as much as possible from the crooked vendor), and
- a high percentage of business going to one vendor or supplier (the one who's paying off the employee).

Self-Dealing

In a self-dealing scenario, an employee uses his or her position in the company to improperly favor outsiders who are connected with the employee (family members, friends, or the employee's own side business, for example). An employee might hire her husband's law firm to provide legal services, contract to purchase computer training from a friend, or arrange to sell your company's products—at a discount—to her own company, for quick markup and resale.

> **EXAMPLE:** Shawna runs her own crafts business making scented candles and bath salts. Her boyfriend, Tom, works for a chain of gift shops that lease space in upscale hotels. Tom arranges for the company to purchase Shawna's products at a hefty markup, even though it already sells several similar items.

WARNING SIGNS

Self-dealing. The whole point of self-dealing is to favor certain vendors and suppliers over others. This favoritism sometimes leads to discovery.

Here are some red flags:

- new or unknown vendors
- vendors who have the same name, address, or telephone number as an employee
- complaints from vendors who are not receiving special treatment or who were frozen out so the employee could favor a relative or friend
- higher than usual costs for products or services, and
- a high percentage of business going to one vendor.

The "Typical" Workplace Thief

In 2011, KPMG International released a report, "Who is the typical fraudster?" Although workplace theft can, of course, be committed by anyone, the report found that the "typical" perpetrator is a man between the ages of 36 and 45, who holds a senior management position in a finance-related role, and has worked for the company for more than ten years. Interestingly, the report also found that workplace thieves are more likely than not to collude with others in their scheme, rather than working alone.

Ten Steps to a Successful Theft Investigation

This section explains how to apply the basic investigation steps covered in Part I of this book to an investigation of employee theft. If you haven't read Part I, you should do so before getting into this more specific material; the discussion that follows assumes that you are already familiar with basic investigation procedures discussed in Part I.

Decide Whether to Investigate

Once you learn about employee theft, you should always investigate, regardless of how much is missing. Studies have shown that workplace thieves tend to start small, then expand their operations. They take small amounts of money or items that aren't very valuable, then wait to see what happens. If nobody catches on, pretty soon the sky's the limit. Investigating a $50 register shortage or slight increase in inventory shrinkage today could save your company from a much more expensive theft scheme tomorrow.

How Employers Learn of Theft

According to the Association of Certified Fraud Examiners, employers find out about workplace fraud—including theft by employees and managers—in a variety of ways. The most common way is a tip from another employee. Somewhat less encouraging is the second most common method by which employers learn of workplace fraud: by accident. Here are some others:

- internal audits or internal controls
- external audits
- tips from vendors or customers
- anonymous tips, and
- notification by law enforcement personnel.

Your investigation will also serve as a deterrent to others. If other employees see a coworker getting away with stealing from the company, they are more likely to start taking a five-finger discount as well.

Investigating will also shield your company from legal hassles down the road. If you want to take action against an employee whom you believe is stealing from the company, you will want some solid evidence to back up your decision. Otherwise, the employee might sue for defamation.

EXAMPLE: Maurice is a sales clerk at a clothing store. Another clerk, Rhonda, tells you that she saw Maurice putting several expensive leather jackets into a bag and taking it out to his car. You immediately fire Maurice. If Maurice actually stole the jackets, then there's nothing to worry about. Because truth is a defense to a defamation claim, treating Maurice as a thief doesn't constitute defamation if he actually is a thief. But if Maurice didn't steal the jackets—if Rhonda made the whole story up to cover her own theft, for example—then you have a major problem. Not only did you falsely treat Maurice as a thief, but you also didn't even bother to look into the allegations. Now you're facing a potential lawsuit and you still have a thief on the payroll.

Also, if the thief stole from someone outside of the company—for example, a customer, client, or vendor—then your company could be liable for any future losses that person suffers if it fails to take reasonable precautions to stop the theft. And reasonable precautions include investigating to find and stop the culprit.

Employee Theft and the Sarbanes-Oxley Act

In the wake of Enron and other corporate accounting scandals, Congress passed the Sarbanes-Oxley Act of 2002. This law is intended to increase the accountability of publicly traded companies for their reported financial results, thereby making sure that investors have accurate information on which to base their decisions. Among the law's many requirements is a mandate that all publicly traded companies must establish procedures by which employees can anonymously and confidentially submit concerns about questionable accounting and auditing matters. Certain kinds of employee theft might fall within this category, particularly if they result in doctored financial records. The Act also imposes obligations on public companies that discover errors or falsifications in their financial reports.

The 2010 Dodd-Frank financial reform law gives employers added incentive to quickly investigate and resolve claims of financial wrongdoing: a bounty program. Someone who reports possible violations of federal security laws directly to the Securities and Exchange Commission (SEC) may be entitled to a share of what the agency recovers. If the whistleblower voluntarily provides the SEC with original information that leads to a successful enforcement action, resulting in an award of more than $1 million in monetary sanctions, that person qualifies for a bounty of 10 to 30%, depending on a number of factors. Here's the most relevant one for investigators: If the whistleblower is an employee of the company, a higher amount may be awarded to someone who first tried to use the company's internal complaint process before going to the SEC.

Take Immediate Action, If Necessary

If you suspect employee theft (or you know that someone is stealing, but you don't know who), there are a few actions you can take right away, before you start investigating. Of course, the options available to you will depend on what you know, what type of theft you suspect, and who might be responsible.

Enhance Security and Safeguards

If you can isolate the theft to one area of operations, you can take some steps to make stealing more difficult. An effective way to do this is to simply add more people to any process where money might be disappearing. Because most workplace theft is committed by employees acting alone, increasing the number of people who have to be involved in any transaction will foil opportunities for theft. Fraud experts call this "segregation" of job duties: If you make sure that no one employee is responsible for every step of a transaction, you will make it much more difficult for any employee to use the transaction as a vehicle for theft.

For example, if you know that there is something amiss in the bookkeeping department, your company could require a second signature (of the company president or other high-ranking official) on all outgoing checks, or have someone outside the department open all incoming mail and log any payments received. If there's a problem in the receiving department, the company could require two employees to check the items received against the purchase order, invoice, and/or packing slip.

There are other ways to increase workplace controls against theft. Requiring additional paperwork—particularly paperwork that involves other people—is another good way to cut down on theft. For example, if you suspect that a cashier is giving false refunds, your company could require all cashiers to fill in a form with the name, address, and phone number of every customer who received a refund. Let employees know that you will follow up with the customers, then do it. Or, if you are concerned about inflated expense reports, require employees to submit a dated, itemized receipt for all claimed expenses.

TIP

Make safeguards permanent once the investigation is over. The same procedures that will help you draw the brakes on theft while you conduct your investigation will help your company prevent theft in the future. (See "Follow Up," below, for more information on preventing theft.)

Another way to deter employee theft (at least temporarily) is to tell employees that the company will be conducting a routine audit for the next couple of weeks. (This will also give you a good cover for your investigation.) Of course, you can't do this forever, but most workplace thieves will put their schemes on hold if they know that scrutiny will be especially high.

Suspend the Suspected Wrongdoer

If you have a pretty good idea who is behind a theft problem, you might consider suspending that employee with pay while you conduct the investigation. One benefit of this approach—other than immediately stopping the theft—is that the employee won't have time to destroy workplace evidence. On the other hand, by tipping your hand at the outset, you lose any chance you might have to catch the employee in the act. You'll have to weigh the company's risk of further losses against your need for this kind of evidence of the theft.

> EXAMPLE: Rick is the night manager of a department store's warehouse. In the past several months, the warehouse has had some serious "shrinkage" problems, particularly in big screen televisions. The store owner suspects Rick because the thefts are taking place at night and Rick is the only worker who has a key to the loading dock area, the only place where the televisions could be removed without attracting suspicion. If he suspended Rick right away, the owner could stop the theft problem, but he might never get proof that Rick is behind the thefts. Instead, the owner decides to hang around outside the loading dock for a few nights after the store receives a large shipment of television sets. When he sees Rick and a couple of his friends making off with a few TVs, the owner has all the proof he needs.

Suspending an employee before you conduct an investigation also poses some legal risks. If your hunch proves wrong, the company could be liable for damaging the suspended employee's reputation. For this reason, you should only suspend an employee if you have strong, objective evidence of wrongdoing, and you should not publicize the suspension in the workplace. You should also make special efforts to wrap up your investigation quickly.

Contact Your Company's Insurance Carrier

Most businesses carry insurance for a variety of potential mishaps. Believe it or not, a company can insure itself against employee theft. If your company has a fidelity bond or a crime loss or employee dishonesty policy, contact the insurance agent right away to find out how to file a claim. If an employee theft is covered under one of these policies, you will ordinarily have a short period of time after you discover the loss to notify the insurance company. Your agent or a business lawyer can tell you what documents and information you need to file a claim.

> ⓘ **CAUTION**
> **If theft may be covered by insurance, contact a lawyer before you investigate or report the loss.** When your company buys an insurance policy, it gives the insurance company the right of "subrogation." This means that the insurance company has the legal authority to proceed against anyone who causes a covered loss in order to get back the money it had to pay out on the policy. If you take any action that compromises the insurance company's subrogation right, your company may not be entitled to collect on its policy. If your company's insurance covers employee theft, talk to a lawyer right away to get some advice on conducting an investigation that won't run afoul of the insurance company's rights. Otherwise, the insurance company may refuse to make good on your company's claim.

Choose the Investigator

You'll find general information on choosing an investigator—including the importance of impartiality, experience, and professionalism—in Chapter 2.

While those qualities are important when investigating any kind of workplace problem, investigating employee theft often requires some additional qualifications, including subject matter expertise and interview skills.

Bringing in the Police

Should you call the police to investigate your workplace theft? It depends on the situation. Once you bring in the police, the investigation will be out of your hands. You'll also have the law in your workplace. This can lead to all kinds of problems, from discovery of things that you wish they hadn't found to serious morale problems in your workforce. On the other hand, the police can use investigative tools that are pretty much off limits to private employers. They are very experienced at conducting interrogations and getting suspects to confess.

Ultimately, it probably isn't worth bringing in the police unless your company has a very serious problem that it can't handle alone, such as an employee who has stolen controlled substances or weapons. Investigating these types of situations yourself could lead to greater problems, such as liability for personal injuries that result from use of the dangerous items or from your investigation. In situations that are less urgent, your company might lose more than it gains by calling the police. And unless the problem is fairly sizable, the police may not be willing to spend many resources going after your workplace thief.

If you do bring in the police, make sure that the information you give them is accurate and fair. Employees who are ultimately exonerated can sue for malicious prosecution if there was no good cause for the prosecution and your company maliciously gave the police false or misleading information. The likelihood of being sued for malicious prosecution is quite low, but you should still consult with an attorney if you are considering going to the police.

Subject Matter Expertise

As you can see from the discussion above, unraveling an employee theft scheme sometimes requires a good deal of technical knowledge.

Depending on the type of theft you are facing, you may need some special expertise to complete the investigation. For example, investigating the theft of intellectual property might require a background in computer technology or science. Investigating a complex vendor fraud or lapping scheme might require accounting or auditing skills.

If you're facing a large-scale or highly sophisticated theft problem, you should consider using an outside investigator who has the necessary expertise. Another option is to team up an in-house investigator with an expert who can provide the necessary information. You can use an internal expert (for example, the head of your company's technology services division or its chief financial officer) or bring in an expert from the outside. If you decide to bring in an outside expert to assist with the investigation, remember that your company will ultimately be responsible for any actions the expert takes. This means that someone on your company's payroll should be overseeing the expert's work. In addition, if the theft is related to confidential company information, you should have the expert sign a nondisclosure agreement.

CAUTION

Don't use an internal expert unless you're sure that person isn't involved in the theft. If you need a particular type of expertise to ferret out a theft, chances are good that your thief also has some experience in that area. This means that your in-house expert could also be your prime suspect and, ultimately, your thief. To avoid this "fox guarding the henhouse" problem, make certain that any internal expert you use could not have committed the theft. If you aren't sure, bring in an outsider.

Here are some examples of experts who might be valuable in an employee theft investigation:

• **Forensic accountants.** These experts review a company's financial documents for signs of fraud. They comb through the books looking for missing paperwork, financial improprieties, unexplained transactions, and other red flags of theft. (Although their title makes them sound like crime scene specialists, "forensic" means only that the work is done in possible preparation for legal proceedings.)

- **Certified fraud examiners.** These specialists—who come from many different professional backgrounds, including criminology, accounting, and law—are trained in the prevention and detection of fraud. Like forensic accountants, they can help uncover signs of fraud in your company's books.
- **Document examiners.** These experts examine disputed or suspect documents and determine how old they are, whether they are copies or originals, whether they have been altered or supplemented, and whether handwriting and signatures are genuine, among other things. If you are facing a document-intensive investigation— particularly if there is a question about whether documents have been altered—these experts may be useful.
- **Computer specialists.** Sometimes, you just need a techie to help you sort things out. A computer specialist can help you figure out whether certain files or documents were accessed, altered, deleted, or copied. They can also track who has been where in your company's computer system, which could help you uncover bookkeeping fraud or intellectual property theft.
- **Experts in your company's field.** If you are trying to figure out whether your company's intellectual property has been copied, taken, or handed off to others, an expert who is familiar with the type of work your company does can help.

Interviewing Skills

An investigation of employee theft has a slightly different focus than other investigations. Unlike a harassment or discrimination case, in which your ultimate goal is to find out what happened, your goal in a theft investigation is to gather the proof you need and then get a particular employee to admit committing the theft.

This means your investigator will have to be skilled not only at gathering information, but also at eliciting confessions. Some techniques for interviewing a suspected employee are described in "Interviews," below. However, if you don't have anyone on your staff who has some experience in these types of interviews—including how to press for admissions without crossing any legal lines—it might be a good idea to hire an outside investigator or certified fraud examiner to help out.

Plan the Investigation

In a theft investigation, you have several goals. First and foremost, you have to figure out whether theft occurred or there's some other explanation for the problem. If you conclude that you are dealing with theft, you will want to find the thief, extract a confession if you can, and get back as much of the stolen property as possible. This means that you'll want to gather as much information as you can up front, before you interview the suspect, so you'll have lots of ammunition and evidence to encourage a confession. The point of your investigation planning is either to come up with a suspect or list of suspects or to figure out what evidence of theft might exist that exonerates or implicates your suspect. So your planning will depend on whether or not you have a suspect at the outset.

If you learned of the theft through a complaint, anonymous or otherwise, you can begin with those allegations. If theft is suspected because of anomalies in paperwork, problems in bank balances, or inventory shortages, you can start there.

Starting Without a Suspect

If there is no immediate suspect, start by figuring out what you know. Did someone make a complaint about theft? If so, review the allegations. What was stolen? When and where? Some complaints are quite detailed; others are more enigmatic ("Your employees are robbing you blind!"). In either situation, catalog the information carefully.

> EXAMPLE: The XYZ Corporation supplies canned food products to hospitals, schools, and other institutions. The food is shipped to XYZ's warehouses, where it is stored until it is packaged and loaded in response to customer orders. XYZ receives an anonymous complaint, dropped in a company suggestion box, that says this: "Wonder why the Seattle warehouse is missing so much inventory? You might want to check out what the night shift is up to."
>
> Pretty sparse complaint, right? Well, yes and no. The complaint doesn't indicate exactly what is happening and who is responsible. But it does indicate that there is some kind of inventory theft going on during the

night shift at the Seattle warehouse. Based on this complaint, you might immediately pull inventory records for all of the company's warehouses, get an employee roster of the night shift workers in Seattle, and plan to visit the Seattle warehouse at night, unannounced, to see what's going on.

Whether you start from a complaint or simply some management suspicions or "funny numbers," you'll want to figure out two things: what's missing and who had access to it. Often, this will require you to review financial records and other documents. (See "Gather Documents and Other Evidence," below, for information on documents that might be helpful to a theft investigation.) Before you actually begin interviewing anyone, you'll want to have the best possible handle on what has been stolen, how, when, and where. This information will help you narrow down your list of suspects.

As you review what you know, start piecing together the information you need to figure out who's behind the theft. Depending on the circumstances, you may need to find out who makes bank deposits; who works each cash register and when; what the inventory, sales, and bookkeeping records show; or who has access to altered records or missing cash. Gather any information you can behind the scenes, before you start your interviews.

Starting With a Suspect

If you are beginning your investigation with a suspect in mind, your first steps will depend on why this person has come under suspicion. Do you know what the alleged theft is? If so, consider what documents, witnesses, or other evidence will help you figure out what (if anything) is missing and how it was taken.

If you have only a name and little other information to go on (as might be the case if you receive a vague, anonymous complaint, such as "John is crooked" or "Kathy is a thief"), consider what types of assets the suspect has access to. Then, think about documents, witnesses, or other evidence that might help you figure out whether anything was taken, and how.

> ⚠ CAUTION
>
> **The theft you know about may be just the tip of the iceberg.**
> Some thieves aren't satisfied with one type of scam. Like the murderer who is discovered by police after being pulled over for a traffic violation, a workplace thief may be caught for a relatively small offense but be guilty of much more. For example, you might catch a manager submitting reimbursement forms for expenses he never incurred but never discover that he is also accepting bribes from clients. Once you have evidence of a theft, don't stop there. Examine everything the employee had access to and every transaction the employee was involved in to make sure you know all of the bad news.

Privacy Issues

This section offers some basic tips that will help you plan an investigation that won't violate employees' privacy rights. Generally, however, the best strategy to avoid privacy problems is to gather only the information you need to know, through the least intrusive means possible. Usually, this means you should investigate by interviewing employees and reviewing company documents, rather than through searches, surveillance, or lie detector tests.

For an overview of privacy issues, see Chapter 1. This section focuses on a couple of issues that are of particular concern in a theft investigation: workplace searches and polygraph testing.

Workplace Searches

Workplace thieves have to put the money and property they steal somewhere. And an employee who is running a complicated bookkeeping scam (such as a lapping scheme) probably keeps an extra set of books nearby, to help keep track of things. To uncover this kind of evidence, you may need to search an employee's desk, locker, or other work space, or to look inside an employee's personal belongings, such as a purse or knapsack. But whenever you conduct a workplace search, you risk violating your employees' privacy rights, particularly if your company doesn't have the right policies in place.

When judges evaluate whether a particular workplace search is legal, they usually try to balance two competing concerns. First, the law considers the employer's justification for performing the search: An employer with a strong, work-related reason for searching has the best chance of prevailing. The court then balances the employer's reason for searching against the worker's reasonable expectations of privacy. An employee who reasonably expects—based on the employer's policies, past practices, and common sense—that the employer will not search certain areas has the strongest argument here.

The court considers the relative strengths of these two competing interests to decide whether a particular search passes legal muster. The more steps employers take to lessen their workers' expectations of privacy and the stronger the employers' reasons to search, the more likely a court is to find the search legal.

> EXAMPLE 1: The owner of a large jewelry store notices that several expensive rings are missing from the display case. He immediately cuts the locks on every employee's locker and rifles through the employees' personal belongings. The store has no search policies, employee lockers have never been searched before, and the store has made no efforts to warn employees that their lockers might be searched. This search might violate employees' privacy rights.

> EXAMPLE 2: Now assume that the jewelry store has a search policy warning employees that all company property, including lockers, is subject to search. The store also requires employees to give the store owner a copy of their locker combinations or duplicate keys to their lockers. In this situation, the store has a much better argument that the search is legal. By warning employees that their lockers might be searched and by driving this point home by insisting that employees provide the store with a means of entering their lockers, the store has done all it can to diminish the employees' expectations of privacy.

CAUTION

Privacy is a highly volatile legal issue. Each year, workers bring lawsuits claiming that employers have invaded their privacy by conducting improper searches. The outcome of each of these cases depends on the judge's view of the worker's misconduct and the employer's methods for getting to the bottom of things, as well as the effect of any state laws on the topic. If a court rules against your company in an invasion of privacy lawsuit, the company may have to pay financial damages or be subjected to a court order prohibiting it from taking similar action in the future. Because there are no guarantees in this area of the law, most employers should consult with a lawyer before conducting any but the most routine searches.

Going Undercover

Many private investigators and investigation firms advise placing an operative undercover to unravel complicated employee theft schemes. For example, if you suspect an employee of stealing expensive merchandise for resale, an undercover investigator could pose as a potential purchaser. If you are facing a kickback/bribe scheme, the investigator could pose as a vendor. Or, if you believe several employees are working together in a theft ring, the investigator could come in as a new employee hoping to get in on the deal.

However, using an undercover agent can get fairly complicated. Because the agent must be someone unknown to your employees, you will have to bring in an outsider. And because undercover work is difficult and nuanced, you'll want to bring in a professional, which will quickly run up some significant costs. Only if your company is losing substantial assets will this make financial sense.

There are also legal pitfalls to watch out for. Remember, your company is legally responsible for actions taken on its behalf by an outside agency. This means that if the undercover worker invades an employee's privacy rights by, for example, conducting an illegal search or getting too involved in an employee's life outside the workplace, your company could be on the hook for damages. For all these reasons, if you are seriously considering using an undercover operative, you should hire an experienced and highly recommended investigation firm. For more information on using undercover agents, see *Undercover Investigations in the Workplace*, by Eugene F. Ferraro (Butterworth-Heinemann, 2000).

Here are a few tips that will help you stay on the right side of the law:

- **Make sure policies are in place before you need to search.** If your company warns employees in advance that certain areas (like desks or lockers) may be subject to search, employees will have lower expectations of privacy in those areas, and less reason to complain about a particular search.
- **Search only when necessary.** You need the strongest possible justification for your search, especially if you will be digging through employees' personal belongings.
- **Never search an employee's body.** Some employers become so zealous that they want to physically search workers for stolen items. This is always a bad idea. All of us have a very strong privacy interest in our own bodies and the clothing worn on them. Before you frisk workers, talk to a lawyer (or call in the police).
- **Restrooms and changing areas are off limits.** Most employees legitimately expect that they will not be watched while using the bathroom or changing their clothes. This expectation is highly reasonable. Some states even have laws prohibiting surveillance of these private areas. If you really think you'll need a bathroom monitor to catch a workplace thief, talk to a lawyer.

CAUTION

Learn the law on vehicle searches. In some situations, you may want to search an employee's vehicle (for example, to look for stolen items or illegal drugs). If the car is owned by the company and provided to the employee to use, your company is likely on safe ground, as long as it has a clear policy warning employees that vehicles are subject to search at any time. However, for vehicles owned by employees, the law is less clear. If the employee parks on the street or otherwise not on company property, you almost certainly may not search the employee's car. (That would be akin to searching the employee's home or other private property that hasn't entered your workplace.) If your company owns the parking lot, your right to search depends on state law. In some states, an employer's right to search might be limited, particularly if the state allows employees to keep weapons in their cars. Talk to an experienced lawyer—and adopt a clear policy based on that legal advice—before searching an employee's vehicle.

Polygraph Tests

As discussed in Chapter 1, a federal law called the Employee Polygraph Protection Act (EPPA) generally prohibits employers from requiring or even asking employees to take a polygraph test. However, the law carves out several exceptions, and one of them applies to investigations of workplace theft.

Under the EPPA, a private employer may ask an employee to take a polygraph if all of these conditions are met:

- The test is administered in connection with an ongoing investigation of economic loss or injury to the employer's business (see "What the Ongoing Investigation Exception Doesn't Cover," below).
- The employee had access to the property that is the subject of the investigation.
- The employer has a reasonable suspicion that the employee was involved in the incident or activity under investigation.
- The employer gives the employee, at least two working days before the test, a written statement that:
  - describes the specific incident or activity under investigation and the basis for testing the employee
  - identifies the specific loss or economic injury under investigation
  - states that the employee had access to the property in question
  - describes the basis for the employer's reasonable suspicion of the employee
  - is signed by someone who is authorized to legally bind the employer, such as an officer or director of the company, and indicates the time and date when the employee received the statement, and
  - is signed by the employee.

Even if your situation fits within this exception, you still have to follow a lengthy list of technical requirements, from giving the employee extensive written notices before the test (including an exact list of every question to be asked), to observing a number of rules during the test, to providing the employee with a copy of the test results. You must also use a polygraph examiner who meets specified qualifications. And you can't take any action based on the test results alone, even if you follow all of these rules; you must have additional evidence of the employee's guilt.

Given all of these rules, it probably isn't worth using a polygraph in most theft investigations. If you think that a polygraph is necessary to get to the bottom of things, talk to a lawyer who is familiar with the law, and hire an experienced polygraph examiner.

What the Ongoing Investigation Exception Doesn't Cover

The ongoing investigation exception applies to many types of workplace theft, but not all of them. Because the exception applies only to an investigation into a specific incident or activity, an employer cannot rely on the exception to require polygraphs to find out whether theft has occurred or to look into a continuing loss, such as regular inventory shortages that occur all of the time. Testing is allowed only in response to a specific, identifiable incident of loss.

In addition, an employer can test only in response to an economic loss or injury to its own business, not to a customer, client, or coworker. So if a workplace thief is stealing from other employees or from clients, the exception probably doesn't apply.

Gather Documents and Other Evidence

Many theft schemes require—or create—paper trails. Think about what types of documents might be generated by the theft you suspect. For example, a refund or void scheme will yield paperwork in the form of cash register tapes and excessive void or refund slips. A phony vendor scheme generally requires invoices or other requests for payment listing the false vendor name.

Depending on what type of theft you suspect, you may want to look at some of these documents, whether in paper or electronic form:
- cash register tape and receipts
- void slips
- refund slips

- credits
- purchase orders
- invoices
- deposit slips
- canceled checks
- bank statements
- vendor records
- financial statements
- tax returns
- expense reimbursement forms
- balance sheets, or
- accounting documents, including ledgers and journals.

You can also collect documents and information outside of the workplace. For example:

- If you suspect an employee of stealing, find out whether the employee is spending lots of money outside the workplace and where that money came from. Is the employee suddenly buying a vacation home or luxury cars, taking expensive trips, wearing valuable jewelry or clothes? If the employee claims that the money came from a legitimate source, look into it. For example, if an employee claims to have inherited a large amount of money, you could check public probate court records and obituaries in online newspapers.

CAUTION

Stick to public records and observable facts. You might be tempted to start covert surveillance of an employee who seems to be living high on the hog, but that's generally a bad idea. To avoid violating the employee's privacy, limit your investigation to documents that are publicly available—such as records filed with a court or agency or information the employee has posted publicly online—and information that is plainly evident. Noticing that an employee is showing up to work in a brand new Lexus is fair game; calling every real estate agent in town to find out whether an employee is in the market for a new home probably is not.

- If you suspect an employee of a phony vendor scheme, check secretary of state filings. Is the business listed? If so, find out the name(s) of the owners; if it is a phony vendor, the employee or his or her friends or relatives may be listed. Check the business address to see if it matches the employee's address. And if the vendor is supposed to be licensed, check with your state's licensing agency to find out whether this requirement has been met.

Interviews

Once you've gathered and examined relevant documents, you're ready to begin your interviews. In a theft investigation, you'll want to interview your suspect(s) last. Unlike a harassment or discrimination investigation, which begins with the victim, moves to the accused employee, then goes to witnesses and other third parties to confirm or contradict the stories of the main players, a theft investigation moves from the outside in. You'll start your interviews with the most peripheral witnesses, then conclude by interviewing the suspect. That way, you'll have all of the evidence you can possibly gather before confronting the potential thief.

Interviewing Witnesses

The types of witnesses available will depend on the nature of the theft. Once you have a sense of what kind of theft you're dealing with, think about who might have helpful information to offer. In a bribe or kickback scheme, for example, you might want to interview vendors, other employees who are involved in the vendor selection process, the suspect's supervisor, and anyone who might have had an opportunity to witness shady deals (for example, a coworker who accompanies the suspect on sales calls). If you suspect an employee of skimming at a cash register, you might talk to the bookkeeper and to employees who work the same register shifts as the suspect.

Getting Started

As in any investigation, it's best to begin your interviews with an opening statement to put the witness at ease and set the tone for your questions. However, unlike other investigations, you may want to keep your purpose secret at the beginning of the interview, to encourage the witness to reveal as much as possible and to try to prevent the suspect from learning of your interest. Because employees may be reluctant to finger their coworkers for theft, you should build up to the topic of your interview slowly, to give yourself time to establish a rapport with the witness.

Experienced investigators advise taking a somewhat vague approach when opening a witness interview. Rather than explaining the purpose in detail, they'll simply say, "The company has asked me to look into something, and I'm hoping you can answer a few questions for me." Or, they might be a bit more specific about the topic: "I've been asked to gather information about our procedures for selecting vendors. Can I ask you some questions about that?"

Of course, if you're dealing with a complaint from a known person, whether employee or outsider, you can be less circumspect in your approach. For example, you might start an interview with a vendor who complained that an employee solicited a bribe by saying, "I understand that you've made a complaint about one of our employees. I've been asked to look into the matter. Can you tell me what happened?"

Questions

The questions you ask the witness will depend on the purpose of the interview. However, your approach should be the same with most witnesses: Move from the general to the specific. If you believe a witness may have seen a coworker stealing from a register, for example, start by finding out what shifts the witness works, when the witness is on the register, and who usually works the nearby registers. You might then ask a general question about theft, such as "Have you ever seen anyone steal from the company?" If the employee responds negatively, get more specific by asking, "Have you ever seen anyone steal from a register?"

Be more direct with a witness who has complained of theft. If the witness has made a complaint about theft, you can start right in with the facts of the complaint. However, you'll want to make sure to cover basic background questions at some point in the interview, to make sure the witness had the opportunity to see or hear the incidents and to find out about any potential animosity between the witness and the suspected employee.

Closing the Interview

Once you have finished your questions, review your notes with the person you interviewed. Make sure you got everything right and that your notes include all of the important details. Have the employee sign your notes or a written summary of the interview. Ask the employee not to talk about what you've discussed with any coworkers. And ask the employee to come to you immediately with any new information.

> **TIP**
> **Perhaps no theft occurred.** Theft is not the cause of every shortage or loss a business suffers. In some investigations, you will conclude at this point that you are not dealing with employee theft. After examining relevant documents and talking to knowledgeable witnesses, you may decide that accounting mistakes, shoplifting, or faulty inventory procedures better explain the apparent discrepancies or shortages in question. If this happens, be sure to take steps to shore up any security or procedural problems your investigation uncovered.

Interviewing Suspects

You may find yourself in one of two situations when interviewing a suspect. In some cases, your review of documents and interviews with witnesses will lead you to believe that a particular employee is the culprit. In other cases, you may have narrowed down the range of suspects to two or three employees who had the opportunity to commit the theft. Either way, you'll want to carefully structure your interview to give yourself the best chance of eliciting a confession.

> **CAUTION**
> **You may have more than one thief.** Many workplace thieves operate alone. Every once in a while, however, more than one employee is in on the scheme. If you have more than one suspect, remember that all of them may be guilty. In this situation, getting one to confess may bring down the whole operation.

False Confessions and False Imprisonment

We've all heard about false confessions in the criminal justice system: suspects interrogated for hours, deprived of sleep, faced with threats or promises, and finally pushed so hard that they confess to crimes they didn't commit. Believe it or not, false confessions can happen in private industry as well. Certain interviewing techniques can be so forceful and frightening that they push employees to falsely admit to theft.

AutoZone, a chain of stores that sells car parts, has faced this allegation. According to *The New York Times*, the store's internal investigators have confronted employees suspected of theft by, among other things, insisting that the company knows the employee is guilty, claiming to have proof (such as security tapes) that the employee is guilty, and even pretending to call the police. One employee who was interrogated by these methods signed a confession that he had stolen $820 to pay family debts; the store later discovered that the money had simply been misplaced, not stolen.

In these cases, the employee often makes a legal claim of false imprisonment, alleging that the employer held the employee against his or her will, by leading the employee to believe that he or she was not free to leave the interview. False imprisonment is a personal injury claim. A successful employee can ask the court not only for actual out-of-pocket losses, but also punitive damages and damages for emotional distress.

To avoid these claims, don't overstate your case and never detain employees. You are free to discipline or even terminate an employee who won't cooperate with your investigation. However, you cannot physically restrain an employee or psychologically pressure an employee to remain in the interview room. And, although you certainly want the employee to confess if possible, don't falsely claim to have evidence or knowledge of the employee's guilt. This won't help you get to the bottom of what really happened, and it could lead to claims of defamation and wrongful termination.

Getting Started

As with witnesses, you should begin your interviews with suspects in an innocuous way. This will allow you to develop some rapport with the employee before you start in on the hard questions. Start by saying something like "I've been asked to take a look at our accounting practices" or "I'm gathering some information on sales and inventory procedures," then tell the suspect that you need to ask a few questions.

Preserve the element of surprise. When you're interviewing suspects, time your approach carefully. Make sure that the employee doesn't have something pressing to take care of or a scheduled appointment. Once you tell the employee you want to ask questions, you should conduct the interview immediately. If you delay, the employee may suspect the true reason for your interest and take steps to foil the investigation (such as destroying documents or getting rid of other evidence) or hide the proceeds of the theft.

Questions

The questions you ask a suspect will, of course, depend on what type of theft you're dealing with and what you already know about it. Because there's such a wide variety of types of theft, it's impossible to provide a list of sample questions. Instead, let's follow the hypothetical case of Mary, the bookkeeper.

> EXAMPLE: Sarah, the HR director of GetGo Enterprises, has been asked to investigate whether Mary, the bookkeeper, is running a lapping scheme. There have been significant lags in posting customer payments; in fact, several customers have complained of receiving a second notice of payment due after they've already paid their bills. To make certain that these discrepancies weren't due to simple errors, Sarah compares the payments the company actually received in the last week (by looking inside the envelopes, already opened in the company mail room, that are being routed to Mary and adding up the checks she found inside) to the amounts Mary has deposited. There is a shortfall of several thousand dollars.

A witness, whose desk is near Mary's, has told Sarah that Mary often writes in a notebook while she is posting to the company's accounting system, and that she takes this notebook with her everywhere, including to lunch and home at night.

Most interviews will follow the same general pattern:

- **Start with general, open-ended questions.** This will help you get the suspect talking, hopefully before he or she realizes the true purpose of the interview. It will also give you a chance to observe the suspect's body language under fairly normal circumstances. You can compare this to the suspect's demeanor when you start in on the tough topics.

    EXAMPLE: Sarah approaches Mary as she's returning from her lunch break. "Hi Mary," she says. "I've been asked to gather some information on our internal accounting procedures. Could you answer a few questions for me?" Mary says that she has to get back to work. "I won't keep you too long," Sarah responds. "Let's go to my office."

    Once both are settled, Sarah begins with a few general questions, such as "Please describe your job responsibilities," "Describe a typical day as the company bookkeeper," and "Could you briefly explain the company's accounting software? What information do you enter, how often do you enter it, and what reports do you run?"

- **Hone in on the particular procedures or transactions at issue.** Begin with general questions.

    EXAMPLE: After Mary has described general bookkeeping procedures, Sarah is ready to ask about customer payments. "You're responsible for processing customer payments, right? Please explain how that works." Sarah's goal is to get Mary to walk her through the process, step by step. Once she's committed herself to a set procedure, she'll have a harder time explaining why she deviated from that procedure for particular customers.

- **Get more specific, and be prepared to lay out documents or other evidence that contradicts the suspect's statements.** If the employee becomes flustered or can't explain the contradictions, raise the possibility of theft in general terms, but don't get angry or speak harshly. If you appear to be sympathetic and nonjudgmental, you'll have better luck getting the employee to admit to something.

> EXAMPLE: Mary has explained the procedure for recording and depositing customer payments. Sarah reiterates what Mary has said: "So, you post customer payments on the same day you receive them? And then you deposit the checks immediately?" Mary confirms what she has already said. Sarah then says, "But Mary, you waited several days to deposit this customer's check," and shows her the document. At this point, some employees will realize that the jig is up and will confess. Others will give a justification for the discrepancy. Mary offers an innocent explanation, so Sarah continues presenting evidence: "Last Thursday, the company took in over $6,000 in payments, but you deposited only $3,575. I know that because I added up the checks myself. And here's the deposit slip, filled out in your handwriting." Mary doesn't respond. Sarah says, "Mary, I know you've worked for this company for a long time, and you would only have done something like this if you really needed the money." At this point, Mary—like many suspects in a similar situation—admits to at least some role in the theft.

Getting the Money Back

This interview may be your only chance to convince the suspect to volunteer information that will help you recapture the stolen money or goods. Here are some sample questions that should help you get what you need:

- What happened to the money?
- Is there anything left, or have you spent it? What have you spent it on? Do you still have the items you purchased with the money?
- Have you deposited any of the money in a bank account? Where do you bank? Would you be willing to sign an authorization for us to look at your bank records? [Have such an authorization available, or have one written up while sitting in the interview.]
- You understand that this is the company's money. If you return whatever's left voluntarily, that might help the situation. Will you do that?

Evaluate the Evidence

In theft cases, you will almost always have a strong sense of what happened and who did it by the end of your investigation. If you were successful in getting the suspect to admit to stealing, you will also have a confession. Obviously, in these situations, you won't have to spend much time sifting through the evidence you gathered.

It's relatively rare to close a theft investigation by concluding that you can't decide who, among a group of people, committed the theft. More common is a conclusion that you aren't sure whether you have enough proof that the person you suspect is guilty. For example, if a relatively small amount of money or property is missing, and the loss may be due to shoplifting, accounting errors, or shoddy inventory procedures, it might be tough to pin the blame on an employee you suspect of theft.

If you can't figure out whether an employee is guilty, you should close the investigation without reaching any conclusions (Chapter 4 explains how) and take immediate steps to tighten workplace controls.

Take Action

If you find that employee theft occurred, often the only appropriate response is to fire the employee. There may be exceptions to this general rule. For example, the employee's actions may have been condoned by management, and the employee had reason to believe they were not serious. But these situations will be rare. Remember, two-thirds of employees will steal if they see others stealing and getting away with it. To show employees that your company means business, anyone who steals from the company should probably be fired.

Document the Investigation

Document the investigation, following the guidelines in Chapter 4. Make sure to stick to the facts. Theft investigations can lead to defamation lawsuits, in which employees accused of theft claim that you spread false and damaging information about them (in other words, that you called them thieves). Avoid this unhappy result by laying out the facts that your investigation uncovered and detailing the reasons for your conclusions.

Convincing a Suspect to Confess

So how do you get from making the suspect uncomfortable to actually eliciting a confession? It varies from person to person, of course, but here are a few tips from experienced investigators:

- Keep your documents and other evidence hidden, and lay them out one piece at a time. Virtually every workplace theft results in some kind of evidence, and the only person who knows exactly what evidence is available is the thief. If you show your hand only a little at a time, the thief won't know how much evidence you have (and may anticipate evidence you didn't know about).
- Give the suspect an out. Try to think of some way to make confessing to the theft more palatable to the suspect. For example, you could say, "I know you wouldn't do this unless you had a very good reason."
- If the employee confesses, gather as much information as you can about the scope of the theft, whether anyone else was involved, and, perhaps most important, what happened to the proceeds. Get the basics of the confession in writing, if possible. Seek this information right away; once the employee leaves the room, the chances of voluntary cooperation diminish significantly.

EXAMPLE: Mary has broken down and admitted that she has "borrowed" money from the deposits on occasion, but only because she was financially strapped after her divorce. Now's the time for Sarah to ask questions like these: "When's the first time you borrowed money from a customer payment? This must be hard to keep track of. Do you have a written record of which payments you've deposited and which you've withheld? I understand you keep a personal notebook at your desk. Is this why? May I see it now? What have you done with the money? Do you still have any of it?" Mary is reluctant to talk, so Sarah prods her further by adding, "Mary, you can understand that we could run into serious problems with our customers if we don't credit their accounts properly. In fact, several customers have already complained. The first step toward making this right is to undo the damage to our customer relations. For that, we need to know which accounts have been affected."

Follow Up

When you've finished your investigation, it's time to think about the future: how to get the company's money or property back (if possible) and how to prevent theft going forward.

Recouping Your Company's Losses

Unfortunately, there's no surefire way to get back money or property a workplace thief has stolen. If you're dealing with a thrifty thief who has carefully deposited theft proceeds in a savings account, you might be in luck. In most situations, however, the thief will have spent most of the money already; that's usually why people steal, after all.

There are several avenues of recovery that might be available to your company, depending on the situation. This section will give you some basic information about each. If your company is facing major losses, however, you should talk to a lawyer before deciding how to proceed.

Criminal Prosecution

A criminal prosecution may offer the best opportunity to get money back. Many judges will order a thief who is convicted (or pleads guilty) to make restitution—that is, to pay back what was stolen—to the victim, as part of the sentence. Restitution may also be ordered as a condition of probation. This gives you tremendous leverage to get the company's money back, because the thief risks going to jail for failure to pay. Even if the criminal case never goes to trial, your company can ask the district attorney to require restitution as a condition of any plea bargain or settlement of the charges.

If you want the thief prosecuted, you will need to show the police—and the district attorney—that there is a case to be made against the thief. Among other things, this will require you to be able to present evidence that there was a theft (as opposed to an accounting error, a loss, or a mistake), to show how much was stolen, and to show that the suspect committed the theft. A lawyer can help you figure out how best to convince those in the criminal justice system that your company's case is worth prosecuting.

Civil Lawsuits

Another method for recouping losses is to file a civil lawsuit. The most obvious candidate to sue is the thief, but only if he or she either has the assets to pay a judgment or is likely to land a job in the near future (which would allow your company to garnish his or her wages to guarantee repayment). There's not much point in paying the costs of a lawsuit against an indigent thief whose financial prospects look dim.

If the thief is unlikely to be able to pay a judgment, you might consult with an attorney to figure out whether any third parties could be liable for your company's losses. For example, someone who bought obviously stolen goods from the thief, or a financial institution whose loose controls allowed the thief unauthorized access to your company's accounts, might be legally responsible for at least some of the losses.

Agreement With the Employee

An employee who has confessed to theft may agree to restitution, or to sign a promissory note for the stolen amounts. However, such agreements often aren't worth the paper they're written on. Some employees sign such agreements with no intention of ever making good on their promises. Even if they do intend to pay the company back when they sign the agreement, they might change their mind once the feelings of the moment have passed.

If you try to come up with a restitution agreement, remember these tips:

- **Don't agree to payments over time.** The more time the employee has to pay the money back, the less likely your company is to collect the money. Instead of agreeing to installment payments, require the employee to pay the full amount within a few days or a week of signing the agreement. Let the employee figure out how to come up with the money, through a loan, help from friends and relatives, or some other source.

- **Write a binding contract.** Make sure that your agreement will be enforced as a contract if you ever have to show it to a judge. Inform the employee that the company will go to court to enforce the agreement if necessary.

• **Negotiate carefully.** Remember the old adage about a bird in the hand? It applies to restitution as well as fowl hunting. If the employee can scrape together a large part of the amount owed, it may make sense to accept that money as payment of the debt. But don't give up too easily. Consider the employee's ability to pay and your company's chances of collecting through a lawsuit to decide whether to settle for less than the full amount. Remember, you can always take whatever the employee can give now and retain the right to go after the rest.

Deduct Unrecoverable Losses

Your company may be able to take a tax deduction for losses suffered through theft or embezzlement, including stealing by employees. Generally, the IRS will allow businesses to deduct theft-related losses from their income for tax purposes if the business lost more than $100, the loss wasn't repaid from some other source (such as restitution or insurance), and the theft was illegal under the laws of the state where the business is located.

To deduct a business loss due to theft, you'll have to fill out IRS Form 4684, *Casualties and Thefts*, and file it with your tax return. For instructions on filling out the form and more information on qualifying for the deduction, see IRS Publication 547, *Casualties, Disasters, and Thefts (Business and Nonbusiness)*, and Publication 584-B, *Business Casualty, Disaster, and Theft Loss Workbook*. You can find these materials on the IRS's website, at www. irs.gov/Forms–&–Pubs.

Insurance Claims

If your company has a fidelity bond or some other type of employee theft or employee dishonesty insurance, the company may be able to recover at least part of the losses from the insurance company. However, it can be pretty tough to get an insurance company to pay up.

In order to recover, you'll have to follow the insurance company's requirements carefully, and you'll have to be able to prove that your company suffered a covered loss (that is, you'll have to prove the amount of the loss and prove that it was caused by theft). If the company's losses have been substantial and may be covered by insurance, you will probably want to retain a lawyer to represent the company's interests in negotiating with the insurance company.

Minimize Opportunities for Theft

Now is also a good time to think about how your company can prevent theft in the future. An accountant, auditor, or fraud examiner can review your company's internal systems for weaknesses that give thieves an opportunity to go to work. Here are some basic steps your company can take to reduce the risk of theft:

- **Segregate job duties.** Make sure that no employee is solely responsible for any financial transaction from start to finish. In other words, make sure that every financial transaction requires the involvement of more than one employee. Requiring a second signature on checks, making sure that the employee who counts a deposit is not responsible for taking it to the bank, and requiring a second employee to count out cash register drawers are all examples of segregation of duties.

- **Require authorizations.** Don't let money leave your company through the back door. Adopt rules that require the signature or oversight of a high-ranking official (or the owner) for major transactions.

- **Adopt a proper accounting system.** Loose accounting procedures give employees all kinds of opportunities to steal. An outside accountant or auditor can help you set up a system that leaves less room for money to disappear.

- **Conduct regular audits.** The simple truth is that employees are less likely to steal if they believe they may be caught. Periodic audits of your company's books and inventory will deter theft, or at least, uncover it in its earliest stages.

- **Impose paperwork requirements.** Put some extra roadblocks in the way of workplace thieves by requiring documentation for cash outflows. Require receipts for reimbursements for expenses or petty cash. Make employees submit licenses and other paperwork from new vendors, to make sure they're on the up and up. Don't allow refunds unless an employee fills out a form that includes the customer's name, address, and phone number.

- **Get involved.** Remember the old saying, "When the cat's away, the mice will play"? Company officers and high-ranking managers are the cats in this scenario. Don't allow any checks to leave the building without an officer's approval and signature. Have all bank statements sent to the president's home address. The greater (and more public) role company officers play in the company's finances, the fewer problems you will have with theft.

- **Don't bend the rules.** Some companies that follow all of the tips listed above still have significant theft problems. The reason is that they allow employees to ignore or override the rules. It's not hard to avoid this mistake: Simply insist that employees toe the line, and discipline those who don't.

- **Make employees happy.** Surveys show that employee satisfaction plays a major role in deterring workplace theft. Employees who feel appreciated are less likely to steal and more likely to report a coworker for theft.

Investigating Threats and Violence

A ll of us have heard the horror stories: A disgruntled employee, a worker's former lover, or an enraged client bursts through the door, shooting first and asking questions later. Although workplace violence is not as common as the news might lead us to believe, it is a major problem in the United States. Government studies estimate that there are about two million assaults and threats of violence made against workers each year. According to the Workplace Violence Research Institute, workplace violence costs businesses more than $36 billion each year.

Sometimes, violence comes out of the blue, without warning. Much more often, however, violent workplace incidents are preceded by threats, verbal bullying, and/or physical intimidation. This means that, in most cases of violence by employees and former employees, your company can avert more serious problems by immediately investigating threats and other signs of aggression.

An immediate investigation of every potentially violent situation, no matter how minor it seems, sends the message that violence will not be tolerated. It also gives your company an opportunity to avert more serious problems. Because workplace violence often escalates from threats, outbursts, or an obsession with weapons to physically harming others, you have a chance to stop this cycle if you investigate at the first sign of trouble.

Investigating threats and violence by employees can be distressing. After all, you don't want your investigation to be the very thing that triggers a violent outburst, and you certainly don't want to make yourself a target for a violent employee's rage. You will have to move very quickly, act decisively, and perhaps rely on outside experts to help you assess the situation and figure out how to handle it.

This chapter will help you navigate this rough terrain. It explains the types of workplace violence and when an employer will be held legally responsible for violence in the workplace. It also applies the ten investigation steps to situations involving violence and threatening behavior.

> ⓘ **CAUTION**
> **This book covers workplace violence by current or former employees only.** This book focuses on investigating employee misconduct, not problems caused by people outside the workplace. For this reason, it includes only limited information about third-party assailants: people who come to the workplace solely to commit theft or other crimes, angry customers or clients, or family members or acquaintances of employees. There are certainly steps you can take to prevent third-party violence. "Types of Workplace Violence," below, briefly discusses these other sources of violence and suggests resources that can provide more information.

Workplace Bullying

This chapter addresses violence and threats of violence. But what about workplace bullying, in which someone—often a manager—belittles and mistreats other employees? According to a 2014 poll conducted by Zogby International, 27% of workers surveyed reported that they had been the victim of workplace bullying, and 21% more reported that they had seen another employee being bullied.

Bullying can take many forms, from verbal abuse to sabotaging (or taking credit for) someone else's work, excluding someone from meetings and social events, or intimidating and humiliating another employee. Bullying doesn't raise all of the same concerns as workplace violence, where employees may be in immediate physical danger. Nonetheless, bullying is a serious problem, which can lead to decreased productivity, high turnover rates, and employee health problems. For help dealing with a workplace bullying problem, check out *Stop Bullying at Work: Strategies and Tools for HR and Legal Professionals*, by Teresa A. Daniel (SHRM).

Threats and Violence in the Workplace

The trick to a successful investigation of workplace violence is to start your inquiry at the very first sign of trouble. This means, in turn, that you have to recognize the early warning signs that often precede violence. If you wait until an employee has seriously injured or killed someone, all you'll have to investigate is what went wrong and what your company should have done differently.

Types of Workplace Violence

Contrary to popular belief, the great majority of violent incidents in the workplace are perpetrated by outsiders—strangers intending to commit a crime—rather than employees. For example, according to the Bureau of Labor Statistics, most workplace homicides are committed by robbers trying to steal from the business, not by current or former workers.

However, employees (particularly former or soon-to-be-former employees), people who know employees (such as romantic partners or family members), and customers or clients also commit workplace violence. This section explains some common types of workplace violence.

Violence by Outsiders

Nonemployee assailants commit most workplace homicides, as well as a substantial proportion of workplace assaults. Motives for this type of violence run the gamut from robbery to revenge to a misguided sense of honor or principle. Consider these examples:

- In 1993, Gian Luigi Ferri, a former client of the law firm Pettit & Martin, entered the firm's offices at 101 California Street in San Francisco. Ferri killed eight people and wounded six more before taking his own life.
- In 2003, a doctor was beaten and strangled to death during a physical examination of a patient at a psychiatric hospital in San Leandro, California.
- In 2000, seven workers at a Wendy's restaurant in Flushing, Queens, were shot and five of them killed during a robbery. One of the men convicted in the shooting was a former employee.
- In 2011, a gunman opened fire at a community event called "Congress on Your Corner," held in the parking lot of a Safeway

supermarket in Arizona. Congresswoman Gabrielle Giffords and several of her staff members were seriously wounded; Giffords's community outreach director was among those killed, the first Congressional staffer to be killed in the line of duty.

High-Risk Occupations

Government statistics certify what common sense suggests: Workers who deal with the public are more likely to fall victim to outsider violence. Those at particularly high risk include workers who exchange money with the public, deliver goods or services, work alone or in small numbers during the late evening/early morning hours, or work in jobs that require extensive public contact. Certain industries—including health care, security (including police officers), and retail—are targeted more frequently than others.

It's difficult to predict and prevent violence by outsiders. While some acts of violence (particularly those committed by angry customers or clients, or by those who oppose a company's practices) may be preceded by threats and acts of vandalism, most are committed without warning.

However, there are a few things you can do to reduce the odds that an outsider will target your company. The Occupational Safety and Health Administration (OSHA) offers tips for employers hoping to protect their workers from violence. These include:

- training employees on how to recognize and respond to threatening situations
- securing the workplace by installing surveillance cameras, extra lighting, and alarm systems, and by minimizing workplace access by outsiders through the use of identification badges and guards
- limiting the amount of cash kept on hand, particularly at night
- giving outside workers cell phones and alarms, and requiring them to keep in touch with a contact person throughout their shift, and
- telling employees not to go anywhere where they do not feel safe, and providing an escort in potentially dangerous areas.

RESOURCE

Want more information on preventing violence by third parties?
Go to OSHA's website, www.osha.gov/SLTC/workplaceviolence, where you'll find
fact sheets and tips on how to prevent and minimize violence in various types
of businesses. For information on your state's workplace safety rules, contact
your state's occupational safety and health agency. You can also find articles and
resources on violence and violence prevention at the website of the Workplace
Violence Research Institute, at www.noworkviolence.com.

Domestic Violence

According to the American Institute on Domestic Violence (www.aidv-
usa.com), 18,700 acts of violence are committed by intimate partners
and spouses (current and former) every year against women in the
workplace. Victims lose almost 8 million paid workdays a year, with
a total cost (in lost earnings and productivity) of more than $1 billion
annually. And sometimes these incidents go beyond the intended victim
to harm other employees as well.

It's not just victims of domestic violence who face lost productivity.
A 2004 survey conducted by the state of Maine found that more than
three-quarters of male domestic violence offenders used workplace
resources to check on, threaten, get angry at, or express remorse to their
victims. And, more than 40% of these offenders had been late to work
because of their abusive behavior at home.

Experts tell us that domestic violence frequently follows a fairly
predictable cycle, in which pressure, threats, and coercion precede acts
of violence. By the time a batterer shows up at the victim's workplace
intending to do harm, chances are good that he has already made
threats and committed other acts of violence or property damage. If
you encourage employees to come forward and let you know when they
fear an abusive partner, you can take steps to prevent that violence from
coming to work.

Here are some strategies a company can adopt:
- Establish a confidential way for employees to report domestic
  violence. Victims of domestic violence are often extremely reluctant

to come forward, so you must encourage employees to report abuse and to report any potential new problems or developments (if the employee's abuser is getting out of jail or has threatened to come to the workplace, for example).

- Increase workplace security by, for example, requiring workplace visitors to sign in and have an escort at all times, installing a locking door between the reception or greeting area and the rest of the workplace, and providing secure, well-lit parking facilities for employees.

- Get a restraining order on behalf of the victim and/or your company, requiring the abuser to stay away from the workplace.

- If you know that an employee has been threatened, make sure that the security staff in your office or building are aware of any outstanding restraining orders or threats against your employee, and know what the abuser looks like. You may also want to move the victim so she cannot be easily located by her abuser (for example, to a different floor, wing, or work site), for protection and to buy your company some time to defuse a potentially violent encounter.

If both partners to the relationship work for you, you can investigate using the tips and strategies described below. You also have the option of immediately suspending the abuser. Most often, however, the perpetrator won't be your employee. In this situation, you may need help from the police or a violence consultant.

RESOURCE

Need more information on domestic violence? There are a number of websites that offer information, training, sample policies, and strategies for dealing with domestic violence in the workplace. They include:

- Legal Momentum (formerly the National Organization for Women's Legal Defense and Education Fund), at www.legalmomentum.org
- the Safe at Work Coalition, at www.safeatworkcoalition.org, and
- the American Institute on Domestic Violence, at www.aidv-usa.com.

Discrimination Against Domestic Violence Victims

Some states protect victims of domestic violence from discrimination, harassment, or retaliation at work. In New York, the Bon-Ton department stores recently settled such a case with an employee who was sent home after telling her manager that her estranged husband had threatened to kill her. Her manager told her to immediately leave the workplace and not to return until she had a restraining order against her husband. Although the employee was eventually paid for this forced time off, she didn't know at the time whether she would be paid. As part of its settlement with the state attorney general, the store agreed to no longer require employees to get restraining orders as a condition of returning to work.

"Settlement in New York Domestic Violence Case May Set Broader Precedent," *The New York Times* (Nov. 18, 2015).

Violence by Employees and Former Employees

This chapter focuses on investigating incidents in which a current or former employee threatens or assaults others in the workplace. This is the most foreseeable (and therefore, preventable) type of violence. After all, the perpetrators are people you know, sometimes people you see every day. And very few of them simply snap one day and go on a rampage; instead, the problem builds up slowly, and the perpetrator usually sends up a few red flags that violence may in the offing. Here are some examples:

- After the receptionist at the Housing Authority in Richmond, California, was fired, he pulled out a gun and opened fire on his coworkers. In the days before he was fired, he told a coworker that he felt like committing a mass murder. The coworker reported his comments, and the receptionist was fired—but was allowed to return to his desk (where he kept his gun) on the way out the door. ("Bulletproof Practices," by Robert J. Grossman (*HR Magazine*, November 2002).)
- In 2009, Timothy Hendron shot several coworkers and took his own life at ABB Group, in St. Louis. Hendron was one of a group of employees who were suing the company and its trustee for charging excessive fees in connection with their retirement benefits.

Tips for Preventing Violence

Investigating threats and aggressive behavior will help you limit opportunities for violence in the workplace. Other ways to prevent violence include:

- **Screen applicants before hiring.** Check for past criminal convictions (if your state allows it), restraining orders, or a history of difficulties with coworkers.

- **Conduct evaluations and impose discipline only when it's warranted.** Experts say that employees are more likely to become violent if they believe they have been treated unfairly. Prevent these reactions by giving employees fair warning and a chance to improve on most problems.

- **Treat employees with respect.** Always treat workers decently, especially when you have to discipline or fire them. Don't disparage the employee in front of others or call him or her names.

- **Adopt a workplace violence policy.** Create a policy that states that violence of any kind will not be tolerated.

- **Prohibit weapons in the workplace.** Unless employees have a compelling need to be armed (for example, they work as security guards), don't allow weapons in the workplace. However, be aware that in some states, employees have the right to keep weapons in their personal vehicles on company parking lots. If your state has such a law, talk to a lawyer about a sensible weapons policy that doesn't violate the law.

- **Consider an employee assistance program.** Workplace violence often begins offsite, with a failing marriage, a substance abuse problem, or money troubles. Help employees manage these difficulties with an employee assistance program (EAP). An EAP might include counseling, rehabilitation services, or anger management classes.

- **Develop a safety plan.** Instruct employees on what to do if violence starts. Plan escape routes, know where first aid supplies are, and have emergency phone numbers on speed dial.

- **Encourage reporting.** Ask employees to come forward and report any incident of violence that they witness.

- **Train managers.** Make sure that managers know the warning signs of violence and how to implement the safety plan.

• In 1999, Byran Uyesugi opened fire on his coworkers at Xerox in Honolulu, killing seven. Uyesugi had been hospitalized six years earlier, after kicking in an elevator door and threatening to kill his supervisor. According to news reports, Uyesugi, a gun collector, was scheduled to attend a meeting to discuss his work performance on the day of the killings.

• In 2000, Michael McDermott, a software developer, killed seven coworkers with an assault rifle at Edgewater Technology. McDermott was having financial problems; the human resources department had just complied with an order to garnish his wages. On the day of the shootings, his car was repossessed from the company parking lot.

• In 2012, the streets of Manhattan erupted in gunfire outside the Empire State Building. Jeffrey Johnson, who had been laid off from his job a year before, shot and killed his former coworker; the two had filed harassment complaints against each other stemming from a workplace dispute. Police shot and killed Johnson, and injured nine bystanders on the busy sidewalk during the morning rush hour.

Workplace violence runs the gamut from vague threats ("They'll be sorry if they fire me") to pointed threats ("I'm going to bring in a gun tomorrow and take out my supervisor"), bullying, physical and verbal intimidation, stalking, assault, and killing.

Warning Signs of Violence

Experts agree that an employee or former employee who commits a violent act often exhibits certain signs of trouble before becoming violent. This is "good" news for employers because it gives your company a chance to prevent violence if you can read these signals and take action immediately. Of course, no single one of these signs, taken alone, is a sure indicator that an employee may turn violent. And some employees resort to violence without any warning. But managers and human resources professionals should be on the lookout for clues that intervention may be necessary. These include:

- an unexplained rise in absences
- substance abuse
- outbursts at coworkers and customers or poor impulse control generally
- verbal abuse or threats toward coworkers and customers; harassing phone calls or emails
- strained workplace relationships
- overreaction or resistance to even minor changes in workplace routine; insubordination and belligerence
- lack of attention to personal appearance, including hygiene
- interest in firearms or other weapons; access to weapons
- signs of paranoia ("everyone's out to get me") or withdrawal
- fascination with violent acts or fantasies, or a history of violence
- seeing oneself as a victim and others as persecutors; blaming others for one's problems
- obsessive behavior toward a coworker or customer, up to and including stalking
- comments about suicide
- mood swings, and
- domestic problems, including money troubles or family disputes.

The Workplace Violence Profile

Relying on a profile to determine which employees might act violently is dangerous. Although perpetrators tend to be white men in their 30s or 40s who have few family ties, workplace violence can be committed by anyone, male or female, of any racial and ethnic background, marital status, and age. Using a profile rather than looking at an employee's actual behavior can cause you to miss important clues that violence may be in the offing or to suspect employees who have no violent intentions. Also, profiling employees could lead to discrimination claims, if employees feel you are making decisions based on their race or gender, for example.

Violence is often a response to stress, whether in the workplace or in other areas of life. In many cases of workplace violence, there is some kind of triggering incident or "last straw" for the perpetrator, who then decides to resort to violence. Often, this last straw is a disciplinary action or termination; in some cases, it may be a complaint against the employee for harassment or violation of another work rule. Some violent incidents are triggered by layoffs, economic difficulties outside of work, or an emotional crisis.

Employer Liability for Violence

Generally, employers are legally liable for workplace violence only if they failed to take reasonable steps to prevent or discourage it. Courts have allowed victims of workplace violence (and their survivors) to sue under several different legal theories.

OSH Act Violations

Under the Occupational Safety and Health Act (OSH Act), employers must provide employees with a workplace free of recognized hazards that are causing or are likely to cause serious harm or death. Traditionally, this requirement has applied primarily to hazards created by machinery, poor ventilation, dangerous chemicals, and so on. More recently, however, the Occupational Safety and Health Administration (OSHA), which enforces the OSH Act, has said that workplace violence may also constitute a hazard. This means that employers that don't take reasonable steps to prevent or abate a recognized violence hazard can be punished by OSHA.

OSHA suggests that employers take a number of steps to prevent workplace violence (some are described above). Foremost among these is adopting a zero-tolerance policy toward workplace violence and enforcing that policy through prompt investigation of violence claims and immediate corrective action.

Harassment Laws

In some situations, workplace violence and threats may constitute legally actionable harassment or discrimination. For example, an employee who touches a coworker against her will or threatens to harm her if she dates someone else, may be guilty of both sexual harassment and violence. Or, an employee who gets in a fistfight with another worker after calling him racist names could be committing both racial harassment and violence. (For information on harassment, see Chapter 6.)

Negligent Hiring, Retention, and Supervision

Someone who is injured by one of your company's employees may be able to sue your company if it failed to take reasonable care in selecting and retaining its workers. Under the legal theories of negligent hiring, negligent retention, and negligent supervision, employers can be sued if they knew or should have known that an applicant or employee was unfit for the job yet did nothing about it. Here are a few situations in which employers have been found liable:

- A pizza company hired a delivery driver without looking into his criminal past, which included a sexual assault conviction and an arrest for stalking a woman he met while delivering pizza for another company. After he raped a customer, he was sent to jail for 25 years, and the company was liable to his victim for negligent hiring.

- A car rental company hired a man who later raped a coworker. Had the company verified his resume claims, it would have discovered that he was in prison for robbery during the years he claimed to be in high school and college. The company was liable to the coworker.

- A furniture company hired a deliveryman without requiring him to fill out an application or performing a background check. The employee assaulted a female customer in her home with a knife. The company was liable to the customer.

- An Amtrak employee who had a history of violent workplace incidents shot his supervisor twice after the supervisor reprimanded him for being absent from work. A jury found that Amtrak's failure to take action after the earlier incidents led to the shooting and ordered it to pay the supervisor $3.5 million in damages.

Although these lawsuits have not yet appeared in every state, the clear trend is to allow injured parties to sue employers for hiring or keeping on a dangerous worker.

TIP

Background checks are a conscientious employer's best friend. To avoid liability for negligent hiring, run a background check before you hire anyone—especially if you are hiring for a position that will have a lot of public contact. If you hire an outside agency to run a background check, you will need to follow the requirements of the Fair Credit Reporting Act—including, among other things, getting the applicant's written consent beforehand. (For more on FCRA, see "Reporting Requirements for Outside Investigators," in Chapter 2.)

Workers' Compensation Laws May Prevent Employee Lawsuits

In every state, workers' compensation laws require employers to purchase insurance that provides benefits to employees who suffer work-related injuries or illnesses. The system strikes a compromise between employers and employees. Employees are entitled to benefits no matter who caused their injuries. In return, the employer gets protection from personal injury lawsuits and the large damages awards that come with them.

Not all workplace injuries are covered by workers' compensation, however. The injury must be connected to the job. For example, an accident that occurs hours after an employee leaves the workplace probably is not covered. And an employer cannot use the workers' compensation system to escape responsibility for its own intentional or reckless acts.

How does this relate to workplace violence? Some violent incidents are covered by workers' compensation. This means that the employee victims cannot sue their employers for their injuries (although they may be able to sue the person who attacked them). However, if the violence is committed by a supervisor, manager, or officer of the company, or if the company has acted recklessly in allowing violence to occur (for example, by retaining an employee who has already engaged in violence), then the incident probably won't be covered by workers' compensation. This means that the victim can sue the employer in court.

The rules on what workers' compensation covers varies from state to state. To find out about your state's laws, contact your state's workers' compensation office or talk to a lawyer.

Ten Steps to a Successful Investigation of Violence

This section explains how to apply the basic investigation steps covered in Part I of this book to an investigation of workplace threats or violence. If you haven't read Part I, you should do so before getting into this more specific material; the discussion that follows assumes that you are already familiar with basic investigation procedures.

After a Violent Incident

This section assumes that you have learned of threats or relatively minor incidents of violence in time to prevent escalation. However, when serious injuries have already occurred, you are in a different predicament. In this situation, you should immediately contact the police and, if necessary, emergency medical personnel. Make sure that victims receive immediate medical treatment. You will also want to make counseling available to employees and discuss ways to prevent similar incidents in the future.

At some point (and probably with the help of the police), you will have to investigate what happened, to try to figure out what could have been done differently and what should be done to prevent further violence. However, that is a very different investigation from the type covered in this section. You may also be investigating in the shadow of legal action against the perpetrator and/or your company. In this situation, you will definitely want professional help. See "Take Immediate Action, If Necessary," below, for information on finding a workplace violence consultant.

Decide Whether to Investigate

Whenever you learn of a threat or aggressive behavior by an employee, you need to look into it. Remember, most employees who commit violence give some warning, often in the form of threats, intimidation, and minor acts of physical violence. If you ignore these early warning signs, you are only allowing the problem to escalate toward violence. And if you take a "wait and see" attitude, you might miss your chance to head off a disaster.

TIP

Employees will appreciate your efforts. Employees are very concerned about workplace violence, and they are understandably fearful about working with someone who has made threats or seems to be out of control. If you don't do anything in the face of this kind of misconduct, workplace morale will suffer, absentee rates will rise, and productivity rates will drop. If you take action right away, on the other hand, employees will see and appreciate that the company takes their safety seriously.

Learning About Threats

Sometimes, you'll learn about a threat of violence directly from an employee who has been threatened or treated aggressively. That employee might file a formal complaint, talk to a supervisor, or confide in a coworker. Even if no threat has been made, employees might come forward to report that a coworker is acting strangely: talking to himself or herself, mentioning violence, losing control, or looking unusually disheveled and scattered.

You may also hear of anonymous threats: emails or written notes that threaten harm but don't indicate the author. Some acts of violence—such as defacing an employee's car, vandalizing someone's work space, or damaging equipment—might also be committed anonymously.

And in some situations, a concerned friend or family member might report the employee. If the employee is ranting to family and friends that he or she wants to kill coworkers or has a plan to harm the boss's children, someone might decide to tip off the company. These reports are sometimes made anonymously, perhaps in a voicemail or an unsigned letter.

So you can't ignore violence. At the same time, you can't take action based solely on a complaint. Not every employee who makes a threat or has an angry outburst moves on to commit violence, and, of course, the truth may be different from what was first reported.

Some employers are so fearful of potential violence that they fire first and ask questions later. This is a big mistake. If you are too quick to judge, you might mistakenly assume that an employee who poses no actual threat is violent. This kind of mistake may have disastrous consequences for the employee and possibly for your company, if the employee decides to sue. You might even provoke the employee into committing a violent act that could have been avoided.

The solution is to investigate every threat and potentially violent act, but to do so very quickly (and often, with professional assistance). The sections that follow explain how.

Take Immediate Action, If Necessary

Once a threat or violent incident has been reported, your first concern is safety. To keep the workplace safe while you investigate, there are a few things that you'll need to take care of right away. If the threat is serious and immediate, start by contacting a workplace violence consultant to help plan your next moves. Next, you'll have to decide what to do with the suspect while you investigate. And you must figure out whether the company needs to step up security until the matter is resolved.

Lining Up Expert Help

Unless you have an in-house expert on workplace violence (as some larger companies do), your first decision after hearing about a violent or threatening incident should be whether to bring in a consultant. Sometimes called "workplace violence consultants" or "threat assessment specialists," these experts are trained and experienced in figuring out whether or not a particular employee poses a real danger to others.

They can also help you with other aspects of the investigation, including planning, interviewing employees (including the accused employee), giving advice on what disciplinary action to take (and how to deliver the news), following up with police and security personnel, developing antiviolence training and policies, and helping your company avoid violent incidents in the future.

Generally, you should call in a specialist whenever you feel like you are in over your head or don't know what to do. Although hiring a consultant can get pricey, it will be well worth the cost if it helps to head off a violent incident. You should probably talk to an expert if:

- an employee brings a weapon to work, shows a weapon to other employees, talks frequently about owning weapons, or otherwise shows a serious fascination with weaponry
- an employee threatens serious physical violence against another employee or makes repeated references to the possibility of committing violence
- an employee physically harms another employee, in a situation that is neither an accident nor the product of mutual aggression (such as horseplay that gets out of hand)
- an employee stalks or follows another employee, or
- an employee shows a dramatic decline in mood, mental acuity, or awareness, or appears to be losing control.

RESOURCE
Finding a consultant. The best way to find a workplace violence consultant—and any other workplace expert—is to ask those you know and trust for a referral. Of course, not every company will have used a workplace violence expert, but some larger companies may have one on call. Another good source of referrals is your company's business or employment lawyer. Your local or state police may also be able to help you find a workplace violence expert.

Dealing With the Suspect

In every situation involving workplace conflict, you will want to separate the alleged offender and the alleged victim while you sort out what happened. Workplace violence presents a slightly different scenario, however. If a worker has threatened or committed violence against another worker, separating the two won't necessarily solve the problem, even temporarily. For one thing, a worker bent on committing violence can follow through, no matter how far away the victim works. The violent worker can accost the victim in a parking lot, a common space, or the victim's work area. And an employee who has been threatened or treated violently isn't likely to feel much safer if you simply move the offending worker to a different floor or shift.

 TIP

Refer an employee accused of violence to your EAP program. If your company has an employee assistance program (EAP), let the accused employee know about it. Many larger companies have these programs, designed to help employees with problems from anger management to relationship difficulties to debt counseling and more. Particularly if the accused employee admits to feeling stress or having difficulties off the job, providing immediate help through the EAP could head off further workplace incidents.

A worker who has resorted to threats or violence could well do so again. Even if separating the workers offers temporary protection to the first victim, it does nothing for the employees who work in the area to which the potentially violent employee is moved, who may quickly become the latest targets of his or her rage and frustration.

All things considered, the best course of action is to immediately suspend an employee accused of violence or threats, with pay. When you tell the accused employee about the suspension, emphasize that it's temporary, that no conclusions have been reached about the truth or falsity of the allegations, and that the suspension is not intended to be punitive. Explain that the alleged acts violate company policy and that you must investigate before deciding what to do. Explain that the employee is not to return to the work site until further notice and that you will be in touch to arrange an interview as part of the investigation. And don't allow the employee to return to the work area after the meeting, except under the escort of a security guard.

Keeping the Accused Employee in the Loop

In a violence investigation, it's especially important to let the accused employee know exactly what's going on, what you plan to do, and why. As the warning signs of violence indicate, employees who commit violent acts are often suspicious and distrustful of others. They sometimes feel that others are out to get them. They are under stress, and they feel isolated to the point that violence seems like a viable solution to their problems.

One key to preventing a violent reaction to the investigation itself is to keep the accused employee informed. Rather than forcing him or her out of the workplace without an explanation or sending security to march him or her out the door, meet with the accused employee immediately; describe the allegations; tell the employee that the allegations, if true, violate company policy; explain that you will investigate and interview anyone who might have relevant information (including the accused employee), and that the company will make a decision only when all the information has been gathered; and convey that the employee will be immediately suspended, with pay, until the situation is cleared up.

By taking this approach, you accomplish two important objectives: You let the employee know that his or her behavior has been noticed and may result in discipline, and you include the employee in the process, thereby counteracting the employee's feelings of isolation and persecution.

Of course, there may be situations when you have to act more precipitously. For example, if you learn that an employee has gone to the parking lot to retrieve a weapon or has threatened to harm a supervisor when he or she returns from lunch, you won't have a chance to hold this meeting; you'll need to immediately dispatch security to deal with the danger. But, in most cases, you should meet directly with the accused employee to explain where things stand. (For information on safety concerns during the meeting, see "Interviews," below.)

Restraining Orders

Some states allow employers to get a restraining order against anyone who has threatened or committed violence against their employees. Generally, a restraining order is a court order that prohibits someone from doing something. The prohibited actions depend on the reason for the order. Restraining orders are used for a number of purposes, from preventing a neighbor from cutting down a shared tree to prohibiting the government from allowing a new law to go into effect.

In the last few decades, restraining orders have been used as a tool to fight domestic violence. A victim of violence fills out court papers explaining the incidents that have taken place and why he or she fears further harm. If a judge signs the order, the person accused of violence must stay a specified distance away from the victim (and sometimes also from locations where the victim spends time, like his or her home or school). If the abuser violates the order (for example, by approaching the victim on the street or coming to his or her home), the police can arrest the abuser for violating the order before any violence takes place.

In recent years, a number of states have passed laws that allow employers to get restraining orders against anyone who has threatened or committed violence against employees. State laws differ regarding what the employer has to prove to get an order, whom the order can protect (that is, if it applies to all employees or only to those whom the offender has threatened), and other details. (You can find out whether your state has a law—and what the law requires—at www.legalmomentum.org by searching "restraining orders.")

> **EXAMPLE:** Lynette, a department manager at USS-Posco Industries, learned that Ezell, one of her employees, violated work rules. Lynette warned Ezell that he would be disciplined for any further violations. Lynette later heard that Ezell had threatened the employees who brought the violations to her attention. Ezell had also made other threats towards his coworkers and bragged that he kept a gun in his car. Ezell was later fired.

The company got a restraining order requiring Ezell to stay away from Lynette and from the workplace. Ezell challenged the order, claiming that he shouldn't be required to stay away from Lynette because he hadn't threatened her directly. The court denied Ezell's challenge, finding that his general threats of violence against employees was enough to allow the company to get the order on behalf or itself and Lynette.

Restraining orders are most effective against terminated employees and other outsiders. It makes sense to apply for an immediate restraining order (if your state allows it) if your company is facing a threat of imminent violence from a former employee or another person who is off-site (such as a customer or the domestic partner of an employee). However, you'll have to weigh the information you have to go on and the severity of the threat. If the threat looks serious and you have credible information to back it up (for example, several employees heard the threat), you may want to get a restraining order even before you investigate. On the other hand, if the threat is unclear and witnesses' stories are conflicting, it may be wiser to wait until you've dug a little deeper. After all, when you seek a restraining order, you are telling a court that you have legitimate reason to fear another person; if you don't have evidence to back that up, you won't get the court order, and you may create some legal trouble with the accused former employee.

Restraining orders are not as useful for current employees. Because they are required to come to work, a legal order prohibiting them from doing so won't do you much good. In this situation, it's best to complete your investigation before deciding whether a restraining order is necessary (and it may well be, if you decide to terminate the worker for violence). If you suspend the worker while you investigate, you can instruct the worker not to come to the workplace, and enforce that instruction by telling guards and reception personnel that the worker is not to be admitted until you instruct them otherwise.

Security Measures

You will probably want to step up security at your company, at least until you complete the investigation. Depending on the nature of the threat (and how extensive existing security measures are), you may want to adopt some or all of the following precautions:

- Require all workplace visitors to check in, receive a security badge, and be escorted at all times.
- Require all employees to wear a badge or picture ID while at work.
- Install surveillance cameras (check your state's laws first; some prohibit cameras in certain workplace areas), extra lighting, and alarm systems.
- Install a locking door between the entrance or reception area and the rest of the workplace.
- Make sure every employee knows what to do in an emergency.
- Bring in security guards (or additional security guards); if you suspect a particular person, give security a recent photograph and a complete description, with instructions not to allow that person into the workplace.

Choose the Investigator

Chapter 2 explains the qualities that make an investigator particularly effective, such as professionalism, experience, and impartiality. Those considerations always apply, no matter what type of problem you're investigating. However, there are some additional issues to consider in a violence investigation.

Using an Outside Investigator

If you are dealing with a workplace violence or threat assessment consultant, that person may be able to handle the investigation. Of course, the consultant can't make decisions on behalf of the company, especially about what discipline should be imposed following the investigation. However, the consultant should be well equipped to handle the interviews, review documents, and write a report summarizing his or her conclusions. Most experts will also be able to help you decide what to tell other employees, whether you need changes to security plans or personnel policies to deal with violence, and how to train employees and managers to prevent future violence.

Getting the assistance of a consultant is a very good idea in any investigation of serious threats of violence or violent incidents. Experts tell us that much can be learned from reading the nuances of a suspected employee's presentation: key phrases, body language, facial expressions, and gestures. Consultants have years of experience deciphering these signals based on interviews with many employees who have committed or are suspected of commiting violence. On the other hand, you and your staff may have no training or experience in dealing with violent employees, up until now. Given the high stakes, it's often a good idea to have an expert on hand to help out.

Some consultants will want to handle the whole investigation, while others will be willing to advise you throughout the investigation without taking over entirely. For example, the consultant may give you advice about what steps to take right away to secure the premises, how to get the suspected employee out of the workplace, what documents to gather, and how to handle the interviews (and interpret the responses). Or, the consultant may interview the suspect and victim, while leaving other interviews to you. During your initial contact with a consultant, ask whether the consultant is willing to handle any of the investigative chores or to be available to advise you throughout the investigation.

Investigator Qualities

In a violence investigation, two of your most important goals are:

- **Laying down the law with the accused employee.** Violence happens, in part, because it is allowed to happen. An employee who has been getting away with intimidating and threatening coworkers may not fully understand that these actions are unacceptable. The longer this situation continues, the more resistant and resentful the employee will be toward any efforts to correct it. The person who interviews the accused employee must be able to clearly explain why the alleged behavior violates company policy and why the company is obligated to take action. This will convey that the employee's actions have consequences, which, in turn, can diminish the chances for further violent incidents.

- **Including the accused employee in the process.** Remember, employees who commit violent acts often feel persecuted and misunderstood. Part of the investigator's job is to convey to the accused employee what is going to happen and why, to make the investigation a transparent process so the employee doesn't feel that the outcome is inevitable or that the company is engaged in a plot against him or her. An accused employee who is included in the process is less likely to see the investigation as a reason to escalate the violence.

The investigator must be able to successfully handle both of these goals. To set limits for the employee, the investigator must have a certain amount of gravitas within the company. This means that a lower-level supervisor or human resources representative might not be the right person for the job; a member of upper management or a company officer might be in a better position to get this message across.

To make sure that the employee sees the investigation as fair and open, you must take special care not to choose an investigator who has had any run-ins or unpleasant dealings with the accused employee. If your investigator has a "past" with the accused employee, the employee may see the investigation as just another workplace conspiracy. Even more distressing, the accused employee may fixate on the investigator as a source of his or her problems in the workplace, which means that the investigator may become a target for violence.

Plan the Investigation

If violence has been threatened or committed, your investigation will have to be especially speedy. With this in mind, you should limit your investigation planning to the bare minimum once you've dealt with any immediate safety concerns.

As always, your first step is to consider what you already know. What happened? If a threat was made, what were the exact words used? If aggressive, intimidating, or violent acts are alleged, what was done? Do you know who made an alleged threat or committed a violent act, or was it done anonymously? Where did it take place? Who was the victim? Who else had the opportunity to witness it?

Your answers to these questions will help you plan your next moves. Specifically, you'll need to figure out:

- **Whom to interview.** The victim or recipient of threats should be first on your list. You'll also want to interview anyone who saw or heard the incidents and, of course, the suspected employee. Other possible candidates include the suspected employee's supervisor or manager and anyone else who may have had an opportunity to witness the work relationship between the victim and the suspect.

- **What documents and evidence to gather.** Start off with the personnel files of the suspected employee and the victim, to see if anything similar has been reported before. If any threats have been put in writing, collect those as well. You'll also want to secure any physical objects that relate to the situation, such as defaced or damaged property (or photographs of the property), weapons, or unsolicited gifts or other objects left for the victim.

- **Whether you will need to review other records.** For example, it may be prudent to run a background check on the accused employee, to find out if he or she has a criminal record, a history of violent behavior, or prior incidents of violence or similar trouble at previous employers. (See "Gather Documents and Other Evidence," below, for more information).

Interviews

Once you've finished your investigation planning, you're ready to start your interviews. Generally, you'll want to interview the victim first, followed by witnesses, and save the accused employee for last. This will give you a chance to gather as much information as possible so you can get the accused employee's response to every allegation.

No matter whom you're interviewing, you should start the interview with some opening remarks to set the employee at ease and explain the process. Next, proceed to your specific questions, remembering to follow up on any new information raised by the witness's responses. Close the interview by letting the witness know what will happen next and inviting him or her to come to you with any concerns or additional information. And conduct follow-up interviews if any new information comes to light.

The Victim

The purpose of your interview with the victim is to find out as much as you can about what happened: what was said or done, when, in what context, how the victim responded, whether similar incidents have happened in the past, and so on. However, most victims will have a different goal during the interview: to find out what is being or can be done to secure their own safety. This is an entirely reasonable concern, and you should address it at the start of the interview.

Getting Started

At the outset, explain that the company is investigating the complaint or incident and that the purpose of the meeting is to gather as much information as possible. Make sure to cover any measures the company has taken to keep the employee safe, such as increasing security, placing the accused employee on leave, consulting with a violence expert, getting a restraining order, and so on. Cover safety measures the employee can take outside the workplace, such as changing established routines, not going out alone, and improving home security. The local police or a violence consultant can help come up with a comprehensive list of security measures for the victim.

Explain how the investigation will proceed and that any employee who has committed misconduct will be disciplined. Ask the victim to come to you immediately if anyone retaliates against him or her for coming forward. Explain that you will protect the victim's confidentiality to the extent possible. Finally, find out if the victim has any questions or concerns about the investigation.

Questions

When you question the victim, you want to find out exactly what happened. Being attacked or threatened is obviously a very upsetting experience; as a result, some victims may be so caught up in how the incident made them feel that they will have trouble relating the facts.

For example, a victim might say, "He threatened to kill me!" or "I can't work with someone who attacked me," but this doesn't really tell you very much about what was actually said or done. Although it's important to find out how the victim felt and reacted, remember not to lose sight of the basic facts: who, what, where, when, and how. Here are some sample questions to consider (of course, the actual questions you ask will depend on the facts of your case).

Sample Questions
- What happened?
- Where and when did the incident take place?
- What did [the accused employee] say or do to you?
- How did you respond?
- Did [the accused employee] touch you in any way?
- Did [the accused employee] threaten you? What were his or her exact words?
- What was [the accused employee]'s demeanor? Did he or she make any gestures? What was his or her facial expression? Did he or she yell, speak loudly, use a normal tone of voice?
- Did anyone else see or hear the confrontation?
- What was going on immediately before the incident? Were you interacting with [the accused employee] at all?
- Has [the accused employee] ever threatened or intimidated you before? Please describe each incident.
- Did anyone witness these prior incidents?
- Have you experienced any unexplained acts of vandalism or property damage? Have you received any unsolicited gifts or other items?
- Do you work with [the accused employee]? What is your working relationship (that is, are you coworkers, does one of you report to the other, do you work together on projects)?
- How long have you worked together? Describe what your working relationship has been like. Have you worked well together in the past? Have you had difficulty working together in the past?
- Do you know of anyone else who has had similar problems with [the accused employee]? If so, please describe what happened to them.

- Is there anything else you want to tell me about [the accused employee] or about this incident?
- How have the incidents affected you? Did you take any time off as a result of the incidents? Did you seek medical treatment or counseling?
- Are there any documents or other kinds of evidence relating to the incidents? Did you take notes or keep a journal recording these incidents?
- Have you spoken to anyone about this? To whom, and what did you say?
- Is there anything else you'd like to tell me?

Closing the Interview

Once you have finished your questions, review your notes with the person you interviewed. Make sure you got everything right and that your notes include all of the important details. Have the employee sign your notes or a written summary. Remind the employee about retaliation. Ask the employee to come to you immediately with any new information. And let the employee know what will happen next.

Witnesses

Witnesses might be coworkers who heard or saw the incident, others who have had trouble with the accused employee in the past, or the accused employee's supervisor or manager. Like the victim, witnesses may also be concerned about safety, which could make them reluctant to tell you anything that they feel might make them a target.

Getting Started

For witnesses, your opening remarks can be brief. The witness doesn't need to know who complained, who is accused, or what the specific allegations are (although they may already know). Once you have explained that you are investigating a workplace problem and talked about retaliation, you can begin asking your questions.

If the witness raises safety concerns, explain some of the measures you have taken to improve security in the workplace.

Questions

When questioning witnesses, your goal is to gather information without giving too much away. To plan your questions, consider who suggested the witness and why. Did the witness see or hear the incident? Was the witness told about the incident? Is the witness privy to some details of the relationship between the victim and the accused?

Start with general questions about the witness's work; these questions will help you figure out if the witness could have seen or heard the alleged incidents. Next, move on to the specifics of the alleged incidents. Here are some sample questions to consider:

Sample Questions

- Describe your typical workday or workweek. Who is your supervisor? Where is your workstation? What time do you typically arrive at work each day? What time do you leave?
- Do you work with [the victim] and/or [the accused employee]? How would you describe their work relationship? What is your work relationship like with each of them?
- Has [the victim] ever spoken to you about [the accused employee]? Has [the accused employee] ever spoken to you about [the victim]?
- Have you seen any incidents or heard any communications between [the victim] and [the accused employee] that made you uncomfortable? Describe them to me.
- [If the witness may have seen or heard any incidents, ask questions to figure out whether the witness was there and what happened.]
- Have you heard this or other incidents being discussed in the workplace? When, where, and by whom?
- Have you ever had any problems working with [the victim] or [the accused employee]?
- Do you know of anyone else who might have information about the incident? Are there any documents or other evidence that you know of relating to the incident?
- Is there anything else you'd like to tell me?

EXAMPLE: The victim claims that the witness heard the accused employee say, "If you were smart, you'd give me a higher rating. I know you work late sometimes, and it's a long, dark walk to where you park your car. Anything could happen to you." The victim says the accused employee made this statement in the hallway outside her office, late Monday afternoon.

You should start by asking general questions to figure out if the witness was there. For example: "Were you in the office on Monday? What did you do on Monday afternoon? Did you see [*the victim*] and [*the accused employee*] in the hallway? What time? What did each of them say?"

If these questions don't get you the information you need, you'll have to ask more specific questions, like: "Did [*the accused employee*] say anything about his rating? Did he say anything about [*the victim's*] work hours? Did he say anything that you considered threatening?"

Closing the Interview

Once you have finished your questions, review your notes with the witness. Make sure you got everything right and that your notes include all of the important details. Have the witness sign your notes or a written summary. Remind the employee about retaliation. And ask the employee to come to you immediately with any new information.

The Accused Employee

You have several goals in mind when you interview the accused employee. Of course, you want to hear that person's side of the story, so you can figure out what actually happened. But your primary goal should be threat assessment: determining whether the accused employee really poses a violent threat (and if so, to whom).

CAUTION

Get expert help. Although this point has already been made in this chapter, it's worth repeating: Assessing whether a particular person will act violently is difficult work, and the consequences of guessing wrong can be disastrous. You should hire an expert for help and advice in any situation that has the potential for violence. The material in this section provides general guidelines, not the comprehensive and individualized assistance that only an expert can provide.

Keep the Interview Safe

Any time you meet with an employee who has the potential for violence, you'll want to take steps to maintain your own safety. First and foremost, you should hold the interview in a room that offers you an escape route, such as a door that opens directly to the outside of the building. If there is only one door to the room, make sure that the employee doesn't sit between you and that door (rearrange furniture, if necessary).

During the interview itself, be sure to listen to the employee and let the employee know that you are interested in what he or she has to say. Acknowledge the employee's feelings about the allegations, but explain that you need to find out what happened in order for the company to deal with the situation. If the employee becomes agitated or upset, make a special effort to stay calm and focused, to avoid letting the situation escalate. Don't be confrontational in your questioning. Maintain the demeanor of an objective fact gatherer. Don't crowd the employee physically or make any agitated movements.

If you have any concerns about safety, bring another person into the interview with you. And make sure that you have security waiting nearby, available to come in if things get out of hand. You should have a telephone in the interview room and a prearranged signal that will let security personnel know that you need some help.

Getting Started

At the outset, explain the purpose of the meeting. Emphasize that the company has not reached any decisions about what happened and that you are interested in hearing what everyone involved has to say before making a decision or taking any action. Because you will probably have to reveal the name of the alleged vistim, spend some extra time discussing retaliation: what it is, that the company prohibits it, and that employees who engage in retaliation will be subject to discipline.

Questions

Let the accused employee know that you are investigating alleged threats or violent behavior. State that this behavior, if it happened, violates company policy and will result in discipline. Be very clear that violent behavior has consequences; this will not only set the proper tone for the interview, but may also help dissuade the accused employee from resorting to violence during the interview.

Although the accused employee will probably want to know the specific allegations right away, you are better off postponing this discussion until later in the interview, after you have had a chance to gather some important background information. Assure the accused employee that he or she will have the opportunity to hear and respond to the allegations before the interview is over. Here are some sample questions to consider.

Sample Questions

- When did you start working for the company? What was the first position you held? Who was your supervisor? What were your job responsibilities? How long did you hold that position?
- What was the next position you held at the company? [Ask the same questions for each position, up to the current job.]
- What is your current job? Who is your supervisor? What do you think of your coworkers? Do you like your current position? What are some of the things you like about it? Is there anything you dislike about it?
- What is your typical workday or workweek like? What time do you arrive, what time do you leave? What are your job responsibilities?
- Do you supervise any employees? What are their names and positions?
- How would you characterize your working relationship with your direct reports? Your coworkers? Your supervisor?
- [Tell the accused employee what misconduct is alleged or suspected.] What is your response to these allegations?
- Did these things happen? [If the accused employee does not completely deny the allegations:] What did happen? When and where?
- How did [the victim] respond?

- Did anyone witness these incidents?
- Have you told anyone about these incidents?
- Have you kept any notes or a journal about these incidents?
- What is your work relationship like with [the victim]?
- [If the accused employee denies the allegations:] Could another person have misunderstood your actions or statements? Do you think someone made up these incidents? Why?
- Have you ever used foul language in the workplace?
- Have you ever threatened anyone in the workplace? Have you ever had a physical confrontation with another employee? When and where?
- Do you own any weapons? Do you own any guns? Have you ever used a gun?
- Has anyone ever filed a restraining order against you? Have you ever had any dealings with the police? Please describe the circumstances.
- [For complaints of stalking or romantic obsession:] Have you ever seen [the victim] outside of work? Have you ever had a social relationship with each other? A romantic relationship? Have you ever asked [the victim] out on a date? What was [his or her] response?
- Have you ever been accused of making threats or acting violently, at this job or at previous jobs you've held? Where and when? How were the accusations resolved?
- Do you know of anyone who might have information about these incidents?
- Do you know of any documents or other evidence relating to these allegations?
- How do you think this situation should be resolved?
- Is there anything else you'd like to tell me?

> CAUTION
> **You must allow the accused employee to respond to the allegations.** Some investigators are so eager to keep the interview civil—or to protect the complaining employee's privacy—that they never confront the accuser with the allegations against him or her. This is a big mistake, one that could undermine the legitimacy of the entire investigation. Courts have held that accused

employees who never learn precisely what they are accused of haven't had a fair opportunity to tell their side of the story, to offer the names of relevant witnesses, or to explain why the victim might have made the accusations. You don't necessarily have to say who complained, but you should say whom the employee is accused of threatening or harming. And don't worry about privacy concerns. You have a very compelling business reason for revealing this information.

> **RESOURCE**
> **Need interviewing tips?** For more information on interviewing the accused employee, check out *Dealing With Workplace Violence: A Guide for Agency Planners*, available at www.dol.gov/oasam/hrc/policies/dol–workplace–violence–program–appendices.htm. Written for federal government agencies, this informative resource is now widely used by private companies as well. It offers case examples, planning tips, policy guidance, advice on handling the aftermath of a violent incident, and much more. Although some of the information is relevant only to government workplaces, most of it applies to public and private employers alike.

Follow-Up Interviews

If any new information comes up during your investigation, you should conduct follow-up interviews with the victim or accused employee. Both employees should have the opportunity to respond to new allegations or defenses, to make sure that you have a complete understanding of the facts when you make your decision and to give you the opportunity to gauge credibility. It is especially important to let the accused employee know of any additional allegations that come up during the investigation. If you don't, you may be accused of unfairness for failing to give him or her an opportunity to respond.

Gather Documents and Other Evidence

Except in very rare circumstances, workplace violence doesn't strike out of the blue, but escalates from threats, conflicts with coworkers, and intimidation to actual violent acts. This means that, if your company is doing its job right, there may be a paper trail. Check the accused employee's personnel file for any history of problems working with others, abusive behavior, physical altercations, and so on. Find out if anyone has complained about the accused employee before. And review the personnel files of any other employees involved in the incident as well, to see if there's any indication of prior problems with the accused employee.

In addition to official company records, there may be other types of documents and evidence that will help you reach a decision. Here are some examples:

- **Records of threats by the accused employee.** For example, if the threats were made in writing—either on paper or in email—you can get those documents. If threatening messages were left on an answering machine or voicemail service, see if you can get copies. And make sure to ask the victim and witnesses if they've kept any records (for example, a log of threatening phone calls or notes of an intimidating encounter).

- **Medical records or records of treatment sought by the victim.** If a physical assault has occurred, the victim's medical records (if the victim sought treatment) can help you assess what happened. And if the victim has sought counseling or other help to deal with stress caused by the accused employee, you might ask for a note from the treatment provider to that effect. (The victim will have to consent to the release of any medical records.)

- **Items collected by the accused employee.** Sometimes, an employee with a propensity for violence collects news articles on other violent incidents, weapons paraphernalia, photographs of or information about the victim, or other items. If the accused employee keeps these things at work, you may be able to collect them. (See Chapter 7 for information on workplace searches.)

- **Nondocumentary evidence.** For example, if the victim's property has been damaged or defaced, you might collect that property (if it's small), or take photographs of the damage. The victim may have received gifts, photographs, or other items from the accused employee, which you can gather and review.

- **Official records.** You may wish to find out whether the accused employee has a criminal record, has been subject to restraining orders, or has been sued for harassing or injuring someone. Many of these records are publicly available; some states restrict an employer's ability to review criminal records (check with your state's department of labor or ask a lawyer about your state's laws).

Evaluate the Evidence

In some violence investigations, the accused employee admits that the incident happened as the victim described. An accused employee who acted under extreme stress and realizes that his or her actions were inappropriate may be willing to own up to the misconduct, while explaining what led to the problem.

> **EXAMPLE:** Marjorie is accused of suddenly turning on a coworker who was walking behind her in a hallway, pushing him away, and screaming, "Just stay away from me! Don't crowd me!" She then ran down the hall to her office and slammed the door. Marjorie's coworkers have noticed that she's been acting strangely for the last month or so. She's been showing up late, falling behind on her assignments, crying, and looking exhausted at work.
>
> When Marjorie is interviewed, she begins crying. She admits that the hallway incident happened just as her coworker described but explains that her ex-husband has been stalking her and threatening to kill her. She is fearful and jumpy, and she thought momentarily that her coworker was her ex-husband; when she realized her mistake, she was so embarrassed that she ran away.

An employee who feels justified in resorting to violence or intimidation may also admit to the incident while claiming, in effect, that the victim deserved it. In this situation, the employee feels entitled, inappropriately, to bully others.

> **EXAMPLE:** Marcus is accused of threatening his boss, Sharon, after she promoted one of his coworkers instead of him. Sharon says that Marcus told her, "You'll be sorry for passing me over. You're going to find out what it means to be on my bad side."

When Marcus is interviewed, he readily admits to making the statement but claims that he didn't intend to threaten her with physical violence. "She's been hard on me ever since I started reporting to her, and she never even gave me a chance for that promotion. I wanted her to know that she'd made a mistake and that I wasn't going to forget it."

In many cases, however, the accused employee will deny the allegations, or at least some part of them. For example, the accused employee might claim to have been joking, to have said something slightly different, or to have spoken in a calm tone of voice rather than a shout. To figure out what really happened, consider the factors listed in Chapter 4. In cases of threats and violence, plausibility, demeanor, corroboration, and prior incidents are often especially important.

- **Plausibility.** Whose story makes sense? Does one story defy common sense or (as may be true in a threat situation) ordinary rules of conversation?

    EXAMPLE 1: Charlotte claims that Harry has threatened her and that she has seen him parked outside her house. Harry first denies knowing where Charlotte lives; when confronted with a photograph her husband took of his car, he admits that he may have been in the neighborhood, but it was to visit a friend. He refuses to give his friend's name or address.

    EXAMPLE 2: Jamal says that Larry has been angry with him ever since he received a promotion that Larry wanted. Most recently, Jamal claims that Larry told him, "You better hope you don't run into me in a dark alleyway, like the one where you park your car." Larry denies intending to threaten Jamal; he claims that he said, "I worry about you walking to your car at night. You could get hurt." Larry can't explain why he was worried about Jamal or why he thought Jamal wouldn't be safe walking to his car alone.

- **Corroboration.** Did anyone else hear or see the incident? Should someone else have been able to see or hear it, if it happened the way the victim or accused employee claimed it did?

- **Demeanor.** Victims or recipients of threats or violence are often pretty stressed out and frightened. Does the victim's demeanor make sense, given the allegations? Does the accused employee exhibit the behaviors attributed to him by the victim? Demeanor can't tell you the whole story, but extreme or inappropriate reactions might indicate that things are not what they seem.

  > EXAMPLE 1: Karen says that Curtis threatened to bring a gun to work and open fire on his coworkers. She says that Curtis said he felt like he was going to explode and couldn't take the pressure of work anymore. Karen relates these statements in a calm tone of voice, then asks, "Can you really keep someone like Curtis here? I mean, what if he goes through with it?" Curtis appeared to be under no particular stress until he was told of Karen's allegations, which he vehemently denies, saying, "Why would she say something like that?" Curtis denies owning a gun and points out the bumper sticker on his car in support of strict gun control. In this case, there may be more to Karen's story than meets the eye.

  > EXAMPLE 2: John says that Rex has been physically intimidating towards him and other coworkers. John claims that Rex blocks their way in the halls, looms over John when he's sitting at his desk, and gets in John's face whenever he is upset about something. Lately, John says Rex has threatened to harm him. John looks pretty freaked out; he has dark circles under his eyes and expresses concern several times that Rex might hurt him if he finds out that John has complained. During Rex's interview, he crowds the interviewer, raises his voice, and tries to talk over the interviewer. Both John and Rex are acting in ways that support John's story.

- **Prior incidents.** Because violence is usually preceded by warnings, prior incidents of threats or abusive behavior are important evidence. Although it isn't conclusive evidence that the incident in question occurred, a history of violence lends a lot of weight to the victim's version of events.

Take Action

If you conclude that the accused employee is capable of violence, deciding what discipline to impose won't be your only concern. The danger to the victim and other employees doesn't necessarily end once the accused employee is out of the workplace; in fact, firing the accused employee, if handled improperly, could actually increase the risk of a violent incident. In addition to any discipline you will impose, you need to come up a plan to deal with the accused employee and keep the target employee (and workplace) safe.

Disciplinary Action

In some cases, you may conclude that no discipline is warranted for the accused employee. If there appears to have been a genuine verbal misunderstanding, for example, you may reasonably decide to simply end the matter with warnings all around and renewed training about workplace violence.

In some circumstances, you may decide that some form of aggressive behavior occurred but that the accused employee should be excused to some degree. For example, consider the case of Marjorie, discussed above, who pushed a coworker but was under extreme stress because of threats and stalking by her ex-husband. Because Marjorie understands that her behavior was inappropriate, it has never happened before, and her current situation is highly unusual, you might choose to give Marjorie a written warning and direct her to some sources of help for her problem with her ex-husband (such as the police and an employee assistance program).

However, if you decide that the accused employee made a threat or committed violence absent special circumstances, you will have to decide whether firing is warranted. Generally, you will probably have to fire most employees who actually threaten or physically assault someone. Your company has a legal obligation to keep its employees safe, and retaining an employee who has shown a propensity for violence is not in keeping with that obligation. If the accused employee recognizes that his or her conduct was wrong, is willing to seek help with anger control and appropriate workplace behavior, and can work with you to figure out how to prevent similar problems in the future, it might be worthwhile to keep the employee on board, as long as the behavior was not extreme and you are willing to monitor the situation closely. If you are considering keeping on an employee who has made threats or committed violence, consult with a lawyer and/or workplace violence consultant first.

How Serious Is the Threat?

Experts say that it is often possible to tell, from the language of a threat or the nature of aggressive behavior, how likely it is that a person will commit violence. Of course, there are no absolutes here; this is all a matter of interpretation and degree, not an exact science. Generally speaking, however, the more detailed and advanced a person's violent thinking has become, the more that person should be considered an immediate danger.

Here are some examples:

- An employee who has focused his or her attention and anger on a particular person is more dangerous than an employee who has vague, general complaints against the company.
- An employee who has threatened someone is more dangerous than an employee who has not.
- An employee who has followed or approached the intended victim, or who has gathered information (such as home address, a favorite route home, or where children go to school), is more dangerous than one who has not.
- An employee who owns or has practiced with weapons is more dangerous that one who has no access to or experience with weapons.
- An employee who has conveyed a detailed plan for harming the victim (such as how the victim will come to harm, what type of weapon the employee will use, when and where the assault will take place) is more dangerous than one who has not.
- An employee who has rehearsed committing violence is more dangerous than one who has not.
- An employee who feels that he or she must act right away is more dangerous than one who threatens to act at some undefined point in the future.

Coming Up With a Safety Plan

Once you've taken disciplinary measures, you'll have to come up with a plan to keep the workplace safe going forward. This is especially important if you are firing the perpetrator. Remember, termination just gets the employee off your company's payroll; it doesn't solve the underlying problem of the employee's willingness to resort to violence.

Consider whether you should pursue any criminal law options, such as informing the police, getting a restraining order, or reporting the accused employee for violating weapons, stalking, or assault and battery laws. Consider taking additional steps to enhance workplace security; talk to your local police for ideas. And make sure to inform your company's workplace security staff that the accused employee is no longer welcome on company property and that police should immediately be called if he or she shows up. A workplace violence expert can help you craft an effective safety plan.

Breaking the News

You will have to inform the accused employee and the victim of the results of the investigation. If you have decided to fire the accused employee, you will want to have security available to assist you, if necessary. Explain what your investigation revealed and why the company decided to fire the employee. Explain exactly what you expect of the employee in the future, including that he or she must stay away from the workplace. Give the employee the name of someone in the company to call to wrap up final details, such as continuing health insurance, getting the final paycheck, and so on.

If the employee becomes agitated or threatening, bring in security immediately. Explain that this kind of behavior won't be tolerated and that the employee will be escorted from the workplace immediately. If a termination meeting ends in further threats or aggression, you should probably contact your local police to report the incident.

When you meet with the victim, explain the action you have taken and why. Describe the safety plan, including steps you have taken to enhance security, and any criminal proceedings you've set in motion. Make sure the victim knows what to do if he or she sees or hears from the accused employee. For example, if there is a restraining order in effect, the victim should call the police immediately and inform you of the incident.

Always Be Respectful

It is extremely important to treat an employee you are firing with respect and dignity. Hold the termination in private, and don't belabor the employee's failings. Never belittle an employee, and be sure to mention the employee's hard work for the company. Studies show that the way a termination is handled plays a major role in how the fired employee views the company. If you're dealing with an employee who has the potential to commit violence, you'll want him or her to view the company in the best possible light.

Find out whether the victim has concerns about his or her own safety. If so, offer to put the victim in touch with someone who can help develop a safety plan for outside the workplace (your local police or a violence consultant can help with this). Ask about the victim's feelings about what happened; in some cases, the victim may be traumatized by the incidents. If the victim needs time off work to recuperate, make that available as an option. You might also offer to have the company pay for a few counseling sessions, if the victim wishes.

Document the Investigation

Document your violence investigation just as you would any other workplace investigation. (See Chapter 4 for details.) Be sure to include any legal actions taken, such as applying for a restraining order or reporting the incident to the police. Also, include your plans for following up with the accused employee or the victim.

Follow Up

Even after you've finished your investigation, there will be quite a few things to do. First of all, you'll want to check in with the victim from time to time, to make sure that he or she feels secure in the workplace and is satisfied with your company's efforts to ensure safety. If you haven't fired the accused employee, you'll also want to meet frequently with him or her, to make sure that any required counseling is completed and to keep track of the accused employee's progress.

In addition to these follow-up meetings, there are several steps you should take to get the workplace back to normal and prevent violence in the future.

Counseling

If actual violence or significant threats have taken place, employees may be traumatized. In addition, after handling the investigation, you may be feeling some stress. If you or others need some help getting back to business as usual, you might consider bringing in some trauma counselors or other workplace advisers, so employees have a chance to express their feelings and have their questions answered.

Policies, Planning, and Training

Most companies learn at least a few things they should be doing differently after investigating a violent incident. Try to use this as an opportunity to figure out how better to prevent and address violence in the future. As part of your violence prevention efforts, consider the following strategies:

- **Adopt an antiviolence policy.** Every organization, no matter how small, should have a clear policy prohibiting all kinds of workplace violence, from horseplay and intimidation to threats and assault. You can find a sample policy at this book's online companion page; see Appendix A for information on accessing the page.
- **Assemble a workplace violence team.** Experts agree that the best way to prevent and address violence is to put together a violence prevention team from different areas of the company: human resources, security, legal, labor, and so on. The team can work together to develop an antiviolence policy, come up with a security plan, decide how to respond to violent incidents, audit potential

trouble spots, develop a working relationship with a violence consultant or local police, and figure out how to handle the aftermath of a violent incident.

- **Train your team, managers, and employees.** Once you've got a team in place, consider bringing in a violence consultant to train the team in violence prevention and response techniques, including threat assessment. Managers and employees should also be trained on the company's antiviolence policy, how the company handles reports of violence, the warning signs of potential violence, and so on.

- **Do a workplace security audit.** Ask the police or a workplace violence consultant to do a walk-through of your workplace and provide ideas on how your company can improve employee safety.

Investigating Drug and Alcohol Use

A lcohol and drug problems are all too common, on and off the job. Employees who abuse alcohol and drugs can cause a number of problems for their employers, managers, and coworkers, from diminished job performance and low productivity to excessive tardiness and absenteeism, as well as increased workers' compensation claims, more accidents, and higher health insurance costs. And, the effects of drugs and alcohol can reach much further than being actually impaired at work: Symptoms of substance abuse, like hangovers, cravings, fatigue, irritability, and inattentiveness, can affect worker safety and productivity, too.

Workplace substance abuse may pose different problems for the investigator than a harassment or theft complaint. Investigating drug or alcohol use can be easier than other types of investigations simply because a full-scale investigation might be unnecessary. Often, there's no major incident or event that spurs an investigation. Instead, the company will learn about possible drug or alcohol use from a manager who believes an employee's declining performance, attendance, or behavior may be due to substance abuse. In this situation, no investigation is required: The manager can deal with the employee's work issues through the usual disciplinary channels and make an appropriate referral to your company's EAP or other resources available to employees facing problems outside of work.

Even if the investigation results from a workplace incident, drug and alcohol use may not be the subject of the initial complaint or problem. Although an employer might suspect—or receive a complaint—that other employees are drinking, using drugs, or selling drugs at work, substance abuse often comes up during an investigation into other problems. For example, a rash of accidents in one department might lead to a safety audit, which might reveal employee drug use. Harassment complaints stemming from a company holiday party might reveal that excessive drinking contributed to an inappropriate atmosphere. Or, a series of thefts might be carried out by an employee with a mounting— and increasingly expensive—drug addiction. In these situations, you'll need to know how to deal with the underlying drug or alcohol use to fully resolve the problem.

Investigations into drug and alcohol use also raise some unique legal concerns, mainly due to the fact that these workplace hazards are caused by primarily personal—and in some cases, socially acceptable—behaviors that can spill into the workplace from an employee's private life, sometimes stemming from addiction or medical problems. Clearly, employees who sell or use illegal drugs at work or show up drunk must face discipline. But what about, for example, an employee who has an occasional drink at lunch with clients; excels at work, but fails a drug test because of infrequent marijuana use on the weekend; or has some performance problems caused by prescribed medication?

A complex patchwork of laws may apply when investigating employee use of drugs and alcohol. Employee privacy is often implicated in these investigations, particularly if your company searches employee belongings or conducts drug or alcohol testing. Because drug or alcohol use may be a sign of an underlying impairment—whether the disease of addiction or another ailment for which the employee is taking prescribed drugs—the Americans with Disabilities Act may also come into play. Depending on the circumstances, you may also have to contend with drug testing laws, drug-free workplace laws, and laws that prohibit employers from making decisions based on employees' off-duty conduct.

This chapter will help you sort through these issues. It explains how the law treats different types of drug and alcohol use. It describes drug testing laws, drug-free workplace laws, and other measures that might dictate how you respond to these problems. It explains some common components of workplace programs to combat drug and alcohol abuse, including issues to consider—in consultation with an attorney—if your company plans to drug test. And, it applies the ten investigative steps described in Part I to situations involving drugs and alcohol.

Workplace Drug and Alcohol Use

Employee drug and alcohol use can lead to serious problems with performance, productivity, attendance, and safety. Although this gives employers a strong incentive to root out employee substance use, the law limits how far employers can go in investigating and responding to these problems.

The High Cost of Workplace Drug and Alcohol Use

More employees use illegal drugs or drink on the job than you might think, and they can create significant liabilities for their employers, from higher absenteeism and accident rates to a greater likelihood of lawsuits.

How Big Is the Problem?

Surveys and studies show that 9% of Americans over the age of 12 have substance abuse or substance dependence problems. And most of them are employed: Government statistics reveal that more than 8% of full-time employees are current illicit drug users, and about 3% admit to working while under the influence of illegal drugs. Marijuana is by far the most commonly used illicit drug, followed by cocaine, methamphetamine, and pain relievers that are being misused (taken without a prescription or in excess of prescribed amounts).

Which Industries Are Hardest Hit?

Although employees in virtually every field use illegal drugs, some have higher levels of drug use than others. According to the National Surveys on Drug Use and Health, food service workers and construction and extraction workers had the highest rates of illegal drug use, with more than 15% of employees reporting that they currently use illegal drugs. The entertainment industries (including arts, design, sports, and media) were close behind at more than 12%. You probably won't be surprised to hear who's on the low-use end of the spectrum: teachers, protective service employees, community and social service employees, and librarians.

Although drug testing and drug use tends to get most of the attention, most workplace substance abuse problems are related to alcohol, a drug that is not only legal, but allowed or even encouraged in some workplace situations. In the United States, two-thirds of adults consume alcohol. And, alcohol has long been woven into the fabric of the workplace, from the former (and for some, continuing) tradition of the two- or three-martini lunch to the after-work happy hour at a local watering hole to the keg at the company's Fourth of July picnic to the open bar at the holiday party.

Alcohol is known to lower inhibitions, which is probably why it's such a popular social lubricant. But many of its effects are more dangerous, particularly in a work situation. Drinking even a moderate amount of alcohol can cause impaired judgment, lack of coordination, and delayed reaction time, which can quickly translate into poor performance, inappropriate behavior, and workplace accidents. So it's alarming to learn that almost 9% of employees are heavy drinkers (defined as having five or more incidents of binge drinking in the past month). And, more than 7% of employees admit to drinking during the work day.

Smaller Businesses, Bigger Risk

About half of all employees in the United States work for small and medium-sized businesses, defined as those that have fewer than 500 employees. But nine in ten illicit drug users and almost nine in ten heavy drinkers who are employed work for these smaller businesses, as do nine in ten full-time employees with substance abuse or dependence problems. This could be because larger companies are more likely to test for drugs and alcohol and more likely to have EAP services available to employees who want to kick their habits.

All of this indulgence takes a heavy toll on employers. Here are some sobering statistics from the federal government on the effect of employee drug and alcohol use:

- Problems related to drug and alcohol abuse cost American businesses more than $80 billion in lost productivity each year.
- Employees who use drugs are three times more likely to be late for work; employees with drinking problems are more likely to have skipped work more than twice in the last month, and use twice as much sick leave as other employees. Experts estimate that 500 million workdays are lost each year due to alcoholism.

- Employees who use drugs are 3.6 times more likely to be involved in a workplace accident—and five times more likely to file a workers' compensation claim—than other employees; 40% of industrial fatalities and almost half of industrial injuries can be linked to alcohol use.
- Employees who use drugs cost employers about twice as much in medical claims as other employees.

Drunk Manager + Dangerous Job = Punitive Damages

If you're wondering just how much an employee with a substance abuse problem can cost a company, look no further than the case of the *Exxon Valdez*, the oil tanker that ran aground and dumped 11 million gallons of crude oil off the coast of Alaska, creating an environmental disaster. The captain of the ship, Joseph Hazelwood, had undergone a monthlong alcohol treatment program, but dropped out of a prescribed follow-up program and stopped going to Alcoholics Anonymous meetings. Members of Exxon management apparently knew that Hazelwood had fallen off the wagon, yet he was not monitored upon his return to work.

The night of the crash, Hazelwood drank at least five double vodkas on shore. After the ship sailed, Hazelwood received permission from the Coast Guard to change course in order to avoid an icy passage. The new route took the ship near an underwater reef. Minutes before the ship had to turn to avoid the reef, Hazelwood left the bridge and went to his cabin, telling his third mate and a nonofficer—neither licensed to navigate those waters—to make the turn. The turn wasn't made and the ship hit the reef, causing the oil spill.

Exxon's liability to various groups of people for the resulting damages was litigated for more than a decade, all the way to the United States Supreme Court. The Court had to rule on the punitive damages award against Exxon: $2.5 billion, based primarily on Exxon's liability for Hazelwood's drinking. The Court reduced the punitive damages award, but didn't overturn the underlying premise that Exxon could be held liable, under maritime law, for the reckless misconduct of its managerial employee, Hazelwood—to the tune of a possible punitive damages award of $500 million.

Exxon Shipping Co. v. Baker, 554 U.S. 471 (2008).

Employer Liability for Drug and Alcohol Use

Lost productivity and increased administrative expenses aren't the only costs associated with employee alcohol and drug use: In some cases, employers can also be sued for the harm caused by an intoxicated employee. Here are some of the ways employers can be held liable for the actions of an employee who drinks or uses illegal drugs:

- **OSH Act violations.** As explained in Chapter 8, employers have a legal duty to keep the workplace free of recognized hazards that are likely to cause serious harm or death. OSHA has stated that an employee's impairment due to drug or alcohol use might qualify as an avoidable workplace hazard. OSHA encourages employers to adopt drug-free workplace programs, although such programs are not explicitly required by any OSHA standard.

- **Respondeat superior.** Under this legal doctrine, an employer is liable for damage caused by its employees when they are acting within the course and scope of employment. If the employee is doing his or her job or acting on the employer's behalf, the company will be held liable for the employee's actions as a cost of doing business. If the employee is acting independently, out of purely personal motives, however, the company won't be liable. For example, the employer shouldn't be held liable if an employee gets drunk at home on the weekend and hits a pedestrian while driving, even if the employee happens to be driving a company car. If, however, an employee who is encouraged or allowed to drink alcohol on the job (for example, while entertaining clients) hits a pedestrian while driving back to the office after having a few drinks at a business lunch, the company could be held responsible. In these cases, someone who is harmed by the employee doesn't have to show that the employer was careless; if the employee causes injury in the course of the job, the employer is liable to those who are hurt.

- **Negligent hiring, retention, and supervision.** As explained in Chapter 8, some states allow lawsuits against employers that fail to take reasonable care in selecting and retaining employees. This legal theory might be used if, for example, an employer knew or should have known that an employee was drinking or using illegal drugs on the job, yet allowed the employee to drive or operate dangerous equipment.

- **Workers' compensation claims.** Employees who are intoxicated by drugs or alcohol when they suffer a workplace injury are generally not eligible for workers' compensation benefits. However, other employees who get hurt by an intoxicated coworker may still be eligible for workers' comp. And, if an injured employee can show that the company acted recklessly in allowing the incident to occur, the employee may even be able to sue the employer in court for damages.

Drug and alcohol use can also lead to liability simply by making other types of legal claims against the company more likely. For example, sexual harassment claims may arise from drunken behavior that takes place at a company-sanctioned event, such as a company party, dinner with visiting clients, or business trip. Alcohol or drug abuse are often associated with incidents of workplace violence, as well.

Laws that May Apply to Employee Alcohol and Drug Use

Given the facts discussed above, employers have good reasons to put a stop to workplace drug and alcohol use. However, there are some legal requirements that might dictate an employer's response, as well as some legal limits intended to protect employee privacy and civil rights.

The Americans with Disabilities Act

The Americans with Disabilities Act (ADA) is a federal law that prohibits discrimination against people with physical or mental disabilities. The ADA applies to companies with 15 or more employees. (Most states have also adopted laws prohibiting disability discrimination; you can find out whether your state is among them by checking the chart, "State Laws Prohibiting Discrimination in Employment," in Appendix B.)

Employees who use (or have used) alcohol or drugs may have a disability under the ADA. The disability may be drug or alcohol addiction, or it may be a separate condition for which the employee must take medication. The rules depend on what the employee is using and why.

ADA Basics

As explained in Chapter 5, a disability is a physical or mental impairment that substantially limits a major life activity, such as the ability to walk, talk, see, hear, breathe, work, or take care of oneself. Employers may not make job decisions based on an employee's disability, the fact that an employee has had a disability in the past, or the employer's perception that the employee has a disability (even if this perception is incorrect).

The ADA doesn't require employers to hire or retain someone who can't do the job. The law protects only "qualified workers" with disabilities: those who can perform the job's essential functions, with or without a reasonable accommodation. Accommodating a worker with a disability means providing assistance or making changes to the job or workplace that will enable the employee to do the job. (See "Reasonable Accommodation," in Chapter 5, for more information about, and examples of, reasonable accommodations.)

The ADA also imposes some limits on medical tests. You may not require applicants to submit to a medical examination unless you have already made a conditional job offer and:

- all entering employees must take the exam (in other words, not just those you know or suspect have a disability)
- the medical exam is the last stage in the screening process, and
- you keep the results of the exam in a separate, confidential medical file (this rule applies to all records relating to an employee's disability).

You may require current employees to take a medical examination only if you reasonably believe that:

- the employee is unable to perform the essential functions of the job due to a medical condition, or
- the employee poses a direct threat—a significant and immediate risk of substantial harm—to the health or safety of himself or herself or others because of a medical condition.

Tests for alcohol are considered medical examinations under the ADA, but tests for illegal drug use are not.

Alcohol

Alcoholism is a disability covered by the ADA. This means that an employer cannot fire or discipline an employee solely for being an alcoholic. For example, you may not take action against an employee because the employee claims to be an alcoholic, attends Alcoholics Anonymous meetings, or takes prescription medication to curb the urge to drink.

However, an employer may fire or discipline an alcoholic worker for failing to meet work-related performance and conduct standards imposed on all employees, even if the worker's problems are caused by drinking. In other words, the disability itself is legally protected, but drinking alcohol is not. And employers are free to prohibit employees from consuming alcohol at work or from showing up to work under the influence of alcohol.

> **EXAMPLE:** Carol works in a call center as a customer service representative for a credit card company. Carol and the other reps all have personal items posted in their cubicles; in Carol's cubicle is a sign that says "Easy Does It." When Carol's manager, Tom, asks what the sign means, Carol explains that it's a slogan from Alcoholics Anonymous that she finds meaningful, and that she has been attending AA meetings since she quit drinking several years ago.
>
> If Tom decided to fire Carol because she's an alcoholic, or to discipline her for having an AA-related sign in her cubicle while allowing other employees to post whatever they want, Tom could be violating the ADA by making decisions based on Carol's disability of alcoholism. If, however, Carol's sobriety comes to an end and she starts coming to work intoxicated or missing work because of binge drinking on her days off, Tom can discipline or fire Carol for failing to meet the standards of her job. The fact that Carol is an alcoholic doesn't excuse her from having to follow the rules that apply to all employees, even if her lapses are caused by drinking.

An employer may also have a duty to provide reasonable accommodation for an employee who is an alcoholic. For example, if an employee's prescription medication for alcoholism causes the employee to feel nauseated after eating, you might allow the employee to take a longer lunch and make up the time at the end of the workday. Other reasonable accommodations for alcoholism might include allowing an employee to take a couple of hours off each week for counseling sessions or granting an employee's request for unpaid leave to enter a rehabilitation program.

Illegal Drug Use

The ADA makes a big distinction between the legal and illegal use of drugs. Illegal drug use includes the use of illegal drugs (such as cocaine or heroin) as well as the misuse or abuse of drugs that are legal, such as prescription drugs. The ADA doesn't protect employees who currently use illegal drugs. These employees are not considered to have a disability, so employers are free to prohibit the illegal use of drugs at work, and to discipline or fire employees based on their ongoing illegal drug use. Employees who currently use illegal drugs are also not entitled to reasonable accommodations.

An employee's use of illegal drugs is "current" if it occurred recently enough to justify an employer's belief that the employee has an ongoing problem. Employees may be considered current drug users even if they didn't actually take drugs that same day or week. This issue comes up sometimes in drug testing, which might show a positive result from drug use that occurred in the past.

Current use of illegal drugs is not protected by the ADA. However, drug addiction is a covered disability, as long as the employee isn't currently using. An employee who is receiving treatment for drug addiction or who has successfully completed a drug rehabilitation program is protected by the ADA from discrimination on the basis of drug addiction. A rehabilitation program includes not only inpatient treatment, but also outpatient treatment, an EAP program, or a self-help program such as Narcotics Anonymous.

CAUTION
Don't "regard" employees as addicts. As explained above, an employee is protected by the ADA if the employer mistakenly perceives the

employee as having a particular disability. (Lawyers call these "regarded as" claims of discrimination.) Employers can get into trouble in a couple of ways here. An employee who doesn't use drugs or alcohol at all but shows some signs of impairment could be mistakenly regarded as an addict. In this situation, another disability might be behind the employee's behavior, or the symptoms might be the result of the proper use of prescription drugs for a disability. Similarly, an employer might mistakenly perceive that a casual drug user is a drug addict, which could give that employee a valid legal claim if he or she were fired for the perceived addiction rather than for actual drug use.

Legal Drug Use

Many of us use legal drugs—like over-the-counter remedies or prescription medication—from time to time. If an employee is using legal drugs to treat a disability, the ADA applies. This may mean, for example, that you have to provide reasonable accommodation for the employee's use of drugs and their side effects.

> **EXAMPLE:** Jerry works at the onsite child care center at a large technology company. The center is open from 6 a.m. until 8 p.m. Jerry has been working the morning shift, from 6 a.m. to 2 p.m. After he was diagnosed with depression, Jerry began taking medication prescribed by his doctor. Jerry is late for work a couple of times and realizes that he is suffering from a common side effect of his medication: lethargy after first waking up. Jerry asks his manager to allow him to switch to the afternoon shift, coming in at noon and staying until the center closes at 8 p.m. Jerry's manager allows the change as a reasonable accommodation for Jerry's disability.

Sometimes, the side effects of legal drugs mimic intoxication. In this situation, employers must be careful not to assume that the employee is using alcohol or illegal drugs. The best approach when an employee appears to be impaired is to discuss the work problem, pointing out the specific behavior that's creating trouble at work, and allowing the employee to explain. If you find out that the employee's condition is due to legal medication to treat a disability, you can then start a conversation about reasonable accommodations.

What About Medical and Recreational Marijuana?

About half of the states—and the District of Columbia—allow residents to use marijuana for medical purposes. Called "medical marijuana" or "compassionate use" laws, these measures typically require the user to have a doctor's written authorization to use marijuana, often for particular diseases or disabilities. If a patient meets the criteria, he or she cannot be prosecuted under state law for crimes relating to the use, possession, or cultivation of a certain amount of marijuana. Federal drug laws still apply, however.

These laws raise a concern for employers that want to discipline employees who use marijuana at work, who arrive at work obviously stoned, or who test positive for marijuana use on a drug test. Can the employee claim that the employer must accommodate his or her use of marijuana because it was prescribed by a doctor for a disability?

The California Supreme Court has said no, ruling that the state's medical marijuana law applied only to criminal prosecution, not to the workplace. The Oregon Supreme Court also found against the employee in a medical marijuana case, but didn't decide the ultimate question of whether an employee who is using prescribed marijuana for a disability is entitled to an accommodation for his or her drug use. If you do business in a state with a medical marijuana law, and an employee requests an accommodation for marijuana use, talk to an employment lawyer about your options.

In 2012, Colorado and Washington legalized the recreational use of marijuana. The Department of Transportation quickly announced that these laws would have no effect on its drug testing requirements for transportation and safety-sensitive positions. Experts so far agree that these laws probably won't change private employer practices, either. The laws don't explicitly apply to employment, nor do they outlaw drug testing for marijuana. As more localities legalize marijuana for some or all purposes, however, the strain between allowing people to use marijuana and allowing their employers to fire them for doing so may bring about some changes. Some marijuana advocates suggest, for example, that employers test only for actual impairment, not for the presence of marijuana metabolites (which show only that the employee used marijuana at some point in the recent past). It's too soon to tell how this will play out, so stay tuned.

Testing Laws

The rules that apply to drug and alcohol testing are complex. On the one hand, testing is required for certain employees in the transportation industry and other safety-sensitive positions, and encouraged by state laws that provide incentives for maintaining a drug-free workplace. On the other hand, state and local laws may limit the circumstances in which an employer may test and the types of tests an employer may conduct. And, employees may claim that their privacy was violated or that they were wrongfully discharged on the basis of an improperly administered test. For all of these reasons, employers that plan to test must consult with a lawyer to come up with a policy and procedures that will pass legal muster, as explained in "Voluntary Programs to Combat Drug and Alcohol Use," below.

When Testing Is Required

Most private employers are not required to test for alcohol or drug use. The big exception to this rule is for transportation and other safety-sensitive industries that are regulated by certain federal agencies, including the Federal Highway Administration, the Federal Aviation Administration, and the U.S. Coast Guard. For example, those in the trucking industry, aviation, or mass transit, as well as those who contract with the Department of Defense or NASA, may be required to test at least some employees for alcohol and drug use. (For more information on these requirements, check out the website of the Substance Abuse and Mental Health Services Administration, part of the U.S. Department of Health and Human Services, at www.workplace.samhsa.gov.)

Legal Limits on Testing

Aside from these exceptional laws that require testing in limited circumstances, federal law doesn't require or prohibit drug testing. However, some states have adopted laws that place limits on an employer's ability to test. For example, some states allow random drug testing; others allow testing only if the employer has some reason to suspect drug use (following an accident or based on the employee's appearance or behavior, for example). States that allow drug testing often impose notice and policy requirements, and some states provide that employees have the right to contest a positive result, ask for a retest, or receive a copy of the test results. To find out about your state's law, see "State Drug and Alcohol Testing Laws," in Appendix B.

Some states have laws that require employers to test if they wish to qualify for a discount on their workers' compensation premiums. These programs are not mandatory, but employers that choose to enroll in them must follow the requirements, including testing, to qualify for the discount. See "State Drug-Free Workplace Laws," below, for more information.

CAUTION

Don't forget local laws. Drug testing is a controversial subject, and one that some municipal governments have weighed in on (typically, to ban or place strict limits on drug testing). If you do business in a city or county that has a local drug testing ordinance, you must follow its requirements. Contact your local government to find out whether there is a drug testing ordinance that applies to your company.

Is an Alcohol or Drug Test a Genetic Test?

The Genetic Information Nondiscrimination Act (GINA) prohibits employers from requiring employees to provide genetic information and from using genetic information as the basis for employment decisions, except in very limited circumstances. Genetic tests are a form of genetic information, and some consider alcoholism and drug addiction to have a hereditary component, which raises this question: Are drug and alcohol tests considered genetic tests prohibited by GINA?

The EEOC has said no. Tests that reveal the presence of alcohol or drugs are not considered genetic tests. However, a test to determine whether someone has a genetic predisposition for alcoholism or drug use does count as a genetic test, and would be prohibited by GINA unless an exception applies. (For more on GINA, see Chapter 5.)

Even in states that don't have drug testing laws, employees might have a legal claim against the employer based on the way the test was conducted, the reasons for the test, or what the employer did with the test results. Here are some examples:

- **Discrimination claims.** If your company singles out certain groups of employees—for example, by race or disability—for drug testing, it could face a discrimination claim. Similarly, if your company tests only union supporters or members, it could face an unfair labor practices charge.

- **Invasion of privacy.** Even if your company has a legal right to test, the way the testing is conducted could lead to invasion of privacy claims. For example, if you require the employee to provide a urine sample while others are watching, this might violate the employee's privacy.

- **Disability-based claims.** As explained above, an employee who is taking medication for a disability is protected by the ADA. Some prescribed medications turn up on drug tests, and some drugs that would otherwise be illegal are legitimately prescribed for certain conditions. If you fire an employee for a positive drug test, and the employee's medication was legally prescribed for a disability, you could be facing a lawsuit.

- **Defamation.** An employee might have a valid defamation claim if the employer publicizes that the employee tested positive, if the employer has reason to know the test might not be accurate. For example, if a retest showed that the first test was a false positive or the employee has appealed the first test, the employer may be liable for revealing the results of the positive test beyond those with a need to know.

Drug-Free Workplace Laws

The federal government and many states have drug-free workplace laws that might dictate your company's response to employee drug or alcohol use. The federal law, the Drug-Free Workplace Act of 1988, applies to all federal grantees and some federal contractors. Some state laws are similar, in that they apply to employers that contract or receive grants from the government. Other state laws are voluntary: They provide incentives, such as discounts on workers' compensation premiums, to employers that follow the drug-free workplace rules.

Which Employers Test—and When?

Despite the legal hurdles, many employers test for drugs or alcohol. According to the National Survey on Drug Use and Health, nearly half of all full-time employees reported that their employers tested for illegal drug use, and more than 35% reported that their employers tested for alcohol use. Testing was more likely to happen during the hiring process: About 43% of employees reported that their employers tested applicants, but only about 30% reported random drug or alcohol testing of current employees.

Employees in the transportation, moving, and protective services industries are much more likely to face random alcohol and drug testing: Almost two-thirds of employees in these industries reported that their employers conducted random testing. Employees engaged in manufacturing, installation, maintenance, and repair also reported high rates of random testing. At the other end of the spectrum, employees working in legal occupations, entertainment industries (including media and sports), and education and libraries reported the lowest levels of random drug and alcohol testing.

CAUTION

Transportation and other "safety sensitive" industries are subject to stricter rules. As explained in "Testing Laws," above, employers in safety sensitive industries that are regulated by certain federal government agencies may be subject to tougher drug-free rules, including mandatory testing.

The Drug-Free Workplace Act

The federal Drug-Free Workplace Act requires covered employers to take certain steps to discourage employee drug use. The Act applies to all companies that receive grants of any size from the federal government. It also applies to companies that contract with the federal government, if the contract is:

- for at least $100,000
- not for the procurement of commercial goods (for example, simple purchase orders are not covered), and
- to be performed, in whole or in part, in the United States.

Contrary to popular belief, this Act does not require drug testing. It requires covered employers to take the following six steps (or face penalties, such as losing the contract or the chance to receive future contracts):

- Adopt and distribute a policy to all employees, stating that the illegal possession, manufacture, dispensing, distribution, or use of controlled substances in the workplace is prohibited, and stating the consequences to employees who violate the policy.
- Establish a drug-free awareness program to let employees know the dangers of drug use at work, explain the drug-free workplace policy (including penalties for violations), and tell employees about available counseling, rehabilitation, and EAP services.
- Notify employees that, as a condition of employment on the federal contract or grant, employees must abide by the drug-free workplace policy and tell the employer, within five calendar days, if they are convicted of a criminal drug violation.
- Give notice to the contracting or granting agency within ten days after receiving an employee's notification of a drug-related conviction.
- Penalize—or require satisfactory participation in a rehabilitation or drug abuse assistance program by—any employee who is convicted of a drug-related crime.
- Make an ongoing, good faith effort to maintain a drug-free workplace, as required by the Act.

State Drug-Free Workplace Laws

As explained in "Testing Laws," above, some states restrict an employer's ability to require applicants or current employees to take a drug test, or give the employees or applicants certain rights (to advance notice or to challenge a positive result, for example). These laws are intended to protect employees and applicants from overly intrusive testing protocols.

Instead of or in addition to these testing laws, some states have adopted drug-free workplace laws that give employers incentives to combat workplace substance abuse. Often, these laws allow employers to qualify for a discount on their workers' compensation premiums if they take certain steps to prevent employee drug use. Depending on state law, these steps might include adopting and distributing a written policy prohibiting drug use, providing employees with an EAP program or outside resources and assistance, and drug testing of applicants and/ or employees. To find out about your state's law, see "State Drug and Alcohol Testing Laws," in Appendix B.

Off-Duty Conduct Laws

More than half of the states have off-duty conduct laws, sometimes called "lifestyle discrimination" laws. These laws prohibit employers from taking action against employees based on certain off-the-job activities, as long as those activities are not illegal. The form of these protections varies: Some states protect an employee's right to engage in any lawful activity, some protect an employee's right to use lawful products off the job, and some protect only an employee's right to smoke or use other tobacco products off the job.

Because these laws protect only lawful behavior, they don't limit an employer's ability to test for illegal drugs or take action against employees who use them. However, taking action against an employee for off-duty drinking or the off-duty use of legal drugs (prescription painkillers used properly, for example) could violate the law, depending on exactly what your state prohibits and allows.

So far, only one state has considered whether medical marijuana use qualifies as "legal" drug use that would be protected under these statutes. In Colorado, at least, it does not: The state Supreme Court found that an employer could fire an employee for off-duty use of medical marijuana, even though it was legal under state law, because it was still illegal under federal law.

These laws typically don't prohibit taking action against an employee for behavior on the job, including performance or conduct problems relating to alcohol. So, for example, while it might be illegal in some states for a manager to discipline an employee simply because the manager saw the employee in a bar after work, it would be legal for the manager to discipline the employee for arriving late to work, even if that tardiness was caused by the previous night's trip to the bar. And these laws don't prevent employers from disciplining or firing employees who come to work intoxicated, even if the drinking technically occurred while the employee was off duty (for example, before the employee left home to come to work). To find out whether your state has an off-duty conduct law, contact your state labor department (see Appendix B for contact information).

Voluntary Programs to Combat Drug and Alcohol Use

As you can see, companies that want to prevent employee drug and alcohol use have to consider a number of different legal requirements in coming up with a program. A system that's perfectly legal—or even encouraged through government incentives—in one state might be unlawful in another. That's why any employer that plans to adopt drug-free workplace rules absolutely must work with an experienced employment lawyer.

Components of a Voluntary Drug-Free Workplace Program

What's appropriate for your company will depend on its size, culture, and resources, as well as the extent and type of its current problems with employee drug and alcohol use. Here are some of the components you might consider, in consultation with a lawyer:

- A **written policy** that explains the dangers of workplace drug and alcohol use, prohibits drinking or drug use at work, and outlaws the possession or sale of drugs. (You can find a sample policy at this book's online companion page; see Appendix A for more information.)

- An **employee education program** that helps employees understand the signs and dangers of substance abuse, as well as the resources available to employees who need help for themselves or a family member.
- A **supervisor training program** that educates supervisors on the signs of possible drug or alcohol use and explains what they should do if they suspect an employee is intoxicated at work or has a substance abuse problem.
- **EAP services** for employees who need help (including help dealing with a family member's substance abuse). An EAP service might include counseling, referrals to outside resources, rehabilitation programs, and so on.

For Employers Considering Testing

If you plan to drug test employees, you must first adopt a written policy explaining who will be tested, when tests will be required, how you will test, what happens to employees who refuse to be tested, and how you will deal with test results (including how employees can appeal or challenge a positive test result), among other things. As explained above, federal, state, and even local laws, along with court decisions in lawsuits filed by employees, determine what is legally allowed. If your company plans to institute a testing program, you will need help from a lawyer to make sure your policy and procedures won't get you into legal trouble.

CAUTION

Employers that are dealing with a union may not make unilateral decisions about drug testing. If your company has already discussed this issue with the union, drug testing might be addressed in the collective bargaining agreement, which dictates what your company may and may not do. If you have not yet negotiated a drug testing program with the union, you must do so before putting any procedures in place. Drug testing is a mandatory subject of bargaining, which means that employers must negotiate with the union rather than unilaterally adopt a program.

Types of Tests

There are a number of different types of drug testing available. A drug test might examine employee urine, saliva, breath, blood, or hair, for example. The test might be limited to certain illegal drugs; for example, the "five-panel" test used under Department of Transportation regulations looks only for cocaine, amphetamines, opiates, marijuana, and PCP. Others cast a broader net, including prescription drugs. Some employers also test for alcohol.

No matter what you test for, you must have procedures in place to determine whether an employee who tests positive is using prescription drugs legally (or has a medical condition that explains the results), and whether the employee has a disability requiring the company to accommodate his or her use of prescription medication. For example, many protocols include an analysis of test results by a medical review officer—a doctor who determines whether a positive test result can be explained by a medical condition, prescribed medications, or other reasons given by the employee.

Whom to Test

Because drug tests impinge on employee privacy, you are generally on the firmest legal footing when you have the most compelling reason to test: safety. For this reason, some employers test only employees whose positions carry a high risk of injury to themselves or others (for example, employees who must carry a weapon or who drive a commercial vehicle). Safety also gives you a good reason to test employees whom you suspect of illegal drug use or who have been in an accident that calls their sobriety into question.

If you decide to test some employees but not others, you must be consistent. For example, you could reasonably choose to test only employees in particular positions (those who provide armed security, transport valuable items, or operate heavy machinery, for example). In this situation, however, you should test every employee who holds that position, rather than picking and choosing whom to test. Ad hoc decision making can quickly lead to claims of discrimination.

When to Test

There are a number of points in the employment relationship when an employer might conduct drug testing. State laws may prohibit or restrict some of these types of testing. For example, some states prohibit or limit random drug tests, and some place more restrictions on testing for current employees than applicants.

- **Applicant testing.** Some employers routinely test job applicants (at least those who reach the final stages of consideration for a position), or even current employees that are moving to a different job with higher security requirements.
- **Periodic testing.** Some employers require employees to take a drug test as part of a regular medical regimen, such as an annual physical examination.
- **Random testing.** For example, an employer might test ten employees every month, on a date that is not announced in advance.
- **Reasonable suspicion testing.** Some employers test employees whom they reasonably suspect are using drugs. For example, if a manager notices signs of impairment, sees a worker using an illegal drug, or finds illegal drugs in an employee's possession, that might trigger testing under the company's policy.
- **Testing after an accident.** Some employers routinely test employees who have been involved in on-the-job accidents, particularly those that may have been caused by human error. Some employers test any employee who has been in an accident that caused injuries or property damage (for example, to a company car).
- **Post-rehabilitation testing.** Some employers require employees who have tested positive for drugs in the past or who have participated in a drug rehabilitation program to undergo periodic testing as a condition of returning to work.

Test Procedures

Some state laws (as well as common law privacy protections) regulate the way employers conduct the test, including how the employee provides a sample, what precautions are taken to make sure the sample isn't tampered with, who does the testing, and how a positive result is handled.

Tips for Avoiding Legal Trouble

As emphasized above, you must work with a lawyer if you plan to implement a drug-free workplace program, particularly one that includes testing. Here are some tips to consider as you sort through your options:

- Draft and distribute a written policy well in advance of any testing. This will put employees and applicants on notice and give them a chance to clean up or move on if they don't want to be tested. (Check out the Department of Labor's Drug-Free Workplace Advisor Policy Builder, www.dol.gov/elaws/drugfree.htm, for ideas.)

- Make sure your policy and testing program fit the culture at your company. If your workplace is creative and employees work independently, for example, employees might view testing as a lack of trust or an unnecessarily bureaucratic gesture.

- When you roll out the policy, tell employees why your company thought it was necessary. Explain any testing requirements you plan to implement, as well as any EAP, rehabilitation, or other resources available to employees.

- Get employee and applicant consent, in writing, to testing.

- Use a reliable, accredited test lab. Your state may require the lab you use to be certified by a state agency.

- Pay for all testing, and pay employees for the time they spend getting tested.

- Never use physical force or restraint on an employee. An employee who doesn't want to be tested should not be required to submit to a test. If your policy requires testing, it should also provide that employees may be fired for refusing to be tested.

- Be consistent and evenhanded in deciding whom to test. Use objective criteria and apply them in the same way to every employee to avoid discrimination claims.

- Train managers to recognize the signs of possible impairment. Reasonable-suspicion testing depends on your managers' observation skills; make sure that they know what to look for and are not playing favorites.

Tips for Avoiding Legal Trouble (continued)

- Document the reasons for each test, such as the signs of impairment that led a manager to believe an employee might be using drugs or the details of an accident that required drug testing.
- Maintain the confidentiality of test results.
- Adopt procedures for employees to challenge a positive test result, including a process for employees to discuss their legal use of prescription or over-the-counter drugs.
- Create effective programs to help employees who have substance abuse concerns, including a robust EAP system. Support employee rehabilitation efforts with referrals, time off, and ongoing monitoring.

Ten Steps to a Successful Investigation of Drug or Alcohol Use

This section explains how to apply the basic investigation steps covered in Part I of this book to an investigation of drug or alcohol use. If you haven't read Part I, you should do so before getting into this more specific material; the discussion that follows assumes that you are already familiar with basic investigation procedures.

Decide Whether to Investigate

You might learn of a possible drug or alcohol problem in a number of ways. An employee might complain that other employees are using or selling drugs. A customer or client might report that an employee smelled of liquor or seemed dazed and inattentive. A supervisor might report suspicions that an employee's recent problems with attendance or performance could be related to substance abuse. An accident, harassment, or violence investigation might lead to evidence of alcohol or drug use. You might even find out about a problem from the police (for example, if an employee is arrested for driving under the influence while making deliveries during work hours, or a group of employees are arrested for smoking marijuana in a local park during their lunch break).

Drugs or Alcohol at Work

No matter how you find out about the problem, any incident involving the possibility that employees are working under the influence of drugs or alcohol should be investigated immediately. (The same is true of drug possession, sale, or cultivation or manufacture at work.) The legal and practical risks of allowing this behavior to continue once your company is on notice are simply too high to ignore. What's more, federal contractors subject to the Drug-Free Workplace Act and employers that are subject to state drug-free workplace rules might be legally required to investigate, in order to show that they are making a good faith effort to enforce their policy and maintain a drug-free workplace.

> CAUTION
> **A fired employee's eligibility for unemployment may depend on the actions you take to prove drug use**. Some states disqualify former employees from receiving unemployment benefits if they were fired for drug or alcohol use. States have different requirements as to the proof necessary to show that the employee was impaired. Some require an employer to provide a positive drug test (or, in some cases, proof that an employee refused to take a test). In these states, if you fire an employee for drug or alcohol use but can't produce a positive test, the employee may still be eligible for benefits.

At the same time, however, employers must not take action based solely on complaints or suspicions. Employers that mistakenly assume drug or alcohol use based on an employee's behavior can quickly get into trouble under the ADA, or be faced with a defamation or wrongful discharge claim. Testing without sufficient grounds under your policy and state and local law can also lead to legal problems. For example, if your policy (and your state's law) allows drug testing only on a reasonable suspicion of drug use, you must make sure you have sufficient facts to warrant a test before moving forward.

Warning Signs of Drug or Alcohol Use

An employer might learn of employee drug or alcohol use after a serious incident, such as an accident, assault, or arrest. Often, however, an employee's alcohol and drug use escalates over time, which gives employers a strong incentive to intervene early, before disaster strikes. The federal government's Working Partners for an Alcohol- and Drug-Free Workplace has identified some behaviors that might signal a drug or alcohol problem, listed below. Keep in mind, however, that these behaviors don't necessarily mean that an employee is using alcohol or drugs; acting on the basis of these signs alone could lead to serious trouble. You should treat these signs only as indications that you should inquire or investigate further:

- coming in late, leaving early, or unauthorized absences
- unreliability, including being away from the assigned work station frequently
- carelessness and repeated mistakes
- being argumentative and uncooperative
- inability or unwillingness to follow directions
- avoiding responsibility
- blaming others or making unbelievable excuses
- taking unnecessary risks by ignoring safety and health procedures, and
- frequent involvement in accidents, mistakes, or damage to equipment or property.

In addition, alcohol and drug use cause physical effects, depending on the drug. An employee who is drinking may smell of alcohol, show a lack of coordination, slur words, or show excessive emotion, for example.

Substance Abuse Off the Job

Sometimes, an employee's off-duty use of drugs or alcohol leads to trouble at work. For example, perhaps a former star performer has had increasing problems with absences, performance, and attitude, and a manager believes substance abuse may be the cause. Perhaps an employee has confided in a manager or coworker that she is having trouble concentrating at work because of substance abuse, whether her own or that of a family member.

In these situations, an investigation probably isn't necessary, unless there are allegations that the employee has been under the influence at work. Instead, your company should counsel the employee on the work-related problems while offering any help you can for the underlying substance abuse. The company's response should have two parts:

- The employee's manager should handle the employee's work problems through the usual performance evaluation and discipline system. Meet with the employee and point out specific incidents or behaviors that need to change, such as unexcused absences, inattention to detail in written reports, or falling asleep in meetings. Ask the employee what's causing the problem, but don't come out and accuse the employee of substance abuse. Although it's legally permissible for an employee's manager to ask about the possibility of substance abuse, it can also lead to problems. As explained above, for example, this might lead the employee to claim that you perceived him or her as having the disability of addiction, which can lead to an ADA lawsuit. By focusing instead on the employee's problems at work, you can give tangible examples and demonstrate that your purpose isn't to engage in a personal attack, but to help the employee get back on track.

- If the employee has admitted to a substance abuse problem or said that a family member's substance abuse is leading to work lapses, refer the employee to your company's resources for substance abuse. If the employee hasn't raised the issue of substance abuse, you can suggest that the employee seek help from your company's EAP. Again, don't insist that the employee has a substance abuse problem; instead, tell the employee that the EAP exists to help employees with personal issues that might be affecting their work performance.

Take Immediate Action

Once you learn that an employee may be (or have been) under the influence of drugs or alcohol at work, your first steps will depend on whether the incident happened in the past or is unfolding in real time. If an employee may be currently impaired by drugs or alcohol, safety must be your first concern. For incidents that have already taken place, you should consider the scope and nature of the problem in deciding whether you need to act immediately.

If an Employee Is Impaired at Work

An employee who is working or attending a work event while intoxicated poses a significant safety risk. If you receive a report that an employee is working under the influence of alcohol or drugs, your first step is to find the employee and stop him or her from working. If the employee is off-site, you may need to go to wherever the employee is working. The employee should not be allowed or required to drive.

> EXAMPLE: Jack works for a vending machine company. He has a regular route of clients who use the company's machines. Jack goes to each client once a week to restock, collect the money from the machines, and talk to the facilities manager about any problems or concerns. A client calls you to let you know that Jack is in their building, behaving erratically. He parked the company van on the curb and left a door open, seemed to have difficulty loading products on his cart and wheeling them into the building, and appears to be slurring his words; he also smells of alcohol. You should ask the client to keep Jack there while you get to the client's building. If Jack really is drunk, you don't want him to drive that van.

If your company has a drug or alcohol testing program, you should immediately determine whether you have cause to test under the policy. If the employee has been reported by another employee or manager, ask that person to detail the reasons why they believe the employee is using drugs or alcohol, and put the response in writing. If you aren't certain that you have the right to test, consult with another company official or legal counsel.

If you conclude that testing is required, start the process, following the protocols in your company's policy. Particularly if you suspect that the employee has been drinking alcohol, time is of the essence: Alcohol metabolizes relatively quickly and may not show up in a test taken hours after the employee is reported.

If the employee appears to be intoxicated, you should take detailed notes of the facts that lead you to believe the employee has been drinking or using drugs. You should also tell the employee why you have stopped him or her from working and ask for the employee's explanation. Take careful notes of the employee's response to your questions.

EXAMPLE: Several employees who work in the warehouse have told their manager that for the past few weeks, Siobhan often comes back from lunch smelling like marijuana and acting like she's stoned. Everyone in the warehouse has to occasionally operate a forklift to move boxes, and they all have to work together frequently to unload shipments. Siobhan often refuses to drive the forklift or asks another employee to remind her of how to operate the controls. She has been unreliable when helping coworkers move boxes; often, she loses track of where items are supposed to go. On several occasions, she has tripped while carrying a box or dropped her end of a box she's helping to move. Her coworkers are increasingly unwilling to work with her because they're afraid they'll get hurt.

The manager immediately reports the situation to you. You ask the manager to write down all of the facts the employees have told him, as well as anything he has observed personally about Siobhan's behavior. You also ask the manager to have each employee who reported to him write down the facts they have observed that lead them to believe Siobhan may be using drugs.

Next, you go to the warehouse and ask Siobhan to return with you to your office. Once there, you tell Siobhan that several employees have expressed concerns about their safety in working with her, and that you can't allow her to work if she poses a danger to others. You briefly mention the specific incidents employees have reported, then ask her for an explanation of her behavior. Siobhan admits that she has had trouble working in the afternoons and claims that it's because she is tired and has been suffering from insomnia since she broke up with her boyfriend. During your conversation with her, you notice that Siobhan smells of marijuana, her eyes are bloodshot, and she appears to be somewhat dazed.

What should you do next? If your company's policy and state law allow for reasonable suspicion testing, you have good reason to require Siobhan to submit to a drug test. Although she has given an alternative explanation for her behavior, there is plenty of evidence to suggest that she might be using marijuana at work. Armed with the written statements of her coworkers and manager, as well as your written notes from your meeting with her, you would have more than sufficient legal grounds to require a test. If Siobhan refuses to take the test, you shouldn't force her to do so. However, you may terminate her employment for refusing to take the test, as long as your company policy allows for it. No matter what happens, you should arrange for Siobhan to be taken home. Don't allow her to return to work, and don't allow her to drive.

Once you have spoken to the employee, gathered notes on the reasons why you believe the employee is intoxicated, and completed any drug or alcohol testing, you should arrange for the employee to be taken home. Again, don't allow the employee to drive.

Company-Sponsored Events

Some companies choose to serve alcohol at social events, such as a holiday party, celebratory dinner, or summer picnic. If your company is one of them, you should set ground rules ahead of time for how much employees may drink and how you will handle intoxicated employees. For example, some companies serve alcohol only for the first hour of an event, limit how many drinks an employee may have (by giving out two drink tickets per person, for instance), have a company meeting before the event to talk about appropriate behavior, charge for alcoholic drinks while serving all other beverages free, and/or provide a car service for all employees who choose to drink alcohol.

If you receive a report that employees are overindulging, you'll need to make sure employees get cut off when they've had too much. You should also arrange rides home for everyone who might need one, if this hasn't already been taken care of.

CAUTION

Don't test employees without a policy in place. Even if you have strong, objective reasons to believe that an employee is under the influence, you shouldn't ask or require the employee to submit to a drug test unless your company already has a written drug testing policy—that has been reviewed and approved by a lawyer—allowing for a test. Many states allow drug testing only if the employer has a written policy and employees have been notified of the circumstances when testing will be required and the consequences of testing positive.

Events That Have Already Taken Place

If you receive a report or complaint about a past incident involving drugs or alcohol, you may still want to take immediate action, depending on how serious the event was and how many employees may be involved. If the employee appears to have an ongoing drug and alcohol problem, you may want to suspend the employee, with pay, while you investigate. For example, if a manager has reported that an employee has shown signs of intoxication twice in the last week, you will want to stop that employee from coming back to the workplace until you can find out what's going on. Or, if an employee has endangered other employees or caused an accident, the employee should not be allowed back to work until you find out what happened. Again, the employee should be suspended, with pay, while you investigate the situation. (For the reasons explained in Chapter 2, you shouldn't suspend the employee without pay.)

If it looks like your company may have a serious drug problem involving a number of employees, such as a possible drug dealing ring or a group of employees who are stealing controlled substances from the company itself (a hospital or pharmaceutical manufacturer, for example), you should immediately talk to a lawyer. Particularly if you aren't sure who may be involved, it might make sense to bring in the police and/or a private security firm that specializes in undercover workplace operations. This will allow you to gather evidence, find out which employees are causing the problem, and root out the troublemakers. On the other hand, involving the police can lead to problems (as explained in Chapter 7, "Bringing in the Police"). A lawyer can help you sort through the pros and cons here.

RESOURCE

Want more information on undercover drug investigations at work? In a typical undercover drug investigation, an "operative" poses as a new employee in the department that seems to have a problem. The operative builds relationships with suspects, branching out (and up the chain) and eventually— with police authorization and supervision—attempting to buy drugs. Once the operative has identified the main players and gathered proof against them, the investigation is brought to a close, sometimes followed by criminal prosecution. For detailed information on undercover drug investigations, including plenty of harrowing tales from the field, see *Undercover Investigations in the Workplace*, by Eugene F. Ferraro (Butterworth-Heinemann).

Choose the Investigator

As is true of any workplace investigation, you must choose an investigator who can successfully get to the bottom of the problem. The investigator may also have to testify about the company's actions in a professional, believable manner, should your company have to defend its handling of the investigation in court. Chapter 2 explains the qualities you should look for in an investigator. Here are a few special concerns that might come up in a drug or alcohol use investigation.

Professionalism

In a case involving drug or alcohol abuse, employees may reveal deeply personal facts, such as a family history of alcoholism or addiction, relationship problems that have contributed to abuse, or the problems substance abuse has caused in the employee's private life. Employees may be in denial about having a problem, may offer rationalizations and justifications, and may refuse to accept responsibility for how their alcohol and drug use is affecting their ability to do their job.

The investigator you choose must be able to listen sympathetically while controlling his or her response. Even if an employee starts the conversation, asking too many questions about an employee's addiction could lead to trouble under the ADA. Similarly, even if the employee is the first to raise the issue, getting too far into an employee's personal life could lead to an invasion of privacy claim.

Instead, the investigator should focus squarely on the employee's behavior at work. While it's important to offer help to employees who need it, the investigator shouldn't get so wrapped up in the employee's explanations and rationalizations as to lose sight of the ultimate goal: to improve performance and correct misconduct at work. Ultimately, it's the employee's job to figure out why drugs or alcohol have become a problem in his or her life. It's your job to determine whether those problems have found their way into the workplace and, if so, to take corrective action.

Expertise

The investigator may need some special expertise in drugs and alcohol: what they look like (and perhaps smell like), how they are used, what paraphernalia are associated with them, what effects they have on users, and so on. If your company allows testing on a reasonable suspicion, knowing what particular drugs look like and how people ordinarily react to them will help the investigator make sure that threshold has been met. It will also help the investigator evaluate all of the evidence at the end of the investigation. In lieu of the investigator having this expertise, you could make an expert available to assist the investigator, if necessary.

When to Use an Outside Investigator

You may want to bring in a professional investigator for a drug or alcohol problem (and possibly private security or law enforcement assistance) if the problem looks to be larger or more serious than you can handle comfortably handle in-house. For example, you might consider an outside investigator if:

- It appears that serious illegal behavior—such as drug sales or manufacture—are occurring on company property.
- The problem seems to be widespread and you aren't sure who's responsible.
- A possibly impaired employee has already caused serious damage (for example, killing or seriously injuring a pedestrian in a car accident) for which your company is likely to face legal liability.

Plan the Investigation

When investigating drug or alcohol use, you may be starting with a complaint or report of inappropriate behavior by a particular employee, such as slurred speech, erratic driving, or the odor of alcohol or marijuana. If the employee was reported while intoxicated, you may also have the results of your preliminary work—such as your notes from talking to the employee, notes taken by the employee(s), client, or other person who made the original report—and perhaps the results from a drug or alcohol test. You may even have the employee's own admission of drug or alcohol use.

In some cases, however, you may suspect alcohol or drug use without knowing the culprit. For example, perhaps a manager has found obvious signs of drug or alcohol use, such as empty bottles, drug paraphernalia, or drug-related trash (marijuana cigarette butts, for instance). Perhaps someone found drugs in a common area, such as a locker room or restroom. Maybe there have been a series of accidents in one department that could be related to drug or alcohol use. Your planning and approach will depend on how you found out about the problem.

When You Have a Complaint or Report

If an employee has complained about, or a manager has reported, potential drug or alcohol use, start with the facts at hand. Consider these questions as you begin to shape your investigation:

- **Who complained or reported the problem?** What's the relationship between that person and the employee who may be using drugs or alcohol? Did another employee or a manager complain, or did the information come from an outside source, such as a client, customer, or even the police?
- **What allegedly happened?** Did the person reporting the problem actually see the employee use drugs or alcohol? If not, what facts led that person to believe the other employee was impaired?
- **Who is the suspected employee?** Does the suspected employee have any prior misconduct involving drugs or alcohol? If your company conducts drug or alcohol tests, has the employee tested positive? Is there more than one accused employee?

- **Where and when did the alleged incident(s) take place?** How many incidents were there? Were others in a position to see the accused employee's behavior?
- **How did the company respond to the incident at the time?** If the employee was tested for drugs or alcohol, were the results positive? Did the employee admit to using drugs or alcohol? Are there notes—your own or from witnesses—detailing why others thought the employee might be intoxicated?

These questions should help you decide whom to interview, what evidence might be available, and what kinds of questions you'll need to ask. If the employee was reported while impaired, and you took the steps laid out in "Take Immediate Action," above, you can sensibly scale back your investigation; you've already done some of the work. Especially if the employee tested positive or admitted to drug or alcohol use at the time, you should have much of the information you'll need to make a decision (although you will probably want to talk to the accused employee again, and perhaps his or her manager and coworkers, to find out the magnitude of the problem).

Because drug and alcohol use may happen around company outsiders —particularly clients and customers—you may need to consider whether and how to approach these potential witnesses. (See "Interviewing Nonemployees," in Chapter 3, for advice on handling these conversations.)

When There's No Complaint or Report

If no complaint or report points to a particular wrongdoer, consider the facts. How did you find out about the possibility of drug or alcohol use? If drugs or alcohol were found in the workplace, where were they found? Who found them? Who has access to that area? When were they found?

If a rash of accidents or complaints of inappropriate behavior have spurred your investigation, consider who was involved in each incident. Do the same names keep coming up, or were many different employees involved? How did you find out about the problem? Does the problem seem to be isolated in one department? Does the same person manage all of the employees involved?

Gather Documents and Other Evidence

As in a theft investigation, you should gather documents—and particularly, physical evidence—of potential drug and alcohol use before conducting your interviews. A suspected employee's first act after being questioned about possible workplace drug use is likely to be destroying the evidence. And, you may need to gather evidence first to decide whether drug or alcohol testing is warranted under your company's policy. Having evidence in hand when you interview the suspected employee can also help you elicit more truthful answers to your questions.

Documents

Although documents may not play a major role in every drug and alcohol investigation, they are still important. Before you begin your interviews, pull together all of the relevant paperwork, including:

- the company's drug and alcohol policy, including any provisions relating to testing
- the personnel files and performance evaluations of the suspected employee (if there is one)
- the results of any drug or alcohol testing involving the suspected employee, and
- any documents pertaining to the incident, such as police paperwork for an employee's DUI arrest while driving for work, a customer's written complaint about the employee's behavior, or your notes from your first encounter with the suspected employee (if you had to intervene immediately).

Physical Evidence

In a drug and alcohol investigation, physical evidence often makes or breaks the case. For example, you may be able to find actual drugs or liquor, drug paraphernalia (such as rolling papers, a razor blade, or hypodermic needles), and items commonly used to mask drug or alcohol use (breath fresheners, eyedrops, or even a clean urine sample or substances used to adulterate or dilute a drug test specimen).

There are also special considerations when it comes to gathering physical evidence in these types of situations. First of all, you may be collecting evidence that is illegal to have in your possession. And to find that evidence, you may have to conduct a search, which means you must tread very carefully to avoid legal problems. You'll also need to keep detailed records of where evidence was found, what it looked like at the time, and what's happened to it since, so you can show that it hasn't been altered or otherwise tampered with.

Types of Physical Evidence

The evidence available in a drug and alcohol use investigation depends on what an employee is suspected of using, where, how often, and so on. Here are some physical items that you may find:

- alcohol, whether in bottles, cans, or containers typically used for other types of beverages, in which the employee is concealing alcohol (such as a water or soda bottle or a commuter mug)
- drugs
- items for consuming drugs, such as pipes, water pipes, rolling papers, razor blades, hypodermic needles, and roach clips
- trash from drug or alcohol use, such as vials, marijuana cigarette butts, glassine envelopes, baggies, empty containers of glue or other inhalants, and paper bags, or
- items used to mask alcohol or drug use, such as mints, mouthwash, eyedrops, and substances used to adulterate or dilute a urine sample in a drug test.

Finding and Preserving Evidence

When dealing with physical evidence in a drug or alcohol investigation, there are a few special considerations. First and foremost, if you find illegal drugs, talk to a lawyer immediately. They're called "illegal" drugs because it's against the law to have them in your possession (among other things). So, if you confiscate illegal drugs from an employee or find someone's workplace stash, you should immediately consult with a lawyer to figure out how you should handle the drugs and whether you should turn them in to law enforcement.

Sometimes, a workplace search can help you turn up evidence of drug or alcohol use. For example, if you suspect an employee of using drugs at work, you may want to search the employee's desk or locker, or to check the employee's personal belongings, such as a purse, briefcase, or vehicle (a common spot for using drugs during the workday). However, you must make sure you don't compromise employee privacy rights in your efforts to uncover evidence of wrongdoing. (See "Privacy Issues," in Chapter 7, for tips on conducting workplace searches that won't lead to legal trouble.)

CAUTION

Consult with a lawyer if you plan to install surveillance equipment. Because it's illegal, drug use and dealing typically take place in private, often in restrooms or locker rooms. To gather actual evidence of these activities, some employers use surveillance cameras or recording devices. However, the law strictly limits an employer's right to record employees: Some states flat out ban cameras in changing rooms or restrooms. Even if your state doesn't, you must tread very carefully when intruding this far into employees' privacy. A lawyer can help you figure out whether you have sufficient legal justification for surveillance.

You must be especially careful to preserve what lawyers call the "chain of custody" with evidence in drug and alcohol cases. This means you should be able to prove where the evidence was found and what happened to it after it was found, in order to counter an employee's claim that the evidence was manufactured, changed, or tampered with.

Start by taking photographs of any evidence you find, exactly where and as you found it. For example, if you find marijuana in an employee's drawer, take a picture of the open drawer with the marijuana sitting in it, before you touch anything. If you find liquor bottles in the trash, take a picture of the trash can with the liquor bottles in it, then another picture of the bottles once you've removed them from the trash, showing how many there are and what condition they're in.

After you've photographed the evidence where you found it, you may need to hand it over to the police, as explained above. If not, you should isolate it in some way that prevents tampering, then store it in a place where others can't access it. For example, if you find rolling papers and a roach clip in an employee's work area, you could seal them in an envelope, mark the envelope to indicate what they are and the date you put them there, and then put the envelope in a locked filing cabinet in your office.

Be sure to take notes on what you find. What's apparent to you on day one may not be so evident months or years later, if the employee chooses to challenge your conclusions. For example, if you find a plastic water bottle with a small amount of liquid in it that smells like gin, you should not only photograph and preserve the bottle, but also take notes on how much liquid there is and its smell. Liquid evaporates and odor fades; your notes will demonstrate how the evidence looked when you found it.

TIP

You may need to test evidence. If you find liquor or marijuana, you'll probably know exactly what you've found, based on the distinctive smell and appearance. In some cases, however, you might find pills or powder that you can't identify, or that the employee claims is perfectly innocent. ("That's my blood pressure medication!") The only way to get to the truth may be to ask an expert to analyze the substance. If you are handing the evidence over to the police, they can likely tell you exactly what you've got. If not, however, you may need to get some testing done; a lawyer can help you figure out when and how to do this.

Interviews

Once you've finished gathering evidence, you're ready to start your interviews. An investigation of drug or alcohol use is different than a harassment, discrimination, or violence investigation, because there is typically no "victim." Generally, your main concern will be that employees are using alcohol or drugs, not that they are making another employee a target of inappropriate behavior. Even if an employee has complained or a manager has reported possible drug or alcohol use, the person who brings the behavior to the company's attention is usually acting as a witness, not someone who was directly harmed by the suspected employee(s).

In these cases, you'll start by interviewing witnesses (including the person who reported the behavior, if there is one), then move on to the suspected employee(s). You'll want to have all the evidence at your fingertips when you talk to the suspected employee, so you can require a drug or alcohol test (if your company allows them on a reasonable suspicion) and/or encourage the employee to admit any underlying substance abuse problem so you can direct the employee to treatment.

Interviewing the Reporting Employee

If an employee or manager has come forward with suspicions about alcohol or drug use, start your interviews with that person.

Getting Started

As always, you should get the interview rolling with an opening statement that briefly explains the process. Tell the employee that you've been asked to look into the complaint or report of possible drug and alcohol use, and you need to gather as much information as you can. Explain that retaliation is prohibited, and ask the employee to come to you if there are any reprisals for coming forward.

Questions for the Reporting Employee

When interviewing an employee or manager who suspects that another employee is using drugs or alcohol, you will often be trying to figure out if you have sufficient facts to either require the employee to submit to testing or conclude that the employee is guilty. The more facts you have, the better your legal position if you confront the employee directly about drug or alcohol use. Focus on sensory details: What did the reporting employee hear, see, smell, touch, or even taste that raised suspicion? You should also inquire about the reporting employee's relationship to the suspected employee, to find out if anyone has a motive to be less than truthful.

Sample Questions for the Reporting Employee
- What happened that caused you to come forward?
- How many incidents have there been?
- When and where did each incident take place?
- Please describe each incident to me.
- Who else was there?
- Did the employee know you were present?
- Did you speak to the employee at the time of the incident? If so, what did each of you say?
- Did you actually see the employee drink or use drugs?
- If not, what leads you to believe the employee is using alcohol or drugs?
- Were there any facts about the employee's appearance or behavior that led you to believe the employee is using alcohol or drugs?
- Did you smell the odor of alcohol or drugs on the employee?
- Has the employee caused any accidents that you believe are related to drinking or using drugs?
- How many accidents? When and where did they occur?
- Why do you believe they were alcohol- or drug-related?
- Has the employee said anything, to you or to others, that led you to believe the employee is using alcohol or drugs?
- Have you seen the employee with alcohol or drug paraphernalia?
- Do you believe other employees are involved? If so, why?
- Which other employees?
- Are there others who have witnessed the employee's behavior? Who, when, and where?
- Have you spoken to the employee about this? If so, when, where, and what did each of you say?
- Have you reported this to your manager? If so, when, where, and what did each of you say? If not, why not?
- Do you work with the employee? How would you describe your working relationship? Do you have any problems working together? Do you socialize outside of work?
- Do you know of any evidence relating to these incidents?
- Do you know or have an idea where the employee keeps alcohol or drugs?

- Have you taken any notes on these incidents?
- Have you spoken to anyone else about this? If so, to whom and what was said?
- Is there anything else you'd like to tell me?

Closing the Interview

When you've finished your questioning, review your notes with the reporting employee. Make sure that you got everything right and there are no gaps in your notes. Ask the employee to bring any new information to your attention right away, and to come to you if he or she faces retaliation for coming forward.

Interviewing Witnesses

When interviewing witnesses, your approach will depend on whether you have an employee suspect (for example, because a manager reported the problem or the employee's behavior was public, such as drunken revelry at a holiday party). If you are concerned about a particular employee's drug or alcohol use, you can treat other employees who might have seen something just as you would any other witness. You'll want to find out what the witness knows and how. For example, did the witness actually see drug use, hear about it, or see something that led him or her to believe another employee was intoxicated? Your goal is to gather the concrete facts without giving too much away.

If, however, you are dealing with unknown suspects, you'll have to consider whether your witness might be involved. For example, if your investigation began because rolling papers, small baggies, and the butts of marijuana cigarettes were found in the company's loading dock, everyone who has access to that area is a potential witness and a potential suspect.

Getting Started

Begin your witness interviews with a brief explanation of your purpose. If you are dealing with a known incident, you can be more direct. For example, if the holiday party turned into a bacchanal of binge drinking, you can tell witnesses, "I've been asked to look into what happened at the holiday party." Explain that you've been asked to investigate the situation. You shouldn't reveal facts unnecessarily, but you don't need to be overly secretive.

If you're dealing with allegations that aren't generally known in the workplace, you should approach the subject with more caution. Explain the general focus of your questions without getting into details. And, if the employee might be a suspect, you should be the most general of all. As in a theft investigation, these are the interviews you can begin simply by saying, "I'm hoping you can answer a few questions for me about your department," or "I've been asked to look into how we can improve off-site events, and I'd like to get your input," for example.

Questions for Witnesses

Your witness questions will depend on the situation. If you already have a suspect employee, consider what led you to this witness. Should the witness have seen or heard something? Did a reporting manager tell you that the witness works in the same area or on the same projects as the suspect employee? Was the witness present at the incident? Start by asking general questions that focus on the connection between the witness and the suspected employee, such as the incident the witness may have seen. Move toward more specific questions as the witness opens up; if the witness doesn't offer information about the incidents you're investigating, you may need to be more direct.

> **EXAMPLE:** In the last month, a client has raised concerns that Carl, a senior account representative, has been drinking quite a bit when they meet for lunch or dinner. Although Carl has clearly been intoxicated, he hasn't acted boorishly; mostly, the client is worried about this change in his behavior (and about him driving afterwards). You speak to the client who brought the incident to your company's attention, then decide to interview the associates who also service the account.
>
> You could begin your interview with Nicole, one of the associates, like this: "Hi Nicole. I need to ask you some questions about the Straw House account. You're one of the associates who works on the account, right?" Then you could ask who else works on the account, who the contacts are at the client business, how often they meet with the client, and so

on, before moving on to questions like these: "Have you met with anyone from Straw House in the last few months? When did those meetings take place? Do you attend all meetings with Straw House, or were there other meetings during the last few months that you didn't participate in? Who was at each meeting? Where did they take place? When? Did you notice anything unusual at these meetings? What happened, and why did you find it unusual?"

If Nicole identifies Carl's drinking behavior as a problem, you can move to more direct questions about that. If she doesn't, you might have to get more specific. For example, you could ask whether alcohol is served at these meetings, how often, and how much. You could ask whether she's noticed anyone drinking too much, or noticed any changes in how much people drink. You could ask whether everyone drinks or some abstain, and whether everyone drinks about the same amount or some drink more than others. If there really is a problem, Nicole will eventually come out with it. And, if she beats around the bush for quite a while before identifying Carl's drinking as problematic, you should ask her why she didn't say something sooner. It's possible that Carl has asked her not to or even threatened to retaliate if she reveals his problem.

If you have a witness who may be a suspect, hold your cards closer to the vest. You may have to start very generally before focusing in on what you really want to know. Broad questions will net you valuable background information, such as who has access to particular areas, who takes breaks at particular times, and so on. They will also help you build rapport with the witness. If the witness turns out to be your suspect, keeping things general at first may help you catch the witness off guard and get him or her to admit important information.

EXAMPLE: You're asked to investigate marijuana cigarette butts that were found on the loading dock. You decide to start by interviewing the four employees who have access to the loading dock. You might begin with a general statement, such as, "I've been asked to check up on some of our security procedures at the warehouse." Then, move from basic questions to more specific inquiries. For example, "Please tell me who works in each area of the warehouse. When a shipment comes in or goes out, what's the usual process? Who meets the truck? How do you know the truck has arrived?

Who loads and unloads? Is it always the same employees, or do you rotate or have different specialties? Is the loading dock area usually locked when a truck arrives? How do you access it and when? Which employees have access to the loading dock? Do each of these employees have a key? Do employees ever borrow the key? Under what circumstances? Where do you keep your key? Have you made any copies? Have you ever seen employees in the loading dock when they are not loading or unloading? When and which employees?" And so on. If this employee is the one smoking marijuana, you might get him to admit that he is the only one with a key to the loading dock, that he always insists on unlocking the door himself, and that no employees are allowed on the loading dock unless he is present, all before he realizes that you are actually concerned with drug use, not security.

Closing the Interview

Conclude your interview by reviewing your notes with the witness, making sure you got everything down. Have the employee sign your notes or a written summary of the interview you prepare afterwards. Ask the employee to let you know about any retaliation, and to come to you if any new information comes to light.

Interviewing the Suspected Employee

When you are interviewing the employee suspected of using alcohol or drugs, you may have a number of goals. You may be trying to figure out whether the facts warrant testing, under the law and your company's policy. You may want to convince the employee to admit the problem and seek treatment. Or, you may be trying to find out whether other employees are involved.

RELATED TOPIC

If you have a number of potential suspects. If you haven't narrowed your investigation down to one suspect, follow the guidelines for interviewing witnesses who may be suspects, above. Once you've reached some conclusions about who's really responsible for the problem, you can switch to the more direct approach in this section.

Your approach and questions will depend on the facts. Of course, the potential scenarios are endless. The employee may have a known problem: For example, he or she may have attended rehabilitation and been in recovery, only to have fallen off the wagon. The employee may have overindulged at a company event where alcohol was served. The employee may have been seen using illegal drugs, been caught with illegal drugs in his or her possession, or tested positive on a random drug test. The employee may be acting intoxicated; if so, the employee may be using illegal drugs, drinking alcohol, using legal drugs for a disability, or behaving strangely for an entirely different reason.

Given this wide variety, it's impossible to give a list of sample questions. Here are some guidelines and examples that will help you stay on the right track:

- **Start with background questions.** Keeping in mind the suspected or reported problem, ask the employee questions about the incident, area, or behavior.

    EXAMPLE: Jacob is suspected of using illegal drugs at work and of possibly selling them to other employees. He is away from his desk frequently, meets with nonemployees in the parking lot and on the street outside of work, and spends a lot of time on his cell phone and in the bathroom. He is jittery and anxious most of the time, talks a lot to coworkers, and has been losing weight. You might start this interview with basic questions about Jacob's job duties and schedule. What is he supposed to be doing and where? Does his job require collaboration with other employees? How often and which ones? Does his job require him to interface with outsiders? In what way, and who are they? Questions like these will help you evaluate the facts you've learned from others about his behavior.

- **If a report or complaint has been made, you should give the employee a chance to respond.** It's only fair to tell the employee what's been said and ask for the employee's side of the story. But don't reveal the name of the reporting employee.

EXAMPLE: Cora's team goes out for a happy hour once a month or so. Although no one is required to attend, Cora has made clear that she thinks these events are important for team building; not surprisingly, most employees attend when they can. Several have reported that Cora has been drinking way too much at the last few get-togethers, to the point of stumbling, slurring her words, and embarrassing herself. After the last happy hour, an employee had to take away her car keys and put her in a cab.

You don't need to be too circumspect in this interview. You should still start with background information about her team, the purpose for the happy hours, who comes, what people do there, and so on. But then, you can simply say, "How much do you typically drink at these events? What type of drinks do you have? How would you characterize your behavior?" If Cora doesn't come right out and admits that she's been drinking too much, you can say, "Cora, some employees are concerned that you are drinking too much at these events. They have been worried about your driving home, because you've had four or five mixed drinks in just an hour or two. Are these reports correct?"

- **Don't judge or accuse the employee.** You aren't going to get anything out of an employee whom you've just called a drunk, pothead, or coke fiend, except maybe some legal trouble. Even if you don't call an employee names, accusing someone of substance abuse isn't likely to help you convince the employee to get help; if the employee doesn't actually have a problem, you may even be violating the ADA.

EXAMPLE: For the past month, employees have noticed that Dana seems unsteady on her feet. She has also had some memory problems and sometimes seems to be slurring her words or having trouble coming up with the right word. She has been reported as "out of it" and dazed, sometimes even falling asleep briefly at her desk. She's had some absences and tardiness, too, which isn't like her.

You consider telling Dana, "Did you think nobody would notice that you're stumbling around and slurring your words? Obviously, you're willing to risk what was a very promising career because of drinking or drugs. I'm really disappointed in you." That seems too harsh, so you think about saying, "You know Dana, we really value your contribution, so we can't help but notice that you seem to have a substance abuse problem. The company has resources that can help, but you need to come clean with me." You realize that sounds accusatory as well, so you decide on a more objective approach: "Dana, a few employees have noticed that you seem tired at work a lot lately, have trouble remembering things, and are unsteady on your feet. Also, you've been absent or tardy quite a bit. As you can imagine, this is starting to cause problems with your supervisor and other employees. Can you tell me what's going on?"

Good thing you changed your tune! Dana tells you that she was diagnosed with multiple sclerosis, and the behaviors you mentioned are all caused by her disease. She tells you that she was in denial about how fast the disease was progressing, but realized a week ago that she had to go back to her doctor and start a more aggressive treatment regimen to help control her symptoms. She is feeling better, but may need some more time off; she also needs a change in job duties, at least until she gets a sense of how well her medications will work and what side effects they might have. You begin a conversation about reasonable accommodations. Had you gone in guns blazing, Dana would undoubtedly have been insulted and hurt. She also would have had some fodder for an ADA claim down the road, if things didn't work out. ("And then, they accused me of being a drunk or a drug addict, instead of just asking me what was wrong!")

- **If your company has a testing program, ask for the employee's consent to test.** If you conclude that there are grounds to require a test under your policies, let the employee know, and tell the employee that refusing to submit to a test could result in termination (if that's what your policy provides).

> EXAMPLE: Conrad has been seen snorting white powder in the bathroom by a coworker, who also reported that his nose was running, his eyes were red, and he was talking nonstop after his trip to the restroom. You immediately meet with Conrad and notice the same physical traits. You have reasonable suspicion to require an immediate drug test, which your company's policy allows. After you question Conrad about the incident, you tell him, "Conrad, as you know, our

company policy allows for drug testing if we have reason to suspect that an employee is using illegal drugs at work. Based on a statement from your coworker and your appearance and comments right now, I believe we have a reasonable suspicion. Will you agree to take a drug test, and sign this consent form? I have to warn you that refusing to submit to a drug test could lead to employment termination, as our policy clearly states."

- **If the employee opens the door, talk about available resources.** As noted above, you shouldn't accuse an employee of substance abuse. However, if the employee brings the subject up, you can and should talk about your company's offerings for substance abuse. Be careful, however: If the employee is going to be fired, it's both cruel and misleading to discuss all the wonderful treatment options that the employee won't ever be able to use.

EXAMPLE: Back to Carl, the senior account manager who was overdoing it at client dinners. When you meet with him, you follow your general questions about his job, the account, and the client, with more direct questions about his drinking behavior. Finally, you tell him, "Carl, the client has expressed some concern about how much you drink at these dinners, particularly in the last month or so. They like you a lot and are pleased with your work, but they feel that your drinking is detrimental to the relationship. They're also concerned about your safety driving. What can you tell me about this?" After hemming and hawing, Carl confides that he has been drinking more than usual lately. His daughter and her husband have moved back in with him and his wife after losing their home to foreclosure, which has been stressful for everyone. Carl says he hadn't considered that his drinking might be causing problems.

Absent a surprise revelation, the company has no plans to fire Carl: The client does like him, and he's an excellent performer. You tell him, "Carl, I appreciate you telling me that. We will talk later about the specific changes we need to see on this account; I'll need to talk to your supervisor about how we will handle this going forward. In the meantime, you should know that the company has resources available, through the EAP, to help employees deal with stresses outside the job. I recommend that you check in with them and find out which resources might be appropriate for you. These opportunities are there to help our employees, and we want everyone to take advantage of them if they need assistance."

Evaluate the Evidence

In some drug and alcohol investigations, it's relatively easy to reach a conclusion about what happened. The suspected employee may admit to the problem, there may be too many witnesses to the employee's drug or alcohol use to deny, or the employee may have tested positive in a drug or alcohol test. In other cases, however—and particularly if no testing was done—you'll have to weigh the evidence and figure out what happened.

Unlike a harassment or discrimination investigation, a case about drugs or alcohol typically doesn't come down to a "he said, she said" scenario. More often, you'll have to decide whether only one person is telling the truth: the suspected employee. Chapter 4 provides a list of factors you can use when analyzing the evidence. There are a few that are particularly likely to be relevant in drug and alcohol cases: demeanor, corroboration, and plausibility.

- **Demeanor.** Drug and alcohol use causes physical symptoms and traits. Did the employee smell of alcohol or marijuana? Was the employee lethargic, dreamy, out of it, or dazed? Was the employee jittery, talkative, nervous, or paranoid? Has the employee lost weight? Were the employee's eyes red or nose running? Of course, any of these facts could have other explanations. But you should know the signs of using the suspected drug or alcohol and look for them during your interview. If there's enough other evidence, the employee's appearance and demeanor could help you reach a conclusion.

- **Corroboration.** If an employee claims that apparently intoxicated behavior was due to a bad reaction to over-the-counter medication, for example, is that story supported by a doctor's note, statements of coworkers whom he told of the problem when it was happening, or other evidence? If the employee is accused of drinking at her desk, what did the coworkers who sit near her see?

- **Plausibility.** This often comes up when judging an employee's alternate explanation for particular behavior or actions, such as why the employee was in a particular place at a particular time, or what caused the employee's apparently intoxicated behavior. For example, an employee who is suspected of dealing drugs spends a lot of time in the parking lot and is often not where he is supposed to be working. Does he have an explanation? If so, does it make any sense? Similarly, an employee who claims that intoxicated behavior is actually due to a prescription drug might need to explain why that particular side effect only showed up at the company's anniversary party.

Take Action

If you conclude that an employee has used drugs or alcohol at work, you'll have to discipline the employee. As always, your response should depend on the seriousness of the behavior. For extreme misconduct such as selling or manufacturing drugs at work, firing is clearly in order. Many companies also choose to fire employees whose alcohol or drug use has injured other employees or done costly damage to property. At the other end of the spectrum, employees who don't seem to have an ongoing problem but showed poor judgment on one occasion—for example, by getting drunk at the company's holiday party or overindulging at a dinner meeting with a client—can probably be handled through the company's usual disciplinary procedures.

What of employees who clearly have a problem with drugs or alcohol and want to make a change before losing their jobs? Some companies offer employees like these structured help, through rehabilitation and/or last-chance or return-to-work agreements.

Rehabilitation

Studies show that providing treatment to addicted employees costs less than either ignoring the problem or terminating the employee. There are many things a company can do to help employees conquer substance abuse, from funding a stay at a rehabilitation facility to providing counseling and referrals through an EAP service to allowing employees to take time off for rehabilitation efforts.

Laws Regarding Rehabilitation

You might be legally required to provide time off for an employee to attend a rehabilitation program. For example, the federal Family and Medical Leave Act (FMLA) requires employers with 50 or more employees to provide up to 12 weeks off per year to eligible employees who need to recuperate from a serious health condition. Addiction or alcoholism may qualify as serious health conditions under the FMLA; if so, employees are entitled to FMLA leave to seek treatment. Employees are not, however, entitled to FMLA leave for absences caused by the substance abuse itself.

> EXAMPLE: Jonas is placed on a performance improvement plan for attendance, providing that any further unexcused absences will be cause for termination. At the performance meeting, Jonas tells his supervisor that he has been abusing prescription drugs and that his doctor has recommended a rehabilitation program. The company cannot terminate Jonas for entering rehab, as long as he has met all of the FMLA's requirements. However, before his leave for rehab begins, Jonas is again absent without excuse due to drug use. The company is free to terminate him, because his absence was due to drug abuse rather than due to seeking treatment.

Under the ADA, allowing time off for an employee to attend a rehabilitation program might be a reasonable accommodation for an employee with a drug or alcohol addiction. As explained above, however, the employer may apply its usual rules and standards to addicted employees, including prohibiting employees from using drugs or drinking at work. If an employee violates a workplace rule or has had consistent performance problems, the company may impose discipline, even if the problem stems from addiction.

> **EXAMPLE:** Jody has a drinking problem, which has caused her to miss a lot of work and to show up late on numerous occasions in the past year. Her supervisor has given her two written warnings and put her on a performance improvement plan; if she misses work or is late by 20 minutes or more in the next quarter, and her absence is not excused, she will be fired. Jody goes on a bender over the weekend and misses work on Monday and Tuesday. On Tuesday evening, her family holds an intervention with an addiction specialist and convinces Jody to enter inpatient alcohol rehabilitation treatment.
>
> Does the company have to keep Jody employed because she's in rehab? Most likely, no. Jody's alcoholism does not excuse her failure to meet the company's attendance standards, and she already committed a terminable offense by the time she entered rehab. However, there might be very good practical reasons for the company to retain Jody: If she was previously a stellar employee and is successful in seeking help for her addiction, it may make a lot more sense for the company to keep her than to try to replace her. However, the company probably isn't legally obligated to retain her.

Some state laws may also require employers to offer rehabilitation options or leave for employees with substance abuse problems. In a few states, an employee who tests positive for drugs may not be fired unless the employee is first given an opportunity to seek treatment. Before denying rehabilitation leave to an employee with a substance abuse problem, consult with an employemnt lawyer in your state.

When the Employee Returns to Work

Rehabilitation for drug or alcohol addiction isn't like physical therapy to recover from a car accident or broken leg. Addicts who have been through rehabilitation and stopped using alcohol or drugs are said to be "in recovery," not cured. An employee returning to work after completing a rehabilitation program may have special needs or concerns; most likely, your company will as well.

Meet With the Employee

If your company has gone to the trouble to provide time off or greater support for an employee's rehabilitation, you'll want to do everything you can to make sure that the employee's return to work—and continuing recovery—goes smoothly. To that end, you should meet with the employee ahead of time.

At the meeting, ask whether the employee has any special needs upon returning to work. Remember, an employee with a drug or alcohol addiction has a disability under the ADA, and your company may have to make reasonable accommodations (for example, to allow a couple of hours off each week for the employee to go to therapy, or accommodating an employee's use of medication to control the urge to drink or take drugs). If your company will require the employee to sign a last-chance agreement as a condition of coming back to work (see below), you should discuss that at the meeting, too.

For a recovering addict, being around alcohol or drugs can lead to relapse. If there are drugs or alcohol in your workplace, you should talk to the employee about ways to limit his or her exposure. For example, if your company runs assisted living centers for seniors, the employee should not be allowed to dispense or administer prescription medications. If sales representatives at your company socialize with clients over meals, you should make sure the employee feels comfortable declining alcohol in that setting. And, if you're dealing with an employee who has an alcohol problem, your company should consider making its internal social events alcohol-free.

Last-Chance Agreements

A last-chance agreement (sometimes called a return-to-work agreement) is a contract between the employer and an employee who is being allowed to return to work despite a serious performance or conduct problem. Last-chance agreements can be used for any misconduct, such as sexual harassment or unexcused absences. In the context of a substance abuse problem, a last-chance agreement typically provides that an employee must agree to certain conditions, such as successfully completing a rehabilitation program, continuing ongoing treatment, and/or submitting to periodic drug or alcohol testing. If the employee fails to meet the conditions or begins drinking or using drugs again, the agreement provides that the employee will be immediately fired, without the benefit of notice or any progressive discipline procedures the employer might otherwise use.

Last-chance agreements can be quite effective in driving home the message that the employee's behavior has been unacceptable and must stop if the employee wants to keep the job. They allow the employer to lay out exactly what the employee has done wrong and where the employee needs to improve, which lays the groundwork for a legally defensible termination, if necessary. Also, they allow the employer to get the employee's written consent to ongoing drug or alcohol testing, if desired.

Balanced against these advantages are a couple of risks to consider:

- **Compromising at-will employment.** If an employee works at will (and most do, in this country), the employee is free to quit at any time, and the employer is free to fire the employee at any time, for any reason that isn't illegal. (Even an at-will employer can't fire employees for discriminatory reasons or in retaliation for whistleblowing, for example.) Unless it's carefully drafted to preserve your company's right to fire at will, a last-chance agreement can give the employee a contractual right to continued employment as long as the employee does everything the agreement requires. To avoid this outcome, have your agreement reviewed by a lawyer to make sure you've done all you can to preserve the right to fire at will.

- **ADA problems.** As discussed above, you may take action to deal with employee drug or alcohol use and the performance and other work problems caused by that use. You may not, however, treat an employee differently simply because the employee has an addiction to alcohol or drugs. Some employers run into problems when they ask an employee to sign a last-chance agreement solely on the basis of addiction. A last-chance agreement places unusual limits and requirements on an employee, which makes it a disciplinary action. If, for example, an employee had no workplace problems, but was asked to sign a last-chance agreement after the employer found out that he attended Narcotics Anonymous meetings or attended ongoing rehabilitation counseling, that would constitute a disciplinary action imposed solely because of addiction, which violates the ADA.

Document the Investigation

Document your investigation following the guidelines in Chapter 4. Remember, if a lawsuit is filed—by an employee who is fired for drug or alcohol use or a bystander who is injured by an employee who may have been intoxicated—your report could be used as evidence. Clearly state the facts and conclusions you drew from them, but don't speculate. Making unwarranted assumptions can lead to legal problems.

> EXAMPLE: Tony is reported for using cocaine and offering it to other employees at the company's holiday party. Because Tony offered drugs to his manager, among others, he is forced to admit that the allegations are true. The company investigates the incident and ultimately decides to fire Tony.
>
> The investigator writes, "Tony admitted that he used cocaine at the holiday party and offered it to others. In light of how serious this incident was, it's clear that Tony is unable to control his drug addiction. Accordingly, I recommend that he be fired." Oops! The investigator has made a logical leap from the fact that Tony used cocaine on one occasion to the assumption that Tony is a drug addict—in other words, a person with a protected disability under the ADA. The facts don't warrant this conclusion (maybe it was the first and last time Tony used cocaine), and there's no need to go there. Once that sentence is deleted, the report is accurate and unlikely to lead to legal trouble.

Unlike other types of investigations, an investigation into alcohol or drug use often creates or involves medical records, which you must handle appropriately. Any document that contain an employee's disability—including alcoholism or drug addiction—counts as a medical record, as do records of genetic information (which could arguably include, for example, an employee's statement during an interview that alcoholism or addiction runs in the family). The safest legal policy is to treat all records that deal with an employee's alcohol or drug use as confidential medical records. This means your entire investigation file may have to be handled confidentially.

Under the ADA, you have an obligation to keep the employee's medical records and the facts they contain confidential. This information should appear only on documents and in files that are separate from the rest of the employee's personnel records, in a separate, locked cabinet. Although the employee is of course free to share his or her situation with others, the ADA allows the company to make this information available only to:

- the employee's supervisor, if the employee's disability requires restricted duties or a reasonable accommodation
- safety and first aid personnel, if the employee's disability may require medical treatment or special evacuation procedures
- insurance companies that require a medical exam, and
- government officials, if required by law.

 CAUTION

Drug test results may be a "consumer report" under the Fair Credit Reporting Act. If a drug lab conducts testing and reports the results directly to the employer, those test results are not a consumer report subject to the Fair Credit Reporting Act or FCRA (see "Reporting Requirements for Outside Investigators," in Chapter 2, for more on the FCRA). If, however, drug test results are reported to the employer by an intermediary that contributes to the results in some way or compiles the results along with other information about the employee (as an employee screening service might do for prospective hires), the results might be subject to the FCRA's requirements. Speak to a lawyer if you believe this law might apply to you.

Follow Up

Once your investigation is complete, there are still a few things to consider. If you retained an employee who used drugs or alcohol, you'll need to check in with that employee to make sure the rules are being followed. You may also want to consider some changes to company policies and practices, to prevent future problems.

Following Up With the Employee

If your company decided to retain an employee who used drugs or alcohol at work or admitted to a substance abuse problem that was affecting workplace performance or conduct, you'll want to follow up.

If your company decided to require the employee to submit to follow-up drug or alcohol testing, is that testing taking place as scheduled? Has the employee passed the test(s)? Has the employee met any other requirements set forth in a last-chance or return-to-work agreement? Have the workplace problems been resolved? For example, has the employee cut back on unexcused absences?

If the employee entered a rehabilitation program, check in to find out how the process is going. As explained in "Take Action," above, you should have a formal check-in meeting before the employee returns to work. It's also a good idea to touch base periodically after the employee returns, to offer encouragement and to find out how any reasonable accommodations are working. After being back at work for a while, the employee might have a better sense of what he or she needs to stay on the right track. And, of course, those needs might change over time.

Changes in Policy and Practice

Once you've been through the process of investigating alcohol or drug use, you should consider what the company can do to prevent future problems. Here are some questions to consider:

- Were your company's policies on alcohol and drug use sufficient to address the problem? Do those policies clearly explain what's allowed and what's prohibited? Do you want to consider adding a drug or alcohol testing program, if you don't have one already?

- Do company employees understand the dangers of substance abuse and alcohol and drug use at work? If not, you might want to initiate an employee education program, where you can also talk about why your company takes these problems seriously and where employees can go for help. A speaker series, brochures and other handouts, or brown-bag lunches to discuss the problem are all good ways to start. You could even encourage employees to complete self-assessments of their drinking behavior on National Alcohol Screening Day (held every year in April; go to www.mentalhealthscreening.org for more information).

- Do you need to know more about potential drug or alcohol problems at your company? Perhaps you successfully got an employee with a substance abuse problem into rehab, but you're concerned that you may have a larger problem on your hands. Consider asking employees to complete an anonymous survey or questionnaire about drug and alcohol use. Employees may be willing to express concerns anonymously that they wouldn't bring forward on their own. You could ask an outside company to administer the survey and compile the results, or use an online survey tool that allows for confidential responses.

• If your company serves alcohol at company functions, do you want to move to clean and sober celebrations? If not, what steps can you take to make sure that employee drinking stays under control and everyone gets home safely? Are employees clear about the rules that apply when they drink alcohol at a work function, such as a party or a client dinner?

• If you have an EAP, did it offer meaningful help, or do you want to rethink the offerings on substance abuse? Does your EAP help employees with family members who have substance abuse problems? Statistics show that only about 5% of companies with fewer than 100 employees have an EAP. If yours is one of the other 95%, it might be a good idea to reconsider, or at least come up with a list of resources for employees who want help.

• If your company provides or contributes to health insurance coverage, does your plan cover substance abuse and addiction treatment? If employees have to pay a portion of the cost, is that amount high enough to deter employees from seeking treatment voluntarily? Are there any possible changes that would offer employees more affordable treatment options?

Using the Interactive Forms

T his book comes with an online companion page, loaded with materials and extras. On the page, you'll find sample policies, forms, checklists, a sample investigative file, podcasts, and more. You can find the page at:

www.nolo.com/back-of-book/NVST.html

To use the interactive files, your computer must have specific software programs installed. Here is a list of types of files provided by this book, as well as the software programs you'll need to access them:

- **RTF.** You can open, edit, print, and save these form files with most word processing programs such as Microsoft Word, Windows WordPad, and recent versions of WordPerfect.
- **PDF.** You can view these files with Adobe Reader, free software from www.adobe.com. Government PDFs are sometimes fillable using your computer, but most PDFs are designed to be printed out and completed by hand.
- **MP3.** You can listen to these audio files using your computer's sound system. Most computers come with a media player that plays MP3 files, or you may have installed one on your own.

Editing RTFs

Here are some general instructions about editing RTF forms in your word processing program. Refer to the book's instructions and sample agreements for help about what should go in each blank.

- **Underlines.** Underlines indicate where to enter information. After filling in the needed text, delete the underline. In most word processing programs you can do this by highlighting the underlined portion and typing CTRL-U.
- **Bracketed and italicized text.** Bracketed and italicized text indicates instructions. Be sure to remove all instructional text before you finalize your document.

- **Alternative text.** Alternative text gives you the choice between two or more text options. Delete those options you don't want to use. Renumber numbered items, if necessary.
- **Signature lines.** Signature lines should appear on a page with at least some text from the document itself.

Every word processing program uses different commands to open, format, save, and print documents, so refer to your software's help documents for help using your program. Nolo cannot provide technical support for questions about how to use your computer or your software.

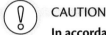

CAUTION

In accordance with U.S. copyright laws, the forms and audio files provided by this book are for your personal use only.

List of Files

All files are available for download at:
www.nolo.com/back-of-book/NVST.html

The following file is in Adobe Acrobat PDF Format:

Form Title	File Name
Sample Investigation Documents	SampleDocs.pdf

The following files are in MP3 format:

Form Title	File Name
Scenario 1: Taking a Complaint	Complaint.mp3
Scenario 2: Interviewing the Complaining Employee	ComplaintInterview.mp3
Scenario 3: Interviewing the Accused Employee	InterviewAccused.mp3

The following files are in rich text format (RTF):

Form Title	File Name
Complaint Policy	ComplaintPolicy.rtf
Open-Door Policy	OpenDoor.rtf
Antidiscrimination Policy	Antidiscrimination.rtf
Antiharassment Policy	Antiharassment.rtf
Antiviolence Policy	Antiviolence.rtf
Complaint Form	ComplaintForm.rtf
Drug and Alcohol Policy	DrugPolicy.rtf
Investigation Notice Form	InvestigationNotice.rtf
Investigation Report Form	InvestigationReport.rtf
Adverse Action Notice Form	AdverseAction.rtf
Checklist: Ten Steps to a Successful Investigation	InvestigationSteps.rtf
Checklist: Avoiding Common Investigation Mistakes	InvestigationMistakes.rtf
Document Checklist	DocumentChecklist.rtf
Credibility Checklist	CredibilityChecklist.rtf
Discipline Checklist	DisciplineChecklist.rtf
Investigation Report Checklist	InvestigationChecklist.rtf

Resources

State Laws Prohibiting Discrimination in Employment

Note: Federal law makes it illegal to discriminate on the basis of race, color, national origin, sex (including pregnancy, childbirth, and related medical conditions), age (40 and older), disability (including AIDS/HIV), religion, and genetic information. The following states have their own laws protecting certain classes from discrimination.

Alabama
Ala. Code §§ 25-1-20, 25-1-21

Law applies to employers with: 20 or more employees

Private employers may not make employment decisions based on:
- Age (40 and older)

Alaska
Alaska Stat. §§ 18.80.220, 18.80.300, 47.30.865

Law applies to employers with: One or more employees

Private employers may not make employment decisions based on:
- Age
- Ancestry or national origin
- Physical or mental disability
- Gender
- Marital status, including changes in status
- Pregnancy, childbirth, and related medical conditions, including parenthood
- Race or color
- Religion or creed
- Mental illness

Arizona
Ariz. Rev. Stat. §§ 41-1461, 41-1463, 41-1465

Law applies to employers with: 15 or more employees

Private employers may not make employment decisions based on:
- Age (40 and older)
- Ancestry or national origin
- Physical or mental disability
- AIDS/HIV
- Gender
- Race or color
- Religion or creed
- Genetic testing information

Arkansas
Ark. Code Ann. §§ 11-4-601, 11-5-403, 16-123-102, 16-123-107

Law applies to employers with: Nine or more employees

Private employers may not make employment decisions based on:
- Ancestry or national origin
- Physical, mental, or sensory disability
- Gender
- Pregnancy, childbirth, and related medical conditions
- Race or color
- Religion or creed
- Genetic testing information

California
Cal. Gov't. Code §§ 12920, 12926.1, 12940, 12941, 12945; Cal. Lab. Code § 1101

Law applies to employers with: Five or more employees

Private employers may not make employment decisions based on:
- Age (40 and older)
- Ancestry or national origin
- Physical or mental disability
- AIDS/HIV
- Gender
- Marital status

State Laws Prohibiting Discrimination in Employment (continued)

- Pregnancy, childbirth, and related medical conditions
- Race or color
- Religion or creed
- Sexual orientation
- Genetic testing information
- Gender identity
- Medical condition
- Political activities or affiliations
- Status as victim of domestic violence, sexual assault, or stalking
- Military and veteran status

Colorado

Colo. Rev. Stat. §§ 24-34-301, 24-34-401, 24-34-402, 24-34-402.5, 27-65-115; Colo. Code Regs. 708-1:60.1, 708-1:80.8

Law applies to employers with: One or more employees; 25 or more employees (marital status only)

Private employers may not make employment decisions based on:
- Age (40 and older)
- Ancestry or national origin
- Physical, mental, or learning disability
- AIDS/HIV
- Gender
- Marital status (only applies to marriage to a coworker or plans to marry a coworker)
- Pregnancy, childbirth, and related medical conditions
- Race or color
- Religion or creed
- Sexual orientation, including perceived sexual orientation
- Lawful conduct outside of work
- Mental illness
- Transgender status

Connecticut

Conn. Gen. Stat. Ann. §§ 25-4-1401, 46a-51, 46a-60, 46a-81a, 46a-81c

Law applies to employers with: Three or more employees

Private employers may not make employment decisions based on:
- Age
- Ancestry or national origin
- Present or past physical, mental, learning, or intellectual disability
- Gender
- Marital status, including civil unions
- Pregnancy, childbirth, and related medical conditions
- Race or color
- Religion or creed
- Sexual orientation, including having a history of being identified with a preference
- Genetic testing information
- Gender identity or expression
- Arrests or convictions that have been erased, pardoned, or rehabilitated

Delaware

Del. Code Ann. tit. 19, §§ 710, 711, 724

Law applies to employers with: Four or more employees

Private employers may not make employment decisions based on:
- Age (40 and older)
- Ancestry or national origin
- Physical or mental disability
- AIDS/HIV
- Gender
- Marital status

State Laws Prohibiting Discrimination in Employment (continued)

- Pregnancy, childbirth, and related medical conditions
- Race or color
- Religion or creed
- Sexual orientation
- Genetic testing information
- Gender identity
- Status as victim of domestic abuse, sexual assault, or stalking

District of Columbia

D.C. Code Ann. §§ 2-1401.01, 2-1401.02, 2-1401.05, 2-1402.82, 7-1703.03, 32-131.08

Law applies to employers with: One or more employees

Private employers may not make employment decisions based on:
- Age (18 and older)
- Ancestry or national origin
- Physical or mental disability
- Gender
- Marital status, including domestic partnership
- Pregnancy, childbirth, and related medical conditions, including parenthood
- Race or color
- Religion or creed
- Sexual orientation
- Genetic testing information
- Enrollment in vocational, professional, or college education
- Family duties
- Source of income
- Place of residence or business
- Personal appearance
- Political affiliation
- Victim of intrafamily offense
- Gender identity or expression

- Status as unemployed
- Tobacco use
- Any reason other than individual merit

Florida

Fla. Stat. Ann. §§ 448.075, 760.01, 760.02, 760.10, 760.50

Law applies to employers with: 15 or more employees

Private employers may not make employment decisions based on:
- Age
- Ancestry or national origin
- "Handicap"
- AIDS/HIV
- Gender
- Marital status
- Pregnancy, childbirth, and related medical conditions
- Race or color
- Religion or creed
- Sickle cell trait

Georgia

Ga. Code Ann. §§ 34-1-2, 34-5-1, 34-5-2, 34-6A-1 and following

Law applies to employers with:
- 15 or more employees (disability)
- 10 or more employees (gender) (domestic and agricultural employees not protected)
- One or more employee (age)

Private employers may not make employment decisions based on:
- Age (40 to 70)
- Physical, mental, or learning disability
- Gender (wage discrimination only)

State Laws Prohibiting Discrimination in Employment (continued)

Hawaii

Haw. Rev. Stat. §§ 378-1, 378-2, 378-2.5; Hawaii Admin. Rules § 12-46-182

Law applies to employers with: One or more employees

Private employers may not make employment decisions based on:
- Age
- Ancestry or national origin
- Physical or mental disability
- AIDS/HIV
- Gender
- Marital status
- Pregnancy, childbirth, and related medical conditions, including breast-feeding
- Race or color
- Religion or creed
- Sexual orientation
- Genetic testing information
- Arrest and court record (unless there is a conviction directly related to job)
- Credit history or credit report, unless the information in the individual's credit history or credit report directly relates to a bona fide occupational qualification
- Gender identity and gender expression
- Status as a victim of domestic or sexual violence (if employer has knowledge or is notified of this status)

Idaho

Idaho Code §§ 39-8303, 67-5902, 67-5909, 67-5910

Law applies to employers with: Five or more employees

Private employers may not make employment decisions based on:

- Age (40 and older)
- Ancestry or national origin
- Physical or mental disability
- Gender
- Pregnancy, childbirth, and related medical conditions
- Race or color
- Religion or creed
- Genetic testing information

Illinois

410 Ill. Comp. Stat. § 513/25; 775 Ill. Comp. Stat. §§ 5/1-102, 5/1-103, 5/1-105, 5/2-101, 5/2-102, 5/2-103; 820 Ill. Comp. Stat. §§ 105/4, 180/30; Ill. Admin. Code tit. 56, § 5210.110

Law applies to employers with: 15 or more employees; one or more employees (disability only)

Private employers may not make employment decisions based on:
- Age (40 and older)
- Ancestry or national origin
- Physical or mental disability
- Gender
- Marital status
- Pregnancy, childbirth, and related medical conditions
- Race or color
- Religion or creed
- Sexual orientation
- Genetic testing information
- Citizenship status
- Military status
- Unfavorable military discharge
- Gender identity
- Arrest record
- Victims of domestic violence
- Order of protection status

State Laws Prohibiting Discrimination in Employment (continued)

- Lack of permanent mailing address or having a mailing address of a shelter or social service provider

Indiana
Ind. Code Ann. §§ 22-9-1-2, 22-9-2-1, 22-9-2-2, 22-9-5-1 and following

Law applies to employers with: Six or more employees; one or more employees (age only); 15 or more employees (disability only)

Private employers may not make employment decisions based on:
- Age (40 to 75)
- Ancestry or national origin
- Physical or mental disability
- Gender
- Race or color
- Religion or creed
- Off-duty tobacco use
- Status as a veteran
- Sealed or expunged arrest or conviction record

Iowa
Iowa Code §§ 216.2, 216.6, 216.6A, 729.6

Law applies to employers with: Four or more employees

Private employers may not make employment decisions based on:
- Age (18 or older)
- Ancestry or national origin
- Physical or mental disability
- AIDS/HIV
- Gender
- Pregnancy, childbirth, and related medical conditions
- Race or color
- Religion or creed
- Sexual orientation
- Genetic testing information

- Gender identity
- Wage discrimination

Kansas
Kan. Stat. Ann. §§ 44-1002, 44-1009, 44-1112, 44-1113, 44-1125, 44-1126, 65-6002(e)

Law applies to employers with: Four or more employees

Private employers may not make employment decisions based on:
- Age (40 or older)
- Ancestry or national origin
- Physical or mental disability
- AIDS/HIV
- Gender
- Race or color
- Religion or creed
- Genetic testing information
- Military service or status

Kentucky
Ky. Rev. Stat. Ann. §§ 207.130, 207.135, 207.150, 342.197, 344.010, 344.030, 344.040

Law applies to employers with: Eight or more employees

Private employers may not make employment decisions based on:
- Age (40 or older)
- Ancestry or national origin
- Physical or mental disability
- AIDS/HIV
- Gender
- Pregnancy, childbirth, and related medical conditions
- Race or color
- Religion or creed
- Occupational pneumoconiosis with no respiratory impairment resulting from exposure to coal dust
- Off-duty tobacco use

State Laws Prohibiting Discrimination in Employment (continued)

Louisiana

La. Rev. Stat. Ann. §§ 23:301 to 23:368

Law applies to employers with: 20 or more employees; 25 or more employees (pregnancy, childbirth, and related medical condition only)

Private employers may not make employment decisions based on:
- Age (40 or older)
- Ancestry or national origin
- Physical or mental disability
- Gender
- Pregnancy, childbirth, and related medical conditions
- Race or color
- Religion or creed
- Genetic testing information
- Sickle cell trait
- Being a smoker or nonsmoker

Maine

Me. Rev. Stat. Ann. tit. 5, §§ 19302, 4552, 4553, 4571 to 4576, 23; tit. 26, § 833; tit. 39-A, § 353

Law applies to employers with: One or more employees

Private employers may not make employment decisions based on:
- Age
- Ancestry or national origin
- Physical or mental disability
- AIDS/HIV
- Gender
- Pregnancy, childbirth, and related medical conditions
- Race or color
- Religion or creed
- Sexual orientation, including perceived sexual orientation
- Genetic testing information
- Gender identity or expression

- Past workers' compensation claim
- Past whistleblowing
- Medical support notice for child

Maryland

Md. Code, [State Government], §§ 20-101, 20-601 to 20-608

Law applies to employers with: 15 or more employees

Private employers may not make employment decisions based on:
- Age
- Ancestry or national origin
- Physical or mental disability
- Gender
- Marital status
- Pregnancy, childbirth, and related medical conditions
- Race or color
- Religion or creed
- Sexual orientation
- Genetic testing information
- Civil Air Patrol membership

Massachusetts

Mass. Gen. Laws ch. 149, § 24A, ch. 151B, §§ 1, 4; Code of Massachusetts Regulations 804 CMR 3.01

Law applies to employers with: Six or more employees

Private employers may not make employment decisions based on:
- Age (40 or older)
- Ancestry or national origin
- Physical or mental disability
- Gender
- Marital status
- Race or color
- Religion or creed

State Laws Prohibiting Discrimination in Employment (continued)

- Sexual orientation
- Genetic testing information
- Military service
- Arrest record
- Gender identity

Michigan

Mich. Comp. Laws §§ 37.1103, 37.1201, 37.1202, 37.2201, 37.2202, 37.2205a, 750.556

Law applies to employers with: One or more employees

Private employers may not make employment decisions based on:

- Age
- Ancestry or national origin
- Physical or mental disability
- AIDS/HIV
- Gender
- Marital status
- Pregnancy, childbirth, and related medical conditions
- Race or color
- Religion or creed
- Genetic testing information
- Height or weight
- Misdemeanor arrest record

Minnesota

Minn. Stat. Ann. §§ 144.417, 181.81, 181.974, 363A.03, 363A.08

Law applies to employers with: One or more employees

Private employers may not make employment decisions based on:

- Age (18 to 70)
- Ancestry or national origin
- Physical, sensory, or mental disability
- Gender
- Marital status

- Pregnancy, childbirth, and related medical conditions
- Race or color
- Religion or creed
- Sexual orientation, including perceived sexual orientation
- Genetic testing information
- Gender identity
- Member of local commission
- Receiving public assistance
- Familial status (protects parents or guardians living with a minor child)

Mississippi

Miss. Code Ann. § 33-1-15

Law applies to employers with: One or more employees

Private employers may not make employment decisions based on:

- Military status
- No other protected categories unless employer receives public funding

Missouri

Mo. Rev. Stat. §§ 191.665, 213.010, 213.055, 375.1306

Law applies to employers with: Six or more employees

Private employers may not make employment decisions based on:

- Age (40 to 70)
- Ancestry or national origin
- Physical or mental disability
- AIDS/HIV
- Gender
- Race or color
- Religion or creed
- Genetic testing information
- Off-duty use of alcohol or tobacco

State Laws Prohibiting Discrimination in Employment (continued)

Montana

Mont. Code Ann. §§ 49-2-101, 49-2-303, 49-2-310

Law applies to employers with: One or more employees

Private employers may not make employment decisions based on:
- Age
- Ancestry or national origin
- Physical or mental disability
- Gender
- Marital status
- Pregnancy, childbirth, and related medical conditions
- Race or color
- Religion or creed

Nebraska

Neb. Rev. Stat. §§ 20-168, 48-236, 48-1001 to 48-1010, 48-1102, 48-1104

Law applies to employers with: 15 or more employees ; 20 or more employees (age only)

Private employers may not make employment decisions based on:
- Age (40 or older)
- Ancestry or national origin
- Physical or mental disability
- AIDS/HIV
- Gender
- Marital status
- Pregnancy, childbirth, and related medical conditions
- Race or color
- Religion or creed
- Genetic testing information (applies to all employers)

Nevada

Nev. Rev. Stat. Ann. §§ 613.310 and following

Law applies to employers with: 15 or more employees

Private employers may not make employment decisions based on:
- Age (40 or older)
- Ancestry or national origin
- Physical or mental disability
- AIDS/HIV
- Gender
- Pregnancy, childbirth, and related medical conditions
- Race or color
- Religion or creed
- Sexual orientation, including perceived sexual orientation
- Genetic testing information
- Use of service animal
- Gender identity or expression
- Opposing unlawful employment practices
- Credit report or credit information (with some exceptions)

New Hampshire

N.H. Rev. Stat. Ann. §§ 141-H:3, 354-A:2, 354-A:6, 354-A:7

Law applies to employers with: Six or more employees

Private employers may not make employment decisions based on:
- Age
- Ancestry or national origin
- Physical or mental disability
- Gender
- Marital status
- Pregnancy, childbirth, and related medical conditions
- Race or color
- Religion or creed

State Laws Prohibiting Discrimination in Employment (continued)

- Sexual orientation
- Genetic testing information
- Victims of domestic violence, harassment, sexual assault, or stalking
- Off-duty use of tobacco products

New Jersey

N.J. Stat. Ann. §§ 10:5-1, 10:5-4.1, 10:5-5, 10:5-12, 10:5-29.1, 34:6B-1, 43:21-49

Law applies to employers with: One or more employees

Private employers may not make employment decisions based on:

- Age (18 to 70)
- Ancestry or national origin
- Past or present physical or mental disability
- AIDS/HIV
- Gender
- Marital status, including civil union or domestic partnership status
- Pregnancy, childbirth, and related medical conditions
- Race or color
- Religion or creed
- Sexual orientation, including affectional orientation and perceived sexual orientation
- Genetic testing information
- Atypical heredity cellular or blood trait
- Accompanied by service or guide dog
- Military service
- Gender identity
- Unemployed status

New Mexico

N.M. Stat. Ann. §§ 24-21-4, 28-1-2, 28-1-7, 50-4A-4; N.M. Admin. Code 9.1.1

Law applies to employers with:

- Four or more employees
- 50 or more employees (marital status only)
- 15 or more employees (sexual orientation and gender identity only)

Private employers may not make employment decisions based on:

- Age (40 or older)
- Ancestry or national origin
- Physical or mental disability
- Gender
- Marital status
- Pregnancy, childbirth, and related medical conditions
- Race or color
- Religion or creed
- Sexual orientation (including perceived sexual orientation)
- Genetic testing information
- Gender identity
- Serious medical condition
- Domestic abuse leave

New York

N.Y. Exec. Law §§ 292, 296; N.Y. Lab. Law § 201-d

Law applies to employers with: Four or more employees; all employers (sexual harassment only)

Private employers may not make employment decisions based on:

- Age (18 and over)
- Ancestry or national origin
- Physical or mental disability
- Gender
- Marital status
- Pregnancy, childbirth, and related medical conditions
- Race or color

State Laws Prohibiting Discrimination in Employment (continued)

- Religion or creed
- Sexual orientation, including perceived sexual orientation
- Genetic testing information
- Lawful recreational activities when not at work
- Military status or service
- Observance of Sabbath
- Political activities
- Use of service dog
- Arrest or criminal accusation
- Domestic violence victim status
- Familial status

North Carolina

N.C. Gen. Stat. §§ 95-28.1, 95-28.1A, 127B-11, 130A-148, 143-422.2, 168A-5

Law applies to employers with: 15 or more employees

Private employers may not make employment decisions based on:
- Age
- Ancestry or national origin
- Physical or mental disability
- AIDS/HIV
- Gender
- Race or color
- Religion or creed
- Genetic testing information
- Military status or service
- Sickle cell or hemoglobin C trait
- Use of lawful products off site and off duty

North Dakota

N.D. Cent. Code §§ 14-02.4-02, 14-02.4-03, 34-01-17

Law applies to employers with: One or more employees

Private employers may not make employment decisions based on:
- Age (40 or older)
- Ancestry or national origin
- Physical or mental disability
- Gender
- Marital status
- Pregnancy, childbirth, and related medical conditions
- Race or color
- Religion or creed
- Lawful conduct outside of work
- Receiving public assistance
- Keeping and bearing arms (as long as firearm is never exhibited on company property except for lawful defensive purposes)
- Status as a volunteer emergency responder

Ohio

Ohio Rev. Code Ann. §§ 4111.17, 4112.01, 4112.02

Law applies to employers with: Four or more employees

Private employers may not make employment decisions based on:
- Age (40 or older)
- Ancestry or national origin
- Physical, mental, or learning disability
- AIDS/HIV
- Gender
- Pregnancy, childbirth, and related medical conditions
- Race or color
- Religion or creed
- Military status
- Caring for a sibling, child, parent, or spouse injured while in the armed services

State Laws Prohibiting Discrimination in Employment (continued)

Oklahoma

Okla. Stat. Ann. tit. 25, §§ 1301, 1302; tit. 36, § 3614.2; tit. 40, § 500; tit. 44, § 208

Law applies to employers with: 1 or more employees

Private employers may not make employment decisions based on:
- Age (40 or older)
- Ancestry or national origin
- Physical or mental disability
- Gender
- Pregnancy, childbirth, and related medical conditions (except abortions where the woman is not in "imminent danger of death")
- Race or color
- Religion or creed
- Genetic testing information
- Military service
- Being a smoker or nonsmoker or using tobacco off duty

Oregon

Ore. Rev. Stat. §§ 25-337, 659A.030, 659A.122 and following, 659A.303

Law applies to employers with: One or more employees; 6 or more employees (disability only)

Private employers may not make employment decisions based on:
- Age (18 or older)
- Ancestry or national origin
- Physical or mental disability
- Gender
- Marital status
- Pregnancy, childbirth, and related medical conditions
- Race or color
- Religion or creed

- Sexual orientation
- Genetic testing information
- Parent who has medical support order imposed by court
- Domestic violence victim status
- Refusal to attend an employer-sponsored meeting with the primary purpose of communicating the employer's opinion on religious or political matters
- Credit history
- Whistleblowers
- Off-duty use of tobacco products

Pennsylvania

43 Pa. Cons. Stat. Ann. §§ 954–955

Law applies to employers with: Four or more employees

Private employers may not make employment decisions based on:
- Age (40 to 70)
- Ancestry or national origin
- Physical or mental disability
- Gender
- Pregnancy, childbirth, and related medical conditions
- Race or color
- Religion or creed
- Relationship or association with a person with a disability
- GED rather than high school diploma
- Use of service animal

Rhode Island

R.I. Gen. Laws §§ 12-28-10, 23-6.3-11, 28-5-6, 28-5-7, 28-6-18, 28-6.7-1

Law applies to employers with: Four or more employees; one or more employees (gender-based wage discrimination only)

State Laws Prohibiting Discrimination in Employment (continued)

Private employers may not make employment decisions based on:

- Age (40 or older)
- Ancestry or national origin
- Physical or mental disability
- AIDS/HIV
- Gender
- Pregnancy, childbirth, and related medical conditions
- Race or color
- Religion or creed
- Sexual orientation, including perceived sexual orientation
- Genetic testing information
- Domestic abuse victim
- Gender identity or expression
- Homelessness

South Carolina

S.C. Code §§ 1-13-30, 1-13-80

Law applies to employers with: 15 or more employees

Private employers may not make employment decisions based on:

- Age (40 or older)
- Ancestry or national origin
- Physical or mental disability
- AIDS/HIV
- Gender
- Pregnancy, childbirth, and related medical conditions
- Race or color
- Religion or creed

South Dakota

S.D. Codified Laws Ann. §§ 20-13-1, 20-13-10, 60-2-20, 60-12-15, 62-1-17

Law applies to employers with: One or more employees

Private employers may not make employment decisions based on:

- Ancestry or national origin
- Physical or mental disability
- Gender
- Race or color
- Religion or creed
- Genetic testing information
- Preexisting injury
- Off-duty use of tobacco products

Tennessee

Tenn. Code Ann. §§ 4-21-102, 4-21-401 and following, 8-50-103, 50-2-201, 50-2-202

Law applies to employers with: Eight or more employees; one or more employees (gender-based wage discrimination only)

Private employers may not make employment decisions based on:

- Age (40 or older)
- Ancestry or national origin
- Physical, mental, or visual disability
- Gender
- Race or color
- Religion or creed
- Use of guide dog
- Volunteer rescue squad worker responding to an emergency

Texas

Tex. Lab. Code Ann. §§ 21.002, 21.051, 21.082, 21.101, 21.106, 21.402

Law applies to employers with: 15 or more employees

Private employers may not make employment decisions based on:

- Age (40 or older)
- Ancestry or national origin
- Physical or mental disability

State Laws Prohibiting Discrimination in Employment (continued)

- Gender
- Pregnancy, childbirth, and related medical conditions
- Race or color
- Religion or creed
- Genetic testing information

Utah

Utah Code Ann. §§ 26-45-103, 34A-5-102, 34A-5-106

Law applies to employers with: 15 or more employees

Private employers may not make employment decisions based on:
- Age (40 or older)
- Ancestry or national origin
- Physical or mental disability
- AIDS/HIV
- Gender
- Pregnancy, childbirth, and related medical conditions
- Race or color
- Religion or creed
- Sexual orientation
- Genetic testing information
- Gender identity

Vermont

Vt. Stat. Ann. tit. 21, § 495, 495d; tit. 18, § 9333

Law applies to employers with: One or more employees

Private employers may not make employment decisions based on:
- Age (18 or older)
- Ancestry or national origin
- Physical, mental, or emotional disability
- AIDS/HIV
- Gender

- Race or color
- Religion or creed
- Sexual orientation
- Genetic testing information
- Gender identity
- Place of birth
- Credit report or credit history

Virginia

Va. Code Ann. §§ 2.2-3900, 2.2-3901, 40.1-28.6, 40.1-28.7:1, 51.5-41

Law applies to employers with: One or more employees

Private employers may not make employment decisions based on:
- Age
- Ancestry or national origin
- Physical or mental disability
- AIDS/HIV
- Gender
- Marital status
- Pregnancy, childbirth, and related medical conditions
- Race or color
- Religion or creed
- Genetic testing information

Washington

Wash. Rev. Code Ann. §§ 38.40.110, 49.12.175, 49.44.090, 49.44.180, 49.60.030, 49.60.040, 49.60.172, 49.60.180, 49.76.120; Wash. Admin. Code § 162-30-020

Law applies to employers with: Eight or more employees; one or more employees (gender-based wage discrimination only)

Private employers may not make employment decisions based on:
- Age (40 or older)
- Ancestry or national origin

State Laws Prohibiting Discrimination in Employment (continued)

- Physical, mental, or sensory disability
- AIDS/HIV
- Gender
- Marital status
- Pregnancy, childbirth, and related medical conditions, including breast-feeding
- Race or color
- Religion or creed
- Sexual orientation
- Genetic testing information
- Hepatitis C infection
- Member of state militia
- Use of service animal
- Gender identity
- Domestic violence victim

West Virginia

W.Va. Code §§ 5-11-3, 5-11-9, 16-3C-3, 21-5B-1, 21-5B-3

Law applies to employers with: 12 or more employees; one or more employees (gender-based wage discrimination only)

Private employers may not make employment decisions based on:
- Age (40 or older)
- Ancestry or national origin
- Physical or mental disability, or blindness
- AIDS/HIV
- Gender
- Race or color
- Religion or creed
- Off-duty use of tobacco products

Wisconsin

Wis. Stat. Ann. §§ 111.32 and following

Law applies to employers with: One or more employees

Private employers may not make employment decisions based on:
- Age (40 or older)
- Ancestry or national origin
- Physical or mental disability
- Gender
- Marital status
- Pregnancy, childbirth, and related medical conditions
- Race or color
- Religion or creed
- Sexual orientation, including having a history of or being identified with a preference
- Genetic testing information
- Arrest or conviction record
- Military service
- Declining to attend a meeting or to participate in any communication about religious matters or political matters
- Use or nonuse of lawful products off duty and off site

Wyoming

Wyo. Stat. §§ 27-9-102, 27-9-105, 19-11-104

Law applies to employers with: Two or more employees

Private employers may not make employment decisions based on:
- Age (40 or older)
- Ancestry or national origin
- Disability
- Gender
- Pregnancy, childbirth, and related medical conditions
- Race or color
- Religion or creed
- Military service or status

State Agencies That Enforce Laws Prohibiting Discrimination in Employment

United States
Equal Employment
Opportunity Commission
131 M Street, NW
Washington, D.C. 20507
800-669-4000
TTY: 800-669-6820
www.eeoc.gov

Alabama
Birmingham District Office
Equal Employment Opportunity
 Commission
Birmingham, AL
800-669-4000
www.eeoc.gov/field/birmingham/index.cfm

Alaska
Commission for Human Rights
Anchorage, AK
907-274-4692
800-478-4692
http://humanrights.alaska.gov

Arizona
Civil Rights Division
Arizona Attorney General
Phoenix, AZ
602-542-5263
877-491-5742
www.azag.gov/civil-rights

Arkansas
Little Rock Area Office
Equal Employment Opportunity
 Commission
Little Rock, AR
800-669-4000
www.eeoc.gov/field/littlerock/index.cfm

California
Department of Fair Employment and
 Housing
Elk Grove, CA
916-478-7251
800-884-1684
www.dfeh.ca.gov

Colorado
Civil Rights Division
Denver, CO
303-894-2997
www.colorado.gov/dora/civil-rights

Connecticut
Commission on Human Rights and
 Opportunities
Hartford, CT
860-541-3400
www.ct.gov/chro/site

Delaware
Division of Industrial Affairs
Department of Labor
Wilmington, DE
302-761-8200
http://dia.delawareworks.com/
 discrimination

District of Columbia
Office of Human Rights
Washington, D.C.
202-727-4559
http://ohr.dc.gov

Florida
Commission on Human Relations
Tallahassee, FL
850-488-7082
800-342-8170
http://fchr.state.fl.us

State Agencies That Enforce Laws Prohibiting Discrimination in Employment (continued)

Georgia
Atlanta District Office
Equal Employment Opportunity
 Commission
Atlanta, GA
800-669-4000
http://www.eeoc.gov/field/atlanta

Hawaii
Hawaii Civil Rights Commission
Honolulu, HI
808-586-8636
http://labor.hawaii.gov/hcrc

Idaho
Idaho Commission on Human Rights
Boise, ID
208-334-2873
888-249-7025
http://humanrights.idaho.gov

Illinois
Department of Human Rights
Chicago, IL
312-814-6200
www2.illinois.gov/dhr

Indiana
Civil Rights Commission
Indianapolis, IN
317-232-2600
800-628-2909
www.in.gov/icrc

Iowa
Civil Rights Commission
Des Moines, IA
515-281-4121
800-457-4416
https://icrc.iowa.gov

Kansas
Human Rights Commission
Topeka, KS
785-296-3206
www.khrc.net

Kentucky
Commission on Human Rights
Louisville, KY
502-595-4024
800-292-5566
www.kchr.ky.gov

Louisiana
Commission on Human Rights
Baton Rouge, LA
225-342-6969
www.gov.louisiana.gov/index.cfm?md=
 pagebuilder&tmp=home&cpid=45

Maine
Human Rights Commission
Augusta, ME
207-624-6290
www.maine.gov/mhrc

Maryland
Commission on Civl Rights
Baltimore, MD
410-767-8600
800-637-6247 (in-state only)
www.mccr.maryland.gov

Massachusetts
Commission Against Discrimination
Boston, MA
617-994-6000
www.mass.gov/mcad

State Agencies That Enforce Laws Prohibiting Discrimination in Employment (continued)

Michigan
Department of Civil Rights
Detroit, MI
313-456-3700
800-482-3604
www.michigan.gov/mdcr

Minnesota
Department of Human Rights
St. Paul, MN
651-539-1100
800-657-3704
http://mn.gov/mdhr

Mississippi
Jackson Area Office
Equal Employment Opportunity
 Commission
Jackson, MS
601-948-8412
800-699-4000
www.eeoc.gov/field/jackson

Missouri
Commission on Human Rights
Jefferson City, MO
573-751-3325
877-781-4236
www.labor.mo.gov/mohumanrights

Montana
Human Rights Bureau
Employment Relations Division
Department of Labor and Industry
Helena, MT
406-444-6543
800-542-0807
http://erd.dli.mt.gov/human-rights/
 human-rights

Nebraska
Nebraska Equal Opportunity Commission
Lincoln, NE
402-471-2024
800-642-6112
www.neoc.ne.gov

Nevada
Equal Rights Commission
Las Vegas, NV
702-486-7161
www.detr.state.nv.us/nerc.htm

New Hampshire
Commission for Human Rights
Concord, NH
603-271-2767
www.nh.gov/hrc

New Jersey
Division on Civil Rights
Office of the Attorney General
Trenton, NJ
609-292-4605
www.nj.gov/oag/dcr/index.html

New Mexico
Human Rights Bureau
Santa Fe, NM
505-827-6838
800-566-9471
www.dws.state.nm.us/LaborRelations/
 HumanRights/Information

New York
Division of Human Rights
Bronx, NY
888-392-3644
www.dhr.ny.gov

State Agencies That Enforce Laws Prohibiting Discrimination in Employment (continued)

North Carolina
Employment Discrimination Bureau
Department of Labor
Raleigh, NC
919-807-2796
800-NC-LABOR
www.nclabor.com/edb/edb.htm

North Dakota
Human Rights Division
Department of Labor and Human Rights
Bismarck, ND
701-328-2660
800-582-8032
www.nd.gov/labor/human-rights/index.html

Ohio
Civil Rights Commission
Columbus, OH
614-466-2785
888-278-7101
www.crc.ohio.gov

Oklahoma
Office of Civil Rights Enforcement
Office of the Attorney General
Tulsa, OK
918-581-2910
www.ok.gov/oag/About_the_Office/
 OCRE.html

Oregon
Civil Rights Division
Bureau of Labor and Industries
Portland, OR
971-673-0764
www.oregon.gov/BOLI/CRD

Pennsylvania
Human Relations Commission
Harrisburg, PA
717-787-4410
www.phrc.state.pa.us

Rhode Island
Commission for Human Rights
Providence, RI
401-222-2661
http://sos.ri.gov/govdirectory/index.php?
 page=DetailDeptAgency&eid=189

South Carolina
Human Affairs Commission
Columbia, SC
803-737-7800
800-521-0725
www.schac.sc.gov

South Dakota
Division of Human Rights
Department of Labor and Regulation
Pierre, SD
605-773-3681
www.dlr.sd.gov/humanrights/default.aspx

Tennessee
Human Rights Commission
Nashville, TN
615-741-5825
800-251-3589
www.tennessee.gov/humanrights

Texas
Civil Rights Division
Texas Workforce Commission
Austin, TX
512-463-2642
888-452-4778
www.twc.state.tx.us/customers/jsemp/
 jsempsubcrd.html

State Agencies That Enforce Laws Prohibiting Discrimination in Employment (continued)

Utah
Anti-Discrimination and Labor Division
Labor Commission
Salt Lake City, UT
801-530-6801
800-222-1238
www.laborcommission.utah.gov/divisions/
 AntidiscriminationAndLabor/index.html

Vermont
Attorney General's Office
Civil Rights Unit
Montpelier, VT
802-828-3657
888-745-9195
http://ago.vermont.gov/divisions/civil-
 rights.php

Virginia
Office of the Attorney General
Division of Human Rights
Richmond, VA
804-225-2292
www.oag.state.va.us/index.php/
 programs-initiatives/human-rights

Washington
Human Rights Commission
Olympia, WA
800-233-3247
www.hum.wa.gov

West Virginia
Human Rights Commission
Charleston, WV
304-558-2616
888-676-5546
www.hrc.wv.gov

Wisconsin
Division of Equal Rights
Department of Workforce Development
Madison, WI
608-266-6860
http://dwd.wisconsin.gov/er

Wyoming
Labor Standards Office
Department of Workforce Services
Cheyenne, WY
307-777-7261
www.wyomingworkforce.org/workers/
 labor

State Drug and Alcohol Testing Laws

Note: Some states have drug or alcohol testing laws that apply to all employers of a certain size in the state. Other states' laws apply only to employers who choose to establish a drug-free workplace in order to qualify for a workers' compensation discount. These programs may not just allow employers to test, but actually require employers to test in certain circumstances. Finally, some states are not included in this chart because they do not have a general drug and alcohol testing statute governing private employers. However, other statutes or case law (from court decisions) may also apply. Check with an employment lawyer or your state department of labor for more information.

Alabama
Ala. Code §§ 25-5-330 to 25-5-340

Employers affected: Employers who establish a drug-free workplace program to qualify for a workers' compensation rate discount.

Testing applicants: Employer must test applicants upon conditional offer of employment. May test only those applying for certain positions, if based on reasonable job classifications. Job ads must include notice that drug and alcohol testing required.

Testing employees: Random testing permitted. Must test:
- after an accident that results in lost work time
- upon reasonable suspicion (reasons for suspicion must be documented and made available to employee upon request)

- as required by employer's routinely scheduled fitness for duty exams, and
- as follow-up to a required rehabilitation program.

Employee rights: Employees have 5 days to contest or explain a positive test result. Employer must have an employee assistance program or maintain a resource file of outside programs.

Notice and policy requirements: All employees must have written notice of drug policy. Must give 60 days' advance notice before implementing testing program. Policy must include consequences of refusing to take test or testing positive.

Alaska
Alaska Stat. §§ 23.10.600 to 23.10.699

Employers affected: Employers with one or more full-time employees.

Testing applicants: Employer may test applicants for any job-related purpose consistent with business necessity and the terms of the employer's policy.

Testing employees: Employers are not required to test. Random testing permitted. Employer may test:
- for any job-related purpose consistent with business necessity
- to maintain productivity or safety
- as part of an accident investigation or investigation of possible employee impairment, or
- upon reasonable suspicion.

Employee rights: Employer must provide written test results within 5 working days. Employee has 10 working days to request opportunity to explain positive test results;

State Drug and Alcohol Testing Laws (continued)

employer must grant request within 72 hours or before taking any adverse employment action.

Notice and policy requirements: Before implementing a testing program employer must distribute a written drug policy to all employees and must give 30 days' advance notice. Policy must include consequences of a positive test or refusal to submit to testing.

Arizona

Ariz. Rev. Stat. §§ 23-493 to 23-493.11

Employers affected: Employers with one or more full-time employees.

Testing applicants: Employer must inform prospective hires if they will undergo drug testing as a condition of employment.

Testing employees: Statute does not encourage, discourage, restrict, prohibit, or require testing. Random testing permitted. Employees may be tested:

- for any job-related purpose
- to maintain productivity or safety
- as part of an accident investigation or investigation of individual employee impairment, or
- upon reasonable suspicion.

If employer tests, all compensated employees must be included in the program, including officers, directors, and supervisors.

Employee rights: Policy must inform employees of their right to explain positive results.

Notice and policy requirements: Before conducting tests employer must give employees a copy of the written policy. Policy must include the consequences of a positive test or refusal to submit to testing.

Arkansas

Ark. Code Ann. §§ 11-3-203, 11-14-101 to 11-14-112

Testing applicants: Employers who establish a drug-free workplace program to qualify for a workers' compensation rate discount: must test for drug use upon conditional offer of employment. May test only those applying for certain positions, if based on reasonable job classifications. Employer may test for alcohol. Job ads must include notice that testing is required.

All employers: may not test applicant unless employer pays for the cost of the test, and upon written request, provides a free copy of the report to the employee or applicant.

Testing employees: Employers who establish a drug-free workplace program to qualify for a workers' compensation rate discount must test any employee:

- upon reasonable suspicion
- as part of a routine fitness-for-duty medical exam
- after an accident that results in injury, or
- as follow-up to a required rehabilitation program.

Employer may test for any other lawful reason. All employers: may not test employee unless employer pays for the cost of the test, and upon written request, provides a free copy of the report to the employee or applicant.

Employee rights: Employer may not refuse to hire applicant or take adverse personnel action against an employee on the basis of a single positive test that has

State Drug and Alcohol Testing Laws (continued)

not been verified by a confirmation test and a medical review officer. An applicant or employee has 5 days after receiving test results to contest or explain them.

Notice and policy requirements: Employer must give all employees a written statement of drug policy, including the consequences of a positive test or refusal to submit to testing. Employer must give 60 days' advance notice before implementing program.

Connecticut

Conn. Gen. Stat. Ann. §§ 31-51t to 31-51bb

Employers affected: All employers.

Testing applicants: Employer must inform job applicants in writing if drug testing is required as a condition of employment. Employer must provide copy of positive test result.

Testing employees: Employer may test:
- when there is reasonable suspicion that employee is under the influence of drugs or alcohol and job performance is or could be impaired.

Random testing is allowed only:
- when authorized by federal law
- when employee's position is dangerous or safety sensitive
- when employee drives a school bus or student transportation vehicle, or
- as part of a voluntary employee-assistance program.

Employee rights: Employer may not take any adverse personnel action on the basis of a single positive test that has not been verified by a confirmation test.

Florida

Fla. Stat. Ann. §§ 440.101 to 440.102

Employers affected: Employers who establish a drug-free workplace program to qualify for a workers' compensation rate discount.

Testing applicants: Employers must test job applicants upon conditional employment offer. May test only those applying for certain positions, if based on reasonable job classifications. Job ads must include notice that testing is required.

Testing employees: Must test employee:
- upon reasonable suspicion
- as part of a routine fitness-for-duty medical exam, and
- as part of a required rehabilitation program.

Random testing and testing for any other reason is neither required nor precluded by the law.

Employee rights: Employees who voluntarily seek treatment for substance abuse cannot be fired, disciplined, or discriminated against, unless they have tested positive or have been in treatment in the past. All employees have the right to explain positive results within 5 days. Employer may not take any adverse personnel action on the basis of an initial positive result that has not been verified by a confirmation test and a medical review officer.

Notice and policy requirements: Prior to implementing testing, employer must give 60 days' advance notice and must give employees written copy of drug policy. Policy must include consequences of a

State Drug and Alcohol Testing Laws (continued)

positive test result or refusal to submit to testing.

Georgia

Ga. Code Ann. §§ 34-9-410 to 34-9-421

Employers affected: Employers who establish a drug-free workplace program to qualify for a workers' compensation rate discount.

Testing applicants: Employer must test on conditional offer of employment. May test only those applying for certain positions, if based on reasonable job classifications. Job ads must include notice that testing is required.

Testing employees: Must test any employee:
- upon reasonable suspicion
- as part of a routine fitness-for-duty medical exam
- after an accident that results in an injury, and
- as part of a required rehabilitation program.

Random testing and testing for any other lawful reason is neither required nor prohibited.

Employee rights: Employees have 5 days to explain or contest a positive result. Employer must have an employee assistance program or maintain a resource file of outside programs. Initial positive result must be confirmed.

Notice and policy requirements: Employer must give applicants and employees notice of testing and must give 60 days' notice before implementing program. All employees must receive a written policy statement; policy must state the consequences of refusing to submit to a

drug test or of testing positive.

Hawaii

Haw. Rev. Stat. §§ 329B-1 to 329B-5

Employers affected: All.

Testing applicants: Same conditions as current employees.

Testing employees: Employer may test employees only if these conditions are met:
- employer pays all costs including confirming test
- tests are performed by a licensed laboratory
- employee receives a list of the substances being tested for (and medications that could cause a positive result)
- there is a form for disclosing medicines and legal drugs, and
- the results are kept confidential.

Notice and policy requirements: If employer uses an on-site screening test, it must follow the instructions on the package. If an employee or applicant tests positive in an on-site test, the employer must direct the employee or applicant to go to a licensed laboratory, within four hours, for a follow-up test. If the employee or applicant doesn't go to the lab, the employer can fire, refuse to hire, or take other adverse action against the employee or applicant only if the employer provided written notice that:
- the employer followed the required procedures for the on-site test, and
- the employee or applicant could refuse to take the test.

If the employee or applicant refused or failed to take the test, the employer can take adverse action.

State Drug and Alcohol Testing Laws (continued)

Idaho

Idaho Code §§ 72-1701 to 72-1716

Employers affected: Employers who establish a drug-free workplace program to qualify for a workers' compensation rate discount and/or prohibit employees fired for drug or alcohol use from qualifying for unemployment compensation.

Testing applicants: Employer may test as a condition of hiring.

Testing employees: May test for variety of reasons, including:

- following a workplace accident
- based on reasonable suspicion
- as part of a return-to-duty exam
- at random, or
- as a condition of continued employment.

An employer who follows drug-free workplace guidelines may fire employees who refuse to submit to testing or who test positive for drugs or alcohol. Employees will be fired for misconduct and denied unemployment benefits.

Employee rights: An employee or applicant who receives notice of a positive test may request a retest within 7 working days. Employee must have opportunity to explain positive result. If the retest results are negative, the employer must pay for the cost; if they are positive, the employee must pay. Employer may not take any adverse employment action on the basis of an initial positive result that has not been verified by a confirmation test.

Notice and policy requirements: Employer must have a written policy that includes a statement that violation of the policy may result in termination due to misconduct, as well as what types of testing employees may be subject to.

Illinois

775 Ill. Comp. Stat. § 5/2-104(C)(2)

Employers affected: Employers with 15 or more employees.

Testing employees: Statute does not "encourage, prohibit, or authorize" drug testing, but employers may test employees who have been in rehabilitation.

Indiana

Ind. Code Ann. §§ 22-9-5-6(b), 22-9-5-24

Employers affected: Employers with 15 or more employees.

Testing employees: Statute does not "encourage, prohibit, or authorize" testing, but employers may test employees who have been in rehabilitation.

Iowa

Iowa Code § 730.5

Employers affected: Employers with one or more full-time employees.

Testing applicants: Employer may test as a condition of hiring.

Testing employees: Statute does not encourage, discourage, restrict, limit, prohibit, or require testing. Employer may conduct unannounced, random testing of employees selected from the entire workforce at one site, all full-time employees at one site, or all employees in safety-sensitive positions. Employers may also test:

- upon reasonable suspicion
- during and after rehabilitation, or

State Drug and Alcohol Testing Laws (continued)

- following an accident that caused a reportable injury or more than $1,000 property damage.

Employee rights: Employee has 7 days to request a retest. Employers with 50 or more employees must provide rehabilitation for any employee testing positive for alcohol use who has worked for at least 12 of the last 18 months and has not previously violated the substance abuse policy. Employer must have an employee assistance program or maintain a resource file of outside programs.

Notice and policy requirements: Must have written drug test policy that includes consequences of positive result and refusal to take test. Employer may take action only on confirmed positive result.

Kentucky

Ky. Rev. Stat. 304.13-167; 803 Ky. Admin. Code 25:280

Employers affected: Employers who establish a drug-free workplace to qualify for a workers' compensation premium discount.

Testing applicants: Must test for drugs and alcohol after conditional offer of employment.

Testing employees: Must test for drugs:
- upon reasonable suspicion
- following a workplace accident that requires medical care
- as a follow-up to an Employee Assistance Program (EAP) or rehabilitation program for drug use, and
- upon being selected using a statistically valid, random, unannounced selection procedure.

Must test for alcohol:
- upon reasonable suspicion
- following a workplace accident that required medical care, and
- as a follow-up to an EAP or rehabilitation program for alcohol use.

Employee rights: Employee must have an opportunity to report use of prescription or over-the-counter medicines after receiving a positive test result.

Notice and policy requirements: Employer must have a written drug-free workplace policy. Employer must distribute and post notice of how it will determine whether employees have violated the policy and the consequences of violating the policy.

Louisiana

La. Rev. Stat. Ann. §§ 49:1001 to 49:1012

Employers affected: Employers with one or more full-time employees. (Does not apply to oil drilling, exploration, or production.)

Testing applicants: Employer may require all applicants to submit to drug and alcohol test. An employer must use certified laboratories and specified procedures for testing if it will base its hiring decisions on the results of the test.

Testing employees: Employer may require employees to submit to drug and alcohol test. An employer that will take negative action against an employee based on a positive test result must use certified laboratories and specified procedures for testing.

Employee rights: Employees with confirmed positive results have 7 working days to request access to all records relating to the drug test. Employer may allow employee to

State Drug and Alcohol Testing Laws (continued)

undergo rehabilitation without termination of employment.

Maine

Me. Rev. Stat. Ann. tit. 26, §§ 681 to 690

Employers affected: Employers with one or more full-time employees.

Testing applicants: Employer may require applicant to take a drug test only if offered employment or placed on an eligibility list.

Testing employees: Statute does not require or encourage testing. Employer may test based upon probable cause but may not base belief on a single accident, an anonymous informant, or off-duty possession or use (unless it occurs on the employer's premises or nearby, during or right before work hours); must document the facts and give employee a copy. May test randomly when there could be an unreasonable threat to the health and safety of coworkers or the public. Testing is also allowed when an employee returns to work following a positive test.

Employee rights: Employee who tests positive has 3 days to explain or contest results. Employee must be given an opportunity to participate in a rehabilitation program for up to 6 months; an employer with more than 20 full-time employees must pay for half of any out-of-pocket costs. After successfully completing the program, employee is entitled to return to previous job with full pay and benefits.

Notice and policy requirements: All employers must have a written policy, which includes the consequences of a positive result or refusing to submit to testing. Policy must be approved by the state department of labor. Policy must be distributed to each employee at least 30 days before it takes effect. Any changes to policy require 60 days' advance notice. An employer with more than 20 full-time employees must have an employee assistance program certified by the state office of substance abuse before implementing a testing program.

Maryland

Md. Code Ann., [Health-Gen.] § 17-214

Employers affected: Law applies to all employers.

Testing applicants: May use preliminary screening to test applicant. If initial result is positive, may make job offer conditional on confirmation of test results.

Testing employees: Employer may require substance abuse testing for legitimate business purposes only.

Employee rights: The sample must be tested by a certified laboratory; at the time of testing employee may request laboratory's name and address. An employee who tests positive must be given:

- a copy of the test results
- a copy of the employer's written drug and alcohol policy
- a written notice of any adverse action employer intends to take, and
- a statement of employee's right to an independent confirmation test at own expense.

Minnesota

Minn. Stat. Ann. §§ 181.950 to 181.957

Employers affected: Employers with one or more employees.

State Drug and Alcohol Testing Laws (continued)

Testing applicants: Employers may require applicants to submit to a drug or alcohol test only after they have been given a job offer and have seen a written notice of testing policy. May test only if required of all applicants for same position.

Testing employees: Employers are not required to test. Employers may require drug or alcohol testing only according to a written testing policy. Testing may be done if there is a reasonable suspicion that employee:

- is under the influence of drugs or alcohol
- has violated drug and alcohol policy
- has been involved in a work-related accident, or
- has sustained or caused another employee to sustain a personal injury.

Random tests permitted only for employees in safety-sensitive positions. With 2 weeks' notice, employers may also test as part of an annual routine physical exam. Employer may test, without notice, an employee referred by the employer for chemical dependency treatment or evaluation or participating in a chemical dependency treatment program under an employee benefit plan. Testing is allowed during and for two years following treatment.

Employee rights: If test is positive, employee has 3 days to explain the results; employee must notify employer within 5 days of intention to obtain a retest. Employer may not discharge employee for a first-time positive test without offering counseling or rehabilitation; employee who refuses or does not complete program successfully may be discharged.

Notice and policy requirements: Employees must be given a written notice of testing policy that includes consequences of refusing to take test or having a positive test result. Two weeks' notice required before testing as part of an annual routine physical exam.

Mississippi
Miss. Code Ann. §§ 71-7-1 to 71-7-33, 71-3-121, 71-3-205 to 71-3-225

Employers affected: Employers with one or more full-time employees. Employers who establish a drug-free workplace program to qualify for a workers' compensation rate discount must implement testing procedures.

Testing applicants: May test all applicants as part of employment application process. Employer may request a signed statement that applicant has read and understands the drug and alcohol testing policy or notice.

Testing employees: May require drug and alcohol testing of all employees:

- upon reasonable suspicion
- as part of a routinely scheduled fitness-for-duty medical examination
- as a follow-up to a rehabilitation program, or
- if they have tested positive within the previous 12 months.

May also require drug and alcohol testing following an employee's work-related injury, for purposes of determining workers' compensation coverage. Testing is also allowed on a neutral selection basis.

Employee rights: Employer must inform an employee in writing within 5 working days of receipt of a positive confirmed test

State Drug and Alcohol Testing Laws (continued)

result; employee may request and receive a copy of the test result report. Employee has 10 working days after receiving notice to explain the positive test results. Employer may not discharge or take any adverse personnel action on the basis of an initial positive test result that has not been verified by a confirmation test. Private employer who elects to establish a drug-free workplace program must have an employee assistance program or maintain a resource file of outside programs.

Notice and policy requirements: 30 days before implementing testing program employer must give employees written notice of drug and alcohol policy that includes consequences:

- of a positive confirmed result
- of refusing to take test, and
- of other violations of the policy.

Montana

Mont. Code Ann. §§ 39-2-205 to 39-2-211

Employers affected: Employers with one or more employees.

Testing applicants: May test as a condition of hire, but only for applicants who will work in:

- a hazardous work environment
- a security position
- a position that affects public safety or health
- a position with a fiduciary relationship to the employer, or
- a position that requires driving.

Testing employees: Same job restrictions apply to employees as to applicants. Employees in these positions may be tested:

- upon reasonable suspicion
- after involvement in an accident that causes personal injury or more than $1,500 property damage
- as a follow-up to a previous positive test, or
- as a follow-up to treatment or a rehabilitation program.

Employer may conduct random tests as long as there is an established date, all personnel are subject to testing, the employer has signed statements from each employee confirming receipt of a written description of the random selection process, and the random selection process is conducted by a scientifically valid method. Employer may require an employee who tests positive to undergo treatment as a condition of continued employment.

Employee rights: After a positive result, employee may request additional confirmation by an independent laboratory; if the results are negative, employer must pay the test costs. Employer may not take action or conduct follow-up testing if the employee presents a reasonable explanation or medical opinion that the original results were not caused by illegal drug use; employer must also remove results from employee's record.

Notice and policy requirements: Written policy must be available for review 60 days before testing. Policy must include consequences of a positive test result.

Nebraska

Neb. Rev. Stat. §§ 48-1901 to 48-1910

Employers affected: Employers with 6 or

State Drug and Alcohol Testing Laws (continued)

more full-time and part-time employees.

Testing employees: Employers are not required to test. Employer may require employees to submit to drug or alcohol testing and may discipline or discharge any employee who refuses, tests positive, or tampers with the test sample.

Employee rights: Employer may not take adverse action on the basis of an initial positive result unless it is confirmed according to state and federal guidelines.

North Carolina

N.C. Gen. Stat. §§ 95-230 to 95-235

Employers affected: Law applies to all employers.

Testing applicants: May test as a condition of hire. Applicant has right to retest a confirmed positive sample at own expense. If first screening test produces a positive result, applicant may waive a second examination that is intended to confirm the results.

Testing employees: Employers may, but are not required to, test. Testing must be performed under reasonable, sanitary conditions, and must respect individual dignity to the extent possible. Employer must preserve samples for at least 90 days after confirmed test results are released.

Employee rights: Employee has right to retest a confirmed positive sample at own expense.

North Dakota

N.D. Cent. Code §§ 34-01-15, 65-01-11

Employers affected: All employers.

Testing applicants: May test as a condition of hire.

Testing employees: Employer may test following an accident or injury that will result in a workers' compensation claim, if employer has a mandatory policy of testing under these circumstances, or if employer or physician has reasonable grounds to suspect injury was caused by impairment due to alcohol or drug use.

Employee rights: Employer who requires drug testing of any applicant or employee must pay for the test.

Ohio

Ohio Admin. Code § 4123-17-58

Employers affected: Employers who establish a drug-free safety program may qualify for a workers' compensation rate bonus.

Testing applicants: Must test all applicants and new hires.

Testing employees: Must test employees:
- upon reasonable suspicion
- following a return to work after a positive test, and
- after an accident that results in an injury requiring off-site medical attention or property damage.

Employers must test at random to meet requirements for greater discounts.

Employee rights: Employer must have an employee assistance plan. Employers who test at random to qualify for greater discount must not terminate employee who tests positive for the first time, comes forward voluntarily, or is referred by a supervisor. For these employees, employer must pay costs of substance abuse assessment.

State Drug and Alcohol Testing Laws (continued)

Notice and policy requirements: Policy must state consequences for refusing to submit to testing or for violating guidelines. Policy must include a commitment to rehabilitation.

Oklahoma
Okla. Stat. Ann. tit. 40, §§ 551 to 565

Employers affected: Employers with one or more employees.

Testing applicants: May test applicants.

Testing employees: Statute does not require or encourage testing. Before requiring testing, employer must provide an employee assistance program. Random testing is allowed. May test employees:

- upon reasonable suspicion
- after an accident resulting in injury or property damage
- on a random selection basis
- as part of a routine fitness-for-duty examination, or
- as follow-up to a rehabilitation program.

Employee rights: Employee has right to retest a positive result at own expense; if the confirmation test is negative, employer must reimburse costs.

Notice and policy requirements: Before requiring testing employer must: adopt a written policy; give a copy to each employee and to any applicant offered a job; and allow 10 days' notice. Policy must state consequences of a positive test result or refusing to submit to testing.

Oregon
Ore. Rev. Stat. §§ 659.840, 659A.300, 438.435

Employers affected: Law applies to all employers.

Testing applicants: Unless there is reasonable suspicion that an applicant is under the influence of alcohol, no employer may require a breathalyzer test as a condition of employment. Employer is not prohibited from conducting a test if applicant consents.

Testing employees: Unless there is reasonable suspicion that an employee is under the influence of alcohol, no employer may require a breathalyzer or blood alcohol test as a condition of continuing employment. Employer is not prohibited from conducting a test if employee consents.

Employee rights: No action may be taken based on the results of an on-site drug test without a confirming test performed according to state health division regulations. Upon written request, test results will be reported to the employee.

Rhode Island
R.I. Gen. Laws §§ 28-6.5-1 to 28-6.5-2

Employers affected: Law applies to all employers.

Testing applicants: May test as a condition of hire.

Testing employees: May require employee to submit to a drug test only if there are reasonable grounds, based on specific, documented observations, to believe employee may be under the influence of a controlled substance that is impairing job performance.

Employee rights: Employee must be allowed to provide sample in private, outside the presence of any person.

State Drug and Alcohol Testing Laws (continued)

Employee who tests positive may have the sample retested at employer's expense and must be given opportunity to explain or refute results. Employee may not be terminated on the basis of a positive result but must be referred to a licensed substance abuse professional. After referral, employer may require additional testing and may terminate employee if test results are positive.

South Carolina

S.C. Code Ann. §§ 41-1-15, 38-73-500

Employers affected: Employers who establish a drug-free workplace program to qualify for a workers' compensation rate discount.

Testing applicants: Employer is not required to test applicants to qualify for discount.

Testing employees: Must conduct random testing among all employees.

Employee rights: Employee must receive positive test results in writing within 24 hours.

Notice and policy requirements: Employer must notify all employees of the drug-free workplace program at the time it is established or at the time of hiring, whichever is earlier. Program must include a policy statement that balances respect for individuals with the need to maintain a safe, drug-free environment.

Tennessee

Tenn. Code Ann. §§ 50-9-101 to 50-9-114

Employers affected: Employers who establish a drug-free workplace program to qualify for a workers' compensation rate discount.

Testing applicants: Must test applicants for drugs upon conditional offer of employment.

May test only those applying for certain positions, if based on reasonable job classifications. May test for alcohol after conditional offer of employment. Job ads must include notice that drug and alcohol testing is required.

Testing employees: Employer must test upon reasonable suspicion; must document behavior on which the suspicion is based within 24 hours or before test results are released, whichever is earlier; and must give a copy to the employee upon request. Employer must test employees:

- if required by employer policy as part of a routine fitness-for-duty medical exam
- after an accident that results in injury, or
- as a follow-up to a required rehabilitation program.

May test employees who are not in safety-sensitive positions for alcohol only if based on reasonable suspicion.

Employee rights: Employee has the right to explain or contest a positive result within 5 days. Employee may not be fired, disciplined, or discriminated against for voluntarily seeking treatment unless employee has previously tested positive or been in a rehabilitation program.

Notice and policy requirements: Before implementing testing program, employer must provide 60 days' notice and must give all employees a written drug and alcohol policy statement. Policy must include consequences of a positive test or refusing to submit to testing.

State Drug and Alcohol Testing Laws (continued)

Utah

Utah Code Ann. §§ 34-38-1 to 34-38-15

Employers affected: Employers with one or more employees.

Testing applicants: Employer may test any applicant for drugs or alcohol as long as management also submits to periodic testing.

Testing employees: Employer may test employee for drugs or alcohol as long as management also submits to periodic testing. Employer may require testing to:

- investigate possible individual employee impairment
- investigate an accident or theft
- maintain employee or public safety, or
- ensure productivity, quality, or security.

Employer may suspend, discipline, discharge, or require treatment on the basis of a failed test (confirmed positive result, adulterated sample, or substituted sample) or a refusal to take test.

Notice and policy requirements: Testing must be conducted according to a written policy that has been distributed to employees and is available for review by prospective employees.

Vermont

Vt. Stat. Ann. tit. 21, §§ 511 to 520

Employers affected: Employers with one or more employees.

Testing applicants: Employer may not test applicants for drugs or alcohol unless there is a job offer conditional on a negative test result and applicant is given written notice of the testing procedure and a list of the drugs to be tested for.

Testing employees: Random testing not permitted unless required by federal law. Employer may not require testing unless:

- there is probable cause to believe an employee is using or is under the influence
- employer has an employee assistance program that provides rehabilitation, and
- employee who tests positive and agrees to enter employee assistance program is not terminated.

Employee rights: Employer must contract with a medical review officer who will review all test results and keep them confidential. Medical review officer is to contact employee or applicant to explain a positive test result. Employee or applicant has right to an independent retest at own expense. Employee who successfully completes employee assistance program may not be terminated, although employee may be suspended for up to 3 months to complete program. Employee who tests positive after completing treatment may be fired.

Notice and policy requirements: Must provide written policy that states consequences of a positive test.

Virginia

Va. Code Ann. § 65.2-813.2

Employers affected: Employers that establish drug-free workplace programs to qualify for workers' compensation insurance discount.

Testing applicants: State law gives insurers the authority to establish guidelines and criteria for testing.

State Drug and Alcohol Testing Laws (continued)

Testing employees: State law gives insurers the authority to establish guidelines and criteria for testing.

Wyoming

Wyo. Stat. Ann. 27-14-201; Wyo. Rules & Regulations, WSD WCD Ch. 2, § 8

Employers affected: Employers that establish a drug and alcohol testing program approved by the state Department of Workforce Services may receive a workers' compensation discount of up to 5% of the base rate for the employer's classification.

Testing applicants: Must test applicants for drugs; may test applicants for alcohol. Job announcements must state that testing is required.

Testing employees: Must test employees:
- upon reasonable suspicion
- following a workplace accident, and
- at random.

Must follow testing protocols prescribed in regulations (including "strong recommendation" that post-accident testing be done by blood sample).

Employee rights: Employee has 5 days to contest or explain a positive result.

Notice and policy requirements: Employer must have written policy including consequence of positive result or refusing to submit to test. Must give notice 60 days prior to testing.

Resources on HR and Employment Available From Nolo

Nolo offers a variety of resources on HR compliance and employment law.

Books

Nolo publishes many titles for employers, managers, and human resources professionals, including:

- *The Essential Guide to Federal Employment Laws*, which explains the requirements, record-keeping obligations, coverage, and deadlines imposed by 20 important federal laws, including the Americans with Disabilities Act, Fair Labor Standards Act, and Title VII.
- *Smart Policies for Workplace Technologies: Email, Blogs, Cell Phones & More*, copublished by Nolo and SHRM, a primer on how to manage employee use of email, instant messaging, blogs, and more, including sample policy language.
- *The Essential Guide to Handling Workplace Harassment & Discrimination*, a step-by-step guide to developing policies, training employees and managers, investigating issues, responding to agency investigations and lawsuits, and more.
- *Dealing With Problem Employees: A Legal Guide*, a comprehensive resource for handling tough employee issues, including detailed information on minimizing legal exposure if you have to fire an employee.
- *Create Your Own Employee Handbook: A Legal & Practical Guide for Employers,* which provides the information and policies you need to draft or update your company handbook, and includes forms that allow you to cut and paste policies into a handbook.
- *The Performance Appraisal Handbook: Legal & Practical Rules for Managers*, which explains how to effectively track and evaluate employee performance without getting into legal trouble.
- *The Employee Performance Handbook: Smart Strategies for Coaching Employees*, a step-by-step guide to handling employee discipline, including information on how to communicate effectively with employees and how to identify, correct, and document problems.

- *The Job Description Handbook*, which explains how to create, use, and update job descriptions effectively, and includes a PowerPoint training presentation on the book's companion page.
- *The Essential Guide to Family & Medical Leave*, a comprehensive resource that explains every aspect of the Family and Medical Leave Act, from figuring out company coverage to reinstating employees when leave is over, including how to handle the overlap between the FMLA and state leave laws, workers' compensation statutes, the Americans with Disabilities Act, and more.
- *The Manager's Legal Handbook*, an introduction to many of the legal issues managers face every day, including discrimination, wage and hour issues, firing and layoffs, employer privacy concerns, protecting trade secrets, and much more.
- *The Employer's Legal Handbook: Manage Your Employees and Workplace Effectively*, a comprehensive guide to employment law, written with the small business owner in mind.
- *Consultant & Independent Contractor Agreements*, which provides all of the information and sample contracts you need to work well with independent contractors—and avoid having them reclassified as employees.

Nolo's Website

You can find free articles on a wide variety of employment and HR topics on Nolo's award-winning website, www.nolo.com. From the home page, click "Employment Law" to view articles on:

- hiring employees
- hiring independent contractors
- wage and hour laws
- personnel policies and procedures
- family, medical, and other types of leave
- discrimination
- workplace privacy
- firing workers, and
- obligations to workers who are leaving the company.

If you select "Small Claims Court" from the home page, you'll find articles on dispute resolution, mediation, arbitration, and working with lawyers.

From the home page, you can also find podcasts on a variety of topics (including employment and HR issues), Nolo's lawyer directory, and much more.

Index

A

AAA (American Arbitration Association), 53

Accent, discrimination on basis of, 127

Accommodation. *See* Reasonable accommodation

Accountants, forensic, 61, 246

Accounting system, that deters theft, 269

Accused employee
  assessing credibility of, 100–101
  cautioning about retaliation, 84, 86, 158, 206, 214, 302
  defensive and combative, 208, 210
  in discrimination investigation, 149–150, 157–158, 161–166, 169–170, 171, 179
  in drug or alcohol investigation, 351, 362–368
  entitled to respond to allegations, 162, 169, 206, 211, 212, 214, 304–305
  entitled to respond to evidence, 95
  finding of no misconduct by, 106–107, 108
  following up with, 117
  in harassment investigation, 205–206, 208–212, 220
  interviews of, 84–86, 95
  in theft investigation, 243–244, 249, 257, 259–268
  in violence investigation, 288–292, 294–295, 301–305, 312–314
  See also Firing; Misconduct; Rank of accused employee; Retaliation; Suspension with pay

Action. *See* Immediate action; Taking action

ADA. *See* Americans with Disabilities Act (ADA)

Administrative charge
  of discrimination, 144–145
  of harassment, 202

Adobe Reader, 378

Age discrimination, 125, 128–129
  based on disparate impact, 139

Age Discrimination in Employment Act, 125

Alcohol at company-sponsored events, 347, 376

Alcoholism
  as disability under ADA, 324, 326–327, 344, 349, 369, 371, 373
  Family and Medical Leave Act and, 369
  See also Drug and alcohol investigation

American Arbitration Association (AAA), 53

Americans with Disabilities Act (ADA), 125
  confidentiality of medical records and, 373–374
  definition of disability and, 129–130
  See also Drug and alcohol use and ADA; Reasonable accommodation

Amphetamines, 320, 338

Anonymous complaints, 36–37, 80

Antidiscrimination laws, 15–16
  agencies enforcing, 123
  harassment and, 183, 184–185
  LGBT employees and, 133–134

See also Investigation
Health benefits, age discrimination in, 129
Heroin, 327
Hiring, disparate impact claims in, 140
Hostile work environment, 184, 186, 187, 188, 191, 202, 216

I

Identity theft, 233–234
Illegal conduct
 company's liability for, 113
 distinguished from inappropriate conduct, 105
Immediate action, 8, 44–46, 64–65
 on discrimination complaint, 149–151
 on harassment complaint, 198–199
 on suspected drug or alcohol use, 344–348
 on suspected employee theft, 242–244
 on threat or violent incident, 285, 287–293
 See also Taking action
Immigration Reform and Control Act, 125
Impartiality of investigator, 82
 of discrimination, 151–152
Improper conduct, not clearly illegal, 105
 discrimination and, 174–177
 harassment and, 186
 sexual favoritism and, 190
 See also Misconduct
Inconclusive investigation, 102–103, 107, 113
Inconsistent treatment, and discrimination complaints, 15–17, 172–174

Insurance policy, covering employee theft, 244, 268–269
Intellectual property theft, 233–234, 246, 247
Interactive files, 378–379, 380
Internet resources. *See* Website resources
Internet use, monitoring, 26–27
Interviews, 9
 of accused employee, 84–86, 95
 assessing credibility of, 100–101
 coercive, 24–25, 260
 of complaining employee, 79–84, 95
 in discrimination investigation, 155–170
 documentation of, 77–79, 83, 86, 88–89, 111, 114
 in drug or alcohol investigation, 356–367
 effective conduct of, 65–79
 to elicit confessions, 247, 265
 employee wanting moral support at, 66, 80
 employee wanting representative at, 66, 85
 focusing on facts in, 70–71, 208
 follow-up, 95
 in harassment investigation, 205–215
 if no one has come forward, 80
 impartiality in, 82
 of nonemployees, 89
 omitting relevant witnesses, 28
 open-ended questions in, 67–68, 208
 planning of, 58–59
 poor questioning techniques in, 28
 safety of interviewer during, 302
 tape recording of, 79
 in theft investigation, 247, 257–263
 union representative brought to, 66, 85
 in violence or threat investigation, 296–305

written notice for all interviewees
about, 81
See also Witnesses
Intimidation
of alleged victim and/or witnesses,
149, 198
bullying as, 273
See also Retaliation
Investigation
benefits of, 5–8
common mistakes in, 10–29
conclusions reached by, 7–8, 9,
98–105
deciding whether to investigate, 8,
41–44
discovery of problems calling for,
33–41
example of good investigation, 11
following up on, 10, 117–118
getting second opinion on, 103
inconclusive, 102–103, 107, 113
new or unexpected information and,
58, 76–77, 95
with outside agency involved, 40–41
planning of, 8–9, 56–61
reopening, 101
roles involved in, 7
scaling to size of problem, 42–43
speaking to other employees about,
116
ten steps to successful conduct of,
8–10
time and resources for, 59–60
See also Discrimination investigation;
Documentation of investigation;
Drug and alcohol investigation;
Evidence; Harassment investigation;
Interviews; Mistakes in investigations;
Theft investigation; Violence or threat
investigation

Investigation file, 113, 114. *See also*
Investigation report
Investigation report, 10, 111–113
checklist for, 115
delay documented in, 65
filing in confidential company
records, 113, 114
See also Documentation of
investigation
Investigator
choosing, 8, 46–56
disciplinary decisions and, 104
for discrimination investigation,
151–152
documenting approval of, 50–51
for drug and alcohol investigation,
349–350
for employee theft investigation,
244–247
false identity used by, 90
gender of, 51
for harassment investigation, 200–202
professionalism of, 51–52
rank of the accused and, 49, 52, 152,
202
team of, 48
training ahead of time, 47
for violence investigation, 293–295
See also Outside investigator
Invoices, fake or altered, 234–236

J

Jokes
derogatory, 185, 215
racist, 193, 210, 213–214, 216
sexually explicit, 188, 189, 194, 198,
203
violent toward women, 191
Judgment calls, 5

O

Obamacare, and age discrimination, 129
Objectivity, 23–24
  of discrimination investigator, 151–152
  focus on facts and, 70
  sympathy with complaining employee and, 82
Occupational Safety and Health Administration (OSHA)
  drug or alcohol use and, 323
  hiring an outside investigator and, 53
  workplace violence and, 275–276, 282
Off-duty conduct laws, 335–336
Officers of company. *See* Rank of accused employee
Online companion page, 378
Open-minded investigation, 67
Opiates, 338. *See also* Painkillers
Oral complaints, retaliation claim arising from, 19
Oral employment contracts, 14
Outside investigator, 52–56
  of discrimination complaint, 152
  of drug or alcohol use, 350
  of employee theft, 246–247
  of harassment complaint, 201–202
  if employee has lawyer, 66
  licensing requirements for, 53
  reporting requirements for, 54, 110
  of threats or violence, 293–294
  See also Investigator

P

Paid leave for complaining employee, 151, 199, 218

Painkillers
  misused, 320
  opiates, 338
  used off-duty, 335
PCP, testing for, 338
PDF files, 378, 379
Performance evaluations
  discrimination claims and, 144, 154, 155, 176
  harassment claims and, 204, 215
Personnel files
  discipline documented in, 113, 114
  discrimination investigation and, 154, 155, 170–171
  drug or alcohol investigation and, 353
  employee's right to inspect, 113
  harassment investigation and, 204, 218
  investigation file separate from, 113, 114
  violence or threat investigation and, 296, 306
  written warning in, 117
Phone calls, monitoring, 26–27
Phony vendor/supplier schemes, 234–236, 257
Planning the investigation, 8–9, 56–61
  of discrimination, 152–155
  of drug or alcohol use, 351–352
  of harassment, 202–204
  new or unexpected information and, 58
  of theft, 248–255
  of threats or violence, 295–296
Plausibility, 102
  in discrimination investigation, 172
  in drug and alcohol investigation, 368
  in threat or violence investigation, 308

⚖ NOLO | *Online Legal Forms*

Nolo offers a large library of legal solutions and forms, created by Nolo's in-house legal staff. These reliable documents can be prepared in minutes.

Create a Document

- **Incorporation.** Incorporate your business in any state.
- **LLC Formations.** Gain asset protection and pass-through tax status in any state.
- **Wills.** Nolo has helped people make over 2 million wills. Is it time to make or revise yours?
- **Living Trust (avoid probate).** Plan now to save your family the cost, delays, and hassle of probate.
- **Trademark.** Protect the name of your business or product.
- **Provisional Patent.** Preserve your rights under patent law and claim "patent pending" status.

Download a Legal Form

Nolo.com has hundreds of top quality legal forms available for download—bills of sale, promissory notes, nondisclosure agreements, LLC operating agreements, corporate minutes, commercial lease and sublease, motor vehicle bill of sale, consignment agreements and many more.

Review Your Documents

Many lawyers in Nolo's consumer-friendly lawyer directory will review Nolo documents for a very reasonable fee. Check their detailed profiles at **Nolo.com/lawyers**.